The Lancashire Lads at War

The Lancashire Lads at War

A Personal Recollection and Unit History of Loyal North Lancashire Regiment Battalions on the Western Front During the First World War

With a Reservist in France

F. A. Bolwell

The War History of the 1st/4th Battalion the Loyal North Lancashire Regiment

Battalion History Committee

LEONAUR

The Lancashire Lads at War
A Personal Recollection and Unit History of Loyal North Lancashire Regiment Battalions on the Western Front During the First World War
With a Reservist in France
by F. A. Bolwell
The War History of the 1st/4th Battalion the Loyal North Lancashire Regiment
by Battalion History Committee

FIRST EDITION

First published under the titles
With a Reservist in France
and
The War History of the 1st/4th Battalion the Loyal North Lancashire Regiment

Leonaur is an imprint
of Oakpast Ltd

Copyright in this form © 2015 Oakpast Ltd

ISBN: 978-1-78282-429-9 (hardcover)
ISBN: 978-1-78282-430-5 (softcover)

http://www.leonaur.com

Publisher's Notes

The views expressed in this book are not necessarily those of the publisher.

Contents

With a Reservist in France   7

The War History of the 1st/4th Battalion the
    Loyal North Lancashire Regiment   83

With a Reservist in France

Contents

The Call, and the Start	13
The Landing in France	16
The Retirement	21
The Battle of the Marne	27
The Battle of the Aisne	31
The First Battle of Ypres	41
The Fight on the Bipschoote-Langemarck Road, October 23rd, 1914	43
La Bassée District	63
The Battle of Festubert, May 9th, 1915	72
Loos	78

To
The Late Colonel Knight
And Officers of the Loyal
North Lancashire

CHAPTER 1

The Call, and the Start

Being a Reservist, I was naturally called to the colours on the outbreak of war between England and Germany on August 4th, 1914, so I downed tools; and, although a married man with two children, I was only too pleased to be able to leave a more or less monotonous existence for something more exciting and adventurous. Being an old soldier, war was of course more or less ingrained into my nature, and during those few days before the final declaration I was at fever heat and longing to be away.

As all the world knows, war was declared on the fourth, which was a sign for all reservists to present themselves at the post offices throughout the country, there to procure their travelling allowance and proceed to the depot named by the authorities on each Identity Life Certificate. This I accordingly did early on the following morning. Late on the night before the General Mobilisation notices had been posted up outside all newspaper offices and public buildings.

I had rather a long journey before me, having to go from a town on the South Coast, where I then resided, to a town in Lancashire, that being the depot of my regiment. During the journey to London I had a conversation with a clergyman, and of course the topic was war. We agreed that it could not last for any length of time, and I remember telling him that I was going to try and get a soft job, and that I expected to have a nice holiday. Little did I think what was in store for me! Waterloo and Euston were packed to suffocation, men flocking to the colours from all parts of the country. The excitement was intense, and the scenes being enacted partially carried away my thoughts of sorrow at leaving home.

That evening I arrived at my depot, and, after reporting myself at the Guard Room, made my way toward the block of buildings which my unit occupied, these particular barracks being the depots of three units.

I met on arrival several old faces, and, after renewing our acquaintances, I there and then fell in with a batch of men going up for medical inspection. We were then examined by two doctors very thoroughly. The next place to visit was the Quarter Master's Stores, there to be fitted up with uniform, equipment, etc. After that, as it was quite dark, we retired for the night, but not before we had all taken advantage of a little refreshment kindly supplied by some ladies who had come forward to release men employed in preparing food for work in the stores. That evening a party of 500 men had been sent to join the Home Battalion then stationed at Aldershot.

Next day a similar body of men had become fit to be sent away, and I proceeded with them to the First Battalion at Aldershot.

On arrival, we were placed into companies and platoons. Most of us had left the service some years ago, and had no idea of the existing new formations. One man, on being asked by an officer where his platoon was, replied: "I don't know, sir. I haven't got it on me."

However, after a week at Aldershot, we were pretty well knocked into shape, and had also been fixed up in accounts and allowances, and other details. We also had a lecture on inoculation by the medical officer, who hoped that every man would consent to be operated on. Another and more interesting speech was given by the commanding officer, Colonel Knight, a man who fully realized the seriousness of the situation and evidently had a good idea of what the present war would be like. His speech was to this effect:

> Men of the 1st Loyal North Lancashire Regiment! I wish to bring home to you the fact that we have a hard task before us. We are out to fight a great nation and men who are out for blood. This regiment have always been top-dogs even with the boys (meaning time-serving men: they had that year won nine football cups out of a possible eleven, besides other sporting competitions). What are we going to do now that we have the men? (meaning the Reservists). None of you men will come back—nor the next lot—nor the next after that—nor the next after that again; but some of the next *might*. But we'll give those Germans something to go on with, and we'll give a good account of ourselves! Remember, men, the eyes of the whole world will be upon us, and I know that you will perform whatever task is allotted to you, like men.

We were then interviewed by the king and the queen; and, later in the day, proceeded to Farnborough Station *en route* for Southampton, arriving that night, every one and everything being embarked by 11.30 p.m. No one of course knew for what port we were bound, though many suggested Belgium.

We had no "send off" whatsoever; no shaking hands or wet handkerchiefs—anyone not knowing a war had been declared would have had no suspicion that these men were starting out on active service. Yet everyone was jolly; every one was happy. They put us aboard an old China boat, and stuffed us into the holds almost to suffocation, with one large electric light burning in a distant corner: it was most unhealthy. After an hour one could have cut the air with a knife.

No sooner had we left our moorings than we ran down a lighter, killing one man on her and knocking a big hole in her side. None of us below had the slightest idea of what was happening; all we heard was an awful noise, with the lowering of the anchor. We all declared that we had been either mined or torpedoed; but after a while things quietened down, and we all tried to obtain a little sleep.

There had been issued out to us on starting seven-pound tins of jam with our other rations. One was placed near the spot I had made for myself to sleep in. It was one of the darkest parts of the hold; and, being tired, I was soon fast asleep. On awakening next morning, to my horror I found myself covered from head to foot in jam—a sorry plight indeed, as we were not allowed to carry more kit than what we stood up in. However, after fighting for a few drops of cold tea, which had to satisfy me for a breakfast, and an hour in the sun and wind on deck, I had become perfectly dry, but my clothes were as stiff as a board. All I could do was to cheerfully declare that at any rate my armour was perhaps more bullet-proof than before. Having set sail on the eleventh of August, we arrived at Le Havre on the morning of the twelfth, after a journey of twelve hours.

Chapter 2

The Landing in France

At Le Havre we were met by two men of the French Army, who to our unaccustomed eyes appeared very strange in their red trousers and blue coats. We promptly dubbed them "The Pantomime Army." They were to act as our interpreters, and came forward with their credentials to the C.O.

After disembarking our transport, etc., we were marched, through the docks, on to the dock road, there to hang about all day long, amusing ourselves as best we could. A sentry was posted to stop any man from going into the town, but we were allowed to let civilians bring us provisions.

At nightfall we were formed up, and marched by way of the seafront through the town and away up a steep hill at the back, where we found a camp already pitched for us. That march and landing I shall ever remember, and so will all those who took part in it. We were among the first English troops of the Expeditionary Force to put foot on French soil, and the excitement was great. Over the whole of the distance we travelled we were hemmed in by crowds shouting *Vive l'Angleterre!* Often they broke our ranks to embrace us. We stayed only the one night at Le Havre, and recommenced our journey on the night of the thirteenth.

At Le Havre Railway Station we were packed into horse-boxes, 36 men and N.C.O.'s in each box, the total often reaching nearly 50 men. In that condition we travelled the whole of the night, and the next day passed through St. Amiens, Rouen, and Arras. At each place we had a wonderful reception—especially at Arras, where the *mairie* and other Civic officials turned out with bouquets of flowers for the Officers; and there was a Guard of Honour of French troops. The free giving of chocolates and sweets by the populace was indeed very gratifying to us: it made us feel more eager for the work which was to follow.

That night (the fourteenth of August) we detrained at a village called Le Nouvain. It had come on to rain, and we were very pleased to find our billets situated in a large schoolhouse with plenty of clean fresh straw for our beds. On the morning of the fifteenth we marched out in brigade order, as we always did on every occasion afterwards. My brigade, which was the 2nd, commanded then by Brigadier General Bulfin, consisted of the 2nd King's Royal Rifles, 2nd Northampton Regiment, 2nd Royal Sussex Regiment, and 1st Loyal North Lancashire Regiment, each brigade consisting of four line battalions. A smarter body of men, all seasoned soldiers, one could not wish to meet (the average of their service was not less than five years, all the younger recruits having been left behind in England as peace details).

Our destination for that day at any rate was not a distant one; we proceeded only to a small village called Esquerries, not more than three miles off. There we again went into billets for four days. On arrival at the farm at which I was billeted, the farmer's wife on seeing us broke into tears—she thought that we were the Germans! But, I am pleased to say, the good woman, and her good man too, were more upset when we left, on account of having become so much attached to us.

We spent those four days in route marches; and all men under the age of twenty-five years were then inoculated. The hard part of that stay was that no man was allowed to write home giving his whereabouts, or even to head the letter with his name or regiment. Of course no Field Service postcards had been issued at that time.

On the morning of the eighteenth we bade goodbye to Esquerries, and continued in a three-days' rush up-country to Mons. The first day we covered something like sixteen miles, and came to rest in the usual farm-buildings. Before we set off the next day, any man who thought that he would not be able to perform the task before us was required to give in his name to the officer commanding companies. I believe we had two sent back, one with a troublesome leg through a break, and the other returned by the brigadier on account of his very low stature. He did not think that he would be able to accomplish any forced marches we might have to undergo. That day we did a matter of twenty miles.

On the third day out we passed through Mauberge. We had only covered some seven miles when a halt was called and we lay on the right of the road for six hours. While there we were told that a force of about 30,000 Germans was on our front, and the cavalry had gone out on a reconnaissance.

At 5 o'clock they marched us into billets, but we had not been settled more than an hour and a half when a staff officer came galloping up with orders to move at once. About four miles from Mauberge we could hear a distant boom of a gun, and all lines of communication had been cut. A halt was called in the centre of Mauberge for one hour, and we were told that no man was to eat his "iron ration," *i.e.* emergency ration, or drink any of the water which he carried in his water-bottle, as we were expecting to go into action and probably should not get the supplies up for four days. On we went, and marched for two hours without a minute's rest. The men began to tire, and their cry became the opposite to that with which we set out. Then it was, "Are we down-hearted?" now it had become, "Dump us in a field!"

After another hour we had passed the outer forts of Mauberge, and were feeling our way very cautiously. Suddenly we would go on with a rush; then more slowly; and this sort of thing continued until 2 a.m. We had had no real rest since 6 a.m. the day before; but at length we arrived at a small village south of Mons, where we found billets, one company of my regiment going further on to find outpost duty. Thankful I was not to be in that company!

Our rest did not last very long. Arriving in as we did at 2 a.m., we were brought out again at 3.30 a.m., with a remark from the colonel that we were a lazy lot of ——. Some of us could barely crawl, being stiff and chafed from our long march of nearly thirty-five miles—not bad for one day, considering that we were fully equipped.

Our next move was to a field two miles off. We were moved so early from the last place because it was thought advisable to shift us before daybreak, owing to the probability of its being shelled by the Germans. In this field the morning was occupied by feet and rifle inspection. A German aeroplane came over us, and we were all ordered to line the hedges and seek cover, which we did in quick time.

During the afternoon we moved higher up toward the enemy, staying in another village for a few hours. We were put into another schoolhouse, which was well stocked with vegetables in the garden, so we set about preparing for ourselves an enjoyable repast. Just on our front the batteries were in action, and, whilst awaiting our dinner, we sat upon the wall of the school and watched the duel. It was a glorious sight! A flock of birds in the distance was mistaken by all of us for a

Zeppelin through the haze. We were, however, doomed to go without the big dinner we had promised ourselves, as we were given our marching orders and were off before it was cooked.

On forming up with the remainder of the brigade, we were ordered to charge magazine, with one round in the breach also. Things began to look exciting, and in their agitation a few men let their rifles go off, narrowly missing their comrades. We then advanced through an avenue for a mile at the double, when the word was given to halt and lie down, no smoking and no talking, as we were now in support to the South Staffords on our front, who were expected to retire through us at any minute. After laying there the whole of the night, and having the pioneer sergeant run over by a pair of mules attached to an ammunition limber, we were not required! All we got for our night out was the loss of the pioneer sergeant, with two broken ribs, and one other man injured. It had been a pitch-black night, and we had not noticed a trench just off the road filled with straw, where we could have rested our aching limbs.

As soon as daybreak appeared, we were ordered off that road; and we had no sooner left it than it was heavily shelled. We dug some more trenches that same day and retired from them just before they were blown up, so we were evidently very fortunate on the twenty-second of August, 1914.

On leaving the road, we retired to a thicket on our left rear, but quitted it, and came to the trenches aforementioned. Two batteries were just behind us there, and they were having a bad time. Also while there the Scots Greys, who were our brigade scouts, came in with a report of meeting with a body of *Uhlans*. They had evidently surprised these *Uhlans*, and had given them a warm time, the losses of the Scots Greys being only one man, I believe, and two wounded. As I pointed out before, we left those trenches in the nick of time; they were not the trenches we have now in France, but only what we call "one-man trenches"—very little more than head cover, dug with our entrenching tools and no good whatsoever against shell fire.

After retiring from them we were kept on the side of the road for the night; and for the next few days were rushed from one position to another.

Early one morning we set off to guard a bridge, and, after going a mile or so, we were again placed in a field. On the way we were handed some corned beef and biscuits, also a grocery ration, *i.e.* a tin of tea and sugar and two Oxo cubes, by some A.S.C. men who had been left with orders to issue them to troops going into action. One of them handed me mine with the remark: "You'll need it, old man, where you're going!" Very cheerful, I thought.

We then advanced over some open fields in artillery formation, the Scots Greys going first, probing all hedges with their swords. In this field we were told to line the hedges.

Two incidents worth relating occur to my mind, one was the bravery of one of our flying-men—he had just flown over the German lines, and on coming back was being shelled by the German batteries—how he escaped being hit I cannot think, as shells were bursting no less than a dozen at once all around him, and the fragments of shells were dropping around us everywhere, though no one was hit. Our colonel, highly pleased with the steadiness of the aviator, remarked that he felt proud to be an Englishman.

The other incident occurred in connection with an order of the C.O. He gave out that the Germans had advanced upon the Middlesex Regiment, driving the civil population of various villages in front of them and thus screening themselves. He was very sorry to say that, if it was done to us, we should have to fire upon them, as it was our duty to those at home. But happily it did not occur then, or on any occasion on which I faced the Germans, so I was spared the horror of assisting in the slaughter of women and children in such a cowardly way.

However, the bridge we set out to guard in the first place had, I believe, been taken by the enemy, so our services were not required.

Our fighting experiences at Mons were not very severe, as the work fell to the lot of other brigades. The 1st Brigade, which contained two battalions of Guards, the 2nd Black Watch, and the Munster Fusiliers, suffered far more heavily than did we, who were moved from one place to another, mostly in support. Operating as we did chiefly round the outskirts of Mons, our casualty list was very slight.

CHAPTER 3

The Retirement

It was from that field that we commenced the great Retirement. My recollections of the villages and towns we passed through on our way are now slight, since we often marched at night, though I have a clear remembrance of some of the larger ones which we traversed by day.

It was the twenty-fourth of August, on a blazing hot afternoon, when we started upon our great task. There was not a soul amongst the officers or the men who had the slightest idea as to what was our destination. The first day or two we tramped along happily enough. It was not, I believe, until the evening of the second day that we obtained an inkling of what was about to happen, when we found ourselves passing through the outskirts of Mauberge once more. Most of us got the impression that we were retiring with a view to taking up a better position. A rumour went the rounds of the regiment that day to say that the C.O. was leaving us for a staff appointment; and he did leave us, but returned again in the course of the next few days.

Most of the next ten days remain in my mind as a nightmare. The weather was exceedingly hot, the long roads with stone sets stretching as far as eye could see were very wearisome, and the men were utterly exhausted. On the third day out we took prisoner a German mounted man, with two others, one of whom got away, and a second was shot.

On one occasion, just before entering a wood, one of our aeroplanes came down near us, and the pilot ran promptly to the general. After a few words, our direction was entirely changed. Had it not been for that aeroplane we should certainly have been ambushed.

We marched in brigades, each day the lead being taken in turns, the last regiment finding rearguard; and the same thing happened by divisions, three brigades to a division, and each brigade taking its turn to lead. The provost marshal and military police went on in front to inform the civilian population of towns and villages to clear out as quickly as possible, and to publish notices of the enemy's advance.

The hardest time of all was when one's particular regiment found rearguard: then we often had to march back for a few miles along the way we had come, dig trenches, hold the enemy the whole of the day, and then at night continue the march until we picked up the main body again. Oftentimes on reaching the main body it was found that they were just ready to start again, so the rearguard would be obliged to continue their march without intermission.

It was a couple of days out of Mons and during a rearguard action that the Munster Fusiliers received a good drubbing, but not until after they had held the enemy at bay for several hours. My regiment was that evening doing rearguard to our own brigade when some of the Munsters retired through us. One poor fellow going through told us how his chum had had his jaw blown away by a piece of shell, and the Germans on reaching the Munsters' trenches had killed all the wounded with the very entrenching tools they had been using. We expected to see them coming in force that night, but after waiting until dusk, we retired on the main body. Unfortunately we did not get clear away without casualties. An unlucky affair occurred in this way: we had, the day before, passed through Soissons, and I remember it was at this village that we caught up with the main body.

On entering the village we had to cross a bridge with a river beneath, and the Northampton Regiment was guarding it while the engineers stood by ready to blow it up when we were all over. My regiment was the last to cross, and we had already done so with the exception of one platoon, and were told to stand in the centre of the village, when someone gave the word that we were all over; and accordingly the engineers blew up the bridge. No sooner had that happened than this platoon came marching down the road. Of course the Northamptons mistook them in the dark for the Germans, and opened rapid fire upon them.

I was afterwards told by a chum who was in that platoon that a body of *Uhlans* came galloping down the road not five minutes afterwards; and he, with one or two others who had survived the Northamptons' fire, were taken prisoners. (This particular man fell ill, so they put him into hospital, and when we fought the Battle of the Marne we retook him; he was sent home, and after a month or two convalescent leave he rejoined us.) Naturally the officer in charge of the *Uhlans* was very wild when he found the bridge had been blown up, as it was eight miles to the next crossing.

Most of our men had thrown away all their heavy kit, such as topcoats, etc., and the Germans of course made good use of them, some of them putting the clothes on.

At one place at which we were billeted five of these Germans stopped in the house next to a barn where a platoon of the Connaughts[1] were. Just before daybreak these Germans gave the alarm, and, as the Connaughts rushed out of their billets to the alarm post, the enemy were awaiting them with machine guns. This I got from a man who on the following night laid himself down to sleep on the pavement where I was doing sentry-go. Poor fellow, he had on no hat or jacket, neither had he any rifle or equipment. He had been following us all day, and had had nothing to eat. So I took him into the room of the house which we were then using as a Guard Room, and the N.C.O. in charge took him before an officer. His story was proved to be correct, so he was allowed to stay with the company for the night; but what became of him after I know not.

Next morning my regiment was finding rearguard, so we marched through the town to an old disused mill. Going through that, and crossing a field, we came to a swiftly running stream, which we waded across through water up to our armpits. On the other side we had a very steep bank to climb, and up which we had to drive two pack animals. One of these, after climbing up a part of the way, fell down and simply rolled over and over till he reached the bottom. We had to shoot the wretched animal, owing to a damaged fetlock. On gaining the summit, we set off in skirmishing order over a mile of open country, going through wheatfields, trampling the ripe wheat underfoot as we went, until we struck a main road which ran parallel with the one we had travelled the day before. Just off this we dug the usual one-man trench, and remained there all day long. The only sight we had of the enemy was a patrol of cavalry too far off to be within range.

Towards four in the afternoon we commenced again to retire, and had no sooner reached the next village before the enemy began to shell us. Again we were lucky in getting off with no damage and no casualty. All this was all very well, but it did not suit the men. This running away from the enemy could not be stood at any price, and the constant cry was: "Why don't we stand and fight them? What are we afraid of? If you bring us here to fight, let's fight—otherwise put us all

---

1. The 88th Connaughts got badly cut up on the Retirement.

on a boat and dump us down in England."

On several occasions we passed food-supplies left on the roadside—left for the Germans: whole cheeses, tins of mustard, one of which I carried for four days, but, on getting nothing to eat with it, I threw it away.

We would arrive outside a village, allotted for billets, perhaps about 7.30 p.m., and, after having marched the whole of the day, we were not allowed to enter the village until eleven or twelve o'clock at night to make ourselves comfy. The reason, I believe, was that it might be shelled by the enemy. No one was allowed to touch a thing—not even fruit—or he would be punished for looting; yet we knew very well that, perhaps on the morrow, the Germans would secure it all.

Various bulletins were issued during that Retirement, I suppose to cheer up the troops. One I remember contained the report of a German who had been taken prisoner, and who had upon him a diary, which—according to the bulletin—declared that the German Army was starving. Another, a very strong rumour, went the rounds, to the effect that we were doing a strategical retirement for the purpose of drawing the main body of the German Army into France, whilst the Russians came in on the East. Two days after that, a report was out that the Russians were marching on Berlin, and were within a few days' march of the capital itself. Imagine our feelings, our delight. Remember, we were absolutely cut off from all outside news. What were we to think? Most of us expected that the war would be over in a very short time.

After the first five days, we were given a day's halt. The whole of the day before we had been marching until three in the morning, and were told on this day's rest that we had done so well, outpacing the enemy and outwitting them so successfully, that we should no doubt be able to rest for the next three days. On that day they paid us out, giving each man five *francs*, which, however, were of no earthly use to us, as we were all brigaded in a large field, and there was not a shop for miles. Our three-days' rest, however, did not materialise: we were off again next morning, with the enemy hot on our heels, having overtaken us by motors. So we had to continue our weary task sooner than we had anticipated.

We were all fairly quiet on the country roads, but as soon as we came to any large towns or villages we would always knock out the strains of "Tipperary." Another good point in Tommy's character manifested itself—no matter how many miles he had covered during the day, during which he would be grumbling the whole of the time, he would, immediately on striking camp, walk if necessary for miles looking for a hay or straw stack on which to find something soft and clean to lie upon.

One turning point on that Retirement was a small town, by name Bernay, I believe, in the Champagne. There we arrived on a Saturday at midday; the afternoon was spent in resting. A few days before we had struck off south from Meaux, and we heard that we were to defend Paris. During the afternoon before we arrived at Bernay, we had passed an encampment of refugees numbering many thousands, and just outside Bernay were many more. I was on outpost duty that night; and a suspicious individual came up to me whilst I was on sentry. I, of course, inquired his business; but, as he could not understand my language, he took no notice. As I could not leave my post, I told another man who was off duty at the time to bring him in. This fellow went out with his rifle, but, although he was one of the fastest runners in my regiment, he could not overtake the stranger, who got away. He may have been only a refugee having a look round, or, on the other hand, he may have been a spy.

That day we finished our retirement from Mons: it was the sixth of September, 1914.

The Advance

The following morning we left Bernay behind, and, going out the opposite side of the town from which we had entered, we marched two miles along the road until we came to a hill on the left of the road about five hundred yards off. There we advanced to the cover of the hill and were ordered to lie down. We were then informed that a four-days' battle was expected, and that a force of 40,000 Germans was on our front. Nothing, however, came of it that day; so we advanced a few more miles, and took rest in a field for an hour. There we were told that all men who wished to do so could grow a beard. From there we marched on to billets in a village.

The next morning we were away early, and during that day we passed through a village from which the Germans had obviously made a hurried exit, for we found that many things had been left behind. We were the ones that were doing the chasing now, and a nice change it was to us! Of course, we could not go very fast, not as fast as we had been made to go when retiring; and we were allowed to march in greater comfort. During the Retirement the infantry had had to put up with many trials for instance: we took the right of the road and on the left we sometimes had cavalry, artillery, and transport, which made marching most uncomfortable, whereas during the Advance we had the road to ourselves.

On the third day out we came across several dead horses and dead troopers, where our advance party had come into contact with the enemy's rearguard.

Chapter 4

The Battle of the Marne

I will make a humble attempt to relate the Battle of the Marne as it was fought by the 1st Division. Our worst day—the one on which we did the most fighting—was the tenth of September. On the morning of that day we marched off particularly early, and we must have done close on ten miles, as we were halted for rest on two occasions. On breasting a hill about two miles from the last halt, we were again called to the halt, and the artillery, brought up from behind, opened out on each side of the road and the crest of the hill. The word was then passed down the ranks that a large German convoy was expected to leave this village, and that we were to capture it. Everyone was in high spirits, as food had been none too plentiful, and we were all looking forward to the capture of this convoy in the hopes of recompense.

The North Lancashires were the second regiment, with the 2nd Royal Sussex leading, they and the King's Royal Rifles taking the left of the road, and the North Lancashires and Northamptons taking the right. We then commenced to advance in artillery formation, three hundred paces distant and fifty paces interval: this we did until reaching the bottom of the hill and to the right of the village half a mile away. In this village, by name Preiz, were the Germans, and running out the other side, but up the hill, was the German convoy retiring, the village itself being in a basin. On reaching the bottom of the hill, we had to cross a stream: once on the other side we opened out in extended order, our idea being to skirt the village and come up with the Germans going over the other crest.

Unfortunately it was a wet morning, and the men had taken the advantage of putting their oil-sheets round their shoulders to keep them dry, the oil-sheets when wet being of a similar colour to the German uniform. In the distance our gunners bombarded us, mistak-

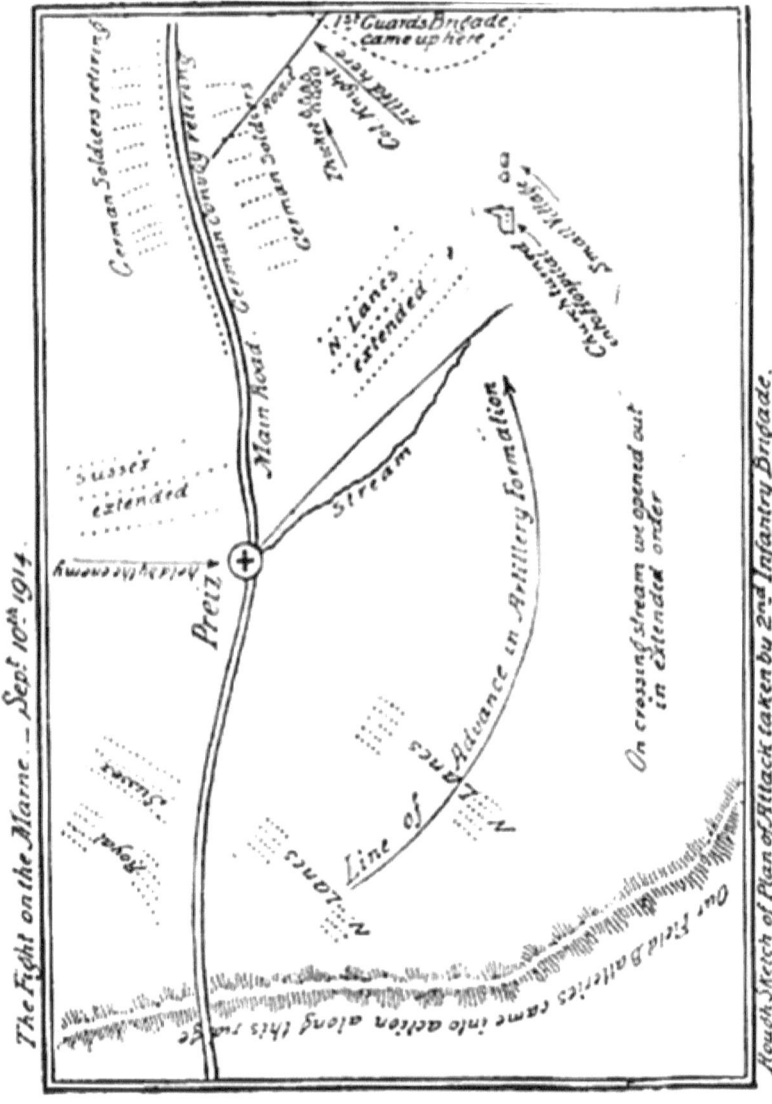

MAP 1

ing us for the retiring enemy; and we had no sooner come into view of our gunners than they let go. However, we plodded on, going up in short rushes by platoons. We had with us at the time a new man who had volunteered for the front at the outbreak of war, offering to enlist provided the authorities despatched him straight out.

This they had done, sending him to the particular platoon to which I belonged. To our sorrow, he happened to be the end man, and should have given the word when the other platoon had halted and got down, to enable us to advance. That first platoon, having got down, opened fire, and instead of our advancing under cover of that fire, that man failed to give the word. I was second man, and, after lying still with our heads stuck into the ground for ten minutes, I asked him if the other platoon had stopped—to which he replied: "I do not know, as I cannot see them." So I gave the order to advance. Consequently as soon as we got up we were met with a heavy fire from the enemy, losing at once one or two men. On crossing a narrow track of road near the crest of the hill we were joined by the C.O., who had come up there by the road to give us final instructions. He got hit by a piece of shell, which passed through his horse's neck and entered his stomach: he died a few minutes afterwards.

We were now getting quite close to the enemy and bearing round on to the main road; but, as the fire became too hot for us and as we had no reinforcements, we had to fall back as far as the stream. A quarter of an hour after that the Guards 1st Brigade came up on our right, and the major who was then in charge of us said he was very sorry that we had not taken the position, but that we would try again: this time it would be an easier task, as we had the Guards on our right to help us.

Once more we opened out into skirmishing order and recommenced our task; meanwhile on the right the Sussex were doing well, and the King's Royal Rifles and Northamptons had succeeded in driving the enemy from the village. So by the time we had reached the crest again, the enemy had flown and the Guards were not required. Coming back into the village, we found the artillery had advanced through the village and from the top of the crest were shelling the departing Germans on the other side of the hill.

We reorganised in the village, and when the roll was called we found we were about fifty men short of the number we attacked with. Needless to say, we did not capture the convoy, neither were our rations increased, but we had the satisfaction of knowing that we had, at any rate, taken the village and driven the Germans off one section of the Marne. Our greatest loss was our C.O.; but we also lost the captain of B Company, who was reported missing and has never been heard of since.

In that battle my section was particularly fortunate, losing only one man. and he the sergeant in charge, who had been hit in the knee by a bullet, but it was only a slight wound. Moreover, on our second advance over the rise we did not get the shelling of our own gunners, as word had been sent back to them informing them of their mistake.

During the next three days we had only running encounters with the enemy.

On the afternoon of the thirteenth of September—a Sunday afternoon—we took up position on the top of a large hill facing the valley of the Aisne. Whilst there, one or two shells came over and we had a few casualties, but the words of our brigadier were: "They will not give battle here, but over there," pointing to some big hills about four miles away, behind which lay the town of Laon. On that morning we had anticipated some street fighting at a place we had come through called Bourge. yet, although they had had the streets well barricaded, they did not show fight, but elected to fall back. That night we were taken from our position on top of the hill nearer the enemy to a village and there put into billets. At eight o'clock everyone was fairly comfortable, and we were settled in farm-buildings with plenty of good straw; but how we managed to sleep so comfortably—with the Germans only three miles off—I cannot say. Why they never blew us off the face of the earth with the big guns they possessed we often wondered—anyhow they didn't! and we got down, to dream of home, huddled into each other the best way we could to keep warm.

Chapter 5

The Battle of the Aisne

We were roused next morning with kicks from the platoon commanders, and, after much struggling and putting on of wrong equipments, we marched out, but not before each man had received two ounces of Gold Flake tobacco, the first English tobacco we had seen since leaving home.

It was the fourteenth day of September, and raining. Leaving the village, we marched down a road for about five hundred yards, bordered on each side by high banks. There a halt was called. On our right we could hear the sound of shots, and the corporal in charge of the range-finder was sent to the top of the bank to take the range. He could not see very far, on account of a heavy mist, but reported the King's Royal Rifles advancing. We then doubled by platoons through an avenue of trees exposed to the enemy's fire, and gained some fields on the further side of the road, lining the hedges. From there into the valley led one road which was little more than a narrow defile; then it wound away to the right front over the crest which the Germans held. Halfway up this road was a small village called Tryon. At the rear and facing the crest held by the enemy was another and smaller hill thickly wooded. Before taking us through the defile and into the valley, the words of the brigadier were: "That ridge has to be taken by nightfall—otherwise we shall be annihilated."

That day witnessed one of the worst battles I have ever experienced, as we were badly equipped with guns, having mostly only eighteen-pounders—"pop-guns," as the boys called them—whilst it was the first day on which we met the really big guns of the Germans—those promptly dubbed "Jack Johnsons."

Our particular front was facing a beet-sugar factory just off the main road, and there the fighting was very furious. By midday we had

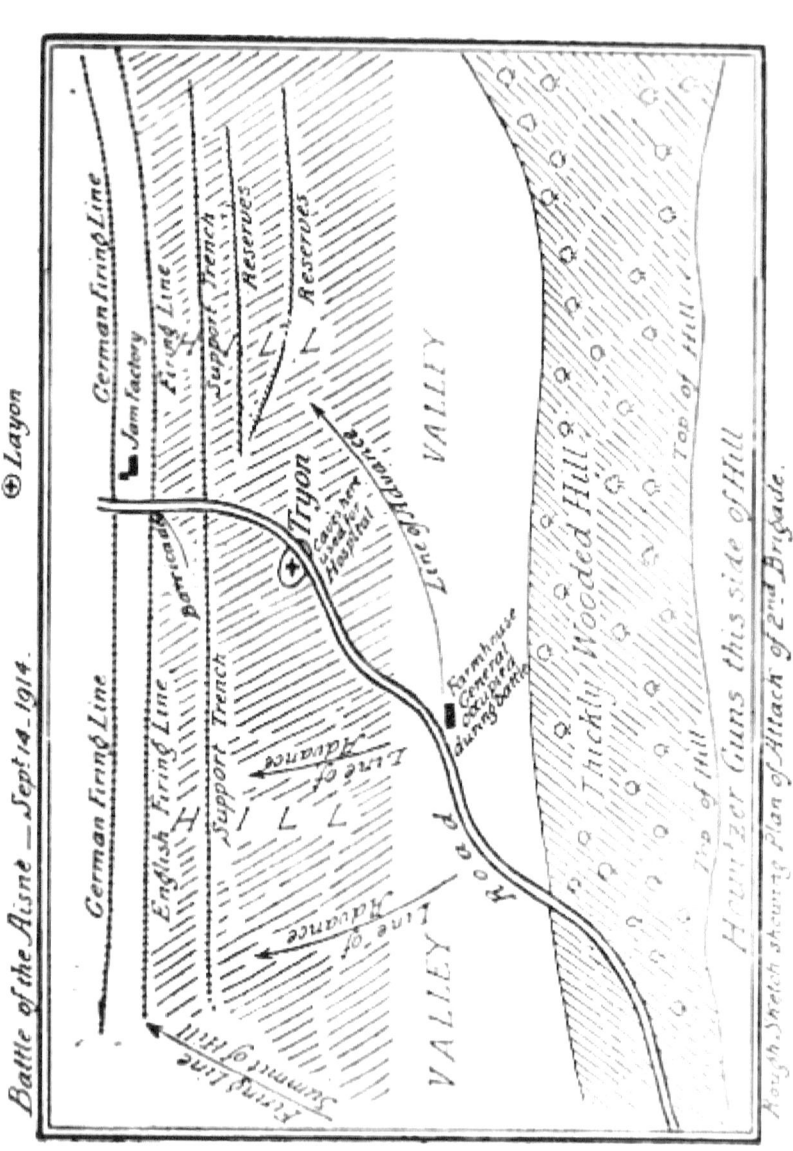

Map 2.

taken several of the Prussian Guard and of the Death's Head Own Hussars prisoners; also report went round that we had captured twelve guns, which news cheered us greatly. One prisoner, a Prussian Guardsman, remarked on the way back: "Never mind, boys; we shall soon be back in dear old London again!"

On one occasion early in the day, having to retire from the top of the crest down into the valley, our company-sergeant-major took us *via* the other hill through the wood to the position at the summit of the hill which the Germans held. It was a splendid move, well carried out, and without the loss of a single man.

On gaining the summit on the first occasion one team of our machine-gunners took up position and held it the whole of the day, helping us greatly to secure the position against all enemy assaults. The men stood their ground splendidly, three of them being recommended for the Distinguished Conduct Medal. On our right was the 1st Brigade, and connected up with us was the Black Watch. One large shell of the Germans which pitched amongst a platoon of theirs standing between two haystacks completely wiped them out with the exception of two men.

We continued to advance and retire the whole day through. First we gained ground and the Germans drove us off again; then we came back with redoubled energy, until towards evening we began to hold on and the Germans to retire. On the right of the road was a haystack on fire, and we were in a small trench just thrown up behind it. The bullets were flying from that rick as if a magazine was on fire and it was very unhealthy. At one time we were in a swede field, and a large shell burst in front of us, covering us with dirt. A chum of mine, being hit very forcibly with a flying swede, up he jumped, shouting: "I'm hit, I'm hit!" but came to the conclusion that he wasn't as bad as he had thought.

As darkness came on we all formed up in line, and the brigadier, coming to the crest, remarked: "The brigade will bivouac on the ground they now hold. Dig in." There and then we commenced a line of trenches, which are there to this day.

It had been a most awful and bloodthirsty day, with two of the finest bodies of men that ever faced each other opposed to one another. There was bound to be a good fight, and it was the cleanest and most sporting day's battle I have ever fought. Of course there was no time for food, and we got none that day; but we had the satisfaction of knowing that we had accomplished what we set out to do. We naturally had very heavy losses, including our second C.O., several other officers and a large number of N.C.O.'s and men—in all nearly four hundred. The rations came up that night while we were digging our trenches; they were brought up under cover of the darkness right to the front line and there dumped. Those who were near when they arrived were fortunate, as they got their shares; others who were further away got none. I was one of the fortunate ones, and filled my pockets with small biscuits and a lump of cheese, on which I kept two chums all next day.

During the night we dug our one-man trenches six-foot long and as deep as we could make them; it was hard work at times, the soil being very rocky. I got fairly well down nearly four feet by daybreak, when my platoon sergeant came along and ordered me to join my section further along the line, another man whose section was near me taking over my trench. It couldn't be helped, as we had all got mixed up in the day action the day before. When I joined my section I found the trench I had to take over only about a foot deep and the whole week following, although I was digging on every possible occasion, I could not get down more than six inches, as I had to go through sheer rock.

Soon after daybreak the Germans were off again, shelling our trenches with shells of every calibre. This continued for an hour, but did very little damage. After that they continued to shell our gun positions in the rear, our guns keeping up a steady reply. One howitzer battery of ours was in a cave, running out by means of rails, situated in the wooded hill behind our lines. The enemy continued to shell with every kind of gun the whole time I was on the Aisne—that is, over a month—and the only casualty that battery had was one man wounded. The German shells would burst round it with a huge roar and a noise very much like "*Krupp*," and this small gun would answer with a short sharp *bang*, for all the world as if a little boy had put his fingers to his nose at a policeman.

Just behind the line and halfway down the slope of the hill was the small village of Tryon, where there was a public wash-house. A large shell had pitched there, but never exploded; its weight was not less than one hundred and twenty pounds. There was another on the roadway, and two or three of them in the valley: one stood up on its base. We were down there one day getting wood, and a chum of mine put his foot on it, knocking it over. An officer passing at the time remarked: "You would have looked well if that thing had gone off!" My chum did not wait to hear any more—he was off.

That valley, when we left it, was like a pepper-box top—simply perforated every few yards. How we managed to remain alive on the Aisne the first week was simply a mystery. Food was scarce; and once we had a single loaf issued out between a hundred men. We tossed for it, the winner to receive the lot, the others going without. After the first week we were much better supplied, having bread or biscuits, with a ration of cheese or bacon, but precious little of that; and oftentimes I tossed for the lot and lost all! Fortunately there were plenty of potatoes and carrots in the ground—these we dug up, boiling them, and, after straining the water off, partook of them with a slice of cold corned beef. Some would boil the beef with the potatoes, thereby getting the salt from the beef into the potatoes: this we called "bully stews."

Our division, I believe, took the extreme right of the British line on the Aisne; anyway, the French were joining us. They were very quiet by day, but as soon as darkness set in they would start a rapid fire all along their line, our boys remarking: "The French have got the wind up." Our orders were not to fire on any account, but to use the bayonet. At night every other man in the front line was posted as sentry, doing one hour, after which the alternate men would do an hour. This continued until daybreak, when sentries were lowered to one in three.

The third night after taking the Aisne we expected an attack from the enemy, and the whole regiment stood to till morning. It was truly beautiful—it rained incessantly, and one could not see more than a yard in front of one's nose! That night a man of the Black Watch came in having been left out since Monday's battle: he had nearly every toe shot off and was almost blind. He had—so he told us—been in one of the boilers of the beet-sugar factory, and a German had fired several shots into the boiler, killing some more men who were in there with him. A Guardsman also came in, shot all over.

On the fourth night I was allotted a nice job. My section sergeant, coming to me just after dark, said: "I've a nice little job for you."

"Oh yes," says I—thinking it was a nice little berth behind with the transport—"what is it?"

"Do you know anything about barbed wire?" says he; "just twisting it around stakes?"

"I don't know," says I: "I may be able to do it; anyhow I could have a try."

"Well, out in front about forty yards," says this sergeant, "you will find a lot of stakes and two reels of barbed wire. Now you go out and I'll send another fellow to knock in the stakes while you can twist the wire round them and make some entanglements."

I can't say I liked the job, because I didn't! The enemy lay only a few hundred yards away, and I had to go out there attracting attention by knocking in stakes and twisting barbed wire around them, a thing the enemy would be sure to try their best to prevent. But it had to be done, so off we started, creeping over the top. We were looking for nearly an hour for this wire and, after twice nearly walking into the enemy's lines, we at length found it, and managed, after several volleys from the enemy, to accomplish our task, and rig up some sort of defence. Every night after that, whenever we occupied the front line, I was one of the men erecting the barbed wire entanglements, and many were the narrow squeaks I had at the hands of the Germans.

At the end of the first week we were relieved by the 21st Brigade, containing the Sherwood Foresters and West Yorkshires. They were a new importation from England, My word! didn't they look smart, while we who had gone through so much looked worse than tramps, absolutely reeking of mud. We were taken back to a village about five miles in the rear, and on the way back we had again to go through the defile by which we entered. Our batteries were still there, but the stench from dead horses was awful. This village was at the back of the wooded hill aforementioned, and there were several caves there, perfectly safe from the shells of the biggest guns yet made. In these caves we were lodged, and we had a chance of a rest—the first real rest we had since commencing the Retirement. At the bottom of the hill was also a river, where everyone indulged in a bathe.

We were in those caves for two days; on the third day we were called out at 4 a.m., and we proceeded to a village on our right previously occupied by the French. To get there we had to cross a sky-line, fully in view of the German observers. We men knew that sky-line, for while we lay in our trenches the whole of the previous week we had watched the Germans shell it when the French troops marched over it. Unluckily for me, my regiment was the last regiment of the brigade to go over. The other three got through safely; but, as the road was thick with mud, we had taken to the field, and thus gave the Germans an even better view of us. Two companies were nearly over before we had it: we were the last two, when over they came in batteries, five shells at a time. We were of course forced to fall back over the crest, but not before we had had twenty-five casualties, though we eventually reached our objective without any further losses.

That village was one of the very worst I had come across—dead horses and dead men everywhere. It was full of caves, in which we were kept; but we stayed there only one day, during which an enemy aeroplane passed over, and on seeing us dropped a silver ball which slowly floated down to where we were, thereby giving the range to the German batteries. But they could not hurt us on account of the good cover afforded by the caves. It was the first silver ball we had seen, and at first we took it for a bomb.

That night we returned to our old caves once more. I afterwards heard that the reason of our being called out was that the 21st Brigade, which had relieved us, had lost the trenches through a great enemy attack, but had regained them by nightfall. Whether that was the true reason or not I was never really able to learn, but, on going back to those trenches at the end of the week, which we did, we found a large grave, with a heading which read:

Thirty-seven Officers and Men
of the Sherwood Foresters
lie here.

It was a Thursday night on which we went back to our old billets in the caves, and on the following Saturday we once more returned to our old positions, only a little further to the right, the 1st Brigade taking over those we had dug in the first place. There we spent another three weeks, two regiments taking the front line and two in trenches in support a little lower down the hill. First of all we worked this arrangement alternately four days in the front line and then four days in reserve, but this was soon altered to forty-eight hours.

It was a fine sight when we were in the trenches in front to see the relieving battalions coming up to relieve us: there were no communication trenches then, and they had to advance in extended order—lines and lines of them; and when the enemy opened fire, as indeed they did occasionally, they all dropped down as one man. As soon as the firing ceased they were off again, and so on until they reached the trenches, when they would fall down just in rear, and on the word of an officer we would get out and they would get in. We would retire in the same order as they advanced.

There was plenty of work on the Aisne during those days, the men in the front line connecting each single trench up with another, so as to form one long continual line; also the making of bunny holes. During the day we had the usual order: one man in three on sentry, now commonly termed in the trenches "look-out"; and, at night, every other man—if a quiet night, one would be on sentry, one resting, and one taken for digging a communication trench, each man taking his turn an hour about. Those in the reserve lines would all turn out with picks and shovels the whole of the night, digging one main communication trench.

One Sunday morning we came in for a bad time. The enemy finding our reserve trenches, which we then occupied with the 2nd Royal Sussex, with enfilading shell-fire, put several sixty-pounders amongst us, causing a lot of damage. After that occasion those trenches were never occupied, but we made up straw dummies in khaki, and set them around each dugout; and we used to get great fun from watching the enemy shelling them, our boys remarking: "That's it, Fritz! Go ahead, and let them have it!" One shell went right through the officers' mess-cart while the officers were at tea, killing two. That cart had a history; how we came by it is worth relating. During the Retirement we were ordered to give in our great-coats, which were placed on the baggage-waggons. There was also on one of these waggons my company's money for paying out the men. This was done early one morning, and, when we marched off, the armourer sergeant and a certain number of men were left behind in charge, to follow on when everything was ready.

I was afterwards told by one of this party that the regiment had not got very far down the road when the Germans entered the village. One of our men, seeing the Germans coming and noticing this Cape cart with horse attached on the other side of the road, made a dash for it, and drove hard after us. He succeeded in getting away and joining the Regiment, but the Germans had done their best to stop him, as the cart was riddled with bullet-holes. The other men rushed out the other side of the village, thereby being cut off; there were about fifty of them from various regiments, and, when called upon to surrender, preferred to make a fight of it. They lost one killed and two wounded; and some then gave in and some made off. One man who joined us again told me they used the open country by night and hid by day, for four days. They went about like that in khaki, and on the fifth day got into a house and, procuring civilian clothing, made their way to Dunkirk, whence, after seeing the British Consul, they were sent to England. Of course, as there was no line established like that which the Germans have now in France, it was possible to do so. The armourer sergeant was amongst those taken, but he escaped from Germany later.

We were much better off now than at any time before; supplies came up more regularly, and we also had an issue of rum, as well as the Paris edition of *The Daily Mail* every day. We learnt whom we were up against—the great Von Kluck, immediately dubbed old "One O' Clock," since every day at that time they used to bombard us. It was here that we first heard that we were "the contemptible little army." Here we also received a draft of reinforcements other than Regulars, the Special Reserve joining the few remaining regulars.

I had here an experience of being a sniper. I was on sentry-go in the front line one morning when an N.C.O. came up to me and inquired "what class shot" I was. I replied "first class"—which I was.

"All right," he said, "you're the man we want. Come with me to the captain." After putting another man on sentry, I followed him. He stated my qualifications to the captain.

"Just the man!" says the captain; "the reason I sent for you is that we are persistently being troubled by a sniper, and I wish you to crawl out in front and bag him."

"Very good, sir," said I—no good saying anything else; so I asked him the position he thought the German was firing from.

"Half right," said he; "if you watch closely until those leaves blow aside, you will see his head"; which I did after a minute or so. "I want you to get that man," said the captain. Off I crept over the top with loaded rifle, and, after going a couple of hundred yards, I lay down and waited, rifle ready cocked. As soon as the leaves moved I let drive my whole magazine at him. Then I waited again. The leaves moved once more, so he was still there. I got suspicious and crawled nearer; but found no enemy sniper—nothing but a post stuck in the ground! No more sniping for me!

Our stay on the Aisne was drawing to a close, but I heard afterwards that two civilians—one an old man and the other a girl—had been shot as spies, the man for working an underground telephone and the girl for sending off carrier-pigeons. These people had lived the whole time along with other civilians in the little village behind the line; they were found out by the French Division who relieved us. Every day, as regular as clockwork, the enemy had shelled us for an hour after daybreak, and for an hour at midday, and again another hour at dusk, with an occasional burst during the night. Rifle-fire was always plentiful on the Aisne at night on both sides.

We left the Aisne in the small hours of the morning of the sixteenth of October, being relieved by a French Division, after we had been in the trenches the whole of the time since the battle of the fourteenth of September. Whilst the French Division was coming up at midnight with the utmost quietness and on a pitch-black night, the enemy poured shrapnel into them, causing the loss of fifty-two to that division, which simply went to show that the Germans had a pretty good idea of what was afloat.

That morning we marched to Braine, and there we entrained for what we all thought was going to be a rest, but really proved to be a harder task than anything we had had before.

Chapter 6

The First Battle of Ypres

From the Aisne we travelled in the usual fashion, thirty-six to forty in a horse-box, *via* St. Denis to Boulogne, where we stopped until 3 p.m. on the Sunday afternoon of October the eighteenth. As usual, many rumours were afloat, the strongest being that we were going on garrison duty to some quiet little place, to pick up strength once more. That quiet little place turned out to be Ypres! The reason of our stoppage in Boulogne was that a train in front of us, also a troop train, had met with an accident; seventeen men had been killed: so we had to wait whilst the line was being cleared. We were supposed to stay with the train, but a good many men went into the town. Consequently the train moved off suddenly, leaving one hundred men and three officers behind in Boulogne. They eventually joined us, each man receiving fourteen days Number One Field punishment.

Leaving Boulogne, we travelled some way up the line, detraining at a small station called Arneke. Early next morning they marched us on to Cassel, where we stayed one day, marching out next morning in brigade order. We proceeded *via* Beaulieu and Poperinghe, resting for the night a few miles north of the latter place.

The following day we proceeded very slowly, and scouts were sent out to our right into a wood on the look-out for the enemy. Evidently everything was in order, as we advanced through that wood during the night. On the way we met many horse-ambulances returning filled with wounded. Emerging from the wood, we arrived at the town of Boesnighe, and that night we found billets there. Moving off early the next evening in a south-easterly direction, after marching the whole of that night with fixed bayonets and hushed voices, we went into action the next morning.

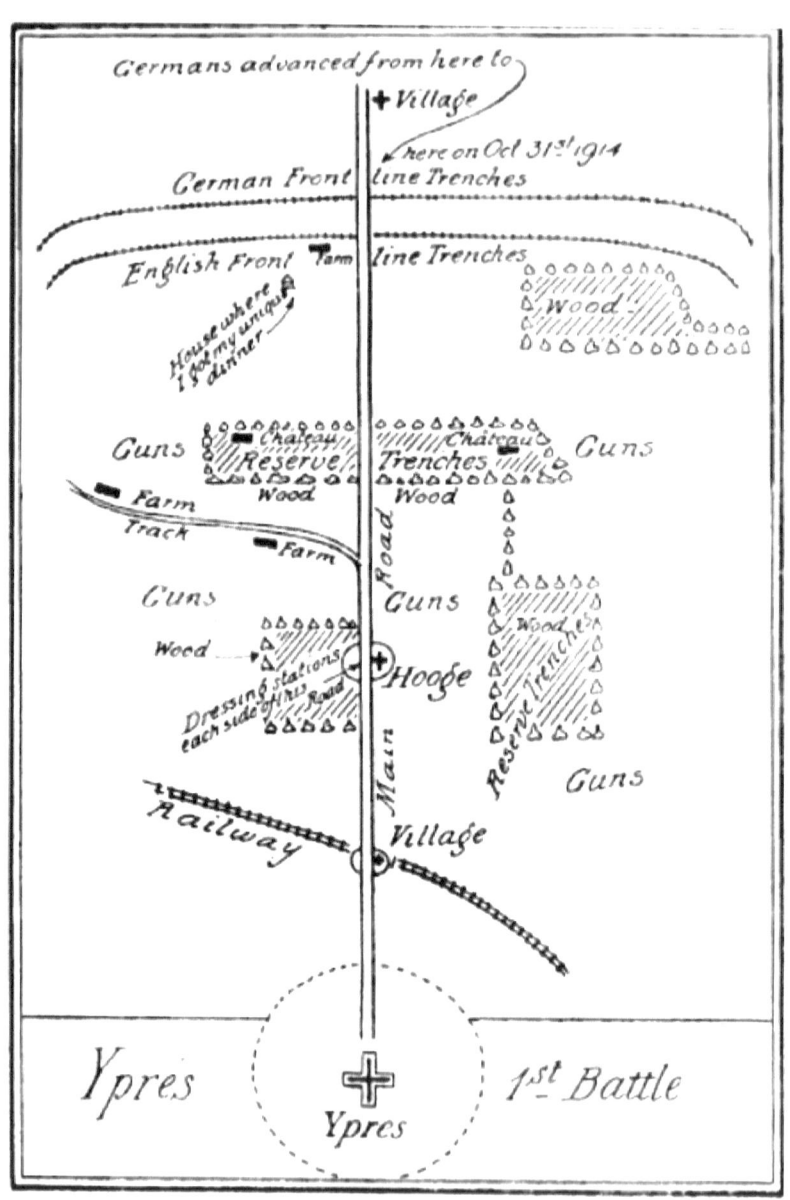

MAP 3

CHAPTER 7

The Fight on the Bipschoote-Langemarck Road, October 23rd, 1914

We were, I believe, sent up in reserve to the 1st Brigade. Whether that is correct or not, it is not for me to state—all I know is that we formed up well behind the front line, two companies taking the first line in extended order and two companies the second line in the same order. Thus we advanced about a mile over flat open country to the front line. We went up in short rushes, and a word of praise is due to the men who took part in it. I never even on the Barrack Square or drill-ground saw a better advance: the men went up absolutely in line, each man keeping his correct distance, and that under heavy machine-gun and rifle fire. Of course some men got knocked over; but it made absolutely no difference. One officer, a Major Powell, carried a chair with him the whole of the way, and, on reaching a hedge, would mount this chair to get a view of the enemy.

Two hundred yards off the front line, we made a combined rush into it. There we found the Camerons, with the usual one-man trench. The man I lay down behind told me that they had been out there three days and had had no rations, and also that they had had many men taken prisoners.

In this front line we had a breather, the German trenches being roughly three hundred yards away, and a hedge was also running parallel between the two lines of trenches, with a big gap facing us. Through this gap we could see the enemy retiring one and two at a time from their trenches. They appeared like so many rabbits running from their holes, and, as they ran, so we took pot-shots at them. After

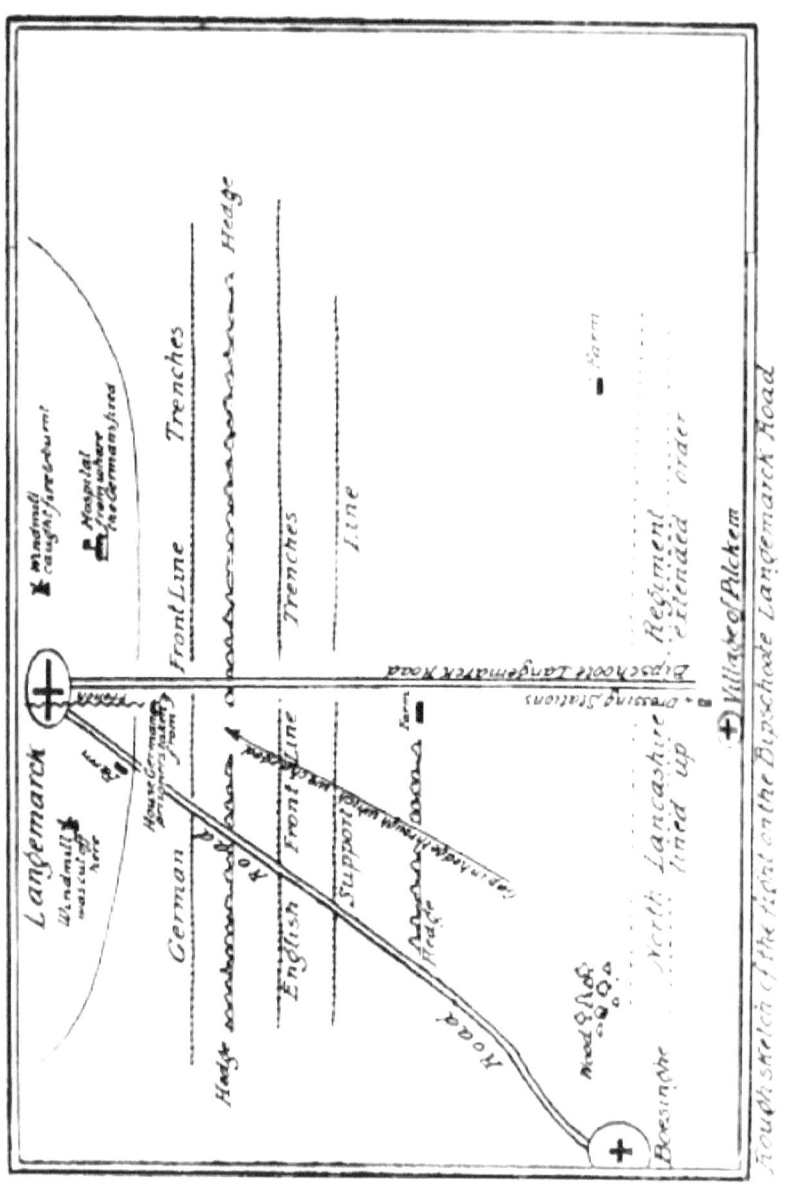

Map 4

we had had our breather, the word was given to charge; and this we did, going through in fine style. Just behind the front line of German trenches was a house from which we took a number of prisoners. The first man of ours to reach it was a corporal. He called upon the Germans to surrender and got a bullet through the brain for his pains. The Germans then saw us, and were obliged to surrender, and were given over to men to take behind. One German officer remarked: "We don't mind we've got Paris, and London is in flames." One of our officers turned round and said: "You know that's not true." Whereon he remarked: "I know, but the men believe it."

The troops we were fighting there were on the whole very young, and they had new clothing and equipment, and told us that they had left Germany for what they thought would be manoeuvres in Belgium, and did not expect seeing the firing line for some months. I myself really thought the war was over that day, as Germans surrendered from all directions and we overran their trenches everywhere.

I went on with the first line, right into the village of Langemarck. We got to a windmill, where we took up position—two officers and thirty-four men, the officers being Captain Craig and Lieutenant Gardiner (afterwards taken prisoner). As it began to get dark, we set about trying to find the other part of the Regiment, and another man and myself were sent out to locate them. Creeping along quietly for about three hundred yards, we came to a trench. Thinking it was occupied by our own men, we walked up, and found it full of Germans! We were off with a volley behind us, but got safely back, reporting the incident to the captain. After studying the map for some time, he came to the conclusion that we were cut off, and had better wait until it was quite dark. This we did, and successfully found the remainder of the regiment.

We had done well that day and set to work with a will during the night on a new line of trenches. These we held the next day, being relieved again at night by a French Division, with the exception of about thirty of us, who were unfortunately left behind.

It had happened this wise: there was a sharp bend in the trench, and my platoon was round the other side of that bend. The French, on coming up the communication trench in the dark, had gone straight on, relieved the remainder of the battalion, and had left us there. The battalion, on forming up in the rear to march off, had found that we were missing; they had waited for us in a field, naturally thinking we should join up as soon as we had been relieved. After waiting for an hour, daybreak came, and the Germans had commenced to shell them; so they had made off, leaving us behind.

We in the trenches were rather worried by a party firing over our heads, apparently from behind, and the Germans were in front. Towards daybreak the men on our left commenced firing heavily, and the officer in charge of us (Lieutenant Gardiner) shouted out to know the reason of it. After shouting several times and getting no answer, he sent an N.C.O. down to inquire. When that N.C.O. came back and reported that the trench was full of French troops, we knew then the regiment had gone and had left us—anyhow, Lieutenant Gardiner went behind and found the men who had been firing over our heads to be French troops also. They were in a ditch, evidently in the dark taking this ditch to be the line of trenches. Of course, on being told their mistake, they cheerfully came up and let us fall to the rear.

On the way back we inquired of everyone if they knew the whereabouts of our regiment, but, as no one knew, we were stranded. We then marched back to our old billets in Boesinghe, which we had left a couple of days before. We found no regiment there, so the officer took us all into an *estaminet* (beer-shop), and ordered us coffee and food. We then heard from a staff officer that the regiment had gone on to Ypres. It was Sunday morning, October 25th, 1914, when we arrived at Ypres. The town was then practically in its normal state, being full of civilians just returning from Mass, and no German shell had yet visited the town. There we found our Corps Headquarters, and the officer in charge of us, having reported the episode of how we got left behind in the trenches and learnt the whereabouts of the regiment, was told that the G.O.C. was highly pleased with our work of the last two days, and that when he reported to the C.O. (Major Carter), who had joined us recently and had led us in the last attack, he was to tell him that the men who had been left behind were to be struck off all guards, fatigues, etc., for the next twenty-four hours and to be given a thorough rest.

Thus ended the Langemarck engagement so far as we were concerned. On October 26th, 1914, General Headquarters issued the report, a copy of which appeared in the current account of *The Times* of November 17th, 1914, as follows:

The Gallant North Lancashires
Special 2nd Brigade Order
26th October, 1914

In the action of the 23rd of October, 1914, the 2nd Infantry

Brigade (less the 2nd Royal Sussex Regiment left at Boesinghe) was allotted the task of reinforcing the 1st Infantry Brigade and retaking the trenches along the Bipschoote-Langemarck Road, which had been occupied by the enemy. In spite of the stubborn resistance offered by the German troops, the object of the engagement was accomplished, but not without many casualties in the brigade.

By nightfall the trenches previously captured by the Germans had been reoccupied, about 500 prisoners captured, and fully 1,500 German dead were lying out in front of our trenches.

The brigadier-general congratulates the 1st Loyal North Lancashire Regiment, Northampton Regiment, and the 2nd K.R.R.C. (King's Royal Rifle Corps), but desires specially to commend the fine soldier-like spirit of the 1st Loyal North Lancashire Regiment, which, advancing steadily under heavy shell and rifle fire, and aided by machine-guns, was enabled to form up within a comparatively short distance of the enemy's trenches. Fixing bayonets, the battalion then charged, carried the trenches, and occupied them; and to them must be allotted the majority of the prisoners captured.

The brigadier-general congratulates himself on having in his brigade a battalion which, after marching the whole of the previous night without food or rest, was able to maintain its splendid record in the past by the determination and self-sacrifice displayed in this action.

The brigadier-general has received special telegrams of congratulations from both the G.O.C.-in-Chief, 1st Corps, and the G.O.C., 1st Division, and he hopes that in the next engagement in which the brigade takes part the high reputation which the brigade already holds may be further added to.

(Signed) B. Pakenham, Captain,
Brigade Major 2nd Infantry Brigade.

On October 26th, 1914, we left our billets on the Melin Road, and proceeded further up, halting about halfway between Ypres and Hooge, called then by us the "black and white village." There we were placed in a field, and, once more lining the hedges, we stopped there the rest of the day. A regrettable incident took place towards evening: one of our own aeroplanes was brought down by our own fire, under the impression that it was an enemy. It caught fire five hundred yards up, and burned furiously: both men, pilot and observer, were killed.

The following morning, October the twenty-seventh, we filed out of these fields, and, passing through Hooge, continued up the road as far as a large wood on the left of the road and about three miles from Ypres town. At the north end of this wood were some batteries of artillery behind a large *château*, and in this wood we dug lines of trenches with entrenching tools.

Next day, the twenty-eighth, we were taken from here to another wood on our left front nearly half-a-mile from the last. We had a little difficulty in reaching it, as the whole of the distance was within view of the enemy. Anyhow, we did the distance, by platoons, at the double and at a hundred paces interval.

This wood was larger than the one we had just left, and we commenced at once to dig in at the rear end. We had had no casualties on the journey, although the Germans had shelled us with eighteen-pounders, all shells, fortunately, bursting at each side of the road. We stayed in this wood until the next morning, then retiring to the one we had come from. We had one or two casualties before we left, losing one or two men wounded and a horse killed, the enemy's observation having been attracted to us by the smoke from a fire.

That afternoon, the twenty-ninth of October, we proceeded to advance once more. Getting nearly a mile up the main road, we took the left side, going out in extended order. Thence we advanced another half-mile, coming under shell-fire; when we reached the rise, we lay down. All this time we had seen nothing of the enemy, though bullets were flying all around us. It was then dark, but we did not stay there. Closing in on the right, we came to a village: here the bullets were very thick, but we continued to cross the village along the main road to the right. The name of this village I never heard; it is now in the enemy's hands. In its centre was what looked like the ruins of a windmill: we could see the arms and sails on the ground, but the remainder appeared to be nothing but a huge pile of stones.

Crossing the village into some more fields, we formed up into line, and there commenced to dig another line of trenches—the King's Royal Rifles on our left and on our right the 3rd Brigade, consisting of the Queen's Royal West Kents, Welsh and South Wales Borderers.

That night we brought in a German sniper, who had evidently been wounded in the stomach. He could not give us any information, as he was too badly wounded.

Later on, while we were digging, the C.O. gave out to us that there was to be no retirement from here: we were to hold the position at all costs. The Rifles on our left were commanding the top of the hill, and, as our line ran down a slope, we were ordered to dig our trenches forty feet long facing the enemy but in step fashion, one behind the other. This we did, bringing the last trench on the right of our line just in front of a wood. We worked all night on these trenches, making them as strong as possible, knowing that there was to be no retirement.

Next morning, the thirtieth, we were very heavily bombarded, and the bombardment increased in violence towards midday, when we were ordered out of our trenches and to advance. We again moved up about a thousand yards, but there was still no sign of the enemy—shells were abundant. In front of a farmhouse we dug in again, and then we began to see our troops retiring on the right. Two or three of the Welsh passing near, we inquired what was going on, when they replied: "It's hell. The Queen's are absolutely cut up"—which was true—what remained of them were sent down the line for garrison duties. We then began to expect a little excitement, but it did not come off that day; and we were once more ordered to return to the line we had left earlier.

Next morning, the thirty-first, the Germans bombarded us more violently than ever. This continued for several hours. The next thing was that we saw the Germans coming; and they did come—in their thousands. We kept them off for an hour or two when the C.O. of the King's Royal Rifles consulted us, or rather our C.O., about retiring. I remember the two officers having a heated argument over it, as they stood by a farmhouse immediately in rear of the line. I do not, however, know what their argument was, but heard afterwards that the King's Royal Rifles had got short of ammunition. The words I did hear from our C.O. were: "It's the general's orders that we hold the position at all costs, and this I'll do if I lose the whole regiment."

We continued to fire until the Germans were on our trenches and coming through the line the King's Royal Rifles had vacated on our left. I was in the third line of steps near the farm-house, where I overheard some of the conversation of the two C.O.'s. Just in front of the King's Royal Rifles' trenches was a huge German officer waving with one hand to the retiring Rifles to surrender and with the other waving his troops on. It did not seem of much good for us few men to attempt to fight that dense mass of Germans, but we did; and out of the thousand, or thereabouts, that we lined up with a couple of nights before very few got away, the enemy taking somewhere about four hundred of my regiment prisoners and our casualties being about the same number.

I had a run for my life that day. A chum of mine who was with us had a cock-fowl in his valise that morning from the farm; he had wrung its neck but he had not quite succeeded in killing him; and, as we ran, this bird began to crow. As for myself, I had no equipment; I had run having left it in the bottom of the trench. It is quite funny as I come to think of it now—the old cock crowing as we ran; but it was really terrible at the time. We were absolutely overwhelmed, not only in our particular spot but all along the line, and had to concede nearly one thousand yards to the enemy. We were also very unfortunate in losing our brigadier, General Bulfin, wounded on the crossroads by a piece of shell, I believe; also our brigade major, who was killed with another piece from the same shell. I am sure every man in the brigade felt very keenly the loss of the brigadier; it was he who took us out from Aldershot, and not a better general or a braver or cooler soldier under fire ever stepped on field of battle.

Most of my regiment being gone and the remainder mixed up with other brigades which had formed another line, two chums and myself went to a farmhouse fifty yards behind this newly made line. There we had a field battery; and, after getting a little rest, started out to find the remnants of the regiment. The enemy were still shelling, and the battle was still going on; but by nightfall, not finding any of them, we came back to the old house and found the battery gone. We decided to rest there for the night with some more stray men of different regiments. Just in front of us, and in rear of the line, lay a wounded German. We decided to bring him in, and did so: he had been hit in the mouth, half of his tongue having been taken away. The poor fellow was in agony, every now and then lying on the ground and kicking. One of our men volunteered to take him back to the field ambulance, and did so.

That night we slept *on beds* in the farmhouse, and next morning, November the first, after a hurried breakfast of biscuits and beef, we all set out to join our respective regiments; but, after wandering about for an hour and seeing no signs of any of ours, my two chums—one of them now holds the V.C.—decided to go back to the farmhouse and make a dinner. There was plenty of vegetables in the garden and an outhouse full of potatoes; and we found a spirit-lamp and a pot; so we commenced to prepare our meal. In a short time it was all in the pot, when—alas!—the Germans began to shell our house, sending over incendiary shells. They let us have it battery fire. The first lot took off the off fore-leg of a cow, which along with some others was grazing at the back of the house; the poor thing hopped around on three legs for a second or two and then dropped, the other cows running up to lick the blood from its wound.

The next lot hit the top of the house, one shell taking away the roof of the scullery, behind which one of my chums was standing; the other had already run into the trenches fifty yards away. I was the last to go, the other two having thought that I had been hit. I did not leave the place until the house was well alight; and three hours after, when the enemy's guns had died down and the fire had burnt out the house, I went over to see how the dinner had got on, and found it done to a turn, cooked by the heat from the burning house. Needless to say, we did full justice to that dinner—all three of us.

We then went into the trenches with the Scots Guards and on the left of them were some of the Gloucesters. On inquiring if they had seen any of the North Lancashires they replied, "Yes; they had gone back to the reserve trenches in the wood, there to reorganise." There we found the regiment, or rather the few that were left of it—about one hundred and thirty.

That night we received from England a draft of reinforcements one hundred strong. After resting in those trenches that night, we were taken a little farther back to a wood in the front of Hooge and on the right side facing the firing line. There we dug new trenches and dugouts, and always came back to them on after occasions to rest. We were never once taken into Ypres or any buildings, since the enemy had during the last few days commenced to shell the town and some parts were on fire. This information we got from our transport drivers, who had gone back some way behind Ypres.

We rested in these trenches for two days, and were then called out—on the afternoon of the second of November—in support of the 3rd Brigade. We went up in the usual skirmishing order, three other men and myself going on in front to warn the C.O., when we came into touch with the Welsh Regiment. We were very heavily shelled going up, but reached the Welsh with insignificant losses. Lying in front of the Welsh and around a farmhouse were a party of French troops. On the word that we had arrived and come into touch with the Welsh, our regiment was made to halt in a wood just behind and lie down. We were only just off the road a little to the right, and I estimate the Germans were about seven hundred to eight hundred yards off.

While we were there a 4.7 gun was brought up on the road, and at the above-mentioned distance fired point-blank into the advancing Germans. An hour afterwards, the Welsh made a charge, and a fairly successful one it was, meeting, as it did, the enemy in the open. They returned to their original position, while we took up a position to their right.

That night we again dug trenches, and next day, November the third, we had very little to contend with—only shell-fire; and we continued during the day to strengthen our trenches. At night we again moved a little nearer to the enemy, and commenced another line of trenches. By next morning we were well dug in, and it was a good job that we were, as the Germans bombarded us very heavily. At that period we did not have lines of trenches where one could walk about; merely the usual one-man trench. The Germans shelled us from early morning until darkness set in and our casualty list was close on fifty, in addition to which we lost our C.O. and our adjutant, Major Carter and Captain Allen, both killed.

I had a fairly decent trench there, as I always had everywhere, knowing that the harder I worked on my trench the more chance I had of safety. I here lost a decent chum, killed on that day, the fourth of November, by a bullet through his brain, whilst he was spreading jam on a biscuit. When it became dark two of my comrades came into my decent trench, and there we soon dropped off to sleep, all three of us, the Germans shelling us all the time. When we awoke, it was nearly nine o'clock; we were roused from our sleep by someone throwing, or rather showering, earth in upon us. Up I jumped and inquired *sotto voce*: "Who are you"

Back came the reply: "Who are you?" On telling him, he replied that he was a Royal Engineer digging a communication trench; we were not sorry to hear that he was not one of the enemy. He then inquired what we were doing there, remarking that the Lancashires had been relieved and gone back some time ago. After wandering about for an hour, we found the regiment in the reserve trenches in the wood. Everyone had settled down for the night, rations and rum had been issued, and we had perforce to make the best of it. I did not sleep so well as usual, feeling the loss of my pal.

However, next morning, November the fifth, we were told that, as we had had such a hard time of it of late, we were to be put into reserve on some fairly easy trenches on the left of the road and just in front of the wood we occupied on our first coming up. All we had to contend with was cross-fire from the enemy's guns. It does not sound very dreadful, nor to us men did it sound hard; most of us thought that we were going to have a fairly easy time of it; so into the trenches we went quite happily. But the shell-fire there was terrible, and the way the shrapnel whistled through those trees, to say nothing of the high explosives, fairly made one's hair stand on end.

I was just in front of the wood, where we had one company entrenched; fifty yards in front and the other side of a hedge was another company. These were the only two companies we had, as we had become very weak. In this reserve trench my company lay for twenty-four hours, exchanging with the company in front of us at the end of that time for another twenty-four hours; but we were kept in that line for another four days through an unfortunate incident. We went into the front line of the reserve trenches on Saturday, November the sixth. In front of us were supposed to be the *Zouaves*. On our right front fifty yards off was a small house beside the road, the hedge just behind us running parallel but gradually getting to a point at the extremity of the trench, which ended in a *cul-de-sac*.

Just over the top and in line with the main trench was a small trench, which we called the Thirteen Trench, as thirteen men occupied it. It was situated just off the road and commanded a view straight up it. Fifty yards along the main trench was a communication trench reaching to the hedge, where it stopped, letting us out on the other side. Sunday morning, November the eighth, broke with a heavy mist; it was one of those hazy mornings that denote heat. Everyone was taking things fairly easy, when a man next to me, on glancing over the top, exclaimed: "Look! here's the Germans."

We thereupon sent for the officer, but he could hardly believe his eyes: we were then supposed to be in reserve. The enemy was advancing upon us in close formation fully a thousand strong, and our full strength could not have been more than a hundred in that trench and a hundred in the trenches behind, as I know that the whole regiment at that time was not more than two hundred and thirty (not including transport).

They were advancing by way of the little house and on to the Thirteen Trench. We kept up a brisk fire for a considerable time into the advancing masses; but we were hopelessly outclassed, and had to fall back on our other company behind. On reaching them, we all retired into the wood, drawing the enemy in behind us. It proved to be a fine piece of strategy, as we drew them on to unfamiliar ground and away from the trenches. We then turned round and made a counter-attack, driving them well back and leaving heaps of them dead and wounded behind.

We had almost reached our original line, when a chum of mine called to me by name. I went over to him, and found him lying on the ground: he had been hit and could not help himself, and he asked me to take him back to the dressing-station. I could not well refuse; so, dragging him and carrying as best I could, I made for the road, and there we nearly both got taken by the Germans, who were coming down that road in hundreds, and were only a few yards off. So I had to drag my man back into the wood, dropping into a ditch with him at the side of the road, where I was able to ascertain the extent of his wound. There was not much to show—only a small bullet-hole through his hip entering his stomach. In this ditch was a *Zouave*; and he gave me some black stuff that looked like coffee. Getting, a little later, into the wood, I was able to take him that way to the dressing-station. I heard a few weeks afterwards that he had died from his wound.

On arriving back, I found that the regiment had again retired a little way behind the trenches we had before occupied; and I also found that I had lost another old and valued chum, the one who had originally enlisted with me and had up till that time been through the campaign unscathed. I am thankful to say he was not badly wounded, although he lost the use of his left hand. There were not many of us left; our ranks were more depleted than ever; not more than seventy or eighty all told remained—nevertheless, they were planning to retake the trenches. On reaching the communication trench unmolested, we started to file in, myself going second man. Of all the trenches I had been in that was quite the worst: we had to absolutely walk the whole of the way over dead bodies—our own men and Germans. It was eight o'clock at night, and of course dark, which made our task more unpleasant; but we reached the end of the communication trench safely, though we had not got more than three or four yards down the main trench to the right, where it ended in a *cul-de-sac*, before a German patrol of about twelve men came walking along the top of the trench.

We waited until they were on top of us—then I let drive. I can hear the yell of the fellow I hit to this day, as he threw up his hands and dropped. The man next to me on my left also let go, and I thought he had blown the top of my head off!—he must have had the muzzle of his rifle quite close to my ear, as I was deaf for some time afterwards. He thought I was hit!

On gaining the end of the trench, I was, with three others, sent into the communication trench to clear out the dead. A London Scottish officer—they had only been out, or rather *in* action a week—came up with his men to relieve us, and remarked to our captain, who was the C.O., that he did not mind seeing dead Germans but he did object to walking upon them; so we had the job of clearing them out, which we did in this way: two men stayed in the trench and two stood on the top of it, the two in the trench each lifting a leg of the dead man up to the two men on top, who then hauled him over. We had been at work for about an hour at this interesting job, when who should walk along the top under cover of a hedge but a German right up to where we were working! He was fully equipped, but we had discarded our equipment, on account of it hindering us at our task. On reaching us, I exclaimed to my pal, who was bending over in the trench: "Look, chummy, here's a German!" The two men on top having just gone further up had not seen him.

On hearing me speak, the German made a motion with his hands and said, "Hush!" I was never more surprised in all my life—he evidently took us for Germans, too.

I then said to my pal: "Find us a rifle": there were plenty at the bottom of the trench. He handed me one up, and, pointing it at the German, I was foolish enough to say: "Hands up!"

He again said: "Hush!"

I said to my pal: "Hand me up some ammunition, quick." He handed me up five rounds, and, pulling one out of the clip, I placed it in the breech of my rifle. When the German heard the bolt of the rifle go home, he turned round and bolted off—but he was too late: I had him right through the back. We thought it best, then, to return to the company; and we did so.

When we had reported this little episode, I remarked to the captain that I thought the man had come from the Thirteen Trench. He replied: "That's all bosh." While we had been away there had evidently been a discussion over this Thirteen Trench, and the captain had asked a man who had been in it early the day before we had been driven out to go over the top—only a matter of ten yards—and see who was occupying it then. This man said that he knew a safer way round, when the captain said: "Take two more men and go over."

Again this man replied, asking if he might not go round. Then the captain, becoming wild, said: "If three of you won't go, thirteen of you go. If you prefer to go the other way round, go, and I'll come and see you do go." I made one of those thirteen, and we filed down the communication trench; and, coming out on the other side of the hedge, we crept along behind it amidst the cries of several wounded soldiers of both sides until we came to the gap in the hedge facing this small Thirteen Trench a few yards away. The captain was leading, then another man, and then myself. We had no sooner reached the top of the trench than a guttural voice challenged "*Halt!*" and then I could see the forms of the Germans: they were packed in there like sardines. Of course, the next minute they had opened fire, our captain and C.O. being killed on the spot; the remainder of us, being unprepared, turned and ran.

The *Zouaves*, who had then taken up a position behind us, thinking it was the Germans coming, opened fire on us, too; and there were we running between two fires! I remember on coming close to the *Zouaves'* line that I took a flying leap clean on top of one of them as he was about to shoot. I knocked him down, of course; but, on getting up and seeing who I was, he clasped his arms around me, very pleased that I was not a German. Then, along with the remainder of the men, I returned to our old trench, reporting to the only officer we had left the death of our captain.

As we could not hand over the trenches complete, the Germans having possession of the Thirteen Trench, we were not relieved by the London Scottish, as it is a rule with the Regular Army that, on being relieved, trenches have to be handed over precisely as they were taken over, any that may have been lost having to be retaken. Consequently we were kept in these trenches another forty-eight hours, and during that time we were, if possible, to retake the one we had lost.

As we were so very weak we were reinforced by a platoon of the 2nd Black Watch and one machinegun belonging to them. The gun was fixed in position at the bottom of the communication trench close to the hedge, so as to cover any movement of the enemy from the Thirteen Trench. At the bottom of the main trench and in that traverse we had eight men ten yards away, and in line were the enemy occupying the Thirteen Trench. At daybreak the next morning each of our eight men received a bullet in his head from the waiting Germans, six being killed outright and two wounded.

I was then sent with five other men to fill their places, and our orders were to lie down in the bottom of the trench and not show ourselves, as our machine-gun was trained directly over the top to the Thirteen Trench beyond us, and on any move being made by the enemy the gun would instantly open fire directly over us. My comrades and myself lay there the whole of the day; the stench from the dead men who had been killed that morning was sickening—indeed, the whole of that trench smelt of blood, warm blood as from a slaughterhouse, which in fact it was. We all got very cramped towards evening, and a great deal of grumbling was going on, as in the ordinary course of events we should have been relieved by that time and back resting.

Someone at length suggested going to the officer to ask for relief and beg him to exchange us with some men higher up the trench, who had more freedom. I was asked if I would be spokesman. Replying in the affirmative, I went to the officer and explained the case, telling him how cramped we had become. He asked me where I had come from. When I told him, he asked me who gave me permission to leave my post: I replied no one, but that I was the oldest soldier, whereupon he came with me to the bottom of the trench, and, addressing the men, promised them he would relieve them as soon as possible. He also said: "You have nothing to fear while I am with you; the Germans are ten yards off." After further promising to send the relief, he departed. We then decided, as night was falling, that three of us should keep watch for the first hour and the other three for the second hour, carrying on like that alternately throughout the night.

The night was very black and the gloom very thick, and we could not see a movement of the enemy ten yards away, but could imagine all sorts of forms and shapes in front of us. I think it was during our second watch that we discerned what we thought to be three forms moving behind the enemy trench and making for the road; so one of us fired. We heard a yell and concluded we had got somebody. During the third watch my two comrades grew very tired, and, getting down with the other men at the bottom of the trench at my bidding, were soon fast asleep. I then pulled two of the dead bodies to the end of the trench and stood them up against the wall facing the enemy to make them appear as if there were more of us.

I had no sooner done this than a German got stealthily out of his trench; and, creeping along behind the hedge and to the rear of our line, up popped another, and then another. Whereupon I sent word of the enemy's movements *via* the next traverse to the officer, asking what I should do. In the meantime I was doing all I could to awaken my comrades; but they were so sound asleep that, although I was kicking them, I could not get them to budge. The word then came back from the officer to say we were to do nothing—not even to fire a shot, as the machine-gun was trained upon the enemy, waiting for them to come up. I was in a very awkward position, as I could see the line of enemy trenches in front, and the one they were coming out of on our flank, and I had to stand there and say nothing whilst they crept around the back of us. I began to get "wind up" (frightened), as by this time they were six to one against me, and, being the end man, I had no chance whatsoever. No doubt I should have accounted for one or two of them, but I should never have got away myself.

This situation continued for about twenty minutes. I had at last been able to arouse my comrades, when an order came down for the North Lancashires to file out: we were being relieved by the West Riding Regiment. I may state that I never heard such welcome words in my life! How the West Ridings fared after that I do not know, but I do know that I was well out of it!

That night we returned to our old reserve trenches for rest at Hooge; and next day a message from General French was read out to us, praising us for the work we had done and regretting that he had had to keep us so long in action without a rest. We had been either marching or fighting since the middle of August, and it was then the middle of November, but he did not think we should have to go into the trenches again before we had had our long-deferred and well-earned rest.

That night the 3rd Battalion Scots Guards, just out from England, came into the wood also, and a fresh regiment of *Zouaves* joined us. We were all very pleased to think that we were about to be relieved, and I remember well taking a dozen field post-cards from different men of the Scots Guards to post as we went down the line. We marched out at eight o'clock, every one convinced that we were going to have our rest, when, on reaching the road, instead of marching towards Ypres, they took us towards the trenches. Even then we thought we were going for our rest, some suggesting that we were on our way to a meeting-place for the brigade; others took it to be another way round—"Yes, *via* Germany," remarked someone. Well, we did *not* get our rest: we went into the trenches again on *two* occasions after that, and for forty-eight-hour stretches. At length we were relieved by the Guards Brigade, and went back to Hazebruck by easy stages.

I should like to say a few words about Ypres before I close the account of my experiences there. We were during the whole of the first battle, from October the twenty-third to the seventeenth of November, 1914, fighting in the trenches all the time, with the exception of the first three days. I was in the Bipschoote-Langemarck-road engagement, in what is now better known as "the Ypres salient." From the time when I first went there until October the thirty-first our front line was fully six kilometres from Ypres town, but between the twenty-third and the thirty-first of October the Germans gained from us quite three to four kilometres. We did not regard this as a defeat to the British arms, as at that time the enemy were, without exaggeration, six to one against us, and they were also much better equipped with artillery.

On the contrary, I wish to pay my humble tribute to all ranks who served during that time, short as they were of men, sometimes even putting the military police into the trenches, to say nothing of the cavalry and cyclist corps. It was there that we finished off the remainder of what was the original Prussian Guards, as well as the Bavarian Guards; and today the British Nation has to thank those troops who fought so well during that time, and put a finish to the chance of the Germans ever reaching Calais, and thence England.

My regiment entered Ypres not less than one thousand strong, and while there we had five lots of reinforcements: we came away with only seventy-five men and one officer, a lieutenant. I do not, however, in my above remarks refer specially to my own regiment any more than to any other regiment in my brigade or division—all the regiments in the 1st Division were splendid: though some may have been a little better than the others where all were very good.

We went then to relieve the 7th Division after it had fought the rearguard action from Antwerp, and we were only just in the nick of time, for the division had suffered very heavily. Altogether with reinforcements the 1st Division must have lost thirty thousand men in stopping the great rush for Calais. When we entered Ypres everything was normal; but when we came out of it the town was in ruins and burning furiously in several parts.

At Hazebruck we rested for close on a month. By "rested" I mean away from the firing line. Of work we had plenty. Two days before leaving Ypres we were joined by a draft of six hundred from home, which had been kept behind with the transport until we should come out of the firing line. Captain Smart, who was with this draft, took over the temporary commanding officer's duties during the three-days' march to Hazebruck, where we arrived in a snowstorm, and were billeted in private houses at the rear of the railway station and running along near the line. Whilst there, we received two further large drafts from England, and we also had a lot of men sent back medically unfit on account of defective teeth, etc. Even there we were not left in peace, doing each day either route marches or brigade training.

To every man new clothes and underlinen were issued; and we all had to have a bath!—an amusing affair, that took place in a rag-shop. A canvas bath had been rigged up, and each company took it in turn to bathe, the water being fetched by the cooks in dixies. We had about four of these dixies filled with about twenty quarts of water to each bath, with some strong disinfectant put in it. About one hundred men would bathe to each bath, the last dozen or so revelling in pea-soup. Everyone *had* to go in—as at that time we all had plenty of live stock crawling over us—under the eyes of the company officer and two or three N.C.O.'s. Enemy aircraft was continually flying over us, and one Sunday morning an airman dropped eight bombs, which killed several civilians, mostly children, and caused sixteen casualties amongst men of my regiment.

We left Hazebruck on Monday morning by motor omnibuses on December the twenty-first, going through Merville to Festubert. Four miles from Festubert we left the buses, and during the afternoon, waiting on the roadside for orders, we for the first time came across our Indian troops. The Meerut Division and 4th Corps were operating around that district. On the cross-roads at Le Touret we waited until dusk, and then moved up the road about a mile to the Rue-de-L'Epinette, Festubert, where we were told that each regiment in the brigade had to attack and take at least one trench. From the Rue-de-L'Epinette we were taken across several fields for about a mile, when the brigade made a charge. It had then become dark and we were on ground that we had never been on before; but we succeeded in taking three lines of trenches—the regiment on our left taking one, though that on our right was not successful. I honestly believe that it was a ruse on the part of the enemy, as we did not take a single prisoner, and had only a few casualties ourselves.

That night I was doing duty as an orderly, bringing up the machine gun section and also two mess-waiters with refreshments for the officers. A funny incident happened on the way up. A house just to the left of the farm where Battalion Headquarters were posted had caught fire, and another orderly on the way down from there said to me: "Be careful which way you go, as I think that house which is burning is in the German lines; so bear off to the right." This the two waiters and myself did; and, after tramping along for some time and crossing several ditches, I gave it up, declaring that I had lost the way. In front we could see some yew trees lining a ditch about a hundred yards off, so we made up our minds to go as far as that, and reached the trees safely; but as we got there bullets began to fall with a plop into the ground at our feet; so we thought we had better go round the other side.

It was, however, just as bad there, and in front we saw a trench; so we thought we would investigate a bit. Creeping up quietly to the parapet, we peeped over: several Germans, unarmed and burdened with two jugs of coffee and a basket of provisions, greeted our eyes. We very soon made off back again, and had not gone more than a couple of hundred yards before we came to a garden surrounding a farmhouse. It turned out to be the very house I was seeking, but of course I could not then recognise it, as it was night-time, nor was it familiar to me, as it had been night-time when I first went into it. We were only about thirty yards off and could hear a babel of sounds, but very unlike the English language. So I suggested that the best thing we could do was to lie down under cover of the hedge, and wait until some one came along.

If he proved to be English, well and good; if German, we should have to get out of it the best way we could. We had not long to wait before three forms loomed in the distance through the gloom; and then we were all of a tremble! Fortunately they turned out to be three of our own Tommies, so we waited till they had passed, and then we went in. Many a laugh over the affair have those two waiters and myself had on after occasions.

Next morning, December the twenty-second, we were properly let in. The enemy commenced to shell us, continuing for some hours; then they came up in force. Unfortunately, by taking those three lines of trenches the night before, we had got too far in front; and consequently we were surrounded before we knew where we were. Anyhow, with bombs and rifle-fire (our machine gun section being behind and not in position by then), we kept them off as long as we could—then we had a run for it, as the company on our left had had to give in. There were very few of us left that day; but our machine gun soon got into action, and held the position until reinforcements came up, when the remainder of us formed up in the Rue-de-L'Epinette. When the roll was called we numbered one hundred and thirty officers and men out of eight hundred and thirty who went into action seventeen hours before. Our C.O., Major Powell, was very much upset, remarking that there had been a grave mistake somewhere, and he would immediately go to the general for satisfaction: we, of course, did not hear how he got on.

That night we were taken to Lacature until all the stragglers had joined up: they made the regiment up to about two hundred; and next day we marched off to Essairs, just the other side of the canal of Bethune, where we spent a quiet but not joyous Christmas Day, as we felt greatly the loss we had sustained two days before.

CHAPTER 8

La Bassée District

Next day, Boxing Day, December the twenty-sixth, 1914, we once more packed our traps, and, marching *via* Beuvry and Annequin, entered Cambrin. The first four days we were billeted in houses and shops, which had been shelled to pieces, and set to work digging ways through the walls of cellars for means to get out should the house be hit again by a shell during a bombardment. That night a night-attack by the enemy was expected and the usual precautions were taken; it came to nothing. Although this village was in ruins and only about two thousand yards from the enemy's front line, civilians continued to live there.

Between the twenty-sixth of December and the twenty-ninth of December there was "nothing doing": most of the regiment were employed in the communication trenches, cleaning up and carrying planks to lay on the bottom, some parts of the trenches being deep in mud and water. In the "Old Kent Road," a trench running from the church at Quinchy to the front line was in a really dreadful state: one had to wade through mud and water like whipped cream up to the armpits.

On the twenty-ninth we received a draft of sixty-nine men and three officers straight from the base. They were sent into the trenches the next day on the Givenchy side of the canal to reinforce the 2nd Royal Sussex. All they had had on leaving the base had been their rations of bully-beef and biscuits, and, on coining out twenty-four hours afterwards, had had to join the regiment and go into a charge with the Scots Guards on the Quinchy side commonly known as the "Brickfields." In these fields, and about two kilometres from La Bassée, were three huge brick-stacks, around which we built fortifications; these stacks were also very useful for our snipers and observers, who

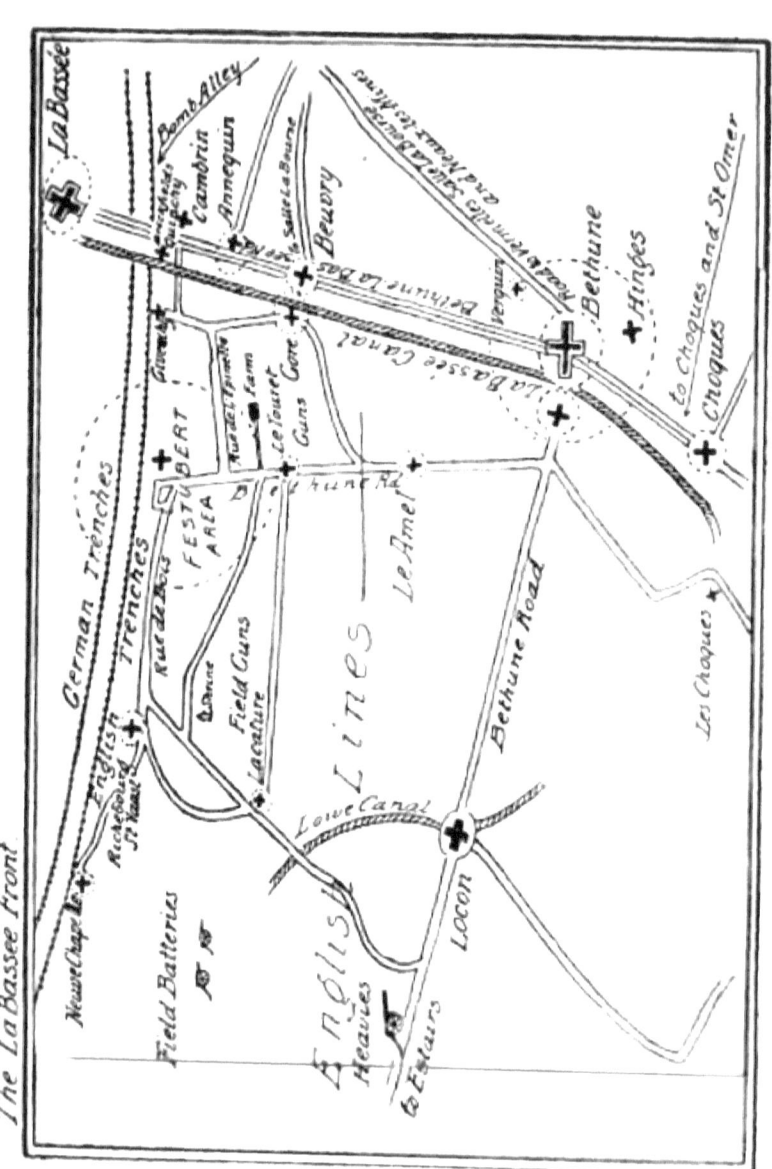

Map 5.

took up positions on the top. On the left of the fields was the railway track, and in rear of that, running parallel to it, was the canal; on the other side of which lay Givenchy.

On Wednesday, December the thirtieth, we had one company in the trenches as I have already stated; on Thursday, the thirty-first, report came through that the enemy had broken through the King's Royal Rifles lines. This was late in the afternoon; and two hours afterwards we were called out and taken into Quinchy. On the way there we passed the Black Watch, who were billeted just in front of us; they were preparing to enjoy New Year's Eve. Arriving at Quinchy, I was sent back to find and bring up the other company from their present trenches to join the battalion, which I did. They fully expected to be taken back to billets, for they were in a terrible condition, as it had been raining all day long. Therefore I did not mention the place to which we were bound.

Fortunately on the way we came across the medical officer, who, on seeing the state they were in, most of them suffering badly from rheumatism, would not consent to let them join up, but posted those suffering the least on barricade guard. I then joined the regiment on the road at Quinchy near the railway track: and, advancing along its side, the Scots Guards taking the right, we succeeded in driving the enemy from the position they had gained earlier that day, and occupied the trenches, where we stayed all next day.

On January the first some shelling and artillery duels took place, otherwise it was calm.

On Saturday, January the second, we were relieved by the 1st Brigade, leaving about thirty men on barricade guard on the main La Bassée Road. We went back into Cambrin.

On Sunday the third we left for Beuvry, three kilometres to our rear and one and a half kilometres from Bethune. We arrived there at 6.30 p.m., and went into billets. A lot of our men were sent back from here with trench-feet, which we then called frost-bitten feet; they were the first cases we had of it. On Saturday, January the second, ninety-four N.C.O.'s and men left us, and next day, Sunday, thirty-four more went off.

On Monday the fourth we rested, enjoying a bathe and change of linen at the Girls' College in Bethune.

On Tuesday the fifth we again left for Cambrin and relieved the King's Royal Rifles from the trenches, Major Powell, who had joined us at Hazebruck, going away sick. We arrived at Quinchy at 5.30 p.m., and the regiment took over the trenches in front of that village, two Companies occupying the front line, one company being in support behind the first brick-stack and the other in reserve behind the other two brick-stacks, whilst Headquarter Company took over and guarded a culvert running from the road under the railway-line to the canal bank.

That night and during the next day little happened beyond artillery duels. Around this sector of the line snipers were very prevalent.

Thursday the seventh was a wet day; nothing occurred with the exception of a German mistaking his way in the early hours of the morning and walking into our machine-gun emplacement. He came in with two cans, one with hot water and the other with hot tea. The boys, after making him taste a little of each, took possession of them for their own use. On being taken down the communication trench this German had the audacity to remark that our trenches were very dirty—not nearly so clean as theirs, as they had working parties cleaning up each day.

On Friday the eighth there was a great deal of shelling on both sides between 10 a.m. and 11 a.m., and also a heavy cannonade and rifle-fire during the afternoon, but no attack.

On Saturday the ninth the part of Headquarter Company doing guard at the culvert were relieved, as they were no longer required, and were put on fatigue duty, carrying all necessary things to the firing line, to save the men in the firing line from becoming continually wet through walking up and down the communication trench. These men continued at this work until the regiment was relieved, retiring at night into a cellar at Cambrin to dry their clothes as best they might. About 1 p.m. there was an hour's bombardment of the enemy's lines.

On Sunday the tenth there was a terrible bombardment, and seven men of each company volunteered to capture an enemy's machine-gun advanced post, which was taken very successfully, with only slight casualties and some prisoners.

Monday the eleventh and Tuesday the twelfth were very quiet, with the exception of a bombardment each day.

On Wednesday the thirteenth I left the regiment early in the morning, and proceeded to Annequin, a small village just behind Cambrin, there to find billets. We found a draft awaiting us there of four hundred and eighty N.C.O.'s and men and three officers, and the regiment was then relieved by the 2nd Royal Sussex, going to Annequin for rest, and staying there the next two days.

On Saturday the sixteenth we fell in, in the afternoon, to return to the trenches; but before we went the brigadier gave us a few words, saying:

> Tomorrow, Sunday, January the seventeenth, is the *Kaiser's* birthday, so be on your guard, as we are expecting an attack in honour of it.

This attack did not mature: the day was one of the quietest I had experienced in the trenches. A mistake had been made: the *Kaiser's* birthday is the twenty-seventh of January.

On Monday the eighteenth we were again relieved by the 2nd Royal Sussex, and returned to Annequin.

Tuesday the nineteenth we spent in resting, going into the trenches again on Wednesday the twentieth, again relieving the 2nd Royal Sussex, who took our billets at Annequin.

On Thursday the twenty-first the whole brigade was relieved by the 1st Brigade; we went to Bethune, where the 1st Brigade had just completed eight days' rest. I was then on the staff of billeting orderlies, and helped to find billets at that town. It was a very unenviable berth, as the majority of French people objected to have soldiers billeted on them, and our officers were often very dissatisfied with the billets we found for them. We settled down to what we thought was to be an eight-days' rest; but early on Monday morning, January the twenty-fifth, the enemy began to shell Bethune—the first occasion on which it was shelled. The brigade got the order to stand to, and moved out of Bethune once more for the trenches, after having had only three days' rest out of our eight.

The report was circulated that the enemy had broken through on the right of La Bassée canal, at the brick-fields at Quinchy. It was true; they had got as far as Quinchy church, and had penetrated the village itself, only to be blown back by the fierceness of our artillery fire, after which we delivered a counter-attack, going up in support to the Highland Light Infantry 5th Brigade 2nd Division, who were then operating around that district in conjunction with the 1st Division, and also in reserve to the 3rd Brigade. We did not on this occasion succeed in retaking all our old trenches; we lost one of the three the enemy had succeeded in taking, and we lost one brick-stack. Our armoured train was in action, and did great work in keeping the enemy back whilst reinforcements were brought up; but we were unfortunate in losing the engine-driver, a Belgian, who stopped a fragment of shell with his head: the naval men in charge of the train buried him with honours, firing the last volley over his grave. That night we returned to Beuvry, and stood to in case of another assault.

On Tuesday, January the twenty-sixth, we had an unfortunate experience. It took place at the time when the regiment was holding orderly room. Nearly all the company officers and N.C.O.'s were attending, besides the C.O., adjutant, machine-gun officer, regimental sergeant-major, pioneer sergeant, signalling sergeant, police sergeant—in fact, every one of note in the regiment. There were also a number of men waiting to be told off for various crimes; and they were holding this office in a farmyard, on hard cobbled stones, when a shell of large calibre dropped amongst them, killing and wounding close on forty officers and men. The C.O. and adjutant had a marvellous escape, as the shell dropped at the foot of the table without injuring either of them, whilst most of the prominent officers and N.C.O.'s were killed, as well as three who held Distinguished Conduct Medals. That afternoon we returned to Quinchy, D Company going in support to the 2nd Royal Sussex.

On Wednesday the twenty-seventh we went into the trenches, taking up bombs in readiness for an attack. It was then 8.30 p.m. We found that the keep, the first two brick-stacks, had now become our firing line.

We did not commence the attack until 4 a.m. on Thursday the twenty-eighth, and succeeded in driving the enemy out with bombs, but returned to our old line of trenches, where we received some casualties. During that day we returned to Cambrin to billets in reserve to the Sussex and Northamptons.

On Tuesday the twenty-ninth the enemy heavily attacked the keep: fully 1,500 Germans got out of their trenches, and, after advancing a couple of yards, lay down, in preparation for a charge. Our artillery then got to work, and, aided by our rifle and machine-gun fire, accounted for every man, only five out of the 1,500 being left, and these we took prisoner. Very excellent work was done that day by both the 2nd Royal Sussex and the Northampton Regiments. That night we were relieved by the Camerons and Black Watch 1st Brigade, and returned to our old billets at Beuvry.

Next day, Saturday, January the thirtieth, we returned to Bethune, and were billeted there in the Ladies' College, standing to at a half-hour's notice if required.

There we also spent Sunday. Next day I set off with the billeting party to find billets at a small place eight kilometres from Bethune and near Choques. After we had arrived there, we arranged billets, when a staff officer came up and ordered us to return to Bethune, as the enemy had once more commenced to attack. Halfway on the road back we were met by the brigade despatch-rider, who ordered us to return to Allouagne, the village where we had secured the billets. All this time there was a heavy cannonade going on in the direction of the trenches; it was close on ten miles away—anyhow, the attack by the enemy did not succeed, and we proceeded as usual.

The regiment arriving here the next day, Tuesday, February the second, we were joined by a new C.O., Lieutenant-Colonel Bowlby. At Allouagne we rested from February the second until the twentieth of that month, having a similar time and doing similar work to that which we had done at Hazebruck, only on this occasion we were not troubled by aircraft. We were joined there by the 5th Sussex Territorials, making in all five regiments to the brigade instead of four.

On February the twentieth we moved a little further up, about one kilometre from Allouagne. On that march one of our men became a little intoxicated: he was placed between an escort. On the road he threw his rifle away, saying: "I'll fight no more." Next morning, on being brought before the C.O., he was told by the C.O., who had overheard what he had said the day before, that he would receive fourteen days' field-punishment and fight on. We stayed at this village, Lozingham, for eight days, leaving on February the twenty-eighth for Mont Bernischon, where we stayed the night, and next day moved on to a small village, by name Les Choques. All this time we were really moving back to the trenches.

On March the second five of our men were overcome by charcoal fumes, Quartermaster-Sergeant Border and Private Sailor losing their lives.

On March the tenth we were awakened by a terrific bombardment of guns, and did not then know that the Battle of Neuve Chapelle had commenced. We were hurried off from our billets at Les Choques and proceeded along the Lowe Canal to Locon, where we were kept until the afternoon, when, crossing the canal and marching to the right, we went on to Le Touret. That night we stayed in a field in reserve, but at ten o'clock went into billets.

Next day, the eleventh, we moved higher up to just behind the Rue-de-l'Epinette and occupied breastworks, where we heard the report of the capture of 2,000 Germans and six guns.

On the next day, the twelfth, we again returned to Les Choques to our old billets, which were not required. We did not, of course, take full part in the Neuve Chapelle battle, but were there in reserve to the 4th Corps, the 4th Meerut Division taking the bulk of the work.

On March the twelfth we moved to Essairs, to the old billets we had occupied on Christmas Day, and renewed many old acquaintances. We stayed there five days, still in reserve and under an hour's notice.

On the eighteenth we removed nearer to La Bassée Canal and behind Givenchy to a place named Goue. This time we found working parties in the trenches between Festubert and Givenchy.

On the twenty-second we left our billets at Goue, and removed to our old position in the Rue-de-L'Epinette, where we had lost so many of our men just before Christmas. We did not relish going there. I went as orderly to the Northamptons in case of communication being cut off by telephone, the Northamptons being more to our left in trenches at the Rue-de-Bois.

On the twenty-third we were relieved by the King's Royal Rifles, and, going round by Richebourg St. Vaast, we took the trenches on the Rue-de-Bois, relieving the Indians. These trenches were really barricades built up with sandbags. We had three companies in them, and one in reserve in billets behind. We found there another implement of torture used by the Germans, a three-pronged steel or iron with sharp points: they were thrown out in front of the trenches for men to step on it—mattered not which part you stepped on: one of the prongs would be sure to run into your leg. That night we had one lieutenant and one private killed, and about thirteen casualties in all. We were in those trenches for a week, until the thirtieth, and it was one of the quietest spots of the whole line—scarcely any rifle fire and little shell fire. These trenches are linked up with from the right Givenchy at the La Bassée Canal end; then come Festubert, Aubers Ridge, Port Arthur, and Neuve Chapelle, all within a distance of five miles.

We did not have many casualties during our stay on the Rue-de-Bois, and returned to our old billets at Les Cheques on March the thirtieth, resting and refitting until April the seventh.

On April the eighth we marched to Neuve Chapelle, and occupied the trenches at Port Arthur, a portion of the line there having been given that name. Another spot there was known as "Windy Corner," on account of its treacherous nature, as it was under a cross fire from the enemy.

On April the sixth we were joined by a new C.O., Colonel Sanderson, who came to us from the 2nd Battalion, which was then serving in East Africa. At Port Arthur we went into reserve, one company occupying the dugout at the rear and on the road. From this road our engineers had erected a wooden track and wooden rails, for the purpose of taking by trolleys all necessities for the trenches. We found this very useful during our stay here of four days, after which we were, on the twelfth, relieved by a Territorial Division.

We then proceeded to Mont Bernischon, for three days' rest, leaving that village for Richebourg St. Vaast, where we occupied billets in reserve. Here I left the regiment to join the 1st Divisional Headquarters for a refresher course in signalling, as that Regiment was at that time short of these specialists. I remained at Locon until May the sixth, when the class was broken up, and all men were sent to rejoin their respective regiments, in view of a great advance that was then supposed to be about to take place.

During the time I was with the class, all qualified signallers and officers of the regiment had been attending lectures held at the 2nd Brigade Office to learn the scheme of the proposed attack, which was to be commenced by a huge bombardment of guns on a front of less than two miles. Before we left our billets at Les Cheques we were told that it was to be the greatest bombardment ever known; and we had detailed instruction in the various parts we were to play. We were all under the impression that we were going to have an easy task of it, as we were to take up our position and start from the Rue-de-Bois, which place had always been so quiet when we occupied it.

That night we were taken to a field near the canal at Locon expecting to proceed to the trenches to be in readiness for the night; however, we did not go up, and stopped there all the next day, May the sixth, until 8 p.m. We were then sent back to billets at Les Choques, the advance having been cancelled for forty-eight hours. Thus we left Les Choques on May the eighth in the evening, and proceeded to the Rue-de-Bois, where we occupied the reserve trenches, everyone being in and ready for the fray at 3 a.m. on the morning of the ninth.

CHAPTER 9

The Battle of Festubert, May 9th, 1915

The signal for the bombardment was given by a big gun at 5.30 a.m., when all the guns commenced to blaze off. It was just as if all hell were let loose! The German trenches, like ours, were built up of sandbags; and within five minutes they represented the waves of the sea beating against the rocks. Debris was flying in all directions, and we men stood on the tops of our trenches to see the fun; but were very soon down again, as the enemy during the whole of that bombardment repeatedly sniped at us. and had the impudence to shout at us: "Come on—we've been waiting for you for twenty-four hours." At 8 a.m. the bombardment ceased, and the attack commenced in earnest. Our position was the centre, and we were led by the 2nd Royal Sussex, followed by the Northamptons, North Lancashires, 5th Royal Sussex, and we also had the 9th King's Liverpools, a Territorial Regiment that had recently joined our brigade. They were in reserve, with the 1st Brigade Black Watch holding the front line whilst we attacked.

The distance between the two lines of trenches was not more than three hundred yards, but we could advance only half-way: we had to yield to the enemy's machine-gun fire. Some of the men had to lie there all day until nightfall, when, at 11 o'clock, the whole of the 2nd Brigade retired to the reserve line of trenches to reorganise, the 1st Brigade still holding the front line. We accounted for 430 of all ranks, not including machine-gun men, who were still in position in the front line.

Another bombardment was commenced again at 2 p.m., and, going into the front line, we prepared for another attack. Towards 4 p.m.

an order came through for the North Lancashires to stand fast, and the Black Watch, sending up two companies, took our places, and then charged the enemy's lines. After repeated attempts, they eventually got into their trenches. Words cannot describe that glorious piece of work—no praise could be high enough. When they got into the trenches the Germans took their rifles and equipment from them, and, turning them out unarmed, told them to get back to their own lines the best way they could, turning their machine-guns on them as they did so.

We, of course, dared not fire, on account of the possibility of hitting our own men. We had the misfortune to lose our armourer sergeant, who had taken part in the charge; also three captains killed, Captains Hay, Hill, and Adcock. Lieutenant-Colonel Bowlby was wounded; Lieutenant Fisher, machine-gun officer, killed; Lieutenant Garrod, sniping officer, killed on the enemy's barbed wire—altogether we lost nearly three hundred of all ranks, the Northamptons losing more than we did, and the whole division losing nearly 8,000 men, without succeeding in taking a single trench.

We held the front line until 3 a.m. of the morning of the ninth, when we were relieved by the 2nd Division and the Highland Light Infantry, 5th Infantry Brigade. Proceeding to Le Touret, the Battalion joined up, and, after calling the roll, we marched on to Lannoy, there to rest.

On the twelfth of May we left Lannoy and marched to Bethune, where we occupied billets for four days. I was fortunate enough to procure a pass, and paid a visit to St. Omer, where my father was stationed with a Motor Transport Company. There I spent two very enjoyable days, but, on getting back to Bethune, I found the regiment had departed, taking with them my rifle and equipment. They had not, however, gone far—only to Beuvry, where I soon found them. That night the 47th Territorial London Division had by mistake taken our billets. We, of course, turned them out, upon which they began to sing:

Though the North Lancs pinched our billets, never mind!
We have slept in the fields before,
And we'll do the same as of yore,
So the North Lancs can have our billets—never mind!

There we stayed six days, finding working parties, etc., and then we moved up to Annequin for three days in reserve. At Annequin there was a coalpit, which was shelled each day and nearly every night, although the civilians still occupied it. The church, typical of churches in the French villages, came under the enemy's fire first. Just behind and in rear was an *estaminet* run by two French girls. How they could live there beats me, as there were three large shell-holes in the walls, and a corner had been knocked off the house. They had placed barrels filled with earth over these holes, and carried on business in the same old way, making quite a good living from the English troops billeted there. On Sunday afternoons they used to take walks with some French officers around what was then the French section of the line; our line finished on the left of the La Bassée Road.

We stayed here four days, and on the afternoon of May the twenty-fourth moved into the trenches, taking over from the King's Liverpools the right of La Bassée Road, originally occupied by the French. We found on this part of the line the trenches very good, with four lines of them, a front line, a support line, and a reserve, called Maison Rouge: there were three red-bricked houses in this line. Some of the dugouts in this line were also splendid, containing beds and furniture brought by the French from the ruined village of Cambrin just behind. Whilst we were here the enemy blew up a mine, but we had few casualties. In this village we had our Transport 1st Line, and also the Brigade Office. The Germans were quite eight hundred yards from us, and in between the two lines was an aeroplane, English or French, which had been hit and brought down by the enemy. On several occasions we went out at night to try to bring it in; but we found the engine had been buried too far in the ground, and all we could do was to take away parts. One day I watched a man go out in broad daylight collecting German helmets.

We were relieved on the twenty-eighth by the regiment which we had relieved four days before, the 9th King's Liverpools; and we returned to our old billets at Annequin. Around this sector of the line we were well backed by the famous French 75 gun.

On June the first we relieved the 9th King's Liverpools from trenches at the brickfields at Quinchy. They had been moved from the trenches on the right of La Bassée Road during our time of reserve to those at the brickfields. We had a rough time here for three days: the enemy exploded two mines, which sent up the largest part of one of our companies (C Company) with them. We were also much nearer the enemy than before, and were continually bombed.

On the fourth we were relieved, and proceeded to Bethune, where we were billeted in a school. The very first night we were again shelled. We spent seven days here, enjoying the luxury of a large swimming-bath.

On June the eleventh we left for Cambrin to relieve the 1st Brigade, and put two companies in reserve on the left of the road and in rear of Quinchy and one on the right of the road at Maison Rouge, one company being in billets at Cambrin. At Maison Rouge we had a transmitting station to the King's Royal Rifles, and from the 2nd Brigade Headquarters, the King's Royal Rifles occupying the front line on the right of the road, nicknamed "Bomb Alley," on account of its being so near the enemy and continually under bombardment. We used sentries on each traverse to look out for bombs: on seeing one coming and at what position it would be likely to drop, the sentry would yell out "Bomb right," or "Bomb left," as the case might be, when the men would at once clear to the opposite direction.

On June the fourteenth we were relieved by the 2nd Division, and left for Bethune, where we went into corps reserve for four days.

On the seventeenth we left Bethune for La Pugnoy, there to rest: whilst here we received a draft of 183 officers and men who had been transferred from a service battalion of the Manchesters, on account of the shortage of our own reinforcements at the feeding battalion then at Felixstowe.

On the twenty-seventh we marched to Cambrin, a distance of about sixteen miles, having our dinner on the road in a thunderstorm; and, on entering the trenches, we received a welcome from the Herts Territorials, who had decorated the fire-step with pieces of chalk (these trenches were of a chalky nature), out of small pieces of which they had built the words: "Welcome to Kitchener's Army." Fancy what the reading of that meant to us men, some of whom had been through the war since the very commencement! We did indeed feel grateful, and we had cause to be so, as we were supposed to have gone back to La Pugnoy for a divisional rest and were expecting at least a month, whereas we got only three days of it. Whilst at La Pugnoy several brigades of Kitchener's Army had passed through us and the 1st Division, those of which occupied the trenches at the time expected to get relieved by them.

However, we had to go, and we were shelled pretty heavily here; we had three companies in the front line, and D Company in reserve. On July the fourth we were relieved from the trenches, after having been in them for six days, and we returned to Salle-la-Bourse. We had then taken over trenches in front of Vermelles, and, after spending a few days at Salle-la-Bourse, we journeyed two kilometres to Noyelles; from there, four days afterwards, we again occupied the trenches for eight days. During this time operations were very calm, and all around the district one could see for some considerable distance—from Vermelles one could see the "Tower Bridge" at Loos; and I often used to gaze at it and wonder when it would become our property, little thinking that my hope would be realized within a couple of months. We did another few days in the trenches, and then went back to Verquin, near Bethune. The observation balloon used to go up here at the back of the village, and on several occasions the enemy shelled it, but never succeeded in hitting it.

On July the twentieth we were again at Noyelles, and on the twenty-third of that month I obtained leave for the purpose of proceeding to England for eight days, after having been on active service for a period of nearly twelve months. I had nearly ten miles to walk, fully equipped, to the railway station to get my train. I need not describe my brief visit home; needless to say I enjoyed myself never better in my life.

Arriving back at Bethune on August the first, we learnt from headquarters that the regiment were in the trenches at Vermelles, and, on arrival at that place, we were just in time to see the Battalion relieved, and had to march back that same night again to Bethune, where we spent eight days, the division holding a horse-show and sports.

From the eighth of August until a fortnight before the Battle of Loos we took our turn, with other regiments in the brigade, to go into the trenches; and a fortnight before Loos we returned to Lozingham to rehearse the coming battle. While at Lozingham we did battalion training, and generally prepared ourselves.

I had become somewhat run down and felt fairly bad with sickness, etc.; when the doctor examined me he found I had a temperature of over 100. He asked me where I felt ill, and on my telling him, he said: "You ought to be admitted to hospital, but I'm afraid I can't do that, as you are a signaller and we are short of signallers." He told me to lie down in my billet and rest. I was like this for nearly a week, and did not feel much better at the end of that time; but, as we were again on the move, I did not trouble him any more.

It was on September the twenty-first that we moved to Marles, a village one kilometre from Lozingham. On the twenty-second we marched to the trenches at Vermelles in readiness for the battle, arriving there at 3 a.m. on the twenty-fourth, throughout which day we were busy teeing in wires, etc., in readiness for our run to the German lines on the morrow.

Chapter 10

Loos

The 1st Division took the centre, with the 15th Scottish Division on the right and the 9th Division on the left. The 1st Division faced a part of the line known as "Lone Tree," named after a tree between the two lines and the only one there. The division had battle headquarters at Larutwar Farm, and brigade headquarters in a part of the trenches known as "Daly's Keep." At 6.40 a.m. on the morning of the twenty-fifth of September the attack was to be launched, first by the Royal Engineers letting off asphyxiating gas; when that reached the German lines or was three parts of the way across, the infantry were to follow. Of the 2nd Brigade the 1st Loyal North Lancashires and the King's Royal Rifles were the two regiments selected, and to them was given the honour of going over first, the King's Royal Rifles on the right. Punctually at the time given the gas was let off, accompanied by smoke bombs, but unfortunately before it had reached half the distance across, the wind changed and blew it back upon us. However, over we went, and, as our distance to the enemy's lines was quite eight hundred yards, we covered them by short rushes.

On reaching the enemy's wire entanglements we found that they had not been sufficiently damaged to admit of our access to the enemy's trench; so we held on for reinforcements, which arrived in the form of the 2nd Royal Sussex; but we could not make headway against the enemy's machine-guns, although the divisions on our left and right had advanced a considerable distance. A brigade consisting of several Territorial regiments in the division was then sent to our aid, and this time we got through, taking several hundred prisoners. The divisions on the left and right of us had advanced, the enemy opposed to them had retired and were to all intents and purposes cut off, so they had perforce to surrender. This gave us practically a clear run of

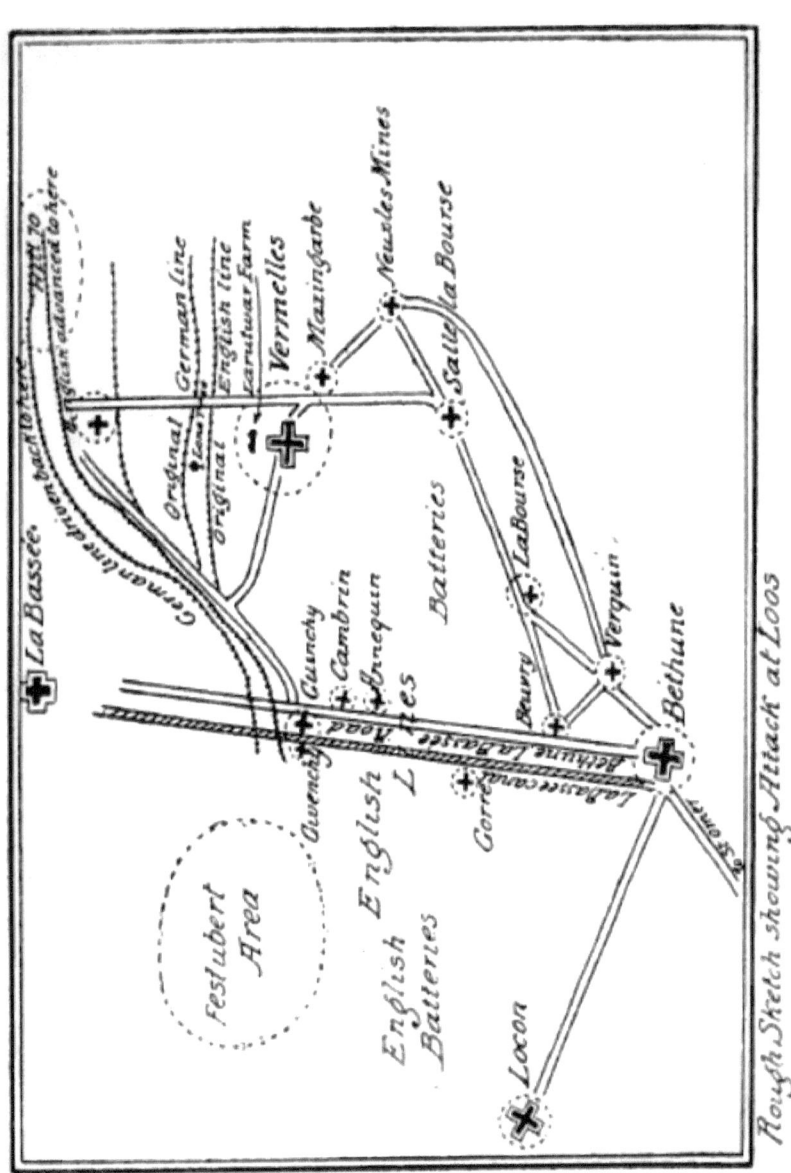

MAP 6.

about half a mile, and we saw, as we passed, that our objective at the chalk-pit was the village of Loos on our left. Fighting in Loos village was very furious indeed. This chalk-pit is situated on the Loos-Lens road, and on the left of it is a wood, where, after charging through it for spare Germans, we dug in.

At 4 a.m. on the morning of the twenty-sixth we were relieved by the 21st Division of Kitchener's Army, as we had obtained our objective. We went back to our old original trenches, leaving the 21st Division to carry on. Our ranks were sadly depleted, having lost many men: it was an awful and ghastly sight coming back over the ground we had taken. About two o'clock that afternoon we heard that the 21st Division were not doing well, and that a couple of field-batteries which had taken up position immediately behind the old German front line had been put out of action, as well as two batteries to the right of Larutwar Farm, which was packed from end to end with wounded, waiting to be taken away. The motor-ambulances worked night and day.

Soon after this, the 24th Division, another of Kitchener's Divisions, came into action to relieve the 21st, very few of whom remained. This division stopped in for nearly twenty-four hours, and retook some of the ground that the 21st had lost. The afternoon before the Guards Division, fresh from ———, where they had been in training, and the New Welsh Guards also went into action, making an attack on the Hohenzollern Redoubt. They did good work, I believe, in taking part of it.

On the night of the twenty-seventh we were ordered out from our old line to the old German support line in reserve; but next morning were taken out again and sent back to Mazingarbe, a small village behind Vermelles. We had eight hours' rest here, and that same night proceeded to the recently captured village of Loos, where were packed piles of dead Germans and men of the 15th Scottish Division. It was indeed an ugly sight. From one cellar we turned out twenty Germans, and we also took one who had been working an underground telephone. We spent one night in this cellar, and the following night proceeded through the village to Hill 70, where we filled a gap and dug a line of trenches, digging most of the time through solid chalk. While there we were heavily shelled, as also was Loos, where houses were crashing to the ground every few minutes.

Three days afterwards we were relieved by a French Division and went back to Neaux-le Mines for a well-earned five-days' respite. After that we were put into the trenches at Vermelles, and on October the tenth the enemy made a determined attack on the 9th King's Liverpools and Gloucesters 3rd Brigade, to whom we had then been attached. The enemy were well driven off, but both regiments had to be taken out that night, and we went up in the place of the King's Liverpools, and were situated in our old trenches near the chalk-pit. Here, on the morning of the eleventh of October, we were badly shelled: we lost a machine-gun team and the gun was knocked out. I was then ordered to take a message into Loos village to the 3rd Brigade Office, requesting them to send up another gun-team at once.

Coming back from this message I received my wound, getting a nasty knock through the leg, severing the arteries and smashing the bone. After binding it tightly, I managed to make my way to the first-aid dressing-station, a distance of nearly a mile and a half. Thence I proceeded to Mazingarbe, but, owing to haemorrhage, I did not get my wound dressed until I was sent back to Lozingham, where I was sent to the operating tent of the 23rd Field Ambulance. Whilst awaiting my turn, I watched the surgeons take from another man's knee a bullet.

Two days later I was sent to Rouen, where I spent ten days; from there I came home to Salisbury Infirmary, and I was in this hospital for twelve weeks undergoing three operations. I was, on becoming convalescent, sent to the Red Cross Hospital, Salisbury; and here I spent another month, and proceeded at the end of that time to the house of Sir Vincent Caillard at Wingfield. At this house I was given massage twice a day; and after a month was sent on to Sutten Veney. After three weeks I was given my discharge, and proceeded to the depot in Lancashire, where I finally signed my papers and re-entered back to civilian life after having had one year and 246 days on active service.

The 1st Division on landing in France consisted of three Infantry Brigades, comprising:

1st Brigade

Grenadier Guards.
Coldstream Guards.
Royal Highlanders (Black Watch).
Munster Fusiliers.

2nd Brigade

1st Loyal North Lancashire Regiment.

2nd King's Royal Rifle Corps.
2nd Royal Sussex Regiment.
2nd Northampton Regiment.

3rd Brigade

The Welsh Regiment.
South Wales Borderers.
Queen's Royal West Kents.
Gloucester Regiment.

The War History of the 1st/4th Battalion the Loyal North Lancashire Regiment

The Colours

Contents

Preface	89
Early History and Training in England	93
Early Days and the Battle of Festubert	99
Trench Warfare	124
The Somme Fighting	136
Trench Warfare in the Salient: October 1st, 1916, to July 14th, 1917	148
The Third Battle of Ypres, 15th July, 1917, to 1st August, 1917	181
Reorganisation, and the Battle of the Menin Road	206
Cambrai, 25th September, 1917 to 6th December, 1917	233
The Givenchy Period, 7th December, 1917, to 3rd September, 1918	251
The Advance	282
After the Armistice	289
Appendixes	292

The Lancashire Foot were as stout men as were in the world and as brave firemen. I have often told them they were as good fighters and as great plunderers as ever went to a field . . . .

It was to admiration to see what a spirit of courage and resolution there was amongst us, and how God hid us from the fears and dangers we were exposed to.

Captain Hodgson,
writing in 1648,
on the Battle of Preston.

DEDICATION
TO
THE MAIN BODY OF OUR COMRADES,
WHO HAVE GONE FORWARD IN TRIUMPH TO
THE UNKNOWN LAND,
WE
THE REAR PARTY,
LEFT BEHIND TO CLEAN UP AND HAND OVER,
DEDICATE THIS BOOK.

LIEUTENANT-COLONEL RALPH HINDLE, D S.O.
He commanded the battalion from February, 1915, till wounded in action at Festubert, and again from August, 1915, till killed in action at Vancellette Farm, on 30th November, 1917.

> *"What do these fellows mean by saying, 'I've done my bit'? What is their 'bit'? I don't consider I've done mine yet."*
> —Lieutenant-Colonel Hindle in 1917.

Preface

The purpose of this book is to supply to the people of Preston and district, for the first time, a complete and authentic record of the adventures of their original local Territorial Infantry Battalion during the Great War, such a record being a chapter of local history which must sooner or later be written; to put into the hands of the relatives and friends of those who have gloriously fallen the story of the unit with which they served faithful into death, with its accompanying tribute from their surviving comrades; to supply to the latter maimed or whole a book which they may hand down to posterity to speak of their service; and last, but not least, to speak to those who shall succeed to our traditions, of comradeship, cheerfulness, endurance, devotion to duty, and all the virtues which go to make up "the spirit of the regiment."

The delay in publication has been unavoidable, and even now the book is not as complete as its compilers would wish; in particular, it is not possible to give the names of casualties as they occurred, except in the case of officers; both company and battalion records have had to be destroyed again and again, and there is little material left to work on except the *War Diary* and individual diaries.

The book is a live product. Every line of it is either written by those who were actually with the battalion during the period of which they write, or is condensed from the *War Diary*. It would have been far easier, and, from a literary point of view, more satisfactory, to have handed over the documents to a professional historian to write up, but it was felt that the vivid descriptions of eye-witnesses, even though lacking in style, were preferable to any such compilation.

A Reduced Facsimile of the Roll of Volunteers for Service Abroad signed in the Public Hall, on 8th August, 1914.

D Company   E Company   F Company

G Company   H Company

CHAPTER 1

Early History and Training in England

The Loyal North Lancashire Regiment has a peculiar history, being descended from the old 47th, the Lanarkshire[1] Regiment, and the 81st, the Loyal Lincoln Volunteers.

In 1881, when these two regiments were at their depot at Preston, it was found convenient to amalgamate them, and they became the 1st and 2nd Battalions of the North Lancashire Regiment. The Lincolnshire men were not pleased at having to drop the epithet "Loyal" (conferred on them[2] in memory of an occasion during the Peninsular War when, on volunteers being told to step one pace forward, the entire battalion moved forward one pace), and they placed their views before the War Office, with the result that the new formation was allowed to retain the epithet, and it became the Loyal North Lancashire Regiment. This little outline of its history explains why the 1st Battalion's March-past is "My love is like a red, red rose," generally known as the "Red Rose," and the 2nd Battalion's "The Lincolnshire Poacher."

A Volunteer Rifle Corps was formed in Preston in 1839 as a consequence of the talked-of possibilities of a French invasion. This corps continued in existence as a Volunteer Corps until the territorialisation of regiments about the year 1878, when it became a Volunteer Battalion of the Loyal North Lancashire Regiment; later, on the formation of the Territorial Force it became the 4th (T.) Battalion of the same regiment.

This Territorial Battalion succeeded to the traditions of the amalgamated units, and strove as best it might to emulate its Regular Bat-

---
1. Changed to "Lancashire" in 1781 when they were sent to that county to recruit.
2. According to tradition.

talions, but the Territorial scheme did not produce the full complement of officers and men, and it should be realised that those who served in it prior to the war did so in the face of a certain amount of ridicule, gave up nearly the whole of their spare time to camps and drills, and in most cases were seriously out of pocket over the whole business.

With the exception of a company which was sent to South Africa to reinforce the Regular Battalion, the unit had not seen active service prior to August, 1914, but those who then belonged to it were keen, and had, in the face of discouragements, done their level best to master their job.

The beginning of August, 1914, found the battalion, under strength in officers and men, in camp at Kirkby Lonsdale. When war was declared on the 4th of August, and the Territorial Force was embodied, the 4th were hurriedly recalled, and took up their quarters in the Public Hall, Preston. Within two or three days they had recruited to strength in all ranks, and had volunteered, practically to a man, for service abroad. Photographs of the original roll signed on that occasion will be found immediately preceding Chapter 1.

That first fortnight in the Public Hall will never be forgotten by any of those who went through it. The companies lived, ate, and slept on the floor, or on the benches in the gallery; the officers slept on the floor of one of the crush-rooms, and the whole business was a bit of a nightmare, but we were firmly under the impression at that time that any day might bring orders to go abroad, and we were kept fully equipped and issued with ammunition according to the mobilisation scale then in force.

On the 8th August, the battalion paraded in the Market Square, Preston, and the colours were handed over to the mayor for safe custody, no one at that time foreseeing that they would remain there for just on five years. A photograph of the colours appears as a frontispiece to this book: in the fullness of time, no doubt, the battle honours earned by the battalion in the Great War will be embroidered upon them.

On the 22nd August, we moved down to Swindon, where the battalion remained for nearly three months, billeted in schools, training, and generally improving discipline, but it was very difficult to get much real work done, as detachments were sent off to guard the main line of the Great Western Railway. These detachments, on the whole, had a pretty good time, as they were stationed at various places along the Thames Valley and the local people took a great interest in them, and were most hospitable. They learnt a good deal, especially in getting used to night sentry work, but no one was sorry when in November they were recalled and the battalion moved as a whole to Sevenoaks.

Here we were allotted good training grounds and serious training was possible. Though the nature of the billets, mostly empty houses, threw us much on our own resources, it had the advantage that we began to learn to make ourselves comfortable under any circumstances.

We spent Christmas here, and had a very elaborate Christmas dinner, followed by a really good concert, in a large marquee provided by the generosity of one of the inhabitants. We found many hospitable folk at Sevenoaks, and made many friends. The two King's Own battalions and the 5th Battalion of the Loyal North Lancashire Regiment were also billeted at the same place, and there was a good deal of unavoidable overcrowding. Up to this time we had been the only 4th Battalion, but in November, 1914, an order was issued that 2nd Line Territorial Battalions should be formed, for Home Service only, to find drafts for the 1st Line Battalions, and we took the title 14th, to distinguish ourselves from the 24th, then in process of formation at Blackpool. The latter was later on—early in 1916—sent overseas, and served in France and Belgium in the 57th Division.

About February, 1915, the 14th, which had previously been worked on the eight-company organisation, with a captain, two subalterns, and a colour-sergeant to each company, was reorganised in accordance with a War Office Order on the four company system. This system had been in operation in the Regular Army for some time prior to the war; why it had not previously been applied to the Territorial Force we never knew, and only surmised that it had been on its trial until the change was actually made.

February, 1915, will always be regarded as the turning point in our history. Major Hindle, then Junior Major, was promoted Lieutenant-Colonel and given command of the unit. A severe process of weeding out started, coupled with vigorous inoculation and vaccination, and we commenced to train in accordance with the new War Office syllabus of training. We trained very hard, but everybody was becoming restive. It is not too much to say that we had daily been expecting to be sent abroad ever since the previous August, and by this time we were beginning to think that we should never go. In consequence there was much muttering, which was not allayed when we saw the

15th Loyal North Lancashires hand in their blankets one morning, and parade for France.

In March, 1915, we were suddenly moved to Oxted, where we were billeted in empty houses. There we began to dig, and completed, to the satisfaction of those who were in charge, a section of the London Defences running over the Downs. This was excellent experience, as there was every kind of soil to be contended with—clay, chalk, sand, and a sort of conglomerate, composed of what seemed to be melted flints, which blunted any pick in about five minutes. Here we first came into contact with elements of Kitchener's Army, which were engaged on similar work.

In April, 1915, it was suddenly made known that at last we really were going to France, and we were moved to Bedford, where we joined the 51st Highland Division. The ten days at Bedford were spent in completely re-equipping the battalion and transport, and in bayonet fighting and route marching, our last route march before crossing to France being one of 18 miles in full pack.

The Lancashire men and the Highlanders fought like anything when they first met, and a keen rivalry sprang up between them, which only became friendly when one evening a fight took place between one of our fellows and one of the Highlanders. It was reported amongst us that our man had won. Probably a similar report was current amongst the Highlanders with regard to their champion! Whatever the truth was, from that day we settled down together and became the best of friends.

It has been impossible to devote very much space to these early days in England. Everyone was as keen as mustard, and we had the advantage of having, besides our Regular Adjutant Captain Norman (Royal Welsh Fusiliers), and Sergeant-Major Farnworth (of the 1st Battalion), a number of senior officers who had made soldiering their hobby for years and passed the examinations necessary to attain their rank. The warrant officers and many of the non-commissioned officers were also thoroughly trained. The disadvantages under which we laboured were that, being a Territorial unit, our equipment had not been up to date, and we were not, at first at any rate, taken in hand and pushed on as the newly-formed Kitchener's Army were; but there is no doubt that at Bedford, when at last we were under orders for overseas, we held our heads high, and in all the glory of a new issue of equipment and clothes were on the whole a pretty smart and likely looking lot. It is most unfortunate that the only photographs taken of companies at Bedford are not now available, the films having been destroyed by fire. Two officers and a number of men had been left at Oxted, and one can never forget the pitiful disappointment shown on their faces as we marched away, leaving them behind. Some of them afterwards came to us as reinforcements.

Officers' group, Bedford, 1915

CHAPTER 2

Early Days and the Battle of Festubert

On the 2nd of May, 1915, Major Foley, Second-Lieutenant Harris (transport officer), the machine gun officer, and 104 other ranks and the whole of the Regimental Transport, entrained at Ballast Pit Siding, Bedford, at one o'clock in the morning, arriving at Southampton at 6.40 a.m., where they embarked on s.s. *Rossetti* and sailed at 4.30 p.m., arriving at Havre at 3 a.m. on the 3rd.

On the evening of that day, the rest of the battalion entrained at Ballast Pit Siding in two trains, and travelled down to Folkestone, where they arrived about midnight, and marched straight down on to the boat, s.s. *Onward*, which cast off at 1.30 a.m.

At last we were really on our way, after all the delays and waitings we were going overseas like the rest! And it had all been done so quickly that only now, as we stood on the darkened boat and watched the lights of England receding, did we begin to realise what it meant—this stealthy journey of nearly a thousand souls across the Channel, which many of us had never seen before, and which many were never to see again.

The adjutant's diary gives our strength (apart from the advance party) as follows:—

Lieut.-Colonel R. Hindle.
Captain and Adjutant C. C. Norman (R. Welsh Fusiliers).
Captains Nickson, Booth, Hibbert, Peak, Whitfield, Crump, H. Parker, Widdows.
Lieutenants Ord (signalling officer), Smith, Rennard, Brindle, Moore, Gregson, Duckworth.

Second-Lieutenants Houghton, Davies, Lindsay, Rogerson, P. Parker, Bryce-Smith, Craven.
Lieutenant and Quartermaster F. W. Baker.
Captain Derham (R.A.M.C).
Rev. Powell, C. of E. Chaplain.
And 895 W.O.'s, N.C.O.'s, and men.

The total strength of the battalion on this date was (including attached) 31 officers and 1,003 other ranks.

No smoking or talking was allowed on deck during the passage, which was calm and without incident, and the boat drew alongside at Boulogne about 3 a.m., where we at once disembarked and marched about two miles to a canvas rest camp at Ostrohove. How strange everything looked in the early morning light, as we swung along against our instincts on the *right-hand* side of the *pavé* road, the French signs with which we grew so familiar later on, the grilles in the front doors, the smells!

On arrival at the camp we were soon told off to our tents, where we slept till eight, when we had breakfast. After breakfast most of us sent off our first Field Postcards to the folks at home, and cleaned up. We stayed in camp all day, resting and sunning ourselves, parading again at 6.30 p.m., when we marched to Pont de Briques Station, where we formed up in groups of 40 and waited for the train, which soon arrived from Havre with the Transport. Cattle trucks! However, we entrained, about 40 to a truck, and presently jolted off; we spent a very uncomfortable night!

On 5th May, about 2.30 a.m., we arrived at Berguette, where we detrained and at 4 a.m. started to march to Lilette, led by a "guide" who took us about two miles out of our way a serious matter, on empty stomachs, to us who were still fresh from "the fleshpots of Egypt"; however, we got there, and went into billets of sorts, many preferring to sleep in the open, so villainously d:rty were some of the outhouses. Here we found the 18th King's Liverpools, the 14th King's Own and Brigade Headquarters being at neighbouring places. All day and all night an almost continuous stream of motor vehicles went through, mostly laden with French troops in their picturesque blue and red. Battalion Headquarters was "*chez M. Rousseau,*" and the officers' mess in a small *estaminet*. As we rested that day, we heard the distant guns for the first time, booming intermittently the whole day through.

On the 6th, about 7.15 p.m., we received orders to move, and marched out at 8 p.m. to Lillers, where we joined the rear of the brigade at 2.47 p.m. Here began the worst march that any of us remember, over strange uneven roads, in pitch darkness. To us, marching in rear of the whole brigade, it seemed interminable; halts were irregular, and by the time "ten minutes' halt" came along to us it was time to move again, and it was impossible to maintain a steady pace. Added to this someone had seen fit to billet from the front of the column instead of the rear, which held us up at each billeting village and prolonged the march considerably. The last mile nearly finished us, but we stumbled into Calonne-Sur-le-Lys at 1 a.m.—dead beat—and slept it off.

We had a pretty easy time for the next few days, as, beyond being required to be ready to move at an hour's notice, we were left alone. The weather was fine, and many of us bivouacked; we did a little training, and tried to teach the local people a little sanitation, a word which apparently did not exist in their language. We, on the other hand, learnt that faggots and soil had a market value; one company, taking soil from a heap in a field, were pounced on by the owner for taking "*ma bonne terre*" to cover someone else's smelly midden, and he was quite rude about it. The officers' mess was in a private house on the main street; one night when an *al fresco* concert was in progress to the great delight of the troops, a man passing on the road enquired what was going on, and received the laconic reply, "Officers' rum issue!"

On the 8th we were visited by Sir Douglas Haig and the divisional commander.

The gunfire about eight or nine miles away increased on the 9th to what must have been a very heavy bombardment—no doubt the second Battle of La Bassée.

On the 11th blankets and officers' kits were allowed to be removed from the waggons on which they had hitherto been loaded, and the state of readiness was relaxed. Respirators for poisonous gas (the old gauze and wadding affairs) were issued. On the 13th there was a thunderstorm, accompanied by torrential rain, which did not add to the comfort of the campers.

Just after midnight on the 14th, orders to move arrived, and after breakfast we fell in and moved to the starting point by Calonne Church, whence we marched as a brigade to Meteren. We arrived there at 2 p.m., and got into billets about 3, mostly on the east and north-east sides of the town, the mess as usual in an estaminet, whose landlord thought fit to start emptying his midden soon after we ar-

METEREN, 1915

rived, causing one man to say to another, who seemed in low spirits, "What's up. Tommy? *Avez vous mal de midden?*"

The country was different from Calonne, where the ground was flat and intersected by ditches full of frogs which croaked all night; here it was undulating, and windmills and hop fields became features. On the south side of the town were a number of graves of officers and men who had fallen in the fighting there on 13th October, mostly Royal Warwicks and King's Own—it was said that the Huns had mounted machine guns on the tower of the church, which commands the country to the south and west, and had simply mown them down. How difficult we found it then to realise the story, and how peaceful the little town seemed to us. The adjutant took the opportunity of teaching the officers a little field sketching—a branch of our training which had hitherto been crowded out. Courses in those days were few and far between, and though we had learnt in the regiment many things of which some of the systematically trained officers of later days were conspicuously ignorant, there were gaps in our knowledge.

Sunday was fine and hot, and all denominations had church parades. On Monday the Ninth Division marched through—what a fine lot they looked, and how we envied them "their cookers." Why hadn't we got cookers? And the old galling comparisons between the treatment of the Territorial Force and Kitchener's Army were rubbed in once more. It is all dead now, but we had something to grouse at. On Tuesday, the 18th, we paraded at 8 p.m. for a night march, through Vieux Berquin and Neuf Berquin to La Gorgue, a suburb of Estaires, where we arrived about 4 a.m. Not for months afterwards did most of us learn that we, the 31st Division, had been moved up by General French to be in reserve for the Second Battle of La Bassée.

The town was full of troops. Our men were billeted in breweries and factories; B and A Companies were in a shell-riddled girls' school; the officers had difficulty in finding even a floor to sleep on, but at last most of them gravitated to one *estaminet*, where they fed on what they could get, and slept. An unforgettable incident rises to the mind. Lieutenant ——, having disposed himself for slumber on three chairs and fallen asleep, tried to turn over and so rolled off in one piece on to the floor, where he lay immovable, only remarking, in injured tones: "I'm fed up with this war!"

On the 19th, the 25th Lancashire Fusiliers left us and went to St. Omer, and 18 of our men were sent to the Tunnelling Company R.E.; this is mentioned because it was our first separation we had been together, in the same sections even, with practically no change for months.

On the 20th we marched to billets in farms on the east side of Logon; when we got there we found them occupied by a battalion of the Grenadier Guards, who had been in action the night before and lost their colonel, sergt.-major, and (57 other ranks, so we formed up in a field opposite a large 18th century farm with a moat round it and stayed there all day; in the evening the Guards moved out and marched off with that inimitable swing of theirs, and we took over their billets—untouched farms within three miles of the line. Here we were close to the lair of a 9in. Howitzer the only one on that front, it was said which had been shelling the Hun all day.

The next day we set to work with zeal to clean up and put the sanitation right covering middens to prevent flies breeding, building incinerators, and fixing up a water supply; we rather specialised in sanitation even in those days, when most people seemed rather to scoff at it. Late at night the 5th Gordons arrived and bivouacked in the field opposite.

On the 23rd, a very hot day, sanitary work continued, and surveys of the billeting area were carried out by officers, and afterwards combined into a composite map; the next day Second Lieutenant Sutherland, of the 2nd Leicesters, two N.C.O.'s, and 11 men reported, to instruct us in trench work needless to say we were keen for anything they could teach us, as we were eagerly looking forward to our first tour in the line. Yes, Reader, you may think this is a figure of speech, but it is not—we really were, and we sharpened our bayonets with zest on the old lady's grindstone, and thought she must be a German spy because she tried to stop us!

All the same, we expected to stay where we were for a few weeks, and were a bit surprised to learn, after a lecture on trench work by Captain Burton, 39th Gharwalis (we were in the Indian Corps), that we were to go into the line on the 25th. We assembled on the road by Battalion Headquarters at 7 p.m. and marched to a cemetery, where we were met by an officer of the 17th Black Watch. He reported that the trenches we were to occupy were being shelled by the enemy, so we halted till 10 p.m., when we moved forward by platoons at 100 yards' distance.

It is quite impossible to try to convey in print the impression of one's first march up to the line: one remembers the dark, strange road, broken trees, loose telephone wires, a long halt in a battered village, then on through interminable miles of breastworks manned by Canadians, crawling cautiously along in single file and breathless silence then a halt, and platoons are sent off down various alleys, to find at the end a trench full of Scotsmen anxiously awaiting relief. The right of the battalion rested on the Quinque Rue, the left on the road from Rue de l'Epinette to Ferme Cour d'Avoue; A and D Companies and Machine Gun Section occupied the front line, No. 2 platoon having an advanced post about 200 yards in front of the main line; C was in support and B in reserve. The fire trench had only recently been built, and the forward bit had 18in. of water in it; no wire had been put up. The support trench was an old German trench about 500 yards to the left rear of the fire trench, while the reserve trench was again 200 yards behind the latter.

The parapets were revetted with, and in some cases entirely built of sandbags; dugouts—very sketchy were built in the *parados!* The trenches were nowhere more than two feet deep, the rest of the cover being above ground; there were narrow communication trenches. Every house in the neighbourhood was in utter ruin, and the ground was a mass of shell holes. Equipment, rifles, ammunition, clothing, tins, both our own and enemy, were strewn everywhere, and dozens of bodies—chiefly of Scots Guards and Germans—lay about as they had fallen in the May Battle of Festubert; the stench was awful. Some old German trenches, not occupied by us, were interesting as showing the elaborate way they had dug themselves in. One dugout was a room about 15ft. square, with doors and a window, lined throughout with wood planking covered with cloth, and furnished with leather-covered chairs and a table; in one a quantity of feminine underclothing was found—what it was doing there could only be guessed.

Most of the above description is taken from the adjutant's journal, written at the time; all we saw that night was mud and sandbags. The platoon which took over the forward trench had to wait for the Scots to climb out at the back, and then stepped down about two feet and found themselves in a good foot of muddy water. There was nothing for it but to wait till dawn; when it came we found ourselves in a shallow ditch, with only two rows of sandbags in front. Immediately to our front was a huge pile of black, red, and yellow sandbags, where the Germans had blocked and strengthened an old communication trench leading into our lines; their main line was further off—from 200 to 400 yards; behind us and in front were the dead bodies, also in our own parapet and under the duckboards of the communication trench, which was soon dubbed "Bluebottle Alley," for as soon as the sun rose clouds of the loathsome insects filled the air and buzzed round our heads.

To our front we could see in the distance the spire of Violaines Church, and on our right was a new parapet, very high and thick, surrounding Canadian Orchard. We were puzzled and annoyed for some days by sniping from that direction, till one early morning we saw a Hun crawling from under that same parapet towards his own lines, but a rifle shot fired from a rifle which had belonged to one of the Scots Guards settled his hash and avenged the late owner of the rifle.

On the 26th we were shelled intermittently all day, and two men were wounded, our first casualties; in the evening two platoons were sent out and extended from the right of No. 2 Platoon at P 11 and started a trench to connect up with the Canadians. On the 27th we were again shelled intermittently, but no appreciable damage was done and we improved our positions greatly. We did not realise then that we had been put in to finish the consolidation of newly-taken ground—a pretty stiff beginning for raw troops. The night was exceptionally quiet—there was less shelling than usual and very little sniping; during the morning our fire trenches were shelled somewhat severely with shrapnel, and again in the afternoon, six men being wounded. As soon as it got dark, working parties went out to get on with the new trench to the right of P 11; the existing forward trench was strengthened and the R.E. put a footbridge across the ditch on our right front; it was very dark and there were no interruptions.

The next day we lost two men wounded by shell fire, which was pretty heavy. A working party of 200, with a covering party under Lieutenant Brindle, started a new trench from the new bridge towards the Canadians, and did good work in spite of bursts of shrapnel at intervals; during the night bearings were taken on gun flashes, and we located the enemy battery which was troubling us.

On the 30th the enemy fire—both shrapnel and H.E. (known in those days as "Jack Johnsons" or "Coalboxes"—was heavier than usual; two years later such activity would have provoked a perfect hurricane of retaliation from our own guns, but in 1915 our gunners had nothing to throw away and no retaliation could be had. That night the working parties continued their work, and our guns at 12.15 a.m. and 2.15 a.m. fired a few shells. The enemy retorted with vigour, wounding Second Lieutenant Bryce Smith and five men and killing one. The working parties were brought in at 1 a.m. The enemy fire died down about 3.30 a.m., but burst out afresh at 11 a.m., being directed chiefly on our fire trenches, which were damaged in several places.

On 1st June we carried out the usual programme, and were shelled fairly heavily during the afternoon; in these early days we had three or six men in every bay of the trench, and the wonder is that our casualties were not much greater than they were. On the 2nd we were relieved by 58th Vaughan's Rifles, and marched back to billets at Cornet Malo, half a mile north-west of Locon Church. We went out by companies, and the leading men set off at about four miles an hour, with the result that those at the back of the long single file were running and stumbling and out of breath, and it was great good luck that we all reached the rendezvous; but we did, and after a short rest, tramped off by companies to our billets, which we reached about 4 a.m. As each company wheeled into its own farmyard a wild cheer went up, for there were our C.Q.M.S. and cooks, a brand new field cooker, like the ones we had seen and envied with the 9th Division, and, best of all, a meal—piping hot and ready. It took about one minute to get the company formed in close column, arms piled, packs off and neatly dressed, and coffee served out.

We rested all day, but in the evening moved to fresh billets between Calonne and Robecq *via* the La Bassée Canal. Lieutenant Gregson and 30 other ranks went to the new grenadier company, and Lieutenant Smith and four to the Trench Mortar class. Two days later, back we went to our old billets at Cornet Malo! That was a horrid march. Starting at 7 p.m., we marched 12 miles as ordered, but on arrival no one knew anything about us, and on enquiring at Brigade Headquarters it was discovered that a counter-order had been issued but had never reached us, so we had to turn about and retrace our steps to Cornet Malo, arriving at midnight. It was during this counter-march that we passed a Battalion of Highlanders, and one of them shouted: "What battalion's that?" Quick as thought came the answer in a tone of pitying contempt: "Battalion! This isn't a battalion; it's a —— walking club!"

Another Scots wit asked: "What are you chaps doing? Marching?" and got prompt answer: "Marching! No; we're resting!"—as indeed we were, technically.

On the 7th Second Lieutenant Lindsay went to hospital with flu'; it was a sultry day and bathing was fashionable, both in the Canal and the clear streams, also the following day, till a thunderstorm with torrents of rain put a stop to it. Captain Parker also went to hospital about this time.

On 9th June we moved up to the trenches along the Rue de Bois, Rue de l'Epinette, through Festubert Village and down le Quinque Rue. for about 800 yards, and relieved the 17th Black Watch. Festubert was the most badly-smashed village we had yet seen—there were remnants of barricades still standing in the streets most of the houses were heavily sandbagged, and some had barbed wire round them. There was a house at the entrance to the village with all the front blown in and the furniture of the upper bedrooms hanging shakily—half in, half out. Where the church had been, now only recognisable by the crucifix which still stood unharmed, we turned to the left. (This description and the pages which follow were written by the late Captain Lindsay at the time, and have been inserted practically as he wrote them.)

Thursday, June 10th, 1915.

The day passed away very quietly; but there were two or three very heavy thunderstorms with torrential rains which rapidly converted the trenches—the communication trenches in particular—into quagmires. These communication trenches became very dirty, in no place being less than boot-deep and in many places thigh-deep in a pestilent liquid mud. The boards placed at the bottom of the trench were quite covered over, and, being extremely slippery, were mainly useful in leading the way to the deeper, wetter part of the trenches! Working parties at night in heavy rain had very great difficulty in making progress. The night was very dark, and the men were loaded with spades and hurdles and sandbags. Only a section of the working party under the command of Captain Crump managed to get through to the fire trench, and took three hours to do it—until midnight—distance not quite a mile! Working parties were under control of engineers.

Lieutenant Holt was admitted to hospital suffering from rheumatism. Second Lieutenant Rawsthorn, Reserve Machine Gun officer, took over the machine guns.

Friday, June 11th, 1915.

Second Lieutenant Lindsay rejoined the battalion.

The morning was finer, but the trenches were still very muddy. Three working parties were sent out in the morning to work in the open between the reserve and the support lines in the making of bridges across the ditches and of tracks through the long grass, of ramps in the trenches to facilitate climbing the parapet, and in clearing up the old German trench which lay in that area. The Germans shelled this old trench of theirs regularly, though it was not occupied.

The battalion was relieved unexpectedly by the 1/7th Black Watch. Relief was completed by 10.15 p.m., and the battalion marched back along the canal to billets near le Cornet Malo, in the wood to the south of that place. The march was a tiring one, but the men lasted out well, and billets were reached about 5 a.m.

Saturday, June 12th, 1915.
The day was passed in resting and cleaning up.

Sunday, June 13th, 1915.
Orders were received to return to the trenches we had left on Friday night, and relieve the battalions which had relieved the 1/8th K.L. Irish and ourselves then. Though no order had been issued, we all knew that the battalion was going up for an attack, and in anticipation of this the officers, or as many as cared to do so, drew men's uniforms from the Quartermaster's Stores. Lieutenant Moore, hearing in hospital word of this impending attack, rejoined us. The battalion marched off at 6 p.m., and relief was completed in the trenches about 1 a.m. This time we took over the fire and support trenches from the 1/6th Black Watch. We found the trenches very much drier than when we left them. There was some shelling at the time of relief. The dispositions of the battalion (646 strong) were: B and C Companies in fire trenches, D Company in support, A Company in reserve.

Second Lieutenant Houghton and one man were wounded going up.

It is a queer sensation going up to one's first battle. The bracing of the nerves to face the unknown—it is the essence of religion, voluntary self-sacrifice for a cause, made possible only by faith, and calling for the strongest effort of will to control the nerves. Happy the man who is not gifted with a vivid imagination—who, like Kipling's oxen, can *plod steadily along, living in the present—blind to the future. Those who fall do so at the moment of their highest endeavour; had they lived they had probably never risen so high again. Surely to them, if to anyone, is granted the peace which passeth understanding.*

Monday, June 14th, 1915.
The battalion had been warned for an attack, and operation orders issued from the brigade in the morning made this clear. With the object of gaining ground in the direction of Rue d'Ouvert, the Fourth Corps was to attack the German positions in the north. The

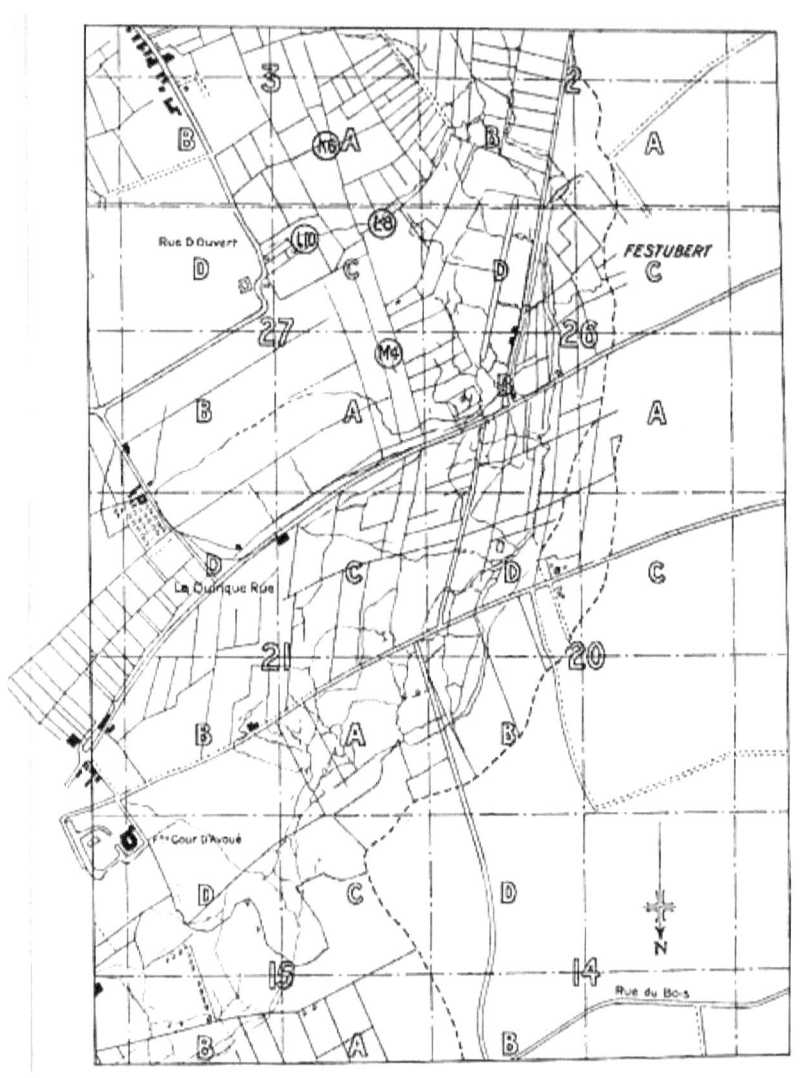

Map No. 1
Festubert

51st Division, the 7th Division, and the Canadian Division were to attack simultaneously.

The 51st Division detailed the 154th Infantry Brigade, and the 154th Infantry Brigade the 1/4th Loyal North Lancashire Regiment (with 10 bombers) on the right, and the 1/6th Scottish Rifles (with 10 bombers), on the left, as assaulting troops. Besides these there were:—

1 2 officers, 7 N.C.O.'s, and 36 men from Grenadier Company.

2. 12 bayonet men from 1/4th North Lancashires.
16 bayonet men from 1/6th Scottish Rifles.

3. 2 N.C.O.'s, 12 men of 1/4th North Lancashires,
Blocking parties.
1 N.C.O., 6 men of 1/6th Scottish Rifles.

4. 1 N.C.O., 6 men of 1/4th North Lancashires,
Carrying parties.
1 N.C.O., 6 men of 1/6th Scottish Rifles.

5. 1 Sections as escort from the 1/4th North Lancashires.
(These North Lancashire details were found by D Company.)

The supporting battalion was the 1/4th Royal Lancaster Regiment, less two platoons, whilst the 1/8th Liverpool Regiment was held in Brigade Reserve.

There was also a Trench Mortar detachment with two guns of the old "Archibald" type, under the command of Lieutenant Smith.

A working party of two platoons from the 1/4th Royal Lancaster Regiment was detailed to accompany one Section of the 2 2nd Highland Field Company R.E.

The attack by the brigade was towards the houses on the road behind the German salient. At these houses a junction would be effected, if the attack was successful, with the 7th Division. The two attacks converged on this point. We were to obtain flanking fire from the rifles and machine guns of the 152nd Brigade in the trenches to our left. They in turn were to advance on the flank when we had consolidated our position.

The whole attack was timed for 6 p.m. on the 15th June, and was to be preceded by a 48 hours' bombardment.

These, in brief, were the operation orders. We had been warned to show no signs of activity during this preliminary bombardment, which began about dawn, and was devoted chiefly to cutting the enemy's barbed wire. Field guns bombarded this, whilst the heavier guns played on the enemy's trenches, and the heaviest on the houses behind. The bombardment was not confined to our front, but extended all along the ridge to the south towards Violaines. This village lay over the ridge, and only the church spire could be seen.

From the support trench, the view was of the usual kind, a flat Flanders plain, with ditches bordered by rows of pollard willows, and wrecked farmhouses with a few scattered trees. The plain very gradually rose to a sky-line, the Aubers ridge being especially marked on the right. The British bombardment was persistent and, from what we could see, effective, whereas the Germans only replied sporadically with some sharp bursts of shrapnel and some high explosive shell on the communication trenches, from which B and C Companies lost a few men. The bombardment continued all along the front, on both sides of us, all night with only two slight stoppages.

In reply to an enquiry from the artillery as to the amount of damage done to the wire by the artillery fire in our line of advance, Major Nickson replied that most of the wire had been destroyed. This was at 11 a.m. on the 15th June, 1915, and shrapnel was still bursting over it. Captain Norman reported to the same effect, and said that all stakes were gone, and such strips of wire as remained did not appear to be an obstacle to an advance. He added that the wire opposite the enemy's main trench could not be observed clearly from our fire trench.

Tuesday, 15th June, 1915.

The British bombardment continued as on the previous day, with the Germans still only occasionally replying. Very heavy artillery (9.2) was brought to bear upon the houses on the road to our immediate left front, some being set on fire. It was particularly interesting to watch this shelling, and to note the regularity and precision with which it was shifted from house to house. The wire and the German sap and the fire trenches were also kept under continual fire. An advanced mountain battery played on the enemy's parapets.

B Company was withdrawn to the support trench to the right of D Company, whilst C Company moved to the right of the fire trench, making room for the charging company of the 16th Cameronians on their left. A Company was still in reserve.

Orders were received in the afternoon that the British bombardment would increase greatly in intensity at 5.30 p.m., and would continue so until 6 p.m. For this first half-hour, the guns would be concentrated on the enemy's barbed wire. At 6 p.m. they would "lift," *i.e.*, increase their range on to the enemy's fire trench and shell this solely for three minutes. At 6.03 the communication trenches would be bombarded for a minute, and the enemy's main trench from 6.04 to 6.15. At 6.15 the guns would lift into the road, and would shell this intensely for half-an-hour, until 6.45. At 6.45 the artillery would form a barrage beyond the road.

At 5.30 promptly the bombardment became terrific. Shells whistled and shrieked overhead in enormous numbers. All the British artillery which was massed behind the line concentrated on the assaulting positions with rapid fire. There were also some French 75 batteries to help. Under this rain of shells B and D Companies moved up the communication trenches towards the fire trench from the supports, and A Company to the supports from the reserve line.

But while the British bombardment increased greatly in intensity; the German shelling, from being merely desultory, also became intense. High explosive shells, in salvoes of four, dropped upon the communication trenches, filling them, in many places, with earth and mud, and in some cases obliterating them. It became a task of extreme difficulty to move up to the firing line under this heavy fire. There were some dead and wounded in the trenches.

At 6 p.m. precisely C Company charged from the fire trench. The leading platoon was a composite one, made up from Nos. 9 and 12 for strength, and under the command of Second Lieutenant Parker; No. 10 Platoon under Second Lieutenant Craven followed at 100 yards' distance, and No. 11 under Second Lieutenant Davies followed this. They had to climb the parapet, and, under a withering fire, form to the left flank slightly and then charge. They did this almost perfectly in line, and were in possession of the trench inside three minutes.

Their losses were chiefly from rifle and machine gun fire. This must have been principally from the main trench, and not the advanced trench of the salient, since they found most of the Germans there sheltering in dugouts; these were dealt with by bombing parties. The bombers worked in two groups: (a) (right) 1/5th Royal Lancaster Regiment under Lieutenant Taylor, and (b) 1/6th Scottish Rifles under Lieutenant Hay (left group). These bombing parties, supported by the various parties told off to them, did magnificent work, and penetrated right through the road to a much greater distance than ever the assaulting battalions reached.

Sketch Map of Trenches

Ditches marked ----------
Trenches marked ~~~~~~~~

Scale about 100 yards to ¼" Square.

Roughly it may be said that the centre of the attack was L8 as marked on the map. The two leading platoons of C Company, with their left directing the whole attack, charged the German T-head sap directly in front, and taking that in the rush, swept to the German fire trench. On their left were the 1/6th Scottish Rifles also charging

When the trench was won, comparatively easily, the Germans holding up their hands and pleading for mercy, the bombing parties extended outwards, down past Z1, K6, and Z4. Their orders were to push ahead as far as possible, since the 7th Division, as detailed, would be attacking at the same time. Another party was to break off up towards the German main trench at X7. The other main party of bombers went towards L10 up the communication trench which was also a firing trench facing M4—at L10 they split off, one towards L9 and the other down the main German trench. These bombers actually went beyond the road so fast that their bayonet men could not keep up with them. They mostly ran along the top of the trench, with the German and British artillery both bombarding the lines all this time very heavily indeed.

Red screens were used to show the furthermost points reached by the infantry, to enable the artillery to support. The bombing parties carried red flags, and a red rocket was to be fired when the infantry reached the houses on the road at L 11. (The artillery had set these houses on fire, and they afforded a good landmark). But the artillery observers could see nothing because of the tremendous smoke and dust cloud, which hid the whole area from their view. All telephone communication was very soon smashed up, and messages had to be sent by relays of orderlies. Lieutenant Ord at L 8 was in charge of this.

The course of the battle becomes a little obscure. The next supporting company was B, but Captain Peak, for some time reported missing, has lately been reported dead, and there is no connected account of what actually happened to this company. At this period the German artillery redoubled in intensity on the deploying companies, and whereas C Company had suffered chiefly from rifle and machine gun fire, B and D and A Companies suffered from shrapnel and high explosive. B Company seems to have reinforced C Company on the right. B Company men say they had to cross a deep ditch with barbed wire entanglements at the bottom. (This must have been the ditch marked in front of the German fire trench at Z1). Here, they say, Captain Peak was killed on the barbed wire in front of the trench.

D Company, coming up the now very badly damaged communication and fire trench, was sent to reinforce the line in the left of the centre of the attacking line across the sap and the fire trench, and then along the edge of the communication trench towards L10. Both B and D Companies moved to support in lines of platoons, through a gap in the trench, under extremely heavy artillery fire.

Meanwhile the attack had swept on, past the German trench, up along the German communication trenches. There were a great number of casualties from rifle fire from the German main trench and enfilading machine gun fire from somewhere about X7 or Z2. But the attack swept on and must have carried the main trench, already bombed, but for being pulled up suddenly by uncut barbed wire, which lay concealed in the long grass on the German (east) side of the ditch which runs parallel to the German main trench, south-east from L10. The attacking line was then within 30 yards of the trench. More enfilade fire came from one of the houses at L11 on the road. This house must have had a good number of machine guns in it.

The position therefore about 7 p.m. was this:—

The Scottish Rifles were attacking on our left with their right resting on the British sap head at L8. Their advance was checked by uncut barbed wire which ran along the northern edge of the communication trench, very early on, and they lay in the open under galling and very heavy fire, losing heavily in attempting to cut it, but were compelled to advance along the communication trench. At 7 p.m. when the advance was checked, they were in this communication trench, which they were holding. Once a part of the German salient, it faced obliquely the British trench at M4; it was also a fire trench, being very narrow, with numerous traverses and some dugouts about Z. The uncut wire here in front of this trench prevented any further advance by them. All their officers except one were casualties. The result of this forced change of front by them was the formation of an angle at L10 in the line of attack, they themselves facing north, whilst the Loyal North Lancashires faced east or perhaps north-east.

The ditch in which C Company lay, now reinforced by D on the left and B on the right, with A coming up from reserve, was bordered by a row of pollard willows. On the left it was comparatively dry, with a slight protecting bank on the east (German) side; but the further it went to the right the more of a quagmire it became. In some places on the right it was thigh-deep in water. It ran parallel to the German trench along the road, at about 30 yards' distance from it. It afforded comparative security after the advance because of the slight cover to

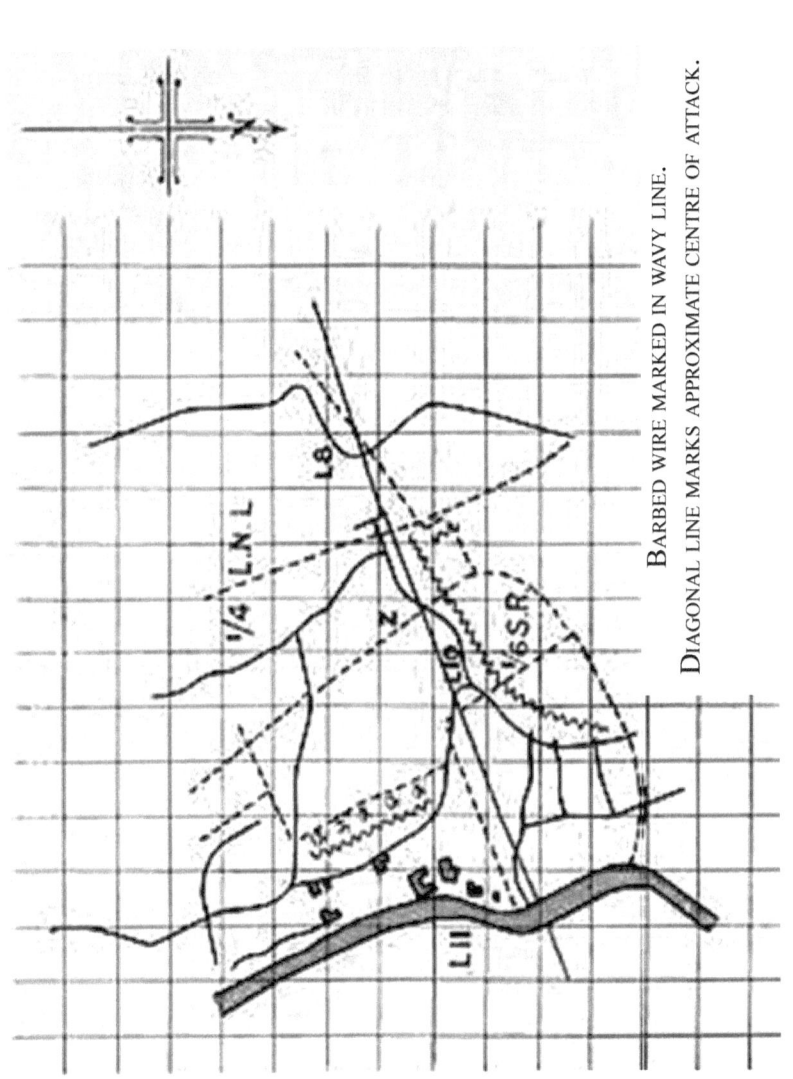

Barbed wire marked in wavy line.
Diagonal line marks approximate centre of attack.

be obtained in it, and because it was too near the German trench to allow artillery fire to be brought to bear. C Company had brought up one sandbag per man and one shovel to every three men, with 20 wire-cutters to the company, and B and A Companies had brought up three sandbags per man and a pick or a shovel carried slung with spun yarn, per man, but some of these were lost in the advance, and only a few men came up with them all.

The battalion entrenched itself in this ditch line as best it could. It was rapidly going dark. A Company, as it came up, was sent to the right of the line to strengthen and extend it and to get into touch with the 7th Division, and several parties were sent out to the right to find them, but fruitlessly. Entrenching in a water-logged ditch with the entrenching tool was slow work. At dusk the 14th King's Own sent up a company to reinforce, under the command of Captain Barrow; Major Nickson was in command of the front line. The colonel had been wounded earlier in the evening, and Major Foley took over command and established his headquarters in the German fire trench opposite L8.

About 11 p.m. there was a slackening of the German fire, both artillery and rifle. The German artillery fire had been directed chiefly against our supports and reserves, and was particularly violent at L8. Some of our wounded had been collected there, and were looked after there all night by Sergeant-Major Farnworth.

By this time, in the front line, a machine gun had been placed in position about L10. The trench junction there had been blocked by sandbags. It was at this point (L10) that the Scottish Rifles were in touch with us. It was found impossible, because of lack of material, to block the further trench (X7), and accordingly the line we held in the ditch was bent back to the right to protect that flank. The line was a bad one. There was a conference of officers held by Major Nickson. Both flanks were in the air. We were not in touch with the 7th Division, and enfilade rifle fire was coming from the right flank, though fairly weak. The ditch was waterlogged, and too wide in places and clearly marked by the row of pollard willows. Spades and picks and sandbags were lacking.

There were no bombs left, and no bombers. (There were two advanced bomb reserves of 1000 bombs each near L8, but no one knew where these were. The bombers sent to reinforce the original party were shelled heavily on the road to the reserve trenches, and out of 33 only five were unwounded.) Impossible to entrench ditch. Therefore proposed line about 20 yards back in the open. This meant beginning afresh without tools. Men too crowded in line. There were no Verey lights. Artillery support had ceased about 8.45 because of uncertainty as to the actual position of the attacking battalions. Major Nickson sent back word to Major Foley explaining this and asking for instructions. In the meantime the German counter-attack began, and prevented instructions arriving.

It was about midnight when the Germans began to throw up flares in great numbers. They had been shelling L10 and the (German) captured salient for some time before. Their counter-attack proper began by bombing at L10 so severely that the machine gun there was damaged and put out of action, and the connection with the Cameronians broken. Almost at the same time, the Germans began to bomb down the right communication trench (X7), and followed this by throwing bombs across the open. There was no means of replying, and no cover to be had anywhere in the ditch. To stay there would have meant the wiping out of those in the line; enfilade fire came from both flanks on the right from the German main trench at K7, and on the left from L9; the Scottish Rifles in the German communication trench were enfiladed down the whole length by artillery and rifle fire. Orders were given, therefore, to retire from the position.

At the point Z (see map) a mixed body of men lined the shell craters and held up the Germans for about two hours, losing heavily. This point Z, which lay on the German side of their fire trench, was an absolute mass of wrecked dugouts. These men finally retired, in the mist of the morning, towards the sap south-west of L8. In the retirement all the attacking battalions were mixed up. The sap at L8 was held by a composite company: 1/4th Loyal North Lancashires, 1/6th Scottish Rifles, 1/4th Royal Lancaster Regiment, Grenadier Guards, 1/8th Liverpool Irish, but the Germans, probably because of their check at Z, did not push their counter-attack on to the British lines.

The attacking battalions were withdrawn to the support trenches about 4 a.m. on the 16th, the men in the sap about 6 a.m., and the lines were taken over by the 1/8th K.L. Regiment (Irish), Motor Machine Guns under Captain Hammond, D.S.O., to left of L8, stayed up through the attack and for four days afterwards.

The casualties were heavy.

The colonel was wounded at the beginning of the attack, when near L8. Almost at the same time the adjutant, Captain Norman, was severely wounded. He advanced with the leading platoon and was on the parapet of the German trench when he was wounded by, it is said, an officer hiding in a dugout.

In C Company, Second Lieutenant P. Parker, who was in command of the charging platoon was seriously wounded, Second Lieutenant Craven was wounded in the leg, and Second Lieutenant Davies, who, wounded slightly twice, would go on, was fatally wounded and died on the field.

In B Company, Captain Peak was reported killed, as previously mentioned, but was posted missing, as there was no definite news of what actually happened to him. Lieutenant Moore was wounded in the wrist, and Captain Crump blown up and injured by a shell.

In D Company, Captain Hibbert was last seen directing the platoons through the gap in the fire trench. After that no news can be obtained of what happened to him, and he was posted missing. Captain Whitfield was seriously wounded in the thighs by shrapnel and died in hospital at Boulogne. Second Lieutenant Rawsthorn, in charge of the machine guns, was killed by shell when leading his team across the open to the German trenches. Lieutenant Brindle was hit on the head and in the arm.

In A Company, Lieutenant Smith[2] was in charge of the trench mortar team during the bombardment, firing from the fire trench. When the order to charge was given. Lieutenant Smith rushed forward with his gun, and was seriously wounded when carrying it across the open. He died in hospital at Lillers two days later, and was buried there.

The officers who came through the fight unhurt were Major Foley, Major Nickson, Captain Booth, Captain Widdows, Lieutenant Rennard, Lieutenant Ord, Lieutenant Duckworth, Second Lieutenant Lindsay.

Second Lieutenant Rogerson was away at General Headquarters attending a Machine Gun Course, and Lieutenant Gregson was attached to the Grenadier Company at the time.

The casualties among the men were heavy, especially among the N.C.O.'s.[3] They were:—

Killed	26
Wounded	266
Missing	110
Total	402

2. C.Q.M.S. Lester and Private Cowburn (S. B.) brought him in to L8.
3. Captain Caldwell. M.O., was specially mentioned for attending to 243 wounded and getting them clear.

It must be assumed that most of the missing are killed. The list therefore stands with a high ratio of killed to wounded.

The respective strengths of the companies on June 30th, according to Orderly Room returns, were:—

A Company	146
B Company	99
C Company	149
D Company	126
Total	520

15 officers on strength. The effective rifle strength was 358.

The German trenches after the two days' bombardment were in a bad state. In many places they had been completely destroyed, and when we took them we found them piled deep with German dead. The dugouts, which had been made in the *parados*, seemed whole, but were full of dead and wounded, probably the work of the bombers. The communication trench was also partially destroyed, and littered with German dead. The whole series of trenches were full of German equipment in great confusion. Like our trenches, they were built of sandbags, but their communication trench was very deep and well traversed, and was probably intended to serve as a fire trench against M4. There was an abandoned German machine gun in the fire trench in a stretcher carriage, which could not be moved. There was a good amount of German equipment outside the trench about the point Z. This place was the wildest spot, a mass of shell holes and fragments of works.

The German barbed wire was very strong, of abnormal thickness in closeness and strength of spikes and in the wire itself. The ditch in front of the sap was heavily wired under the water. The German casualties must have been very heavy. The artillery officers said they caught the reinforcements coming up on the road first with the 4.5 howitzers, and later with the 9in guns. Bombers say something of what they saw there, but not all of them agree on the point. The trenches were occupied at the time of the attack by Bavarians, it is said. The counter-attack was made by the reserve division of the Prussian Guards.

The British trenches suffered severely too. In the morning L8 was a wreck, most of the trench battered down, and the communication trench, which was with hurdles, also badly damaged. The trench was saved in many cases, though, by the hurdles bending and not collapsing as sandbag revetting would have done. It was at L8 that the brunt of the firing was. In some places there the trench lines were completely obliterated, and in very many places so badly damaged as to need extensive repair before being of much use again.

The British report of June 16th, as issued by the Press Bureau, read:—

> Yesterday evening, we captured the German front line of trenches east of Festubert, on a mile of front, but failed to hold them during the night against the strong counter-attacks delivered by the enemy.

The *communiqué* issued at the German Main Headquarters says, according to the *Daily Telegraph*:—

> Wednesday.
> Again influenced by Russian defeats, the French and English yesterday attacked with strong forces of men at many points on the Western front.
> On the other hand, two attacks of four English divisions betweens the roads of Estaires—La Bassée and La Bassée Canal completely collapsed. Our brave Westphalian regiments and reinforcements, consisting of portions of our Guard, repulsed the attacks after desperate hand-to-hand fighting. The enemy suffered heavy losses. We captured several machine guns and one mine-throwing howitzer.

June 16th, 1915—June 21st, 1915.

The battalion regathered at Le Touret and was given breakfast there from the cookers which had been brought up, with a rum issue. The roll was called, and only 243 men answered it.[4] We moved off about 10 a.m. In spite of their exhausted condition and their heavy losses, the men marched well and in good spirits, singing for the first half-hour of the journey, but a halt was made just before reaching billets for the purposes of a rest. The day was very hot and close. The march was resumed about 4.30 p.m., and billets at Le Cornet Malo were reached about 5.30 p.m. Billets were of the usual type—barns with adjacent orchards.

Lieutenant Ord was admitted to hospital on June 17th. The men were very exhausted, and the days passed in resting and cleaning-up and reorganising. All the companies needed reorganising. B Company was without an officer until Lieutenant Gregson came back from the

---

4. Fifty-one men actually answered the roll, the rest being accounted for.

Bomb School on June 19th. There was a great shortage of N.C.O.'s, since most of them were casualties. B, C, and D Companies had an average of five or six each, and A Company was not much better. Platoons were very weak in strength. A few odd men rolled up during the first few days. One, Corporal Smalley, of D Company, came in from the German lines wounded, with German field dressings on his wounds.

The system of officers messing by companies had to be abandoned, and a battalion mess was reinstituted. This system was abandoned on the 9th July, when three messes were constituted: Headquarters, A and B, and C and D, when out of the trenches.

Brigadier-General Hibbert inspected the battalion, together with the 1/8th Liverpool Regiment, on June 18th, and conveyed to officers and men the appreciation of himself and of the corps commander for the services they had rendered. He said that though the attack had failed in its immediate object, yet it had been instrumental in attracting to itself reinforcements which might otherwise have been directed against the French, attacking further south. The G.O.C. Division held an inspection on June 19th, and conveyed to us a message from Field-Marshal Sir John French, congratulating the brigade on the fight it had made.

CHAPTER 3

Trench Warfare

Major Foley took over the command of the battalion on June 16th, 1915, *vice* Lieutenant-Colonel Hindle, wounded; Major Nickson became senior major, *vice* Major Foley, from the same date; Lieutenant Duckworth became adjutant, *vice* Captain Norman, wounded; Captain Widdows took over command of C Company, *vice* Major Nickson; Lieutenant Rennard of D Company, *vice* Captain Hibbert, missing; Lieutenant Gregson B Company, *vice* Captain Peak, missing; Second Lieutenant Rogerson became machine gun officer, *vice* Second Lieutenant Rawsthorn, killed.

The weather was good and sunny, and we bathed in the La Bassée Canal. Most of us were exhausted by the attack and in need of rest. Indents for clothing and necessaries were rendered.

Orders were received on the 21st for the battalion to proceed to billets near Le Touret. A working party of 200, under Captain Booth, was detailed for work under the R.E. building a light railway.

June 22nd—June 24th.

The battalion arrived in billets about 7 p.m., and took over the billets of the 1/7th Royal Highlanders.

There was no working party to be furnished for the night, the 22nd/23rd June, but one of 100 men under the command of Captain Widdows for the night following. This working party was detailed for work in the firing trench. The trench, which needed extra traverses and wider parapets, was protected from the German view by an old ruined communication trench which was to be demolished as soon as the new low fire trench was ready for use, and in neither working party were there any casualties.

This stay at La Couture was quiet, and was devoted to resting and reorganising. There was a little shelling of the village to our right, but none near to us. Second Lieutenant Rogerson rejoined the battalion after a fortnight's machine gun training.

June 25th.
The battalion moved off about 7 p.m. on the night of the 24th June, and marched to Estaires, where it arrived about 11 p.m., and was billeted, the men being in factories or breweries. These billets were very similar to the ones we occupied on May 18th. Estaires is a fair-sized town, a market town in many ways, with some industries. It was interesting to us, because it was the first town we had been quartered in since landing in France.

In the afternoon of June 25th, orders were received to move to the trenches the same night. The battalion marched to the trenches *via* Laventie, which had been heavily shelled by the enemy, but most of the damage centred on the church, as in other villages where we had been. Here the church, and the two roads which crossed near the church, as well as the adjoining streets for a length of about 200 yards, were in ruins; the nearer you got to the church centre the more intensive was the damage. The inhabitants, however, were living in the village and carrying on their business outside this shelled ring.

The trenches were reached at 8.30, and relief was completed by 9 p.m. The battalion we relieved was the 1/1st London Regiment (T.F.).

June 26th—July 4th.
We spent eight days in these new trenches. They are known as "E2 Lines, Fauquissart," and were of the breastwork type, a shallow trench first being dug to a little above the water level and a high parapet of sandbags placed in front of this. The line we occupied was practically, when allowances are made for the fact that it was a fire trench, the equivalent of the reserve trenches which we held about June 10th. It was the same line. The British here had been able to make no headway. The parapet was very good and very thick as a rule, but much of the *parados* was shaky and had to be rebuilt. The long grass in front had already been partly cut by the previous trench holders, and there was a fair amount of wire in front, but not too much.

The enemy was about 300 yards off, but the lines were not exactly parallel, and at one point the enemy must have been nearly five hundred yards away. There was very much less shell fire than in the previous trenches we had held, and very much more rifle shooting. There was a number of fixed rifle batteries with which the enemy tried to break the sandbags. There were also snipers normally to be found firing from a flank. The telescopic-sighted rifle, which had been issued to the battalion just before entering the trenches, proved very useful for sniping in return. These rifles were the short rifles, fitted with telescopic sights, with a crossed hair-line on the object lens and a range dial. One ran to 600 yards and the other 1,200 yards in range.

A, B, and D Companies were in the trench line, with C Company in reserve holding an entrenched post. These "forts" took the place of the support line in the trenches we had been in before and were intended as defensive and rallying points in case of an attack. Battalion Headquarters was in the open.

Second Lieutenant Evans, who had been left behind with Second Lieutenant Norwood at Oxted when the battalion moved to Bedford preparatory to sailing for France, rejoined the battalion from the 2/4th Loyal North Lancashire Regiment on the night of June 26th.

On June 27th, Second Lieutenant R. A. Ostrehan and Second Lieutenant E. G. Baker, from the 2/4th Battalion, joined the battalion, and Second Lieutenant D. H. Ostrehan joined on the night of the 28th.

To the left of our positions, the opposing lines narrowed down until in one place, known as Red Lamp Corner, they were no more than fifty yards apart. A mine was sprung here by us one morning at dawn, and shook the earth around. There was a short bombardment by our artillery of the mine crater and of the enemy line, and a slight reply from the German artillery, which bombarded the position much more heavily two days later, but these bombardments did not affect us.

July 4th—July 9th.

The battalion was relieved in the night of the 3rd/4th July about 10 p.m. by the 1/7th Gordon Highlanders, and marched off to billets in the Estaires—La Bassée road, near La Gorgue, taking over billets from the 1/5th Seaforth Highlanders. The billets were of the usual type, orchards and farm buildings. The officers' mess was established in the local schoolroom.

The six days' rest from the trenches was interrupted by a series of working parties, which swallowed the whole available strength of the battalion, officers' servants, signallers, stretcher-bearers, transport, and machine gunners all having to be empanelled in order to provide the number required. The work done was miscellaneous—digging in communication trenches, improving communication trench parapets, laying a level bed for a light trench railway, &c. This resulted in most of the men sleeping all day. New clothing was issued on the 4th July, and a day was set apart for bathing the battalion in the brewery-bathhouse. This bathhouse had been made by taking vats from the brewery and tubs, and filling these with hot water. Men filed in at one door and gave up their dirty underclothing, and tied their clothes into a bundle, fastened with their identity disc. Each man was issued there with clean shirt and underclothing, whilst his old garments were washed and cleaned. Facilities were provided for bathing a company at a time. Six baths for officers were laid down also. This hot bath was greatly appreciated by the men; it was the first one they had had since landing.

The G.O.C. Indian Corps, to which the division had been attached, inspected the brigade on Wednesday, July 7th. The battalion paraded as strong as possible, and put 293 rifles into the field. The General, Sir James Wilcox, expressed himself as well satisfied with the brigade and welcomed them back to the Indian Corps, which they had temporarily left, expressing a hope that they were back for good.

July 10th—July 15th.

in these six days the battalion was on trench duty in F lines, a little to the right of our previous position. The trenches were of the same type as those of E2 Lines, consisting of a strong breastwork sandbagged trench, only a little sunk below the level of the ground, with several supporting points in rear. The whole battalion was in the line, with the exception of Battalion Headquarters, which were situated about 1,000 yards back from the firing line in a farmhouse. Captain Booth was sent to hospital from here.

Nothing of much moment happened to us in these lines. There was one very wet night, which left the trenches in a very bad condition for the following day. What shelling there was was directed upon the house behind us; very few shells fell on the trench.

Our casualties amounted to one killed and three wounded in this period, mainly from sniping, which was fairly active. We had a sniping post, heavily sandbagged, in an orchard to the rear of the line, and a sniping party with telescopic-sighted rifles to garrison it.

There was an order that equipment must never be removed for any purpose. One day a man emerging from his billet with equipment on but the shoulder straps of his jacket unbuttoned cannoned into the R.S.M., who accused him of having had his equipment off. This he denied, and muttered that he had just been having breakfast.

"Do you need to unbutton your shoulder straps to have breakfast, then?" enquired the R.S.M. in his silkiest tones.

The man stood glowering for a moment, and then in desperation burst out, "Well! Ah've got to saay summat, 'evn't I?"

We were relieved on the night of the 16th/17th July by the 1/4th Royal Lancaster Regiment, about 10 p.m., and moved off to reserve billets near Headquarters. Detachments from A Company, under Second Lieutenant Evans, and C Company, under Second Lieutenant R. A. Ostrehan, garrisoned "fort" supporting points behind the line. There was a heavy trench mortar bombardment of the trenches held by the 2/5th Lancashire Fusiliers on the night of the 19th 20th July, which caused a brigade "stand-to," but nothing happened. The 2/5th Lancashire Fusiliers had rejoined the brigade the week before.

The brigade was relieved on the night of the 23rd/24th July by the 13th Brigade, the battalion by the 1st Middlesex Regiment.

On the 27th we left for La Gorgue Station, where we entrained, and arrived at Calais at 8 p.m., then on via Abbeville and Amiens to Corbie, where we detrained and marched to billets at Ribemont. On the 31st we went to Martinsart, being then in Divisional Reserve. Here we remained for a week training.

This Somme country was a great change from the plains of Flanders, and the air was better.

We relieved the 25th Lancashire Fusiliers on the 6th August in Sector B. A, B, and C Companies were in the fire trench; D Company in support at Poste Lesdos; Battalion Headquarters in Aveluy Wood south of Authuille. The trenches were cut in the solid chalk—hardly any sandbags—and the French had made the dugouts very comfortable. The barbed wire was thick. On the 4th Second Lieutenant W. R. Haggas had reported from the 2/4th Loyal North Lancashires, bringing five N.C.O.'s and men, who had been wounded, from the base, and a week later Lieutenant-Colonel Hindle returned from England and again took over the command of the Battalion. On the 9th a thunderstorm broke and turned the trenches into mud. On the 11th the first party went on leave. Two men were wounded the same day. The sector was quiet, and so was La Boiselle sector, where we went on the 14th, relieving the 1/5th Irish. C and D Companies were in the fire trench; A and B in support at Poste Donnez. The opposing lines were so close that high bomb nets were found necessary.

On the 21st we were relieved by the 1/5th King's Liverpool Regiment, and went into billets at Aveluy. It is chronicled in the *War Diary* that at this time the men began to have hot tea and soup served about midnight and that one-third were allowed to sleep at night. On the 22nd a draft was received from the 2/4th Loyal North Lancashire Regiment of 101 other ranks, and the following day four officers, Second Lieutenants A. B. Bratton and H. M. Strong, from the 3rd Loyal North Lancashires, and Second Lieutenants J. S. Walker and M. W. Nolan, from the 11th Loyal North Lancashires, joined.

On the morning of September 4th the enemy shelled the trenches at Poste Lesdos fairly heavily, and one shell burst in the midst of a working party, killing one and wounding five other ranks of D Company, whilst a week later one other rank was killed. On the 17th Lieutenant-Colonel Foley left the battalion and crossed to England to take over command of a third-line unit. The succeeding day, just before being relieved by the 1/8th Liverpool Irish, the trenches were again heavily shelled, and one company sergeant-major, one sergeant, and one corporal were killed by a single shell, whilst three other ranks were wounded. Captain H. Parker, Captain J. A. Crump, and Lieutenants K. H. Moore, R. Ord, and J. L. Brindle rejoined the Battalion from the 3/4th Loyal North Lancashires, and the first-named three officers took over the command of A, B, and C Companies respectively.

At this time companies of one of the service battalions of the Highland Light Infantry were attached to us for instruction.

On October 1st Brigadier-General J. L. Hibbert was wounded in the shoulder, and Lieutenant-Colonel Hindle took over the temporary command of the brigade, while Major Nickson took over the battalion with Captain Crump as second. Captain Rennard and Second Lieutenant Norwood went into hospital the same day, and Captain Gregson on the 3rd, and on the 4th Captain Green, R.A.M.C, reported for duty, *vice* Lieutenant Sugars transferred to the 3rd Battalion. Lieutenant-Colonel Hindle returned to the battalion on the 7th, and Brigadier-General G. T . G. Edwards, C.B., took over command of the brigade.

On the whole the month was quiet. On the 3rd we went into the line, A, C, and D in front and B in support at Poste Lesdos—being relieved on the 15th by the 2/5th Lancashire Fusiliers, when B and C Companies relieved the 1/8th Irish on the right of F1 sector, A and D being in support at Poste Donnez; here we stayed till the 21st, going back to Aveluy, whence nightly working parties went up the line.

On the 27th, "fur" coats were issued, and we went back to Poste

Lesdos sector.

On the 28th, the enemy bombarded the wire and front line from 7.10 a.m. to 9.30 a.m., doing considerable damage and blowing in 100 yards of trench between Aintree Street and Mersey Street, held by C Company, and 30 yards in A Company's sector. C.S.M. Edwards earned the D.C.M. for manoeuvring his company about during the shelling in such a way as to escape with very few casualties.

The whole of the month was quiet and uneventful, but there was some desultory shelling of the working parties; salvos of H.E. and H.V. shells were sent over hourly, and in one of these bursts on the 30th Major Nickson was killed, whilst Second Lieutenant Bratton and six other ranks were wounded.

On the 31st Captain J. O. Widdows went sick and Second Lieutenant Nolan and 20 other ranks were wounded, the total casualties for the month being:—Officers: killed one, wounded two, sick four; Other ranks: killed one, wounded 35, missing one.

Early in November Second Lieutenant R. S. De Blaby reported for duty from the base. On the 2nd an enemy shell burst in the trench held by A Company, killing two men and wounding one, whilst five others were admitted to hospital suffering from shock. Two mornings later two shells landed at the junction of Aintree Street and the fire trench, killing three men and wounding three others who were waiting as sentry reliefs. About this time, owing to the number of sick and wounded (the trenches were in a very bad state and knee-deep in water through the torrential rains and the men were very wet), it became extremely difficult to find the requisite number of men for the different duties each day.

On the 5th Lieutenant-Colonel Hindle went on leave for nine days, Captain Crump taking over command, and during that period the weather was so bad, snow falling on several of the days, that the programme of training could not be carried out. On the 18th Second Lieutenants T. A. Burnside, F. R. Best, and M. Wilson joined, and on the 20th one man was killed during an enemy burst of 30 small shells in reply to our artillery's work on the German trenches.

On the 25th Bomber Gent did very good work. Taking nine bombs with him, he went out alone, and, encountering an enemy patrol coming from a sap-head, bombed them with good effect. The following day Lieutenant K. H. Moore was killed by a sniper. The month's casualties consisted of one officer killed, and of other ranks eight killed, three wounded, and 95 sick.

On December 2nd, at Bouzincourt, C.Q.M.S. E. E. Lester was presented with the *Croix de Guerre* for conspicuous bravery at Festubert on June 15th. This ceremony took place on battalion parade. Second Lieutenant A. Hague arrived from the 3/4th Loyal North Lancashires, and later in the month Second Lieutenants A. Parker and Fairclough joined for duty, whilst Second Lieutenant Bryce Smith rejoined from the base. As Christmas approached the weather was very bad, and the sides of the trenches were continually falling in. There were pumps in plenty, but the water ran in as fast as it could be pumped out. On Christmas Day we were relieved by the 1/4th King's Own, and managed to get a good dinner, thanks to our excellent quartermaster, Lieutenant Baker. The casualties during December consisted of 2 other ranks wounded and 82 sick, and for the whole year 23 officers (4 killed, 10 wounded, 2 missing, 2 died of wounds, and 5 sick), and 624 other ranks (30 killed, 271 wounded, 146 missing, and 177 sick).

New Year's Day, 1916, dawned wet and dismal in the trenches at Authuille, and though the general situation was quiet our trench mortar batteries were in action for a time. It was during the evening's retaliation that a shell blew in a dugout, killing Second Lieutenant F. R. Best and wounding Second Lieutenants H. Rogerson and R. A. Ostrehan and three other ranks. The following day the battalion was relieved by the 16th Battalion Lancashire Fusiliers, and moved to billets at Lavieville, six miles away. The following day the brigade left the 51st Division, and, moving off from Henencourt, we marched *via* Behencourt to St. Gratien and a day later to Rainneville. The brigade stayed at Rainneville a day and a-half, the time being spent in a much-needed clean-up, and at this point on January 5th we became the 164th Infantry Brigade of the 55th Division.

On the 6th we left the 13th Corps to move to the new divisional area, the 55th Division being then part of the 14th Corps. The march was *via* Bertangles, Vaux-en-Amiens to Argoeuves, the battalion subsequently moving independently to Airaines, *via* St. Sauvneur, Picquigny, and Soues, reinforcements arriving from the base the day after the battalion had been billeted. Company training was carried out, and we had the task of finding control posts for all entrances to the village to prevent British Army horses from entering on account of the number of diseased horses there. On the 14th Second Lieutenants Silveira, Agostini, and Matthews arrived from the 3/4th Loyal North Lancashire Regiment.

The brigadier should have inspected the brigade the following day at Courchon, but the event was cancelled owing to rain, and battalion drill took place instead. In the afternoon the A.S.C.'s Picture Palace was booked and the men given a free show. During the week a bombing school, bayonet course, and rifle range were fixed up, and excellent progress was made with the training. On the 20th of January Major Parker took over the battalion on Lieutenant-Colonel Hindle's departure on leave. During the remainder of the stay there the training was rounded off by an attack over open country, a gas test in the presence of the G.O.C. of the division, and instruction in grenade throwing for all the officers and N.C.O.'s, before, ultimately. General Allenby inspected the division near Hallencourt, on the 29th.

On February 2nd the Earl of Derby inspected the battalion at Vieulaine, and the following day we proceeded to billets at Longpre, whence the brigade, less two battalions, marched to new billets. Brigade Headquarters proceeding to Ribeacourt, 2/5th Lancashire Fusiliers to Beaumetz, and the 1/4th Loyal North Lancashires to Prouville. At Autheux, a few days later, the battalion and platoon bombers were inspected in their work by the G.O.C. of the 55th Division, Major-General Jeudwine. "Old Judy," as he was called, soon found a place in our hearts—he had the gift of inspiring those under him—and we all loved him.

About this time the brigade experienced the French winter at its worst in so far as rain was concerned, conditions being so bad that no training was possible for two days. The men found welcome relief when the downpour ceased by participating in a five miles cross-country run. On the 15th the brigade marched from Hem, *via* Doullens, to Halloy and on to Bellevue, where units broke off to their respective villages, the 1/4th continuing the march *via* Bavincourt and Gouy-en-Artois to Monchiet. Three nights afterwards hostile aircraft flew over the village and dropped two bombs not far from our lines. There were no casualties. Shortly before noon the following day an enemy 'plane again flew over the village, dropping a bomb about 150 yards from the huts, once more without effecting any damage.

On the 23rd orders were received for the battalion to go into the trenches to take over from the 1/5th King's Liverpool Regiment. There was a heavy fall of snow that afternoon, followed by a frost at night, and we moved into the line the following night. The enemy was very quiet on this front and apt to show himself a good deal. Lieutenant-Colonel Hindle took over the command the day following the battalion's arrival. About this time the trenches became very wet owing to the thaw, and the discomforts familiar at these times recurred. Meanwhile the enemy indulged in rather more sniping than usual, while a visit by a dozen hostile aeroplanes one morning was accompanied by activity on the part of his artillery. There were no casualties or cases of sickness during the month—a record.

March also was quite uneventful. A German deserter surrendered to us, and there was only a single casualty during the month, one man being wounded. But on April 1st, while A, B, and C Companies were billeted at Bretencourt, the enemy fired about three salvoes to the west of the village, and one shell burst in a barn occupied by No. 15 Platoon (D Company), killed six men, and wounded eight others. On the 9th Lieutenant-Colonel Hindle went to the 3rd Army School, and Major Crump took command of the battalion during his week's absence.

On the 23rd, while rifle grenades were being fired, one exploded in our lines and would have caused serious loss of life, but Private Carter threw himself upon it and received the full force of the burst. He was killed, and Second Lieutenant Wilson, trying at the same time to grasp the grenade and throw it away, lost his hand. Lieutenant-Colonel Hindle went on leave on the 27th, Major Crump taking over the command. During the month, in addition to the casualties referred to, there were seven men killed and a like number wounded.

On 1st April, while the battalion was at Grosville, four cavalry N.C.O.'s were attached, two from the 1st Dragoon Guards and two from the Inniskilling Dragoons. On the 4th the battalion took over slightly to the right of the former frontage, the left company frontage being taken over by the 165th Brigade. Owing to shortage of officers, A and C Companies worked as one in respect of officers' duties. Lieutenant-Colonel Hindle resumed his command two days before the battalion was relieved. As soon as duty again lay in the shape of trench life, it was discovered that though the enemy was very quiet there appeared to be a great amount of work in progress in his lines. One day the enemy shelled the front line with "Five-nines," but there was no material damage. Obviously the object of the shoot was to discover trench mortar emplacements. During the next two days there was again some shelling, and on the 30th, during a "strafe" of the right company, Second Lieutenant Eccles was killed, the only other casualties during the whole of the month being two other ranks killed and two wounded.

Shortly after midday, June 4th, our artillery and trench mortars opened an intense bombardment on the enemy wire, and this was replied to by heavy fire for half-an-hour, mainly on our support lines and communication trenches, but no severe damage was done, and, although the dressing station behind the support line was blown in, there were no casualties. The following day Second Lieutenant Ducksbury reported for duty from the base. The time was mainly occupied in training bombing parties, scouting, wire cutting and crawling, and cutting new pattern fire steps under R.E. supervision.

A special raiding party was practising and was increased to four officers (Captain Gregson, and Second Lieutenants Martin, Roscoe, and Walker) and 15 N.C.O.'s and men per company, who were billeted separately in the village and trained. Short rifles and long bayonets were issued to the battalion on the afternoon of the 19th, and long rifles and short bayonets withdrawn. The same day the battalion moved up to Agny to relieve the South Lancashires, the raiding party remaining at Bretencourt. Although the enemy shelled and sent over rifle grenades within the next few days, little damage was done and there were no casualties. Here we first met a large trench mortar called "Crashing Christopher"—the "Heavy Minnie" of later days.

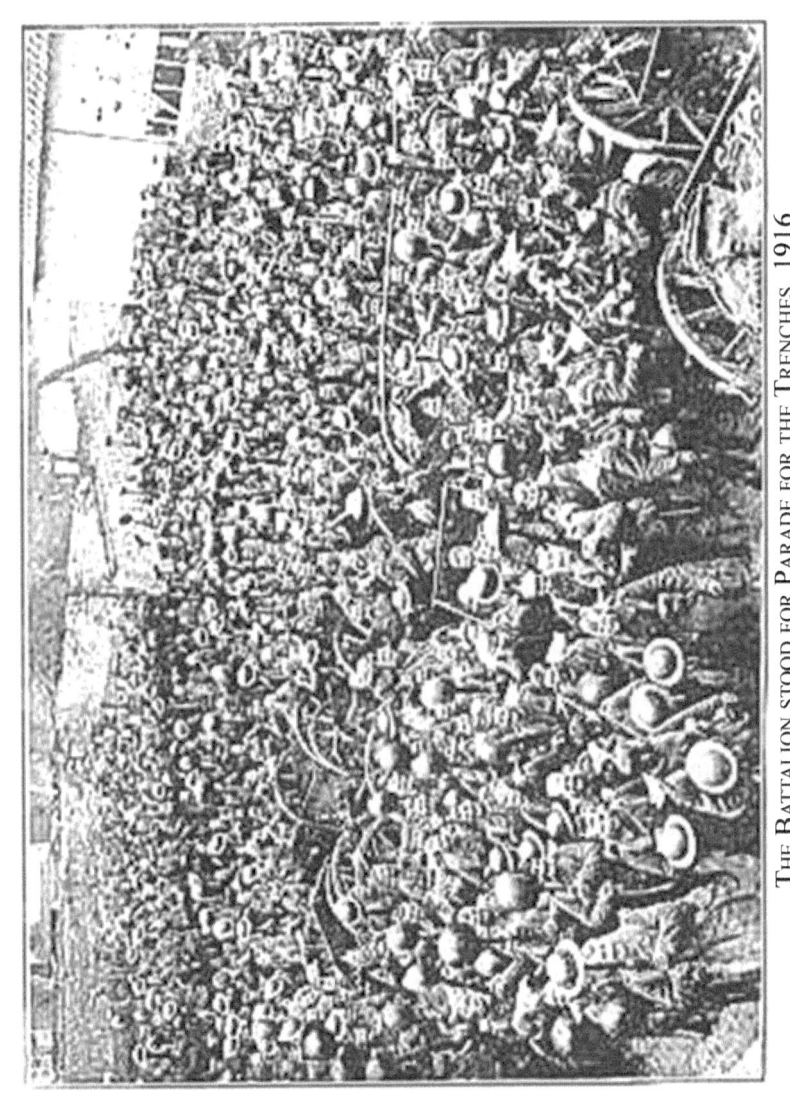

The Battalion stood for Parade for the Trenches, 1916

CHAPTER 4

The Somme Fighting

On the 27th of June we were bombarded by all calibres, but sustained no casualties.

On the 28th the raiding party of three officers and 56 other ranks mentioned in the last chapter left our lines at the junction of Gambler Street with the fire trench at 5.35 p.m. The raid was preceded by the discharge of cloud gas and artillery fire.

This party was working in conjunction with raiding parties from all battalions in the division. They advanced by two rushes to within a few yards of the enemy trenches, where they came under heavy fire and were held up. At 5.50 p.m. they established communication with our lines and reported that they could get no further and were suffering heavy casualties. A sergeant returning and reporting that the enemy were in strong force and further progress was impossible, Major Crump ordered them to retire, which they did in good order in spite of losses which included the whole of the leaders.

The wind seemed to be uncertain and blew back the smoke curtain diagonally across the front so as to disclose our party, which was on the right flank of the division, to the enemy.

The enemy wire had been well cut and presented no obstacle, but the enemy were seen in force in the trenches to the north of Blairville Wood, some of them wearing box respirators. The gas, however, apparently did not reach the wood, but near our lines a number of enemy dead were observed who had obviously been killed by the gas. Corporal Thompson did admirable work in maintaining telephonic communication between the advanced portions and the headquarters of the brigade raiding parties in our own front line. Private Clarke and Corporal Thompson remained in a shell hole not far from the enemy wire until after nightfall and saw them come out of their trenches and carry some of our men who were either dead or wounded across the bridge into their trenches. The ten killed of the raiding party included Captain E. M. Gregson and Second Lieutenant A. Martin, whilst Second Lieutenant A. S. Walker was amongst the 18 wounded.

The Lancashire Fusiliers' party (who also came under command of Major Crump) advanced quickly and rushed the last few yards before effecting an entrance into the enemy trenches. They divided into three parties, which bombed along the fire trench before being attacked by enemy bombers coming across the open. They were then ordered to retire, which they did after suffering casualties. A private of the left party did good work with his bayonet, keeping the enemy at bay until the last of his party had left the trench; for this he was awarded the Victoria Cross. All the parties came under machine gun and rifle fire, but they inflicted a large number of casualties before returning. There were no trench boards in the enemy line where our men entered them, and the trenches had obviously suffered considerably from our artillery fire. The enemy threw "stink" bombs into their own wire, but most of the wounded were brought in by our men, who, however, brought back no prisoners and no material, except a cap taken from a German soldier for identification purposes.

Captain G. C. Hutchinson, of the Lancashire Fusiliers, though severely wounded in the German wire, did capital work in this raid, as he continued to direct operations after being hit. Lance-Sergeant Russ and Private Bennett, of the same battalion, assisted several wounded men back to our lines and later brought in Captain Hutchinson. Sergeant Entwistle, who brought back reports on the progress of the raid, returned to assist in carrying out the retirement, whilst Private Ward and another collected five wounded in a shell hole and brought them in one at a time under heavy machine gun and shell fire.

A private who was with the party writes:—

Captain Gregson was there; I never saw him look better—he was always one of the smartest officers in the battalion, but he seemed to have been got up for the show with greater care than usual. The smoke lifted like a curtain. We were in full view of the Boche trench. We went on till within 50 yards of it and then he opened out with machine guns, rifles, and trench mortars. It was Hell let loose, but someone shouted 'On the Kellys,' and on we went, but were cut down like corn. The 'Jerrys' were two-deep in their trench, and we realised we were done.

Sixteen men answered the roll-call out of 76.

The worst part of a stunt is always after, when they have a roll-call. To stand there and listen to names being called and try to answer 'He's killed'—no one can picture it who hasn't seen one.

The total casualties for the month were two other ranks killed, six wounded, and 26 sick, including four officers.

On the afternoon of July 1st, the enemy shelled our reserve and support trenches and also the village of Agny with 4.2's, whilst late at night he opened fire on the front line with "whizz-bangs" and 4.2's, trench mortars, rifle grenades, and machine guns. He also sent up a large number of flares, but our artillery replied and activities ceased within an hour.

The following day Lieutenant-Colonel Hindle went to hospital, and Major Crump again assumed command of the battalion. There was considerable enemy activity with artillery and trench mortars, whilst our aeroplanes were active. The trenches were damaged by enemy gunfire the following day, when Second Lieutenant Jump and three other ranks were wounded. The battalion was relieved by the 2/5th Lancashire Fusiliers on the 4th, and went to billets at Daineville; Colonel Hindle returned the same day, but on the 7th he again had to go to hospital.

On the 10th we practised over trenches similar to those we expected to attack. The attack was practised several times, and on the night of the 11th the battalion relieved the 1/6th King's Liverpools. Two nights later the brigade made a demonstration, Second Lieutenant Saunders being in charge of a party which went over at midnight to bomb an enemy sap. Though they were unable to enter the sap, owing to wire being uncut, a number of bombs were thrown into it, and it was not until the party returned that the enemy replied with light machine gun and rifle fire.

On the 16th, 76 reinforcements joined the unit, which was relieved by the 1/4th King's Own and marched to Barly, where we rehearsed trench attacks and signalling in conjunction with aeroplanes. Later the battalion marched by stages to Candas, where it entrained for Mericourt. Arriving there on the 11th, we marched to billets in Meaulte and on the following day to Happy Valley, where we bivouacked.

The weather was fine and the billets good at this time, and training was carried out on an extensive scale, the work including practising digging-in with entrenching tools. One afternoon men marched to Bray and bathed in the Somme, where, unfortunately, one man was drowned.

On the 30th July, Church Parade was held, at which Brigadier-General G.T. G. Edwards presented Sergeants Entwistle and Lancaster with Military Medal Ribbons won by them in the raids at Blairville. Late that afternoon orders were received to be ready to move at very short notice, and the same night the battalion left for the trenches at Guillemont, occupying some old German communication trenches (Dublin and Casement trenches), which contained no dugouts. Within in a few hours of the battalion's arrival the enemy opened out on the trenches and battery positions in the vicinity with 5.9's and heavier shell. Second Lieutenants Orrell and Crone were wounded, as also were 15 other ranks. The total casualties for the month were three officers and 34 other ranks.

August was a trying month. The line held extended from Maltzhorn Farm, where we linked up with the French on the right, to a point near Arrow Head Copse. The trenches were incomplete, as they were newly dug, and besides being narrow and shallow, they had not been joined up in several places. The enemy bombardment was more or less severe every day, and on the 3rd Second Lieutenants C. S. Munro and J. Hunt were wounded, along with 16 other ranks, whilst three men were killed. About this time enemy snipers were very active along a ridge about 150 yards ahead, where they appeared to have established themselves. This ridge was on the south side of and abutted on the sunken road which ran from our line to Guillemont. Part of this sunken road was held as a trench by the 2/5th Lancashire Fusiliers, who were thus enfiladed by the enemy snipers on the ridge and consequently had a considerable number of casualties daily, the losses among the officers being especially heavy.

It was decided, therefore, to attack this ridge and establish a strong point there which would deny that ground to the enemy. This minor operation was considered important in view of the casualties mentioned and also because it would afford facilities for reconnoitring Guillemont and the lines of approach, this being most essential in view of the contemplated general attack on the Guillemont—Maurepas line.

At a conference held by the brigadier with Major Crump and Major H. Parker, it was decided that Major Parker should carry out the operation with two strong platoons of D Company on the evening of

Scale 1/20000

the 5th of August; that under brigade arrangements communication trenches (which were exceedingly narrow) should be kept clear to facilitate the movement of the troops taking part in the attack up to the front line; and that a barrage would be put down by the divisional artillery who would also do counter-battery work.

When the attacking party commenced to move up to the starting-off place, it was found that the communication trenches had not been cleared as arranged, and it would have been impossible to get up in time by using them. The party therefore moved up over the open and managed to arrive in time, but, unfortunately, not till after dark.

Second Lieutenant A. Hague and his platoon attacked. The second platoon with consolidating material was kept in reserve in our front line, but the enemy was found to be in considerable force on the ridge, occupying a strong point, and a switch line running back towards Wedge Wood.

The attacking platoon encountered heavy rifle and machine gun fire, and our barrage brought down enemy artillery fire, which caused considerable loss to working parties in communication trenches. Three attacks in all were made, but finally the attempt had to be abandoned for that night. Second Lieutenant Hague was reported missing, two men were killed, and 25 wounded.

Major Parker subsequently reported to the brigadier that he thought that he could attain his objective on the evening of the 6th August, provided he was allowed to attack at dusk without barrage but with only five minutes' preparation with two Stokes' Mortars, and this plan was assented to. The same troops were employed, having been brought up to strength. The attacking platoon, led by Lieutenant R. S. De Blaby, attacked at 20.30 hours. The attack was successful, the position was consolidated, and our troops were relieved by the 1/5th Liverpool Regiment just before dawn. During consolidation Major Parker went out with a patrol and located the enemy switch line, finding it heavily wired and strongly held.

The troops engaged in this operation rejoined the battalion (which had been withdrawn to reserve) on the morning of the 7th August.

After a night in bivouacs, preparations were made to go over the ground prior to an attack on Guillemont on the 8th. The Battalion returned to the line that night and assembled in trenches east and west of the road which ran south from the east corner of Trones Wood, C Company being detailed to consolidate the right of the enemy line and D Company the left on the west side of Guillemont. A and B

Companies acted in conjunction with the 1/4th Royal Lancasters and the 1/8th Liverpool Regiments respectively. The attack was not a success. The right was held up from the start by the switch line which had been reported by our patrol on the 6th, such report having been either overlooked or ignored, and the men had to fall back to the original line, though the 1/8th Liverpools went through the village on the left, and D Company of our battalion commenced to consolidate, but were driven off by the enemy coming behind them and cutting them off from the Liverpools.

Considerable confusion was caused owing to the mist and the employment by the enemy of smoke bombs, the four platoons in reserve not being called upon for this reason, though all their officers were killed and they suffered many other casualties. The operation was a costly one. Nine other ranks were killed, 97 wounded, and 107 reported missing; whilst of the officers, Captain E. M. Rennard and Captain H. Lindsay were killed. Second Lieutenants O. H. Ducksbury and J. H. Holden missing (afterwards found to be prisoners of war), and Lieutenants De Blaby and A. T. D. Evans and Second Lieutenants E. L. Fairclough and T. A. Bigger wounded. Lieutenant De Blaby died the following day.

On the 9th of August the remnant of the battalion was relieved by one company of the 1/5th South Lancashires and marched to bivouacs, where Lieutenant-Colonel Hindle again took over command.

Three days after coming out of the line a large permanent working party of 150 men, under Major Parker, proceeded to the trenches to the 2/5th Lancashire Fusiliers, who were also detailed for the same work, and on the 14th August Major Parker was wounded. The brigade subsequently left the area. The battalion which had been strengthened by drafts of 100 men from the Manchesters and one officer and 110 other ranks from the East Lancashire Regiment, entraining at Mericourt and detraining at Abbeville, marched to billets in Saigneville, *via* Cambron and Gouy. Here training proceeded on the usual lines, whilst a lecture was given to the officers and N.C.O.'s of the brigade by Major-General H. S. Jeudwine. The general used the tail of a cart as a platform without warning it tipped up and sent him sprawling in the road. This was too much for the gravity of the troops and of the general himself. No one laughed more heartily than he did as he picked himself up and resumed the thread of the lecture this time from the ground level.

Battalion sports were held whilst the unit was at rest, and in the closing days of the month the battalion returned by train to Mericourt, marching to a camping ground at Millencourt, whence Captain L. Duckworth went to hospital, whilst the battalion again moved a short distance to another area, where all ranks were accommodated in tents. The total casualties for the month were 13 officers and 289 other ranks. After a couple of days' "rest" at Millencourt, the battalion was sent for instructional purposes to take over the left of an old Corps line trench running between the Albert-Amiens road and the Albert-Millencourt road. On relieving the 8th King's Liverpool Regiment in the corps line, the battalion spent the night rehearsing the numerous phases of trench warfare, one company building a "strong point."

The following day this was repeated, and some of the time was spent in wiring and patrolling. The battalion was relieved by the 1/8th (Irish) King's Liverpool Regiment on the night of September 3rd. Three days later the battalion moved from Millencourt to a camping ground near Fricourt, where it was joined by Captain S. B. Donald, of the 5th East Kents (Buffs), and Captain C. B. Bolingbroke, of the 1/6th Norfolks. Orders to go into the trenches were received the following day, and the battalion marched to Montauban where it was met by guides of the 8th Devons. The sector taken over by the brigade extended from the eastern edge of Delville Wood in the direction of Ginchy, the 1/4th Loyal North Lancashires being in the front line alongside the 2/5th Lancashire Fusiliers, and the remainder of the brigade in support. Captain C. H. Cockrill reported for duty from the 1/6th Norfolks on the 8th, on which day we had four killed and 19 wounded.

The Delville Wood battle started on the 9th September. The British artillery were in action all day, and at 4 p.m. the barrage started; at 4.45 the division on our left attacked. Our objective was to capture Hop Alley with B and C Companies, whilst the Lancashire Fusiliers were to go over with us and take Ale Alley. At 5.25 the battalion went over and the first objective—Hop Alley—was gained, but the second wave did not succeed in reaching Ale Alley, and as Hop Alley had become untenable under intense machine gun barrage and gunfire, the remnant of B and C Companies withdrew and fell back to their original line. Supporting companies from the 1/8th King's Liverpool Regiment and 1/4th Loyal North Lancashire Regiment were sent up to strengthen the lines, whilst working parties consolidated the position. Sergeant H. Farnworth was awarded the D.C.M. for work in this attack.

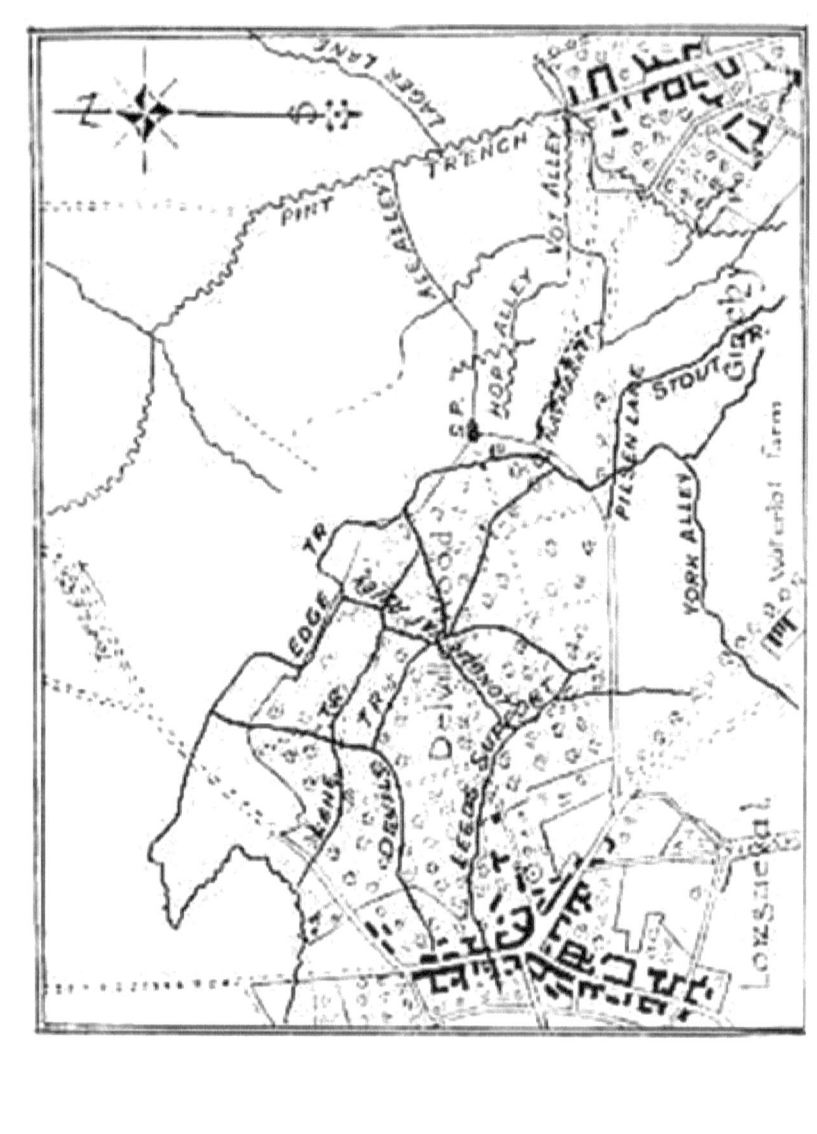

The casualties were heavy; amongst the 24 killed were Second Lieutenants W. E. Pyke and E. F. Falby. whilst, in addition to 125 men, Captains Donald and Bolingbroke, Lieutenant H. W. Strong, and Second Lieutenants W. V. Gray, P. Pollard, F. R. Vipond, C. H. Forshaw, and W. H. Berry were wounded. Under the heading of missing were the names of 79 of the rank and file. As the result of these heavy losses the battalion was withdrawn from the front line to the supports and rested for the day. In the afternoon we stood-to in view of a possible attack by the enemy. Though remaining in support, the battalion was moved 1,000 yards nearer the front line (or the remainder of its stay until the 41st Brigade came up as relief on September 12th, when we marched to bivouacs near Fricourt.

The customary routine was followed during the "rest," during which a move was made to Buire. Brigadier-General Edwards handed over the brigade to Brigadier-General C. I. Stockwell, who was quickly dubbed "Strafing Jimmy." He was a good soldier, and his methods, though often resented by individuals, were effective. He continued to command the 164th Brigade till the Armistice.

On the 19th, after being ordered to go into the line at Fricourt, where were the 1/8th King's Liverpool Regiment, we were suddenly ordered to vacate the trenches and proceed to bivouacs at Mametz, where six days were spent in company training, during which specially large working parties were employed in digging a communication trench through Longueval.

On the 24th a battalion of the 165th Infantry Brigade was relieved by us in front of Delville Wood close to Flers. On the 25th and 26th one other rank was killed and 22 wounded. On the latter day we relieved the 1/7th King's Liverpool Regiment in Gird Trench, close to Guedecourt. That day we had 17 wounded and 3 missing.

Following great activity by our artillery, the 164th Brigade attacked in the afternoon of the 27th, the battalion being in support. The 8th Irish captured the part of Gird Support still occupied by the enemy, and in the course of the evening we relieved the Irish in the captured trench, one company occupying a sunken road running into Guedecourt. The casualties were very slight, but Second Lieutenant R. Forrest was killed and Second Lieutenant G. Duerden and 4 other ranks were wounded.

The following morning mist hung low over the battlefield, and when it cleared a large enemy party was observed to be digging-in along a line rather more than half a mile away. Rifle and machine gun

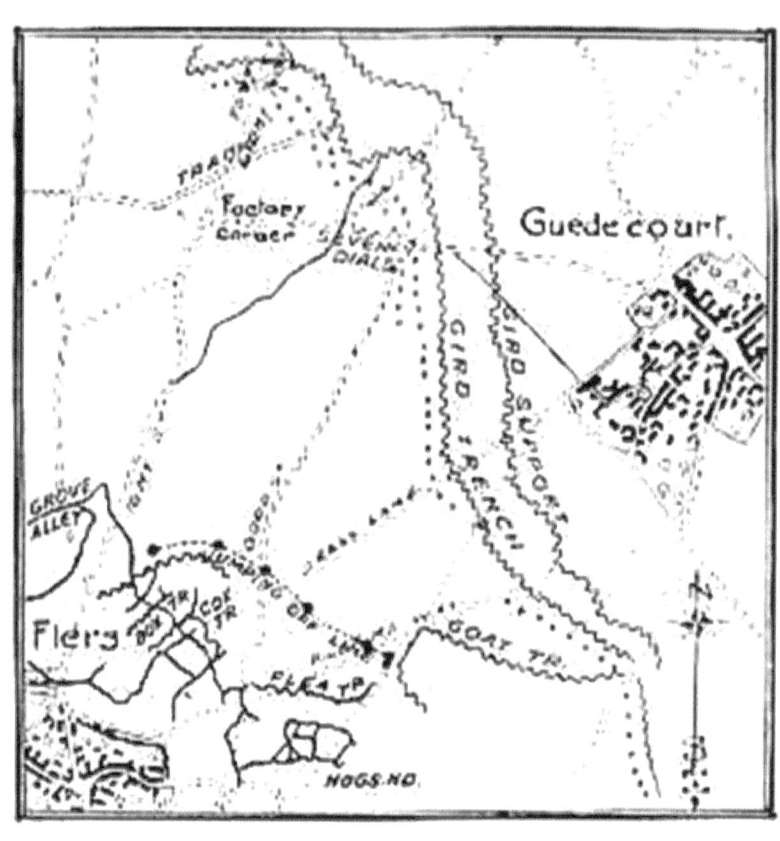

fire was directed at them, and they ceased work abruptly after suffering a number of casualties. During the afternoon the enemy artillery retaliated, killing 6 men and wounding 30.

The 10th Royal West Kents relieved us on the 29th, and we went into billets at Dernancourt. Thus ended an eventful month, in which the battalion had suffered somewhat heavily, the total casualties being 3 officers and 33 other ranks killed, 9 officers and 211 other ranks wounded, 82 other ranks missing, and 2 officers and 54 other ranks sick.

CHAPTER 5

Trench Warfare in the Salient: October 1st, 1916, to July 14th, 1917

On the 1st October we left Manancourt and entrained at Edge Hill, arriving in billets at L'Etoile at 11 p.m. The following day we marched to Longpre, where we entrained for Poperinghe, where we were billeted for the night. The next day we marched to Brandhoek, where we were in huts for the next few days, furnishing a daily working party to dig a cable trench near Rigersberg Château. During this period Second Lieutenant G. Duerden joined us again, and the following officers as reinforcements:—Captain A. Walsh, Second Lieutenants G. Tong, F. C. Jenkinson, V. Mather, A. O. Knight, I. Haworth, F. L. Vernon, E. G. Faber, A. Bardsley, A. Ashton, E. E. Tweedale, H. Holden, H. Swaine, R. V. Reed, B. H. Williams, J. E. Ordish, R. Bissett, J. H. Ogden, and H. K. Vipond.

During these days we did Company training, in preparation for our debut in the Salient.

The Salient! How can one hope to describe it so as to bring home its realities to those who have never seen it? Yet without some such description the history of the next few months would be about as informative as the stereotyped official bulletin, "On the rest of the Front there was nothing to report."

Picture then Poperinghe, a typical Belgian town, with here and there a house partly demolished by shell fire, crawling with troops of all kinds, with shops, restaurants, and *estaminets,* sprinkled with English notices, such as "Divisional Headquarters," "Wind Dangerous," "Officers' Club," "Divisional Canteen," and so on. This was our centre of civilisation. Beyond it stretched eastwards the Ypres road, fringed at first with tall trees and a sprinkling of houses, and peopled with troops, lorries, guns, limbers—coming and going, twelve kilometres of it, with deep ditches on either side, and beyond them fields which had once been cultivated but were now given over to "dumps," camps, battery positions, and so on, a few fields being still under cultivation by women and old men.

After six kilometres we come to Vlamertinghe, badly knocked about, but with a certain number of houses still standing and used by our troops; a thin slice of the tower of the church remaining to give the Hun a range mark; from this point the road is under enemy observation, and one begins to notice shell holes and broken trees becoming more frequent as we near Ypres railway station, to which trains still run, but only at night with all lights out, drawn very slowly and silently by a mysterious engine which shuts off steam and proceeds by electricity or something of the kind as it nears Ypres.

Standing on the "platform" at Ypres station at night, you see the enemy flares going up all round you except on the west, and you realise that you are indeed in "The Salient."

The city of Ypres itself, which at first sight seems like a jumble of ruins, you find presently to contain hiding-places for dozens of guns and hundreds of troops; whole streets of houses remain standing, mostly minus windows or doors. By day, the streets are almost deserted; by night, though no lights are shown, the city is alive with parties of troops, mule-drawn limbers, waggons, and motor lorries, bringing up rations and ammunition and the baggage of incoming battalions.

All these come along the road from Vlam after dusk, and when things are in full swing the road is a wonderful sight—mile after mile of mixed army vehicles tightly packed along both sides, the middle full of marching troops. Sometimes motionless, sometimes crawling cautiously on in the dark, sometimes disturbed by a shell falling and killing a few men or a mule or smashing up a lorry in its crashing burst, hour by hour the stream goes on, the very life-blood of the Infantry in the Salient.

From Ypres to the front line was at this time about two miles, first by road, then tracks, then trenches or breastworks, through wrecked and ruined country, weed-grown and desolate.

Each battalion held a "sub-sector" of the line. Battalion Headquarters being in some group of dugouts or ruined *château* about a mile behind the front line with the reserve and support companies somewhat nearer, and two front line companies. In addition to the infantry battalions, there were posts held by machine guns, this weapon having

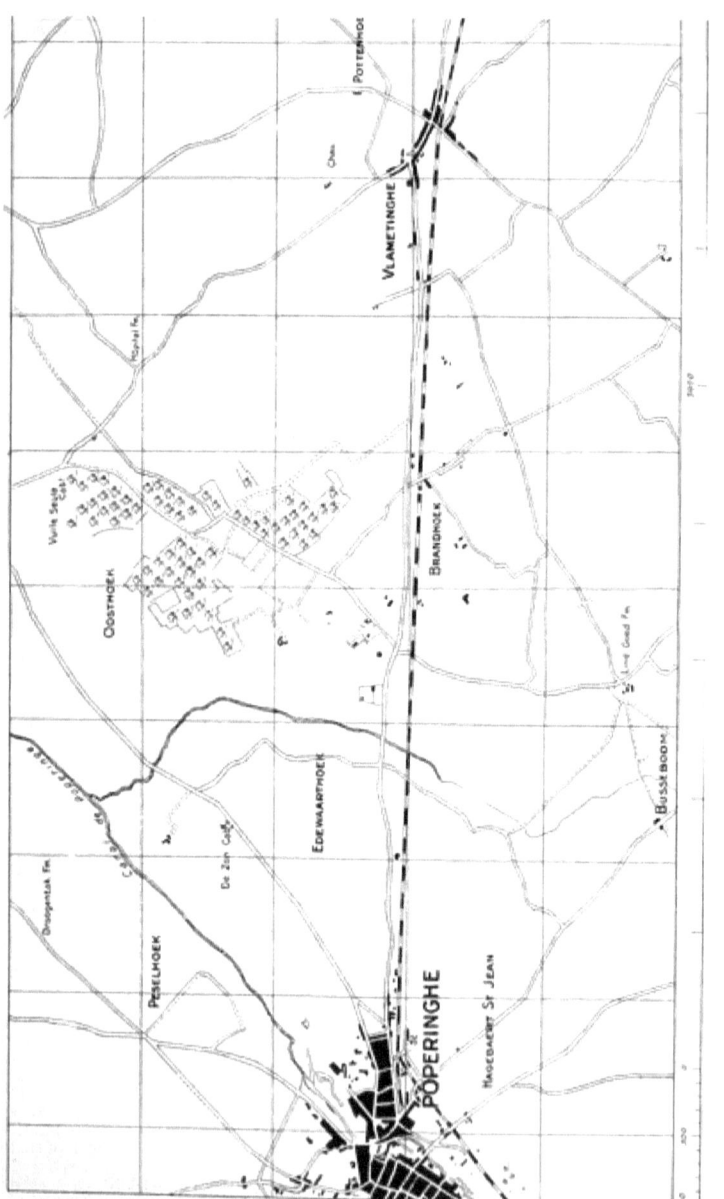

Map No. 2

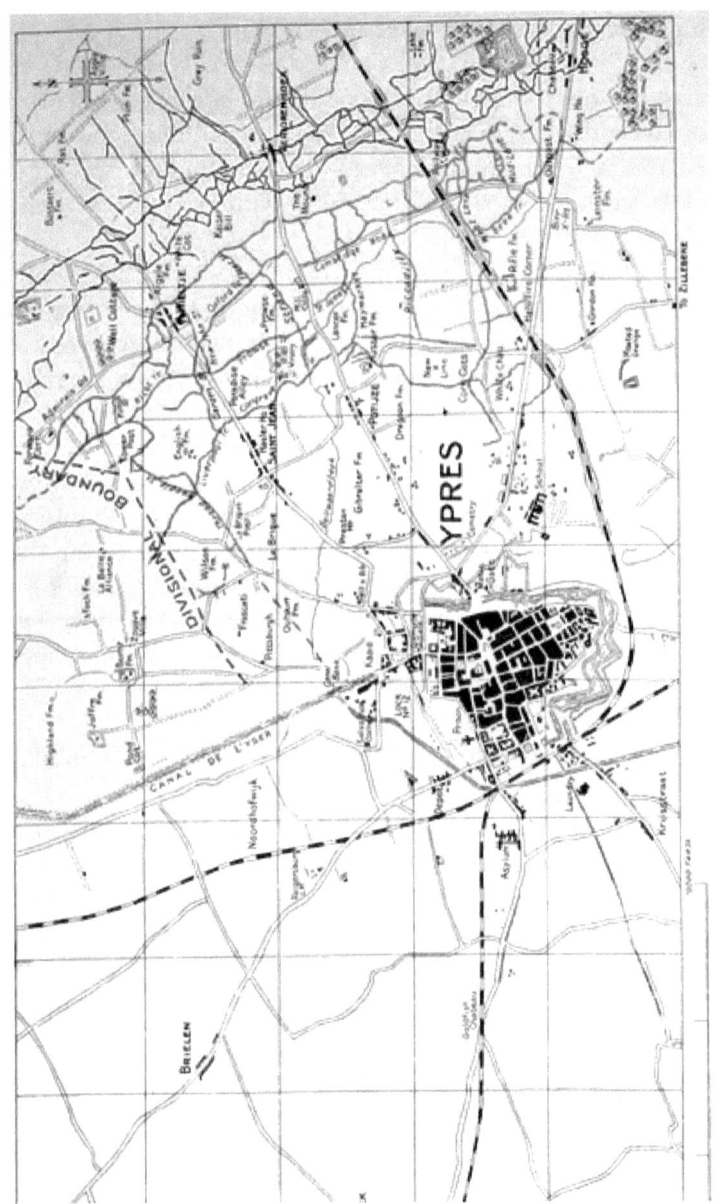

THE YPRES SALIENT

been taken out of the hands of the infantry, trench mortar sections, and other details doing various jobs.

The country in general is rather like Hundred End, the soil being like the Lancashire clay, but wetter and stickier.

On the 15th we moved up to Ypres, where we were billeted in the ramparts. These ramparts billets merit a special description. The city is guarded on the east and south by a rampart and moat, the rampart being about 50 feet high, and of equal thickness and formed of earth taken out when the moat was dug, faced with brick on the outside and crowned with trees.

Under this mines had been made, stuffy, cramped places full of frames and props and dimly lit with electric light, generally overcrowded and always damp and rat-infested, but still places where the battalion in brigade reserve could lie down and sleep in comparative safety, except for the danger of gas. To the south of the Menin Gate, an ugly gap in the ramparts through which the Menin Road issued from the city and where it was never safe to linger, was one of such mines usually occupied by two companies, to the north a similar one and the officers' dugouts. Battalion Headquarters being further back in the city. On the night of a relief, men would arrive in small parties in the pitch dark and stumble along the street, which was always a foot deep in mud, till they found the gas sentry, when they would disappear within the dark entry with a grunt of relief.

During the next few days working parties went up the line every night, and on the evening of the 19th we relieved the 1/4th King's Own in the Railway Wood sector.

Railway Wood had once been, as the name implies, a wood beside the Menin railway; when we made its acquaintance it was just a churned-up, slimy bit of rising ground, approached by a decent communication trench called West Lane crossing the muddy Bellewardebeek, beyond which were the breastworks and dugouts and cookhouses forming Beek Trench, a mass of slime and rotten sandbags which it was part of our job to drain, duckboard, and rivet with corrugated iron. As nearly every trench in the Salient was in a like state, and repairs were soon spotted and strafed by the Hun, and as every available man was daily employed in repairs, et cetera, it will be seen that "Old Bill's" opinion, that the war would only end "when the whole of Belgium had been put into sandbags," had much to justify it.

Going up to the front line from Beek Trench on a dark night was no picnic. You started along a narrow alley winding uphill, your hands feeling the slimy sandbag walls, your feet wary for broken duckboards; now and again a hot, stuffy smell, a void space in the wall, and the swish of pumped-up water under foot proclaimed the entrance to a mine. Gradually the sandbag walls got higher and the alley narrower, and in places you stumbled into daylight where the trench had been blown in and got covered with blue slime wallowing across the block; round corners you dived under narrow tunnels two or three feet high, finally emerging into the comparative open of the front line trench.

When we were in brigade reserve in Ypres, the working parties sent out at night often had this journey to do, after a two mile tramp and heavily laden with shovels, duckboards, barbed wire, and so on, but there was no falling-out, and little grousing.

A feature of this sector was the craters and shell-hole posts out in the open in front, garrisoned by small parties of men; there they lay—cold, wet, and sleepy—for hours on end, visited at intervals by an officer or N.C.O.

On the 20th Captain Ord was appointed *commandant* of the 164th Brigade Officers' School, and Major A. H. Haslam joined us. On the 22nd 16 "Minnies" fell on our front line, wounding Second Lieutenant J. F. Walmsley and J. H. Ogden; the following night we were relieved by the 1/5th King's Liverpool Regiment and went back to Ypres to the prison and magazine billets. These two buildings had not been greatly damaged, and the Magazine was fairly shell-proof. We sent the usual nightly working parties up the line till the 27th, when we relieved the 1/4th King's Own in Weiltje sector, to the north of Railway Wood; here the Hun was further off and things were a bit more comfortable.[1] Second Lieutenants Reed, Tong, Vipond, and Vernon were posted to other battalions on the 29th. The tour was quiet on the whole, and on the 31st a piece of the enemy's parapet fell in, giving our snipers a splendid chance— they claimed three certain hits. That night we were relieved by the 1/5th King's Own and marched back to C Camp, a collection of wooden huts distributed in a roadside copse near Brandhoek, a little bit of Heaven to weary and sodden men coming out of the line. Here we could sleep and feed in peace, do refitting, physical jerks and parades, and play football.

During the month no less than three officers and 55 men had

---

1. On the 26th, R.S.M. Farnworth, who for a long time had been suffering great pain in his limbs, was sent to hospital. He was eventually discharged unfit for further service. A man of arresting personality, steeped in army tradition, and the possessor of a biting tongue, his influence in the battalion was great and lasting.

gone sick and been sent to Field Ambulance (also known as "Fanny Adam")—for which the change to the Flanders clay was no doubt largely responsible.

We remained at C Camp till the 8th November, when we moved up to Ypres again and were billeted in the Ramparts and the school; the latter was a large building on the Menin Road outside the city and made a decent billet till the gunners put a large gun in it, with the usual sequel.

During the next three days we sent a working party of 250 up the line every night. Major Crump rejoined the battalion on the 11th.

On the 12th we relieved the 1/4th King's Own in the Railway Wood sector, B and C Companies being in the front line, A and D in support in Beek Trench. Captain Houghton rejoined the battalion.

On the night of the 13th the moon shone beautifully and disclosed our wiring party to the Hun about 100 yards off. Second Lieutenant Higson was hit; the next night our Lewis guns retorted on Hun working parties.

Every day brought its ration of "Minnies," shells and bullets, and someone got hit; Second Lieutenant Walton was killed by a sniper's bullet on the 16th. The sniper was promptly shot by one of ours.

On the 17th, at 11 p.m., for half an hour, we strafed the Boche with guns, heavy and Stokes' trench mortars and rifle grenades, to stir him up—the usual tactics of the 55th Division; he retaliated feebly and wounded only one man; a fighting patrol then went out, but found no Hun about.

On the 18th, at 8.45 a.m., 18 heavy "Minnies" fell on B Company, wounding two men; our guns retaliated— they always did for "Minnies" to discourage them. I think we all hated and feared the "Minnie" more than anything, chiefly on account of the deafening, nerve-shattering effect of the explosion; if you watched you could see them coming over like an oil-drum describing slowly a parabola in the air and could dodge them and watch the fall from a safe distance, then a pause, then *Crrraaash!* and up went sandbags, earth, wood, iron, and sometimes men, leaving a crater of raw crumbly earth to be dealt with as soon as might be.

In the evening we were relieved by the 1/5th King's Liverpool Regiment, and straggled systematically back to Ypres—billeted this time in the prison and magazine.

The officers now with the battalion were as follows:—

Lieutenant-Colonel R. Hindle, Commanding.
Major Crump, Second in Command.
Second Lieutenant R. N. Buckmaster, adjutant.
Second Lieutenant Burnside, Transport.
Lieutenant Bardsley, quartermaster.
Second Lieutenant Lowe, Lewis Guns.
Second Lieutenant Mather, Bombs.
Second Lieutenant Williams, Sniping and Intelligence.

A COMPANY

Captain A. T. Houghton
Captain A. Walsh
Second Lieutenant Tyldesley
Second Lieutenant Bissett
Second Lieutenant Cooper

B COMPANY.

[2]Captain F. S. Baker
Second Lieutenant Agostini
Second Lieutenant Robinson
Second Lieutenant H. Holden

C COMPANY

Captain Hore
Lieutenant Tautz
Second Lieutenant R. Hall
Second Lieutenant Ashcroft

D COMPANY.

Captain Matthew
Lieutenant Howarth
Second Lieutenant Holmes
Second Lieutenant Brown

The next five days were spent in cleaning up and bathing—a ceremony in which a whole company filed into an old building labelled "Divisional Baths," handed in their underclothing, stood in tubs un-

---

2. Captain Baker formerly quartermaster had volunteered for a combatant commission when we were short of officers after the Somme Battles—and was given command of B Company which he held until killed in September, 1917. The high qualities which had made him an ideal quartermaster, made him equally successful as a company commander.

der a trickle of warm water and washed as best they might, receiving "clean" clothes in return, and came away cleaner and fresher men. The inverted commas in the last sentence are a tribute to the longevity and indestructibility of the louse, or "chat," and her eggs; no process was ever discovered by which they could be extirpated, except "handpicking." Some people may think this reference a little indelicate, but this is a truthful record.

The usual nightly working parties went up the line, until, on the 24th, we relieved the 1/4th King's Own in the Wieltje Sector. A and D Companies were in the front line, C Company in support in "New X Line," and B in reserve, Battalion Headquarters being at Potijze Château.

The relief started badly, a "Minnie" strafe during the morning having blown in the front line in several places, incidentally blowing a company commander out of his dugout; the strafing went on all afternoon, but luckily ceased at dusk, and the relief passed off without incident.

This sector was a distinct improvement on Railway Wood. The Hun was about 400 yards away, and there was consequently hardly any trench mortar activity and no mining, but the wire was thin, the drainage bad, and the Company Headquarters mere shanties, while most of the sentry posts had to make shift with a ground-sheet for sleeping accommodation, the old traverses and dugouts having been knocked in and never repaired. The reserve company in Congreve Walk was more comfortable, being well hidden in dead ground, and their trench was clean and dry a nice change after their tour in the worst bit of Railway Wood.

That night was quiet, and our patrols and wirers were busy in No Man's Land; rain fell during the night, and breakfasts were very late in the morning.

The following description of a typical day in the front line is for the edification of those who have never been there; how we longed to bring *some* of our stay-at-home acquaintances out there and rub their noses in Flanders mud—the real stay-at-homes, the profiteer, C.O., agitator, striker—the folk who, in accordance with what Lewis Carroll called "*the glorious British Principle of Political Dichotomy*," were doing their best to nullify our efforts in the fighting line!

The day begins at "Stand to," about an hour before dawn, when the officer and N.C.O. on duty go round rousing every one with a hoarsely-whispered, "Wake up, there—Stand to!" reinforced by a shake as each man comes slowly up out of the wells of sleep and stumbles to his feet, rubs his eyes, grabs his rifle, and mounts the fire step. The company commander rouses the signaller, or *vice versa*, and every one sniffs the cold night air and hopes that "Jerry" won't come over this morning.

Slowly the darkness thins; faces become visible, then sandbags, then duckboards, then the screwposts supporting the wire in front; suddenly a lark stirs, mounts up and bursts into his fervent song the dawn has come, and the company commander gives the word "Stand down," which is passed along and acted on promptly, so that in a minute only the sentry on each post is left on duty. For we no longer hold the line continuously—our numbers are too small—but with a certain number of sentry posts, each consisting of an N.C.O. and, when possible, six men more often four—some posts being Lewis gun posts, others bombing posts, others riflemen only. This line of posts, weak as it is, is strung out between and in front of a series of "strong points" containing machine guns and an infantry garrison lodged in deep mines, while behind us is the support company ready to come up in case of need, and reserve troops further back; in addition we have the guns, which we can always switch on in a few seconds by telephone or sending up a rocket; all these things give us confidence, weak though we feel ourselves to be.

About this time there appears in the trench an officer from the reserve company, followed by sweating men carrying knapsack food-containers and dixies. The word "Breakfast up" is hardly needed, as already a man from each post is waiting with both hands full of mess tins to draw the bacon and tea for his post—bread and dry stuff was issued by the company quartermaster-sergeant the night before. The sentries are excluded from the ensuing munching until such time as a chum, his meal swallowed, is available for relief; never for an instant, by day or night, must that vigilant watch over No Man's Land cease.

The officers crowd into the Company Headquarters or crawl into their own "caboosh" and eat their food in privacy, the same food as the rest but on a plate, sometimes with porridge and eggs, privately purchased, in addition—the army issues the same ration to all ranks, but extras can be bought at canteens in Ypres.

After breakfast comes cleaning and inspecting rifles, while the company commander, who has already had a look round and detailed the day's work to the company sergeant-major, completes and sends down by runner to Battalion Headquarters his trench state and account of ammunition expended; then adjusting his tube helmet and box respirator and tightening his belt carrying his revolver and glasses (it is a standing order that everyone must wear his equipment all the time in the front line), he sets out to inspect his lines, finding, if he knows his job, a cheery word for all and sundry, and receiving often better than he gives, taking stock of everything, strafing slackers, and generally tuning up for the day, well knowing that, if he misses anything, the commanding officer or, worse still, the brigadier, will spot it and strafe him!

Each sentry post has its standing orders pinned up on a board, with a duty roster showing each man's work through the 24 hours, and ensuring that each gets eight hours in which he may try to sleep, and a sheet for intelligence, which is collected by the intelligence officer every morning when he visits the sniping posts.

"Dinners up" is the signal for a general break and a repetition of the breakfast scene, but the food is stew or roast meat and potatoes or rissoles. At 1.30 p.m. casualty returns and special indents have to be at Battalion Headquarters, and at 3.30 p.m. a report on the situation and direction of wind (this latter with reference to possible gas activities). Having to render this report in the middle of a strafe, some sorely-tried officer is said to have written, "Situation ——, Wind vertical!"

Long before this we have all washed (or dabbed) our hands and faces in shell-hole water and shaved as best we can, and an inspection of box respirators has been carried out by the officer on duty; feet are also inspected and rubbed with whale oil to guard against trench-feet, then work is resumed till tea, after which it is time to stand-to again for another hour.

Then the night routine begins; the men who have worked all day "get down to it," while the wirers begin to slide over the parapet with their rolls of barbed wire and posts; the patrol puts on boiler-suits and cap-comforters—each man leaving behind any possible identification, and slides off into the waste, fitfully lit by enemy flares, in front of us.

The officer and N.C.O. on duty start their tour of the line, candles are lit in Company Headquarters and correspondence is dealt with, while the company commander has another good look round while waiting for the patrol to return; when they come in the leader's report has to be reduced to writing—often no easy matter when an unfortunate reference to "enemy seen" raises a perfect hail of questions from higher authority, truculently asking why they were not instantly gone for and spitted! Picture Second Lieutenant Snooks, on patrol for the first or second time with three men, sent out to examine enemy wire, shivering and squirming his way across No Man's Land, all eyes and ears, suddenly hearing guttural voices and seeing six or more figures looming big in the haze. Of course, he ought to bluff them and bring them in—that is what you would do. Reader, wouldn't you?—but he doesn't; he remembers that he was told to examine wire, not to make trouble, so he crouches motionless in the mud till they pass, and thinks he has done the right thing—till he sends in his report. Then, all at once, the brigadier, the colonel, the company commander send for him, and ask him abruptly, and with degrees of rudeness befitting their respective ranks, what the —— he meant by letting those Boches escape! Needless to say, he never repeats the mistake! And in time he learns that in the division and the battalion it is a criminal offence to let slip any opportunity of killing, capturing, or annoying Boche!

About 10 p.m. is "tea up," and the rum issue is mixed with this or with the breakfast tea at the discretion of the company commander. The patrol and other men coming in cold and wet need theirs at once, followed by a walk down to the brigade drying room, where they can sleep in blankets before a brazier while their clothes are dried.

With the patrol's return operations usually close for the night, and about midnight, having dealt with the last batch of chits which a thoughtful and zealous runner has seen fit to pick off the adjutant's table and deliver, asking searching questions about the "number of sandbags laid" or "the number of screw posts, long, salved" the day before, or the name of a man used to operating an electric light plant or minding pigeons or mixing cocktails ("nil returns to be rendered!" which means "If none, say so"), the company commander, who alone has no allotted sleeping time, takes off his tin hat, loosens his belt, and sleeps. At 3 a.m. the officer on duty, who does a four-hour spell, sends in another "situation and wind report," and waits for the hour when he can stir up everyone else for "stand-to," strolling from one post to another and keeping an eye on things in general and the Boche in particular.

It is very quiet, probably raining a little; nothing on the move, except rats. What brutes they were, those rats of the Salient! huge mangy brutes the size of a cat, a few patches of fur on their otherwise bare pink bodies; getting under your feet, running over your face as you lay trying to sleep, eating through haversacks to get the biscuits within, scurrying, scratching, gnawing all night long!

To resume the thread of the story:—The following extracts from a company commander's diary, given under the dates on which they were written, help to give life to an otherwise bald narrative:

25th. This dugout is very poor and the roof is leaky—my canvas bucket catches most of the drip, however. . . . Have just been entering up logbook sitting in the dugout with a candle for company—caked in mud, sandbags over my boots—feet cold, raining outside, but quite cheerful, as I am expecting some hot stew before long. The old skin-lined coats are no longer issued; instead we have leather jerkins lined with fleece, very warm and comfy.

26th. Today is apparently Sunday, but out here one can't tell it except by the calendar; the daily hate goes on much as usual in fact today we have been hating the Boche rather extra much. Our guns have been slowly and deliberately knocking his front line to blazes all day, but if I know anything of him he will be about half a mile behind down a hole of some sort—we all go to ground in these days:' *They shall go into the caves and dens of the rocks, they shall say unto the mountains, "Fall on us" and to the hills "Cover us," men's hearts failing them for fear and for looking for those things which are coming on the earth*' a wonderful book, the Bible! . . . One of the men said today, 'The Boche isn't here. Sir; he's gone to the Somme and left his missus to look after this place ' . . . How nice a change of boots will be!

27th. A fighting patrol under Second Lieutenant Agostini went out but encountered no enemy. At 7.30 p.m. we were relieved by the 1/5th South Lancashires; they were very strong and all arrived together instead of post by post and the narrow trench was jammed with men so that our fellows had a struggle to get out. However, we got out without a casualty, assembled at Ypres station, and trained to Brandhoek, whence we marched to C Camp for a rest.

28th. 'Cleaning and inspection of kit,' says the *War Diary*. We always lay long on the morning after relief, no one worried anyone else till noon at least.
Today I had a bath! *Oooooooh!* Nothing can describe the utter luxury of it when for several days you haven't even had your revolver off! A real one and lie down in it! I feel another man already! Nothing of special interest, very busy inspecting, clean-

ing up, repairing, and generally getting ready for the trenches. . .
. . It's still very cold and difficult to keep warm; these huts have no glass in the windows, but horn, sacking or linen, so one always writes by candle-light. We have a gramophone in the mess which plays all day and cheers us much. 'O, Cecilia! Don't make those eyes at me!' is a great favourite, especially with the *padre*, who says the sentiment is exceedingly proper!

The following days were devoted to company training, and on Sunday December 3rd, 1916, there was a Church Parade. Our diarist writes:

We are still in rest, and it's still freezing—coke is bad to get in quantity today we are very short; food is plentiful, there are Y.M.C.A. huts and canteens and places about where one can buy baccy, biscuits, fruit, etc. the important thing is that all eatables must be in tins, otherwise the rats get the lot. . . . In spite of cold, dirt, and discomfort, it's a good life on the whole, and one's conscience is at rest; we're part of an army—and a fine army and the army is abundantly cheerful.

Our numbers at this time were very low, three more officers and 37 other ranks having gone sick during the month.

On 6th December, we were inspected in mass by the corps commander, an amusing inspection which rather showed up the lack of horsemanship of some company commanders. As a result a battalion riding school was started, and carried on whenever we were in "rest." The following day we moved up to Ypres (ramparts and school), and on the 8th relieved the 1/6th King's Liverpool Regiment in Railway Wood. The following day our artillery was active, strafing the enemy front line; we received some "Minnies "in exchange. During the night our field guns and machine guns fired on enemy communications; he retaliated with shells and "Minnies."

In the support trench (Beek) were many homemade weather vanes, somewhat out of adjustment, and one day, in directing a stranger to Company Headquarters, someone said, "Keep along the trench and you'll see several weather-cocks."

"Yes," broke in a humorist, "to show the various Norths!"

On the 11th the activity on both sides was renewed, but without serious damage. Of course trenches were blown in and there were many narrow escapes, but only two men were wounded in the three days. It was always a standing wonder that so much metal could fly about in horrid, jagged bits, knocking trenches about, missing men by inches, demolishing dugouts, and yet cause so few casualties. For example, three men were lying in a low dugout with an iron roof; a shell struck the front edge, burying the men and at the same time saving them from its own explosion, which took place simultaneously! Men are sometimes literally struck dumb at these times, as witness the following true story:—

Scene—a slight shelter; officer inside, private at entrance; three shells fall in quick succession, the first and second miss the shelter by a foot or two and make the usual noise and mess, the third hurtles down and buries itself at the very entrance a long pause, then a small, unnatural voice, "That's a dud, sir!" Another pause, another voice of like quality, "Yes, I see it is!"

The 12th was very quiet. A drizzling rain fell all morning, mixed with snow later. The following day we were told to prepare for relief, and had the satisfaction of seeing, during the afternoon, our heavies putting some really big stuff on the Hun lines; in the evening we returned to our Ypres billets.

14th. Ypres was shelled fairly heavily and we had one casualty; our guns were also very active.

What an awful row these big guns make when they go off; if you're anywhere near them the noise seems to box your ears and make you deaf for some seconds.

15th. Our guns were making a fair old row last night and this morning, celebrating the *Kaiser's* peace proposals, I suppose what a difference from the old Richeburg days! Tonight, about 1.30, the Hun suddenly started shelling this place to some tune and kept it up for half an hour; quite a lot burst near our dugout and there was a good bit of stuff flying about, but no one was hit.

During these days the usual nightly working parties filed through the Menin Gate and went up the line to shovel slime for a few hours.

On 17th December, 1916, we moved to prison billets and into the line again—Wieltje—on the 18th.

On the 19th a dozen "Minnies" fell on our front line—again no one was hurt; on 20th December, 1916, the Hun shelled us all day; no casualties, bitter wind and snow, aeroplanes active, a Hun machine being brought down over their lines at 1.15.

21st December, 1916. Great artillery activity. Our front line trenches were cleared with the exception of a few Lewis guns from 8 a.m. to 4 p.m. Our heavies bombarded the enemy trenches from 8 a.m. to 10 a.m. The field guns cut wire opposite our front line from 10 a.m. to 1 p.m., after which the heavies resumed operations. In the evening a patrol located an enemy sentry post in the Long Sap. On the 22nd the artillery programme was repeated; the enemy retaliated and caused one causality. On the 23rd the 1/4th King's Own raided over our heads, entering the enemy trenches and finding them deserted; the enemy retaliated heavily, causing three casualties, one man (Duerden) being killed in the front line by a bit of shell. As the front line was simply plastered with shells, we were lucky not to have more.

The diarist writes:—

There was a pretty heavy strafe this morning early, it went on for about an hour and left one kind of dazed and sleepy.

Christmas Eve was very quiet; the great question was, "Were we to stay in the line over Christmas or not?" Our joy on hearing that we were to go out was tempered by pity for the King's Own, who relieved us.

Christmas Day. Out of trenches! Came out last night and forthwith had a shave and partial wash. We sent an officer on, and when we landed here (Ypres) the men found candles lit and fires going in their billets, and we had *ditto* in ours. Today we gave the men a decent Christmas dinner, and are now about to have one ourselves—a roaring fire, plenty of candles, turkey stuffed with *the* stuffing, beer, *vin ordinaire*, pudding, and sundries have the promise of a very pleasant evening in them, if the Boche will refrain from throwing stuff over—he peppered this place some today! Tomorrow, work—pulling things together—refitting, cleaning, reorganising; tonight, Christmas Day, home thoughts, comfort and God bless everyone, especially those at home, who are always with us in thought—what we owe to their prayers no man knows.

Second Lieutenant Tyldesley was largely responsible for the success of the dinner referred to. The battalion dined in the magazine, two companies at a time, on hastily-made tables and waited on by the officers; there was pork and goose mixed (Tyldesley's tunic bore the marks of goose-grease for long after), and trimmings, plum pudding

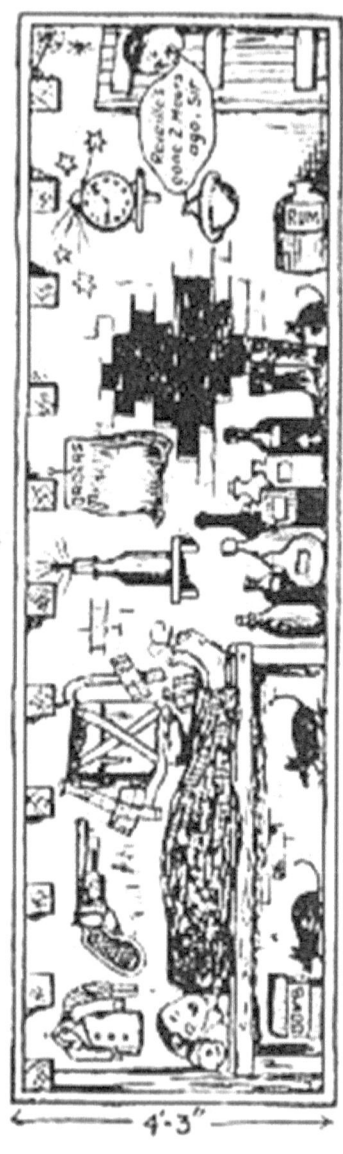

and dessert and fruit and *beaucoup* beer, and we drank "The King" and everyone enjoyed themselves.

26th. Everyone in splendid form after a day's rest and a good feed, a sort of cheery, alert look on everyone's face that I haven't seen for a long time.

220 men were on working parties that day, and on the 27th we were relieved by the 1/5th South Lancashires and went back to C Camp, this time by train—'the Midnight Choo-choo' as some wit dubbed it. The silent assembly of troops at Ypres Station, the entraining, and the gradual withdrawal of the train from that stricken area into cultivated country, are some of the things we shall never cease to recall with complete vividness. The following days were devoted to the usual cleaning and inspections, etc.

Today I have had all my men inspected for deficiencies and paid them; I find an excellent plan is to require a man to produce a chit from his platoon commander stating that he has been fully inspected before he is paid; by adopting this plan I get all sorts of people up for inspection who would otherwise probably have been missed. Tomorrow I get my company on parade for a whole morning—a most unusual occurrence and one to be made the most of.

The 31st December found us still at C Camp—clean, fresh, and ready for another year of war, though fervently hoping for peace.

Our total casualties for the year were as follows:—

	Officers.	Other Ranks
Killed	9	69
Wounded	23	434
Missing	1	290
Do. Believed killed	2	0
Drowned	0	1
Sick to F.A.	16	204
Totals	51	898

The New Year started with a brigade holiday, and in the Church Army hut the men were given a dinner followed by a cinema performance; the sergeants and officers also had dinners in their respective messes.

A dinner of stew, mixed pork, and goose, and plum pudding, and beer in a mess tin, means more to the men today than all the elaborate spread we had at Sevenoaks, which cost £150.

During this period reinforcements of officers and men kept turning up, and were rapidly assimilated; on the other hand, almost every day some officer or man went sick, the weather on the whole being mild and damp.

On 3rd January, 1917, we were inspected by the brigade commander, and were complimented on the turnout, also on the camp; in fact at this time brigade were rather fond of us and let us alone quite a lot.

On the 5th the Lewis gun detachments with their handcarts were inspected by the divisional commander; he caused great mirth by wheeling a handcart violently at a ditch, to demonstrate how easily the shafts broke! At this time the Lewis gun was in a transition stage and the favourite toy of the staff; it was finding its feet as a company weapon, and masses of orders about it were coming in every day, to the joy(?) of all concerned.

On the 6th we returned to Ypres, and on the 7th relieved the 1/6th King's Liverpool Regiment in Railway Wood, where we were badly shelled the following day, six men being wounded. This relief was accomplished without a casualty, although platoons had some narrow escapes. We were singularly lucky that way; we were always hearing that such and such a battalion had had a platoon blown to bits in the square, but it never happened to us; if an officer lost men by taking a known dangerous road when a safer was available, it was not counted unto him for righteousness!

On the 8th the enemy shelled us all day, especially Beek Trench and Battalion Headquarters, and six men were wounded; the 9th was quieter—one man wounded.

On the 10th, after a quiet morning, our artillery bombarded enemy lines opposite B Company, who had their Company Headquarters blown in in the retaliation which followed no casualty.

After a quiet day on the 11th, the battalion was relieved on the 12th, except A Company, by the 1/4th King's Own, A Company being left behind to do a special job—wiring in close support and support lines—the rest going back to Ypres, whence they provided the usual nightly working parties till the 16th, when they were relieved by the 12th Royal Sussex Regiment and marched to P Camp north of

Poperinghe. The next day we marched to Roussel Farm, about a mile east of Elverdinghe, the drums, recently re-formed, playing on the march for the first time. A Company turned up, dead beat, at 5 a.m. Second Lieutenant Faber went sick from sheer overwork; as Lewis gun officer he had tried to do everything himself and broke down. We were sorry to lose such an excellent officer.

During the next few days, except when snowed off, a party of nine officers and 300 other ranks, under Captain Houghton, was employed daily in making the formation for doubling a railway track, supervised by an R.E. officer. As our party included a civil engineer, a railway engineer, and a municipal engineer, there was enough technical skill to have laid the whole railway! During this period another party, D Company under Captain Matthew, were repairing dugouts in Canal Bank, Ypres, and after the first day were billeted there to save marching.

On the 22nd Captain Harris returned to the battalion and took over the Bombing Company, an experimental organisation which did valuable work during its short existence. We were glad to leave this place with its thin huts (the weather was bitter) and march to D Camp on the 23rd, where, on the 24th, we were inspected by the army commander, General Sir Herbert Plumer.

On the 1st February our shooting team were winners in the interbattalion competition and were chosen to represent the brigade. On the 3rd we were relieved in D Camp by the 1/5th North Lancashire Regiment, marched to Poperinghe, and trained to Bollezeele.

The train was a sort of miniature affair, and the railway ran, mostly by the roadside, at about three miles an hour. What a treat it was to get out of the sound of the guns for a bit, and to be in a pleasant little Flemish town, outwardly untouched by war! It consisted of a cheerful-looking market square lined with small shops, with a church in the middle—quite a treat to see a church untouched by shells—with a sort of openwork spire, to let out the sound of the carillons which played every hour and half-hour; how sweetly and peacefully it floated out over the open country on a still, frosty night! There was also a good inn, the "Lion d'Or," known as the "Brass Cat!" The men were mostly billeted in enormous barns; the officers in houses round the square. Here, it was rumoured, we were to have a month's rest, but no one believed it; we actually *got* 16 days.

On the 4th, being Sunday, of course orders for an immediate move were received at 11.30 a.m., and the battalion packed up and concentrated at 2.15 p.m. and marched to Esquelbecq, a distance of five miles; this march will long be remembered by the Lewis gunners, who had to carry their guns there and back again—for this turned out to be a "camouflage" march; much hostile aerial activity had recently been displayed in the back areas, so large columns of troops were made to march eastwards during the day and back at dusk.

It was bitterly cold, snow on the ground and freezing hard—this weather continued all the time we were there. The time was devoted to training—company, battalion, and brigade schemes, and in the intervals we smartened up and overhauled our interior economy.

On the 16th we moved back to C Camp, where we relieved the 14th Hampshires.

On 17th February, 1917, we sent an officer and 20 men to attend an investiture of French soldiers by the army commander, as representatives of the 55th Division—rather a compliment.

On the 18th the brigadier presented military medal ribbons to Company Sergeant-Major Heywood, Corporal Bamber, and 1147 Private Ainscough, T. On the 24th we moved into billets in Canal Bank, Ypres. These were large elephant dugouts on the bank of the canal north of Ypres, comfortable and fairly safe, but we were only there for a night, relieving the 1/5th South Lancashires in the La Brique sector the next night. This was a rotten sector, badly neglected by previous divisions; even the main communication trench was about two feet deep in water when we first saw it, and Bilge Trench well deserved its unsavoury name. It is only fair to say that when we left it it was fairly comfortable. On the 26th the line was rearranged, and we returned to Canal Bank, whence we sent up the usual nightly working parties.

On the 4th March Ypres was heavily shelled during the day, but we relieved the 1/4th King's Own in the line in the evening without casualties; at 7.5 p.m. the enemy sprung a mine on our right brigade front and our artillery opened a heavy bombardment; one man was wounded in Ypres.

The 5th was a quiet day; at night a patrol went to examine Canadian dugouts in the middle of No Man's Land and found them occupied.

On the 8th we were relieved by the 1/4th King's Own and went back to Canal Bank, where some artist did the Regimental Crest in bits of tile in front of a dugout. One wonders if it is still there!

On the 13th we sent a strong fighting patrol up the line to raid two of the Canadian dugouts. The party consisted of one officer, one N.C.O., and 12 men, who constituted the dugout party, and two complete Lewis gun teams.

Presumably the Hun got wind of the enterprise—he always did for Nos. 1, 2, and 3 dugouts were empty and the wire round them destroyed. That evening we relieved the King's Own again. On the 15th Ypres was shelled throughout the day, and again the following day; a patrol of ours had a scrap with a Hun patrol in No Man's Land, but suffered no casualties.

The 17th was a quiet day; the battalion was relieved by the 1/5th King's Own and went back to C Camp, where we remained till the 28th. During this period important reorganisation was carried out, the bombing sections rejoining their companies, thus "washing out" the Bombing Company, the Lewis guns being placed finally under company commanders; companies reorganised their platoons into four sections—one of bombers, one of riflemen, one of Lewis gunners, and one of rifle grenadiers. As a matter of fact we had ourselves suggested and partially adopted this about a month before, but it was now officially sanctioned. Second Lieutenant H. Lonsdale joined us during this period.

On the 28th we moved back to Canal Bank, Ypres; on that day we made 272 barbed wire concertinas and carried 100 up the line. We remained here a few days, supplying nightly working parties—chiefly carrying wire up to the front line; two men were wounded on the 1st April.

During February and March we lost 98 men through sickness alone—our monthly average being between 40 and 60 during the following months also.

On the 2nd April we relieved the 1/4th King's Own in the La Brique sector without casualties; Second Lieutenant Fullerton joined us. The next day was quiet, with slight shelling on the front line, but on the following night a patrol of ours ran into a strong enemy party, who tried to cut them off, but a Lewis gun team being sent for, they thought better of it and retired, covered by two machine guns; we had three killed and one wounded that day.

On the 6th we had a man wounded, and again on the 7th; on the latter day the 165th Brigade on our right carried out a hurricane bombardment on the enemy's front line with Stokes' mortars. The enemy sent up red flares, which, being our S.O.S. signal, brought our artillery into action, and 600 shells were fired on the enemy front line opposite us. Our relief that night by the 1/4th King's Own was carried out, with one casualty, in bright moonlight, and we went back to Canal Bank.

The 8th, Easter Sunday, was a lovely day, and very quiet. The *padre* held four communion services in one of the dugouts, and a large number of us went.

The next few days we spent in doing a certain amount of training on the Canal Bank, with nightly working parties; on the 12th Second Lieutenant R. A. Hall was accidentally wounded in the arm during bombing practice; the same evening we relieved the 1/4th King's Own in La Brique subsector.

On the 13th, during some slight shelling, a Lewis gun post on our right company front had the misfortune to get hit, one man being killed and three others wounded, and on the following day, though "quiet," two more men were wounded. On the 17th we sent out a large fighting patrol, with Bangalore torpedoes, to capture an enemy sentry post in a sap head, but, as usual, "*when they got there the cupboard was bare*," and they came away empty.

On the 17th we were relieved by the 12th Royal Sussex 39th Division)—the relief was not complete till 1.30 a.m.—and we entrained at Ypres at 2.30 a.m. and arrived at Poperinghe station at 3.25 a.m. and marched to Z Camp, where we snatched a few hours' sleep. At 2.30 p.m. we marched *via* Watou to Houtkerque, where companies were billeted in scattered farms; here our medical officer, Captain A. W. Uloth, R.A.M.C, went sick, and Captain R. W. Shegog, R.A.M.C, came in his place. Here we remained for three days, cleaning up and training, till on the 22nd the whole brigade concentrated at 9 a.m. one mile south of Herzeele and marched, with first line transport, to billets in Arneke, where we arrived at 1.45 p.m., leaving again early next morning to concentrate at 9 a.m. four and a half miles west of Arneke, and march *via* Watten (locally known as "Wat") to Houlle, where we arrived at 2 p.m.

These marches, though a stiff trial to men fresh from the trenches, with slack muscles and tender feet, were interesting; we were seeing new country: Houtkerque and Herzeele were nice little towns, though the latter had more troops than it could properly hold; Arneke was still better—the people, who seemed delighted to see us, had a curiously English look, probably due to the fact that Marlborough's troops were once billeted all round this part; just as the Scotch blood in Lancashire is traced to the presence of the Pretender's following.

Houlle is in the midst of the hilly country near St. Omer—strongly reminding one of parts of Kent—an ideal country to train in. Here were large ranges, like the Aldershot Ranges, for musketry, and every day we marched out of billets and up on to the hills for training of some kind, taking our cookers with us and having dinners up there, every day getting fitter and improving in morale—shaking off the trench staleness and thinking more of open fighting—getting more of the "offensive spirit." Second Lieutenant Hall rejoined us on the 26th. The diarist writes at this time:—

> Still in the same place (that in itself, you see, is sufficiently remarkable to be chronicled). There are real hedgerows here, just bursting into leaf, and the fritillaries are out all along the lanes, in fact I am in the middle of real Spring. A lilac in front of my window shows half out, covered with bloom, and the currants are quite green. All this makes one long more than ever for England. The people round here are much better farmers and gardeners than we are—nothing is wasted, and everything done thoroughly and carefully. As I look out of the window a thrush is singing and the view is an English view. *Oh, to be in England now that April's here!*
>
> *30th.* The cuckoo is at it and the nightingale, in fact it is Spring, cloudless day, glorious sun, everything as it should be, only one thing wrong, I'm not where I ought to be, in England—Spring in a foreign land is a painful pleasure to an Englishman.

The point of these extracts is that they express what each of us felt at that time and many other times—an intense longing, carefully smothered, for home and peace; few individuals, if any, went abroad, or stayed there, because they *liked* it.

Until the 6th we remained at Houlle training; it would serve no useful purpose and would bore the general reader to set down the programme of training carried out; enough to say that it was a fresh and merry column that marched back to Arneke on the 6th of May, leaving again by train at 11.45 a.m. for Poperinghe. Here we were met by the divisional band, which played us to L Camp, where we spent the night, returning to Poperinghe the next morning and up by train to the prison billets at Ypres.

During the next five days bathing was carried out, and the usual nightly working parties went up the line. Ypres was distinctly livelier than before, but only one man was wounded during the period.

On the 14th we relieved the 1/4th King's Own in the right sub-sector, Potijze. The sectors had been rearranged. D Company had two platoons in the front line and two in close support; A Company was in reserve and held Mill Cotts, Garden of Eden, Prowse Trench, and St. James' Trench. B and C Companies, in brigade reserve, were billeted in houses on the Potijze Road.

On the 18th the enemy was very active with his artillery, the front line Company, D, calling for retaliation five times during the morning; we had one man killed and one wounded. A fighting patrol had gone out the previous night to try to capture an enemy party, and were supported by an artillery barrage—as usual, the enemy had withdrawn.

At 9.15 that evening the enemy placed a shrapnel, trench mortar, and howitzer barrage on our front line first, then on our support line, and an S.O.S. being sent up by the battalion on our left was repeated by us; as soon as the barrage started our front company stood to and fired rapid over the parapet. No one in the front line saw the enemy leave his trenches, but two snipers, who had been out in No Man's Land all day and were waiting for it to get dark to come in, saw the enemy place a machine gun on his parapet, the team of which they proceeded to knock out; they also saw Huns entering the trenches of the battalion on our left. Our trenches were badly damaged in places, one man was killed, one missing, and Second Lieutenant Francis and four men wounded; B Company relieved D that evening.

> It is curious to notice the different effects intermittent and concentrated shelling have on one—intermittent shelling takes people different ways—on the whole it makes you angry; concentrated shelling, such as a barrage, you rise above altogether by some curious effort of will. I think it is that in the first case one hears each one coming hissing along in a descending scale, and speculates where it will fall, while in the second there is simply a terrific medley of bangs and crashes which you can only accept as a perfect inferno of noise, and leave it at that."

The following night we hit back; Major Crump, who was in command in the absence of Lieutenant-Colonel Hindle, who was commanding the brigade, organised a raid, carried out under an artillery barrage by Second Lieutenant Tautz, three N.C.O.'s, and 20 men, who entered the enemy's lines and bombed dugouts. The party had great difficulty in getting through the wire, and our casualties were two men wounded of the party and one in the trench; three of the raid-

AEROPLANE PHOTO OF OPPOSING TRENCH LINES YPRES

ers were at first reported missing, but Private Metcalfe turned up at dawn, having got entangled in the wire and badly wounded, and in the evening another, Private Cooper, came in, having spent the day in a shell hole.

That day, the 20th, leave reopened, having been closed since January, and everyone began to calculate their chances.

About this time we were encouraged to use our Lewis guns against hostile aircraft, and special mountings and fittings were issued to us for that purpose it was impossible for people behind to deal with machines flying low over our front line. This aeroplane shooting was rather good sport, and though very few were actually brought down by Lewis gun fire, they soon learned to keep out of range. At this time the aeroplane activity in the Salient was great on both sides—on a fine day machines swarmed like midges in the sky.

On the night of the 20th we were relieved by the 1/4th King's Own, and on relief we marched to A Camp, just behind Vlamertinghe, leaving Captain Harris and 200 men of B and D Companies in Ypres as a working party. They had rather a lively time, as Ypres was being heavily shelled daily—a shell actually entered a cellar where several men were sleeping, ricocheted and buried itself in one of the walls without exploding or touching anyone. During the next few days five men were wounded.

On the night of the 20th we relieved the 1/4th King's Own in the Potijze sector, C and A Companies in front, B in support, and D in reserve, and began at once a series of works designed to mislead the enemy and make him think an attack was intended on our front. How much he was deceived appeared from the amount of attention we received from this time onward until the Battle of Messines.

The opposing sides gained much of their knowledge of the other's intentions from aeroplane photographs, which show up with great clearness any newly-dug earth. It was our task then to open up all the disused trenches on our sector, placing along the top a row of new sandbags, and to dig saps out into No Man's Land, at the same time annoying the Hun by every means in our power. Two were killed and three wounded during the next four days, during which we kept throwing things at the Hun—trench mortars, grenades, bullets, etc.—and we really did stir him up. Then came the news that we were not to be relieved, so companies changed over.

On 1st June the gas strafe started; our people started it with a discharge of 500 gas drums on enemy reserves. We heard afterwards that so sudden and concentrated was the attack that a whole company were poisoned where they stood. The enemy retaliated on us, killing one man and wounding three, using everything he had; then he began to bring up gas shells and use them, chiefly at night on lines of communication. The sighing of gas shells going over never ceased during three successive nights before the show, yet the damage done was very slight. But the companies in the trenches kept getting odd ones, and the veering breeze kept clouds of various gases drifting about for quite a long time, and we had a few anxious vigils. The Hun was very angry and horribly afraid and therefore shelled everything he could think of, and we appeared to occupy some of his thoughts, for we certainly got our full share and he took his toll of us.

On the 2nd we sent over more gas drums, and again the Hun retaliated, doing a lot of damage to trenches and killing two men and wounding five others.

On the 3rd we treated him to a combined smoke, artillery, and machine gun barrage, and he replied, but more feebly, killing one man and wounding two; but during the night, from 10 p.m. to 4 a.m., he drenched Ypres with gas shells, our transport suffering slightly. He also, on the following day, put 67 "Minnies" on to B Company, killing one man and wounding Second Lieutenants Hall and Johnson and 11 others. We were glad to learn that Lieutenant-Colonel Hindle had been awarded the D.S.O. in the Birthday Honours List.

That night a minor enterprise by the 1/5th North Lancashire Regiment on our right caused some shelling on our right front company, and a party digging saps in front escaped by a miracle; he also sent a few *granatenwerfer* over into the middle of another party engaged in sap digging, causing several casualties, the total being 14 wounded for the two days. On the 14th both sides were active. We were preparing an elaborate programme of smoke and other bombs, to be discharged at the same hour as the Messines battle was timed to start, also putting scaling ladders against the parapet this work was under Captain Harris. The Hun shelled Ypres pretty heavily in the evening, and set two large dumps on fire.

At 3.10 a.m. on the 7th the Messines battle started with a literal earthquake 19 mines being blown up at once, the barrage starting at the same time en our front among others. The enemy shelled us for about half an hour, by which time he found out that we were bluffing him and stopped. Our casualties were five killed, Second Lieutenant Agostini and 10 others wounded.

Oblique Aeroplane Photograph showing Trench Lines at Ypres.
Taken April 23rd, 1917

On the 8th the enemy shelled the roads with 5.9's and gas shells in the early morning, our guns doing wire cutting with the 106 fuse, a very sensitive fuse which bursts on graze without burying itself; a good many "shorts" fell on our trenches due to defective ammunition, which was just as dangerous to the gunners as to us, as muzzle-bursts were not infrequent. A gunner officer going round the line was at a loss for words when he saw a shell case, which had fallen short, stuck up over a dugout with the inscription, "A present from the R.F.A.!" Sergeant Thompson was killed by a nosecap from one of these "shorts," and during the day four men were wounded.

In the afternoon A and C Companies relieved B and D in the front line.

At 11.9 p.m. the 39th Division on our left sent over gas from projectors; we caught some of the retaliation on Potijze Road 5.9's and gas shells.

On the 9th we had a fairly quiet morning, but the artillery livened up in the afternoon; the 1/4th King's Own carried out a successful raid on our front, bagging six unwounded prisoners, who seemed glad to be taken. The enemy was taken by surprise in mid-relief. We had six men wounded during the day.

Things remained lively during the next two days, five men being wounded, but on the 11th the blessed word "Relief" was whispered. Imagine the joy of men who had never had their clothes off for nearly three weeks—more, in some cases. The relieving battalion, the 1/9th King's Liverpool Regiment, did not arrive till after 3 a.m., so relief had to be carried out in daylight in very small parties, but it went off without a casualty, and we marched to a canvas camp behind Ypres, where we rested till noon on the 12th, when we marched by companies to Poperinghe, leaving by train at 2.45 p.m. and reaching Esquelbecq at 4.45 p.m.; here we were joined by part of the transport, and after dinner had been eaten we marched on to Bollezeele, where we occupied our old billets.

The next three days were spent in cleaning up, bathing, and a little training.

On the 16th the brigade marched *via* Watten to Boisdinghem; it was a broiling day and the sky was like brass, and as the march started at 9 a.m., when the sun was high up, and was mostly uphill, a large number of men were affected with sunstroke and fell out, but the 9th Wing R.F.C. were very good to us and lent us lorries to bring in the stragglers. Here we found the accommodation poor and totally inadequate, but we crowded in somehow, many preferring to bivouac in the open fields rather than occupy the buildings allotted to them: the village lay on the top of the downs not many miles from our old area Houlle, almost out of the sound of the guns. About this time the diarist, reviewing recent events, writes:—

> To be within two or three yards of a big shell when it bursts sounds like sudden death, but it isn't—necessarily; it happens daily to lots of people who survive; I have been several times as close as that, closer in one case; the shock and noise absolutely deafen one for some minutes afterwards, but it seems to pass off; but there must be a good solid bulwark of earth between you and the shell! if there isn't, well shell-shock is the best you can hope for!

On Sunday, the 17th, we had a Church of England parade out of doors, the cornet player of the drums leading the hymns. Second Lieutenants Easterby and Rigby joined us. The following day we were inspected in mass by the brigadier, who gave us a good rating about Saturday's march. We thought this a little unkind, as it might have occurred to the Staff to make a start early in the morning and get it over in the cool of the day, instead of expecting men who were weak from a long spell of trenches to march 15 miles heavily laden in the middle of a hot June day; however, we had no doubt that those responsible would be duly ticked off, so we swallowed the rating with outward calm; after all, the men who fell out had in some cases done so without asking leave, being long past caring what happened, and this was a breach of march discipline.

The remaining days of the month were spent in training; we received a large number of reinforcements, including Second Lieutenant Brooke. Captain Houghton, who had picked up trench fever during the last tour, was sent to Field Ambulance, Captain Harris taking over A Company.

On the 2nd July we marched to Lumbres, thence we went by rail to Brandhoek, and marched from there to Derby Camp. At dusk D Company moved forward to a post called L4 on the Ypres Road, A and C Companies to a strong point called P 1, and two officers and 50 other ranks to Ypres for water duties. Second Lieutenant H. Whitehurst joined us as a reinforcement. Two men were wounded on the 3rd and one on the 5th, on which day Captain Ord rejoined us from the Divisional School, Major Crump leaving the following day for a three months' course at the Senior Officers' School, Aldershot.

On the 9th we relieved the 1/4th King's Own in the line; there was considerable enemy activity during the night, and we had one killed and one wounded.

On the 10th, although considered "quiet," we had three men wounded, while on the 12th, though he put two of our Lewis guns out of action with *minenwerfers* and shelled our trenches intensely, we had no casualty. At 11 p.m. he began to shell Battalion Headquarters steadily and went on till 8.30 a.m.; a wiring party from our left front Company had three men wounded by "Minnies," and had to come in.

One man was killed and eight wounded during the day, one of the wiring party being missing. On the 13th two men were wounded during desultory shelling of our lines, and five on the next day, which started quiet, but things on both sides woke up at dusk, our guns bombarding enemy batteries, the Hun sending gas shells on to us, and barraging the front line, stopping all work, wounding three men and gassing two others that day. In the early morning 20 yards of the front line parapet was knocked in, one man killed and five wounded. Things were getting very hot indeed, and our strength was daily being whittled down, but relief was not yet.

The casualties at this time would have been far heavier than they actually were but for the fact that the N.C.O.'s in the front line had learnt that No Man's Land was the safest place in a bombardment and used to take their posts out in front of our wire as soon as the Hun opened out.

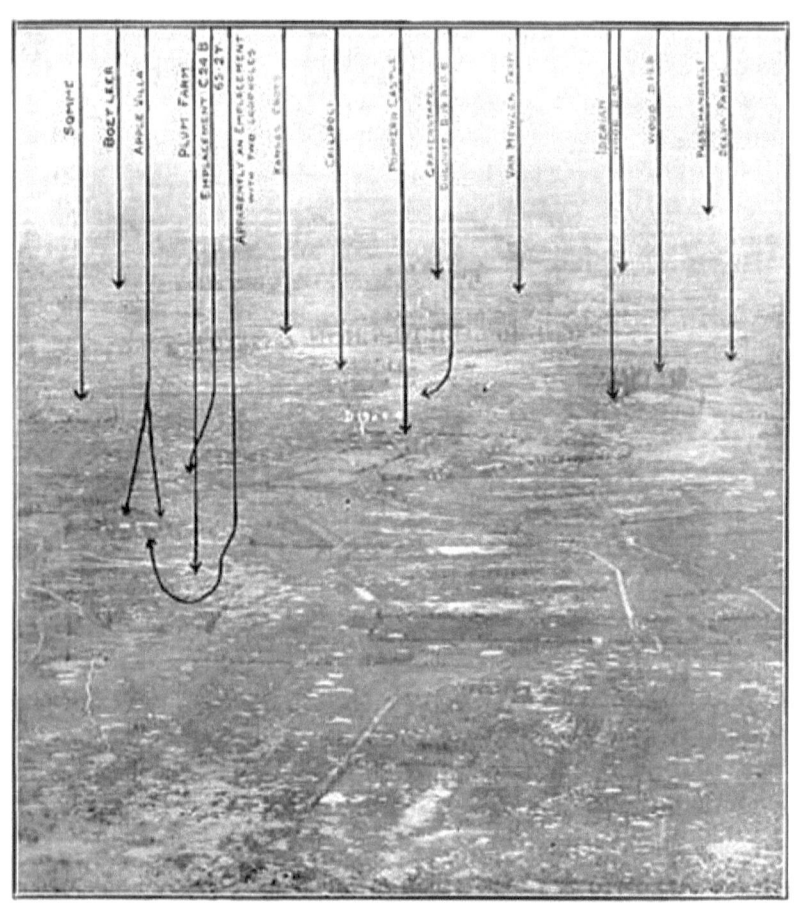

OBLIQUE AEROPLANE PHOTOGRAPH SHOWING OBJECTIVES IN THE 3RD BATTLE OF YPRES.

CHAPTER 6

The Third Battle of Ypres, 15th July, 1917, to 1st August, 1917

On the 17th July, 1917, the preliminary bombardment of the enemy lines by our guns commenced. In the early morning ten shells from a Hun high velocity gun landed on Battalion Headquarters, one actually entering the colonel's dugout and exploding there without injuring him!

On the night following, a fighting patrol of ours had a brush with a Hun patrol in No Man's Land, and did good work, bringing back a dead German, who turned out to belong to the 449th Infantry Regiment, who were expected to be opposite to us. On the 20th Second Lieutenant Vincent took a raiding party of 20 in to the enemy lines and found a post of four men; two fled, one was bayoneted, and one taken prisoner. During these days artillery had been active, and our casualties were 6 killed, 13 wounded, 2 gassed.

On the 21st we suffered rather heavily from enemy artillery, a single shell hitting 9 men, our total casualties on that day being 11 killed and 14 wounded, of whom 2 afterwards died—our worst day since the Somme. The quartermaster, Lieutenant March, was wounded but remained on duty. In the evening we were relieved by the 15th King's Liverpool Regiment, and went back to a canvas camp near Poperinghe, where all had a bath, and then marched on to Watou, resting there for three days and returning to the canvas camp on the 25th. Captain L. Duckworth rejoined us here, and Second Lieutenant Holmes reported for duty. During the night of the 27th enemy aeroplanes dropped bombs near our camp.

The following Operation Order and the details of the attack are taken *verbatim* from the *War Diary*, the official record, and are very complete, but a few prefatory words are necessary to make them intelligible to the general reader.

The 55th Division was at this time in the 19th Corps of the 5th Army, which, with the 2nd Army and the 1st French Army, were to attack the enemy's Gheluvelt—Langemarck line; the task allotted to our brigade (164), was to pass through the other two brigades of the division when they had taken their objectives and capture the third-line system, mostly consisting of concrete blockhouses, which we were to meet for the first time.

The barrage is officially stated to have been the most intense which had ever been put down up to that time, and largely contributed to the success of the attack. Another novelty for us was "B team," a nucleus of officers, warrant officers, N.C.O.'s and men who were kept out of the attack so that the battalion could be reorganised as quickly as possible afterwards; the order had been issued by the Higher Command some months before, and to it was largely due the wonderful speed with which units recovered from battles which in earlier years would have taken nearly all their leaders and specialists and rendered them unfit for action for at least six months.

The following officers actually went up with the battalion for the battle, the remainder being on B team. Of those that went up, only the commanding officer, adjutant, transport officer, and Second Lieutenant Higson came through unwounded.

>Lieutenant-Colonel R. Hindle Commanding.
>Captain Ord Second in Command.
>Captain Shegog, R.A.M.C. Medical Officer.
>Captain Caley Chaplain.
>Lieutenant Buckmaster Adjutant.
>Second Lieutenant Ashcroft Signalling Officer.
>Second Lieutenant Williams Intelligence Officer.
>Second Lieutenant Bardsley Transport Officer.
>
>### A COMPANY.
>
>Captain A. L. Harris
>Second Lieutenant Ordish
>Second Lieutenant Tyldesley
>Second Lieutenant MacSweeny
>
>### B COMPANY.
>
>Lieutenant Ogden

Second Lieutenant Vincent
Second Lieutenant Easterby
Second Lieutenant Rigby

C Company.

Captain Hore
Second Lieutenant Higson
Second Lieutenant Mather

D Company.

Lieutenant Ostrehan
Second Lieutenant Fullerton
Second Lieutenant Holden

The aeroplane photograph read in conjunction with the map will help to give the reader some idea of the country as it actually was, for though July as a whole had been fine, there was a heavy thunderstorm on the 29th, which turned the tracks and roads into morasses and filled the shell holes with water.

> The succeeding days were dull and heavy, making the completion of the artillery preparation peculiarly difficult, and typical Flanders weather prevailed on the morning of the 31st—the moment chosen for the attack.
> Low-lying clouds which made aerial observation and co-operation as difficult as could be imagined; a dampness of atmosphere, threatening rain at any moment; a half-sodden ground, greasy and depressing—such was the luck of the weather when the barrage opened.[1]

The Operation Order for the attack is set out below practically in full. It is impossible to summarize it without losing some detail which may be of interest to readers.

The Operation Order

1. On Z Day, the 55th Division will take part in a general attack. battalion on the right—6th Cameron Highlanders.
   Battalion on the left—2/5th Lancashire Fusiliers.
   165th Brigade will capture the Frezenberg line before the advance of the 164th Brigade begins.
   Brigade support—1/8th Liverpool Regiment, who will, after

---

1. From *The Story of the 55th Division*, by the Rev. J. O. Coop. *Liverpool Daily Post*.

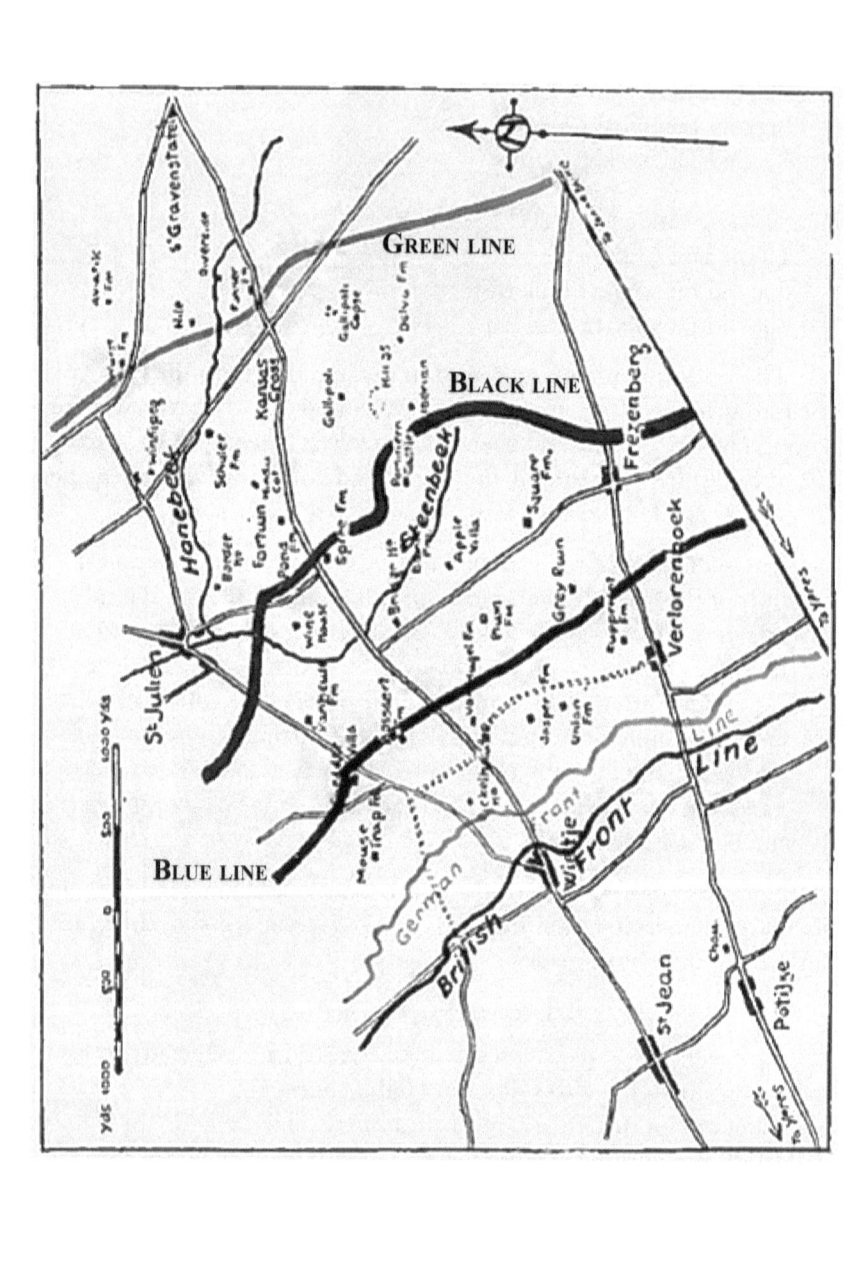

the capture of final objectives, consolidate the general line K of Keir Farm—Schuler Farm.

Brigade reserve—1/4th Royal Lancaster Regiment, who will, after the capture of final objectives, consolidate the general line Gallipoli—Somme—Hindu Cot.

2. At Zero plus 4hrs. 40 mins. the battalion will advance in artillery formation from the position of assembly and deploy as necessary, at the discretion of the platoon commanders, before crossing the black line.

The attack will then be made behind a creeping barrage, in four waves.

The black dotted line will be captured and held as an outpost line, the green line being consolidated.

3. Distribution and Formation for Attack.

    Right Front Company   D.
    Left Front Company   A.
    Right Support Company C.
    Left Support Company   B.

Between assembly line and black line, the formation will be four lines of platoons in file or fours, at 50 yards' distance.

After crossing the black line the formation will be four waves at 50 yards' distance.

The second wave will close up to the first, and the third wave to the second, before the first and second waves reach their respective objectives.

4. Machine Guns.

One sub-section will move in rear of each supporting company. They will occupy the outpost line, one gun being placed in each of the four strong points that will be constructed, upon receiving orders from the O.C. Battalion.

5. Objectives of waves and commanders.

The first wave will capture the line of trenches D20 a 33 90 D14 a 10 20 and all buildings north-west of Kansas Cross within the battalion boundary and on the south-west side of the Zonnebeke—Winnipeg road. A special party will be told off to bomb forward along the trench leading towards the green line from D 14 c. 30 70. This line will be under command of O.C. D Company.

The second wave will capture the green line; this line will be under the command of O.C. A Company.

Third wave will pass through first and second waves, and will capture black dotted line and will be under command of O.C. C Company.

Fourth wave will collect Nos. 4, 5, and 6 mopping-up parties and will help in the consolidation of the green line. This wave will be prepared to assist the third wave in the capture of its objectives.

6. Consolidation.

The consolidation, which will commence at once, will be carried out in depth and will take the form of three lines of strong points, namely, those held by Nos. 1, 2, and 3 waves.

These strong points will ultimately be joined up to form trenches.

One company of the 1/8th Liverpool Regiment will be available to assist in digging.

It is essential that artillery shelters for the garrison should be constructed before dawn on Z plus 1 day.

Strong points will be constructed at the following places:

D 14 d 05 30.

By the second wave, where touch will be gained with battalion on right.

Also at:

D 14 b 20 05, D14 a 9 5, D 8 c 71.

By the third wave, and touch gained with the battalion on our left.

One machine gun will move up into each of these strong points as soon as the ground has been gained and consolidation begins.

7. Battalion Headquarters.

Prior to advance will be in the mined dugout in Congreve Walk. During advance Battalion Headquarters will move between the two rear companies.

A temporary headquarters will be established about Pommern Castle.

8. Assembly.

The battalion, with machine guns, trench mortars, and mopping-up parties, will occupy Congreve Walk between Potijze road and Lone street. Order from right to left:—

15 Platoon.	3 Platoon
Mopping-up party No. 1.	Mopping-up party No. 2
9 Platoon.	6 Platoon.
16 Platoon.	1 Platoon.
Right sub-section machine guns.	Left subsection machine guns.
13. Platoon.	7 Platoon.
12 Platoon.	2 Platoon.
Mopping-up party No. 5.	5 Platoon.
Mopping-up party No. 4.	Mopping-up party No. 6.
14 Platoon.	Mopping-up party No. 3.
Trench mortars.	4 Platoon.
Battalion Headquarters.	

9. Mopping-up Parties.
For during the attack will follow:

1. Trenches north-west of Iberia and dugouts at D19 b 10 65	15 Platoon.
2. Gallipoli dugouts and trenches as far west as Somme exclusive	3 Platoon.
3. Somme and trenches north-west as far as battalion boundary	4 Platoon.
4. Works at D 14 c 12	14 Platoon.
5. Keir Farm	14 Platoon.
6. Buildings 100 yards west of Kansas Cross	4 Platoon.

Parties 1, 2, and 3 will be furnished by 1/4th Royal Lancaster Regiment.
Parties 4 and 5 by C Company 1/4th North Lancashire Regiment.
Party 6 by B Company 1/4th North Lancashire Regiment.

These parties will merge into the waves immediately in front of them before reaching their objectives.
Parties found by the 1/4th Royal Lancaster Regiment will be absorbed by their own unit as soon as it reaches them.
Parties found by the 1/4th Loyal North Lancashire Regiment will be furnished from fourth wave, and upon completion of their task will be absorbed by that wave as it passes over them.
Each mopping-up party will consist of one platoon.

10. Trench Mortars.

One sub-section of trench mortars will assemble in Congreve Walk, close to the mined dugouts, and will move near Battalion Headquarters in the attack, ready to deal with any points of resistance that may hold out. They will take up position on the line D 14 Central-Toronto Farm, after all objectives have been taken.

11. Medical.

Aid post prior to advance I 4 a 64.

During the advance, the medical officer will move in rear of the centre of the battalion and will establish an aid post in the vicinity of Pommern Castle.

12. Communications.

During the advance, communications will be by runner visual being established whenever halted. Second Lieutenant Ashcroft will establish:

1. A battalion command post, about D 19 a 44, and will arrange telephonic communication with 164th Brigade office near Rat Farm.

2. An advance command post about Hill 35, and connect up by telephone with brigade forward station, near Somme Farm.

3. Runner relay post about D 19 a 28.

13. Dress and Equipment.

Dress:—Fighting order with packs.

Ammunition: 120 rounds S.A.A on every man except—

(1) Signallers.

(2) Scouts.

(3) Runners.

(4) Lewis Gunners.

(5) Bombers.

(6) Rifle Grenadiers, carrying No. 20 grenades.

All of whom will carry 50 rounds S.A.A.

In addition, every N.C.O. and man will carry:

(1) In the pack. Towel and soap, spare oil tin, holdall, rations (see para. 14 following), extra water bottle (containing cold tea without sugar or milk), groundsheet, and mess tin.

(2) In each top pocket of the jacket.—One No. 23 rifle grenade complete with rod and cartridge (except Rifle Grenadiers carrying No. 20 grenades).

(3) In each bottom pocket of the jacket. One aeroplane flare.

(4) Under the braces of the pack.—Three sandbags.

In addition to the above—

(*a*) Each bomber will carry eight No. 23 grenades in bomb buckets.

(*b*) Sixteen extra pairs wire-cutters will be issued to each company and will be equally distributed amongst Platoons.

(*c*) S.O.S. signals will be issued at the rate of five per company.

(*d*) All Rifle Grenadiers wearing grenade carriers will carry six No. 20 grenades. These will not be detonated until the battalion arrives at Congreve Walk.

Rifle Grenadiers will carry their 50 rounds of ammunition in a bandolier and will discard their S.A.A. pouches. Orders re carrying of heavy tools will be issued later. Men carrying heavy tools will not carry entrenching tool. All the stores mentioned above will be issued in the concentration area on X/Y night.

14. Supply.

(*a*) Rations.

(1) Rations for consumption on Z day will be delivered to companies from Quartermaster's Stores on X day.

(2) Rations for Z plus 1 day will be drawn at the concentration area on the night X Y.

(3) Rations for Z plus 2 day will be at the Brigade Dump, near junction of Milner Trench and Congreve Walk, and will ultimately be brought forward by pack transport.

Scale of rations for Z, Z plus 1 and Z plus 2 day will be as follows:—

Preserved Meat	1lb.
Biscuits	1lb.
Sugar	2oz.
Tea	5-8oz.
Jam	3oz.
Solidified Alcohol	One 8oz. tin for eight men.

(*b*) Water.

800 gallons of water will be held in reservoirs for 164 Brigade on the line Liverpool Trench—Congreve Walk, and water bot-

tles will be filled from this source on Y;Z night.

On Z day, 800 gallons of water for the brigade will be sent forward in petrol tins for use on Z plus 1 day.

15. Dumps.
Brigade dumps will be formed as follows:—
Advanced dump on road at about D 13 c 18.
Right Forward dump—Gallipoli

The advanced dump will be formed and maintained by transport with the following stores:—

S.A.A.	Flares.
Lewis gun drums.	Blank Cartridges.
No. 23 grenades.	Verey lights.
No. 20 grenades.	

1/4th Royal Lancaster Regiment will be responsible for carrying from the advanced dump to the forward dump and will provide one platoon for carrying from the forward dump to companies.

EXTRACTED FROM WAR DIARY.

Poperinghe.

28th July. Announced to be W day in connection with forthcoming operations. Bombs again dropped during night fairly near our camp.

Second Lieutenant W. Young and three other ranks to Field Ambulance sick.

29th July. X day in connection with forthcoming operations. Preparations made for moving into concentration area. At 9 p.m. the battalion (less party of 100 other ranks and seven officers who were being left out of the attack) marched off from camp by platoons at 300 yards" distance. There was comparatively little shelling, and the concentration area was reached (H 10 c) without casualties. It consisted of camouflaged trenches and bivouac sheets erected under hedges. Battalion Headquarters was established in a ruined farm with a siege battery of R.G.A. at 2.30 a.m. The battalion was fitted out with rations for Y, Z, and Z plus 1 day's, bombs, wire-cutters, aeroplane flares, S.O.S. signals, sandbags, etc.

Vlamertinghe.

30th July. Y day. Strict orders had been issued with regard to restricting movement, so as to preclude the possibility of the concentration being made known to the enemy. As a matter of fact, it was a very dull day, and visibility was never even fair. During the late afternoon, the brigadier and divisional commander visited the battalion and wished us good luck. At 9.23 p.m., in drizzling rain, the first platoon moved off towards the trenches, followed by the remaining platoons at intervals of 200 yards. The mopping-up parties (three in number) provided for our battalion by 1/4th Royal Lancaster Regiment moved with us into such positions as to arrive in their correct position of assembly.

30th July. The route taken was the main Vlamertinghe-Ypres road to the Water Tower I 7 c 85 95. thence by tramline to where it joined No. 5 track, running parallel and in between the Ypres-Potijze road and Ypres-St. Jean road, joining Congreve Walk, our assembly trench, at about I 4 a 45 90. On arrival here, Battalion Headquarters was established in the mined dugout at the vinery I 4 c 65 80. Congreve Walk was reached without a casualty, not a shell being fired during the whole time the battalion was on the roads and tracks. Our artillery was very active, raining gas shells on the enemy continuously for four hours from about 10 p.m. to 2 a.m. At one time about 11.30 p.m. the enemy sent a few mustard-gas shells, in the vicinity of Congreve Walk, causing momentary sneezing and a temporary cessation of the work of drawing tools. After tools had been drawn there was nothing further to do except have hot tea two cookers being concealed near St. Jean with this end in view.

Two other ranks wounded.

31st July. Z day. At zero hour (3.50 a.m.) the 55th Division assaulted, taking part in a general attack of the 5th Army, part of the 2nd Army, and the 1st French Army.

At zero the 165th and 166th Infantry Brigades attacked and captured the blue line. The artillery barrage commenced at zero. It did not provoke any reply in the neighbourhood of Congreve Walk until about 4.15 a.m., when a few 4.2's and 5.9's fell in the trench and caused a few casualties. From 4.30 a.m. onwards, German prisoners came past in continuous streams, in many cases being utilised to carry down our wounded. From the blue line the 165th and 166th Brigades moved on to the black line; the artillery provided a protective barrage to cover consolidation. At zero plus 4 hours 40 minutes, the 164th Infantry Brigade moved off in artillery formation from Congreve Walk, 1/4th Loyal North Lancashires on the right, with 1/4th Royal Lancaster Regiment in support and 2/5th Lancashire Fusiliers on the left with 1/8th (Irish) Liverpools in support.

Second Lieutenant Ashcroft (signalling officer) was killed by a nose-cap as we started off, otherwise everything went off satisfactorily. The enemy were dropping shells, both high-explosive and shrapnel, promiscuously between Congreve Walk and our original front line, but there was no difficulty in eluding the areas to which attention was being paid. It was a dull misty morning, and so there were neither aeroplanes nor balloons in the air to detect the advancing troops. As we passed over No Man's Land, companies were well shaken out into their various squares and the direction was being well kept. The enemy wire in front of his first line system was practically non-existent and provided no obstacle. The trenches appeared very badly smashed in and in places obliterated, though here and there appeared small concrete dugouts apparently still intact.

The advance continued to go well, and the platoon commanders with the help of their compasses maintained their direction. The enemy were apparently preoccupied finding out exactly where their own infantry were and also in moving back some of their guns. Consequently, we were very little troubled by shells, but machine gun fire caused us considerable annoyance. It was mostly coming apparently from our right flank, perhaps from some strong point which had not been sufficiently mopped-up. However, although bullets were flying everywhere, the range had not been correctly estimated, and so we suffered very few casualties in this way before reaching the black line.

At zero plus 6hrs. 20mins. (10.10 a.m.) the 164th Infantry Brigade formed up under the protective barrage, which stood about 200 yards on the enemy's side of the black line, and moved forward to attack and consolidate the green line. Just before forming up under the barrage, we were caused a little trouble by some snipers who had apparently been swept over by the barrage and were lying out in shell holes. From now onwards the artillery barrage was rather thin, owing to the fact that it was out of range for some of the guns which had fired during the initial assault and because it was being provided by batteries who had moved forward since zero to positions in the vicinity of the original No Man's Land.

When the 1/4th Loyal North Lancashires moved off from the black line, touch had been obtained with the 2/5th Lancashire Fusiliers on the left and the 6th Cameron Highlanders (45th Infantry Brigade, 15th Division) on the right. During the subsequent advance from the black line to the green line the casualties, which were particularly heavy amongst officers, were again principally caused by machine gun fire. Reports were received from several officers giving their location, and those machine guns immediately in our line of advance were effectively dealt with, but we were still troubled by guns firing from high ground beyond the green line and also by guns enfilading us from our right flank.

Several strong points had to be dealt with in the course of the advance, particular mention being made of Somme Farm, Gallipoli, and Keir Farm. Somme Farm provided us with 60 prisoners; it consisted of several concrete dugouts, one being an aid post, and had evidently been used as a Battalion Headquarters. There were also concrete dugouts at Keir Farm and Gallipoli, each of which provided us with prisoners.

The green line was reported captured at 11.40 a.m., and consolidation was at once put in hand. While this was in progress, hostile machine guns again proved troublesome, especially from Nile Farm. During the advance to the green line six batteries 77mm. were encountered. The gunners continued to fire them until our advancing waves were within about 200-250 yards, and then withdrew. On arrival at the green line difficulty was experienced in husbanding the available resources of ammunition until a further supply could be brought up. Demands were received from all parts of the line, but they were unable to be met for some considerable time, owing to the fact that the pack animals, which were bringing up supplies, were experiencing difficulties owing to the unexpected quantity of uncut wire.

Meanwhile, while the green line was being energetically consolidated, the third wave moved on to take the black dotted or outpost line. This was established along a line running about 200 yards in front of the green line. Our own barrage appeared to fall a trifle short at this point, and consequently our line was held up slightly and could not be established on the intended line. Fifty prisoners were captured and sent back by the platoons comprising the outpost line. A message timed 11.41 a.m. stated "enemy in full flight."

At 12.10 p.m. our protective barrage ceased. Meanwhile the outpost line was being put into a state of defence by the construction of a series of strong points, though considerable difficulty was being experienced in maintaining touch on the left. On the right we appeared to be in touch, but it was obvious that the right flank company of the 6th Camerons was not up to its alignment, and, consequently, their line was swung back.

The difficulties about ammunition continued to increase. Many Lewis guns were used until every round had been expended, but there was still none available for issue at Battalion Headquarters. Things went well until 2.30 p.m., when a report was received that the enemy were forming up for counter-attack in the vicinity of Boetleer. At 2.35 p.m. a strong counter-attack developed on the right, and the 6th Camerons on our right were seen to be withdrawing. This attempt on the part of the enemy was immediately followed by an attack on our left. With the enemy advancing on both flanks and closing together in the centre, our outpost line, seriously weakened, particularly on the left, withdrew, and was absorbed into the green line. This line in turn then had to withdraw as there was no touch on the right, and the 2 5th Lancashire Fusiliers had had to fall back well behind the green line owing to the green line not having been taken by the divisions on their left.

The withdrawal was carried out in perfect order, the troops fighting as they moved back. By this time our supporting battalion, the 1/4th Royal Lancaster Regiment, had merged itself into our line, and the combined forces of the two battalions formed a line of resistance just in front of the black line. Posts of Lewis and machine guns were thrown out as soon as it was dark, and our protective barrage and S.O.S. line was withdrawn to conform with our new line.

In the evening, about 10 p.m., a warning order was received to the effect that the brigade would be relieved by units of the 165th Brigade.

Further general observations will be made under date August 1st.

Casualties during operations on the 31st July:—

Officers:—

Killed—Captain A. L. Harris (commanding A Company), Second Lieutenant G. Ashcroft (Signals), Second Lieutenant B. H. Williams (Intelligence Officer), Second Lieutenant V. Mather, Second Lieutenant F. Fullerton, and Second Lieutenant J. H. Ogden (Commanding B Company).

Died of Wounds—Captain R. W. Shegog, R.A.M.C.

Wounded and Missing—Lieutenant D. H. Ostrehan (Commanding D Company), and Second Lieutenant C. Rigby.

Missing—Second Lieutenant D. H. McSweeney and Second Lieutenant H. S. Holden.

Wounded—Second Lieutenant H. Tyldesley, Second Lieutenant H. C. Vincent, Second Lieutenant F. C. Jenkinson, Second Lieutenant E. M. Easterby, Captain R. Ord, Captain W. L. B. Caley, Second Lieutenant L. Howarth (with 164th T.M.B.), and Second Lieutenant J. E. Ordish.

Other Ranks:—Killed 44, Wounded 179, Missing 77.

Total Casualties:—Officers 19, Other Ranks 300.

1st August, 1917. Following message has been received:—

Well done, one-six-four. I am very proud of what you did today. It was a fine performance, and no fault of yours you could not stay.

General Jeudwine.

I congratulate all units on having earned this praise, which I know to be well deserved.

C. I. Stockwell,
Brigadier-General,
Commanding 164th Infantry Brigade.

The above account may now be amplified and illuminated by a short summary of the adventures of each company and platoon—taken from the original narratives of the battalion, which, written in most cases from the account of surviving private soldiers, are now in the custody of Colonel C. F. Coop, D.S.O., at Liverpool.

A Company lost its commander, Captain Harris, soon after passing the black line—he was shot by a sniper; C.S.M. Dudley was later on wounded and taken prisoner; No. 1 Platoon had its commander (Sergeant Entwistle) and the Lewis Gun corporal wounded when leaving Congreve Walk. It came under machine gun fire just before reaching the black line, and by the time it reached Kansas Cross only eleven were left.

About 12 45 p.m. a heavy machine gun barrage started on our line, and about 2 pm. the enemy were seen counter-attacking over ridge on our right, and I saw the Highlanders withdrawing. This was immediately followed by an attack on our left. We held on for fully half an hour, when the order came down from the right, 'Go back, one by one.' Only six of our platoon were left. We withdrew to shell holes 50 yards back, though the people on our left and right had fallen farther back. The enemy were then very close to us, and I think he captured one or two prisoners.

At this point we lost touch on both flanks, because we were in advance of the rest of the line; we therefore withdrew as well as we could, fighting and firing as we went. We managed to rejoin our own line just before dusk, and found a few more of our platoon who had become separated.

No. 2 was held up in front of Somme Farm, a machine gun playing on it from there; a tank came up and reported to Second Lieutenant McSweeney and moved to attack.

No. 2 rushed the machine gun and took 60 prisoners. The position consisted of about six very strong concrete dugouts, one of which was a Regimental Aid Post and contained several wounded enemy.

At the green line they came under heavy shell fire. The enemy could be seen in full flight, and our Lewis gunners fired on them. There were 15 or 16 of the platoon left, and they began to dig in; they were in touch on both flanks.

Later they saw the enemy advancing to counter-attack over the ridge in front, in several waves, extending to about one and a half yards between each man, and Second Lieutenant McSweeney was taken prisoner.

Second Lieutenant Tyldsley, commanding No. 3. was wounded just after passing the black line, when it came under very heavy machine gun fire but advanced to the green line without ever being held up.

No. 4 Platoon had ten killed and three wounded by one shell before leaving Congreve Walk, and Second Lieutenant Ordish was wounded during the advance.

They were held up by Somme and by a further line of strong points 150 yards beyond, from which they got about 20 prisoners.

Lieutenant Ogden, Commanding B Company, was killed.

No. 5 went through Somme, and most of the garrison gave themselves up. A few tried to run away, and were fired on.

They went through to the outpost line and began to dig in. Second Lieutenant Mather was siting the trench when he was killed by a sniper's bullet, and Sergeant Nabb took over the platoon.

No. 6, after A Company had dealt with Somme, moved on to a line of posts about 500 or 600 yards farther on, which they passed on the flank and moved on to the outpost line.

No. 7 Platoon, except Lewis gunners, were detached to carry trench mortar ammunition for the 164th Trench Mortar Battery. Eighteen men were detached for this purpose. Ten became casualties before leaving Congreve Walk, one shell hitting the lot. The remaining eight carried up their loads, but quickly became casualties; only two arrived at the green line, carrying four rounds each.

Sergeant Ward was killed.

No. 8 Platoon was detached to mop up Kansas Cross, and was formed up in rear of No. 4 Platoon, A Company. It suffered ten casualties from shell fire before leaving Congreve Walk, all the bombers being knocked out, and had a few more casualties before reaching the black line, and when it got to Kansas Cross it was only about eight or nine strong.

> There were a few concrete dugouts and a trench just on our side of Kansas Cross, also a few ruined buildings. We captured 50 prisoners here, all of whom gave themselves up without a fight—slightly wounded men taking them back. After completing the mopping-up, we moved on to assist in consolidation. Here Second Lieutenant Rigby was wounded.

No. 9 Platoon suffered many casualties from machine gun traversing fire, but went on to the outpost line. Second Lieutenant Jenkinson was badly wounded just before getting to the green line, and four Germans, who gave themselves up, carried him down. Prisoners were coming in in 20's and 30's.

No. 10, under Second Lieutenant Higson, mopped up Keir Farm, where two concrete dugouts were found and a number of prisoners taken, also documents, some of which were taken from an enemy liaison officer. They advanced to the green line, and commenced to consolidate.

> No British contact 'planes flew over; we only saw three enemy 'planes, who flew so low that they fired at us; also an observation balloon ascended from Abraham Heights.
>
> About two hours after reaching the green line the enemy were observed to be forming up on the heights in front of us, and eventually counter-attacked on our right against the 15th Division, who commenced to retire. We formed a defensive flank on our right to get enfilade fire on the enemy and so cover the retreat of the 15th Division, but they retired behind us and could give us no assistance when we were compelled to retire. By this time the enemy had got a machine gun barrage on our

front, also enfilading us on our left, and caused a number of casualties; we fought a rearguard action along with the rest of the battalion until we reached the black line.

S.O.S. signals were sent up from the green line, but they all failed to burst.

No. 11, under Lieutenant Lonsdale, got held up by the belt of wire running down the left of Hill 35. This wire had hardly been touched, but they cut a way through after some time and managed to catch up the barrage.

From Somme Farm came a lot of machine gun fire, so we hung back a bit and waited for our left flank to come up; we trained our Lewis gun on to the farm to assist the people on our left. When they approached fairly close about a dozen of the enemy attempted to make off, but were either caught by our fire or gave themselves up. From the trenches running through D 13 central, the enemy began to retire. We opened fire on them and caused some casualties; some got away and seemed to have left their equipment and rifles. Gallipoli held out for some time, but we engaged it with the Lewis gun while the remainder worked round it. The garrison surrendered—about 25 in number. Men went in the rear side and reported strong machine gun emplacements.

From Keir Farm I saw about six men run without tunics, but a lot held out until we got round them; about 20 men gave themselves up from here. The point D 14 c 12 was searched and found to be a battery position—as far as I could make out, three guns. A corporal and two men were told off to search for papers, documents, etc. I pressed on with the Platoon, and at a line in front and to the left of Martha House we came under point-blank artillery fire from near Kansas Cross, but did not stop our advance; it only seemed to be from one or two guns. At D 14 c 38 we found a battery position, two guns untouched but several damaged, and an officer gave himself up with several men.

We then pushed on to the green line and got in touch with the people on our right and sent out patrols to the left, but could not get in touch. Some of the King's Own then came up and were sent on to the left. Having pushed Lewis guns forward with patrols, we commenced to consolidate, and put in a good two and a half hours. At 2.30 p.m. the patrols reported a counter-attack on the right and left. We stood to and opened a heavy rifle and Lewis gun fire on them, sending up two S.O.S.'s, but neither of them worked.

In the meantime three enemy aeroplanes flew over our lines, dropping flares and opening machine gun fire on us. The machine gun fire from the left began to account for a lot of our men. The enemy appeared in strength, being in open order. I counted six lines, and yet there were more following. The sections on our right began to retire across our rear, and the enemy was beginning to get well behind us. The left were also pressing, so we decided to retire from the left, covering the retirement with rifle and Lewis gun fire. We then took up a line running from approx. D 20 a 89 to D 14 c 72 in shell holes.

We formed a defensive flank of three Lewis guns along a small ridge to our right. The enemy pressed on, although we were accounting for a large number with our rifle fire and the enfilade Lewis gun fire on the right. The Lewis guns ran short of S.A.A. After we had made a stand for about an hour, the S.A.A for the rifles ran short; we collected as much as we could from the dead and wounded, but it was only about ten rounds per man. The enemy again succeeded in working round our right, so we had to retire, fighting a rearguard action on to the old Frezenberg line.

No. 12 ran into two strong points, and in each case the garrison gave themselves up. Fifty prisoners came out of one. Both consisted of concrete dugouts, with trenches in front, and behind one of them there was a concrete gun emplacement. Sergeant Whiteside, the platoon commander, was wounded.

When the enemy counter-attacked on our right the Scots retired, and Lieutenant Hore sent some of our party to form a defensive line on the right flank. We held on for about three-quarters of an hour, and then we withdrew, dropping in shell holes and firing as we went back. They fired machine guns on us as we withdrew. A good number of our wounded were captured, but no unwounded prisoners, as far as I know.

No. 13 got to the green line and consolidated this, but got mixed up with other platoons.

None of us know what happened to Sergeant Yates. We saw him just before the withdrawal, and he was then unwounded. Nobody saw him again.

Second Lieutenant Easterby, Commanding No. 14, was wounded twice, the second time being just beyond the black line.

Two snipers who caused trouble near Gallipoli were captured. The platoon consolidated the green line until 2.30 p.m., when the enemy counter-attacked on the right. The Scots on the right were seen to withdraw, and Second Lieutenant Fullerton, who had taken over command of the whole line, shouted to us to hang on. He himself established a defensive flank on our right, but was shortly afterwards killed.

No. 15, after going 500 or 600 yards, ran into a strong point.

The barrage had knocked out a machine gun which had been playing on us, but rifle fire continued to come from this place. We went straight on, and when we neared the place they gave themselves up. There were about three dugouts—connected—and about 20 prisoners were taken.

On reaching our objective we dug in under machine gun fire from our left. About 1.15 p.m. we saw the smoke of an engine on the other side of the ridge. About half an hour after this the enemy appeared over the ridge, and advanced towards us. We opened on him with Lewis guns. He was covering his advance with machine guns on the left. The 6th Camerons were seen retiring, and took up a position in a strong point about 150 yards behind our trench. We hung on to our trench for 20 minutes or half an hour. Second Lieutenant Fullerton acted with great gallantry during this trying period. He persuaded the whole of our line to hang on—he was the only officer left in the green line—and it was a great loss when he was killed, just before we withdrew.

Only seven of this platoon survived.

No. 16 was first held up at Gallipoli, but continued the advance, and 150 yards further on found another strong point, consisting of a trench and a few dugouts. The garrison of the post—about 25 in all—gave themselves up immediately. They then moved on to the green line, and commenced to dig in. They had been digging for over an hour when the enemy counter-attacked on the right.

Twenty minutes previous we had seen the smoke of a train. For a time he was disorganised by our machine guns and Lewis gun fire; then he advanced on the front of the battalion on our right, which withdrew immediately, and the enemy followed. Second Lieutenant Fullerton ordered us to line the hedge on our right, and we held on there for half an hour. Meanwhile the enemy tried to get round behind us, and to a certain extent succeeded.

Our position was then so bad and our ammunition supply so small that we had to withdraw, moving back step by step in small parties. Gradually we worked back to the black line, though some of our men—including Lieutenant Holden—were captured.

EXTRACT FROM WAR DIARY CONTINUED.

At 12 midnight, July 31st August 1st, the battalion held a line of resistance just in front of the black line. At 1.15 a.m. completion of relief by the 165th Infantry Brigade was reported, and the remnant of the battalion were ordered to concentrate in our original front line between Warwick Farm and Lone Street. This was done, and Battalion Headquarters was established at the mined dugouts in Oxford Trench. At 10 a.m. headquarters was transferred to the mined dugout at Wieltje.

Meanwhile an effort was being made to collect our stragglers. During the withdrawal a great many men had become separated from their platoons, and by 2 p.m. on the 1st of August only 90 of our men had assembled in the old front line. In ones and twos they were eventually brought in, though some remained behind with the 165th and 166th Brigades in the black line till 24 hours or more after the battalion had been relieved.

The weather was desperate; rain was pouring down all day, and the trenches were in a terrible state. Four or five derelict tanks could be counted, stuck deep in the mud, either in our old front line or in the German original front line. The day was fairly quiet, and there was only a little shelling in the vicinity of Wieltje.

About mid-day the enemy counter-attacked on the front of the division on our right, and succeeded in making a small breach in the black line. In the evening of this day a cooker was brought up with hot tea, etc., for the men.

Lieutenant G. J. Fismer, R.A.M.C, reported for duty *vice* Captain

R. W. Shegog, R.A.M.C, died of wounds.

Casualties: Officers: Lieutenant C. L. Hore, M.C., to Field Ambulance sick; Other ranks: Nil.

With reference to the attack in which the battalion took part, the following points are of interest:—

> 1. Ammunition ran short in every company, a proof of the fact that the rifle has again come to its own as the chief weapon of the infantryman.
>
> 2. It is estimated that quite 90 *per cent,* of the casualties were caused by machine gun fire and snipers.
>
> 3. Casualties amongst officers were exceedingly heavy, and great responsibility devolved upon N.C.O.'s. This fact emphasised the necessity for careful preparation, by means of daily lectures and demonstrations to all platoon sergeants and section commanders.
>
> 4. It is generally agreed that on this occasion the men were far too heavily laden. It is thought that in an attack of this kind, when a distance of several thousand yards has to be traversed, it is far better to go lightly equipped, and to trust to the probability of being able to get additional supplies of water and rations from the rear as soon as darkness falls.
>
> 5. All systems of communication, except runners, broke down. Visual was impossible owing to the dull mist which prevailed, and wires, when once laid, were soon broken.
>
> 6. Tanks were a failure (except possibly in one case), the ground being far too wet and heavy. One tank is said to have done useful work in co-operation with the infantry in reducing Somme Farm.
>
> 7. Aeroplanes for some reason failed us, the R.F.C. evidently considering the bad visibility sufficient reason to cancel flying. This was particularly unfortunate, as the enemy were not slow to take advantage accordingly, and three hostile machines are reported to have been flying over our positions practically all the time that consolidation was in progress. In one case a machine gun was fired at our troops.
>
> 8. Lastly, many acts of extreme gallantry and devotion to duty were reported after the fighting of the 31st July, on the part of all ranks of the battalion.

In fact the 55th Division as a whole, and particularly the 164th Brigade, will ever be remembered for its share in the attack which started the third Battle of Ypres. The 164th Infantry Brigade in particular can ever be proud of the advance from the black line to the green line.

Copies of the following messages and letters are attached:—

(1) From Major-General H. S. Jeudwine, C.B., G.O.C. 55th Division, to Brigadier-General C. I. Stockwell, D.S.O., Commanding 164th Brigade.

(2) 55th Division Special Order of the Day.

(3) Letter from 5th Army Headquarters to XIX. Corps.

(4) 5th Army Commander's Congratulations.

Fifth Army.
2nd August, 1917.

Appendix to D.R.O.'s of 7th August, 1917.
Army Commander's Congratulations.

1. The Army Commander wishes to offer his heartiest congratulations to the troops under his command on the success gained by them on July 31st.

2. For a fortnight prior to the attack the enemy has maintained a heavy and continuous artillery fire, including an unprecedented use of H.V. guns against back areas and a new form of gas shell, all of which caused severe casualties. Despite this and the fact that the forward area was dominated by the enemy at all points, the necessary preparations for the battle were completed and the difficult forward march and assembly of nine Divisions successfully carried out and the assault launched. This alone constitutes a performance of which the army may well be proud.

3. As a result of the battle, the enemy has once again been driven by the 1st French Army and ourselves from the whole of his front system on a front of about eight miles, and we are now firmly established in or beyond his second line on a front of seven miles.

4. We have already captured 5,448 prisoners, including 125 officers. Up to date the capture of eight guns, 10 trench mortars, and 36 machine guns has been reported.

5. In addition we have inflicted extremely heavy casualties on the enemy. Owing to losses during our preliminary bombardment, he was forced to bring up six fresh divisions. Since then three more divisions have been withdrawn shattered. Thus, in a fortnight, we have disposed of seven or eight divisions and severely handled 10 more, several of which must be shortly withdrawn.

6. The 2nd Army on our right and the 1st French Army on our left have been as successful as ourselves. The French captures to date number 157 prisoners and three guns. The 2nd Army have also taken 390 prisoners and several machine guns.

7. Despite the weather on the day of the battle, we shot down five enemy machines and one balloon, losing only one machine ourselves.

(Signed)

R. T. Collins,
Lieutenant-Colonel,
For Major-General, G.S.

55th (West Lancashire Division.
Special Order of the Day.

3rd August, 1917.

To All Ranks of the 55th (West Lancashire) Division.

Before you went into action on the 31st July, I told you how confident I was that the division would do its duty and maintain its reputation and the reputation of the grand regiments to which you belong.

You have done more than that.

The attack you made on the 31st is worthy to rank with the great deeds of the British Army in the past, and has added fresh glory to the record of that army.

The courage, determination, and self-sacrifice shown by officers, warrant officers, non-commissioned officers, and men is beyond praise. It is a fine exhibition of true discipline, which comes from the mutual confidence of all ranks in themselves, their comrades, their leaders, and those under them. This in its turn is the product of hard training. Your doings on the 31st show how well you have turned this training to account.

You captured every inch of the objectives allotted to you. It was not your fault that you could not hold all you took. You have broken and now hold, in spite of weather and counter-attacks, a line that the enemy has strengthened and consolidated at his leisure for more than two years.

This will, I believe, be the beginning of the end. When your turn comes to go forward again you will know your own strength and the enemy will know it too.

I am proud of what you have done and am confident that with such troops ultimate victory is certain.

H. S. Jeudwine,
Major-General,
Commanding 55th (West Lancashire) Division.

Fifth Army.
3rd August, 1917.

XIX. Corps.

The Army Commander wishes to convey his thanks and congratulations to the G.O.C. and all ranks of the 164th Brigade on their fine performance on July 31st. They carried out their task in a most gallant manner and fought splendidly to retain their hold on the ground won. All officers showed energy, courage, and initiative in dealing with the situation, and the men under their command, in spite of heavy losses, did their utmost, by carrying out their orders, to ensure our success and the enemy's defeat.

Great credit and praise is due to the G.O.C. 164th Brigade for the magnificent behaviour of the troops under his command.

(Signed)　　　　　　　　　　　　　　N. Malcolm,
Major-General, G.S.

The Brigadier-General commanding has much pleasure in forwarding the above remarks of the Army Commander and directs that these be communicated to all ranks.

He considers that all the credit and praise is due to the officers and men of the brigade.

Captain,
Acting Brigade Major,
164th Infantry Brigade.

6th August, 1917.

CHAPTER 7

Reorganisation, and the Battle of the Menin Road

On the 2nd August, 1917, the remnant of the battalion was relieved by the 9th Royal Irish Rifles (36th-Ulster-Division), and assembled at a camp near Vlamertinghe, where they found the members of B team and food, and had a good sleep. At 10 p.m. that night we moved in motor 'buses to the Watou area, where we took over our old camp. Lieutenant G. M. Fismer, R.A.M.C, and one other rank had been wounded in coming out of the line, and Lieutenant J. E. Ratcliffe reported as medical officer; on the following day Lieutenant W. L. Price and Second Lieutenants R. Grisdale and A. P. Smith and 108 other ranks reported as reinforcements.

On the 5th we marched to Abeele, where we entrained and travelled *via* St. Omer and Watten to Audruicq, arriving there about 5 p.m. Here we found lorries waiting to take us to our new billeting area, Audrehem, a pleasant village just big enough to hold us.

On the 7th, Second Lieutenant Holden came back from attachment to the R.E.'s with 23 other ranks, and Captain C. M. Denton and 34 other ranks reported as reinforcements. During the next few days Captain Houghton, Second Lieutenant Vincent and Second Lieutenant Swaine rejoined us and Major de Wend Fenton. Second Lieutenant F. Shippobottom and Second Lieutenant A. B. Fergie reported for duty along with nine other ranks, while on the 18th Second Lieutenant J. Hailwood and A. Martin, and on the 21st Second Lieutenants A. H. Doleman, S. A. H. Pruden, and Iners joined us, followed by Second Lieutenants H. W. C. Griffiths, H. Dance, and J. Oldham on the 22nd.

The following honours were announced for gallantry in action in the recent battle:—

Bar to D.S.O.	Lieutenant-Colonel R. Hindle, D.S.O.
Military Cross	Second Lieutenant H. C. Vincent, B Company.
	Second Lieutenant H. Lonsdale, C Company.
D.C.M.	24908 Lance-Corporal E. Ashton, A Company.
	201260 Lance-Corporal T. Butcher, A Company.
Military Medal	200057 Sergeant J. Heaps, Headqrs.
	201530 Lance-Corporal P. Norris, B Company.
	200643 Sergeant J. E. Cookson, D Company.
	34879 Sergeant J. Cosgrove, C Company.
	200809 Corporal F. Pitcher, B Company.
	200414 Lance-Corporal W. H. Clarkson, Hqrs.
	202761 Private J. Spencer, D Company.
	200146 Private J. Bates, Transport.
	200357 Private J. H. Parkinson, Transport.
	12910 Private D. Rathbone, C Company.
	31987 Lance-Corporal J. Walmsley, A Company.

It is fashionable among fighting men to belittle the honours which they themselves have earned, knowing as they do that many individuals employed at bases have received decorations which were never meant to be conferred for anything except gallantry in action, while others who have abundantly deserved them have either died before they were granted or have had no witness surviving to report their conduct; it is therefore only fair to mention that when "immediate awards," such as the above, are made to fighting men, it is as a result of reports sent in by eyewitnesses, which, in our battalion at any rate, were tested by cross-examining those mentioned in them as to the deeds of others, the resulting list of recommendations being further checked and often cut down by brigade.

We enjoyed our stay at Audrehem, knowing that our last battle had raised us to the status of Storm Troops, and that when we moved up again it would be for another attack and not back to the demoralising influences of trench life. With this in view we carefully reorganised and trained, all ranks working together keenly with one end in view efficiency, with the result that in six weeks a tired, straggling, muddy, shaken remnant was transformed once more into a smart battalion, well organised and equipped, and trained with special reference to attacking concrete blockhouses. Officers daily attended lectures by one of their number on some phase of the attack, and company commanders held daily conferences of their N.C.O.'s and senior privates, so that however heavy might be the casualties among leaders, someone might remain with the necessary knowledge to carry on.

Every fine day companies marched with their cookers to the training area at Guemy, and remained there all day doing progressive field training; there was football, boxing, a divisional horse show, and other delights, as well as brigade days, and the commander-in-chief himself came one day to see us at work; so the days slipped by until the 14th September. Captain Duckworth went as second in command to the 1/8th King's Liverpool Regiment, and various other officers left us sick or to other units, so that when B team had been detailed the following officers moved up to take part in the attack:

Lieutenant-Colonel R. Hindle, D.S.O.   Commanding.
Captain A. T. Houghton   Second in Command.
Captain R. N. Buckmaster   Adjutant.
Lieutenant Bardsley   Transport Officer.
Second Lieutenant Brooke   Intelligence Officer.
Second Lieutenant Whitehouse   Signalling Officer.
Lieutenant Radcliffe, R.A.M.C.   Medical Officer,

A Company.

Lieutenant E. G. Baker
Second Lieutenant A. P. Smith
Second Lieutenant H. Dance
Second Lieutenant J. Oldham

B Company.

Captain F. W. S. Baker
Major Fenton
Second Lieutenant Holmes
Second Lieutenant Fergie

C Company.

Captain R. H. Tautz
Second Lieutenant Pruden
Second Lieutenant Grisdale

D Company.

Lieutenant Holden
Lieutenant Price
Second Lieutenant Martin
Second Lieutenant Myers

On the 14th the battalion, including B team, marched to Aubruicq,

Aeroplane Photo taken 9th September, 1917, from a point near Pond Farm

proceeding thence by train to a point near Ypres, where we took over a bivouac camp near Goldfish Château— a muddy field with pits dug all over it, each just big enough to shelter two or three men, and covered with sheets of corrugated iron.

Since 31st July, 1917, the ground along the Steenbeek captured by us on that day had been the scene of bloody fighting, two attempts by other divisions to advance beyond the black line of the previous attack having, been made and having failed, so that with small variations the front taken over by us on 15th September was identical with that held when we had come out six weeks before.

The ground over which we had to pass was commanded by two spurs—the Grafenstafel Spur half a mile to the north, and the Gallipoli Spur, part of which was within our frontage, to the south; and apart from the concrete blockhouses on our own front, every yard of our advance was raked by machine gun bullets from innumerable others on our flanks, so that until these were put out of action no advance was possible without appalling losses.

Add to this the total absence of landmarks in that amorphous wilderness, where no trees, no blade of grass remained, every square yard of ground having been churned up by our shell fire—the extreme difficulty of distinguishing one blockhouse from another—the fact that companies had been reduced to three platoons and platoons to only 20 men owing to lack of sufficient reinforcements—and when you have studied the maps and photographs and tried to visualise the ground, you may form some idea of what the battalion had to do on the 20th September, 1917. The Grafenstafel Road was our one hope of keeping direction—the road which, as the photographs clearly show, became utterly indistinguishable from the surrounding mire within 260 yards of our starting point; when this failed, general direction was only kept by use of the compass.

The material paragraphs of the Operation Order and the official account of the battle are as follows:—

The Operation Order.

1. (a) The 55th Division will attack on Z day. The 9th Division will be on the right, and the 58th Division on the left.

(b) The 165th Infantry Brigade will be on the right, the 164th Infantry Brigade on the left, the 166th Brigade less two battalions will be in reserve.

(c) The 1/4th Royal Lancaster Regiment and the 1/4th Loyal

North Lancashire Regiment will be in the right or Keir sector.

The 2/5th Lancashire Fusiliers in the centre or Cotts sector.

The 1/8th Liverpool Regiment in the left or Schuler sector.

The 1/5th Royal Lancaster Regiment will be attached to the 164th Infantry Brigade and be available for the countering of enemy counter-attacks.

2. On the night 13th/14th the (German) 2nd Guards Reserve Division came into the line opposite to the 55th Divisional front and is reported to be holding the line with all three regiments up, one battalion of each regiment being in the line, one in support, and one in immediate reserve.

Those in reserve are located west of the Passchendale Ridge.

3. (a) First pause of the barrage   Red Dotted Line.
First objective in   Yellow Line.
Final objective in   Green Line.

4. It is the intention to capture and occupy as a line of resistance the green line.

The attack will be made in stages under cover of a creeping barrage. There will be a pause of at least half an hour on the red dotted line and again on the yellow line.

5. The plan of attack and objectives will be as follows:—In the Keir sector:

The 1/4th Royal Lancaster Regiment will attack at zero in four waves, the first two waves extended and the second two in columns.

Objectives:—First two waves   Red Dotted Line.
              Second two waves   Yellow Line,
after which they will support the capture of the Green Line.

In the Cotts sector :

The 2/5th Lancashire Fusiliers will attack at zero, in four waves.

Objectives:—First wave   Red Dotted Line.
              Second wave   Yellow Line.
              Third wave   Green Line, an advanced strong point established at Green House.

In the Schuler sector:—

Two Companies 1/8th Liverpool Regiment will attack at zero in two waves.

Objectives:—First wave   Red Dotted Line.
              Second wave   Yellow Line.

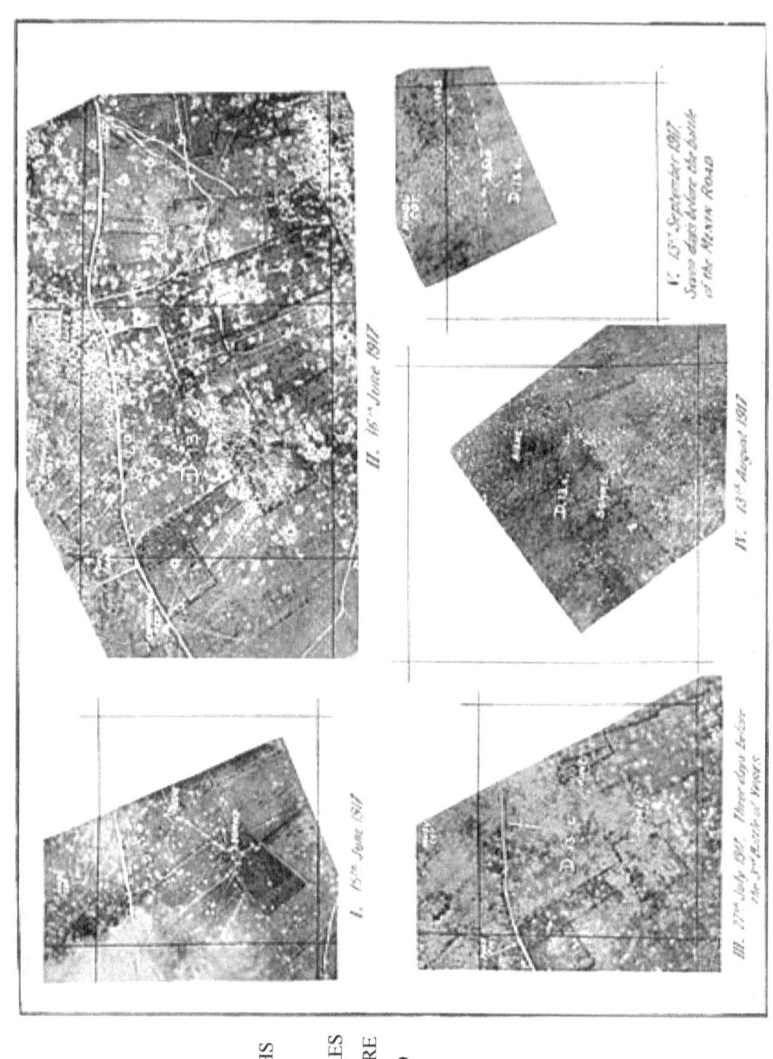

FIVE AEROPLANE PHOTOGRAPHS SHOWING THE GRADUAL DISAPPEARANCE OF ALL FEATURES AND LANDMARKS IN MAP SQUARE D. 13 C. BETWEEN JUNE AND SEPTEMBER, 1917

Two companies will be in the hands of the officer commanding 1/8th Liverpool Regiment.

6. The battalion will assemble in three lines at 20 yards' distance, the leading line being about 150 yards west of the assembly line of the 1/4th Royal Lancaster Regiment in the following order:—

First wave, from right to left—14 Platoon, 13 Platoon, 1 Platoon, 2 Platoon.

Second wave, from right to left—9 Platoon, 10 Platoon, 11 Platoon, 5 Platoon, 6 Platoon, 7 Platoon.

Third wave, from right to left—15 Platoon, machine guns, 3 Platoon.

Captain Houghton will be responsible for the taping of these lines and supplying two guides to each company to lead them to their position of assembly.

7. Distribution of companies during the advance:—

First wave, from right to left—Two Platoons D Company, two Platoons A Company.

Second wave, from right to left—C Company, B Company.

Third wave, from right to left—One Platoon D Company, one Platoon A Company.

The first wave will form two lines of extended order before crossing the Yellow Line.

The objective of the first wave will be an outpost line passing through Fokker Farm D14 c 99 and D 14 d 15.

Garrisons will be detailed in advance:—For Fokker Farm by A Company, and dugouts D 14 d 16 by D Company.

Strong points will be constructed at these points and others in between should it be found necessary, the principle being that the whole front should be:—

(a) Covered by enfilade machine gun or Lewis gun fire.

(b) Under observation.

The objective of the second wave will be approximately the green line.

The garrison will be detailed beforehand for the dugouts D 14 c 49 by B Company.

The objectives of the third wave will be to ensure that the first and second waves reach their objectives.

Garrisons will be detailed beforehand for dugouts D 14 c 44 and Martha House by D Company.

OBJECTIVES IN THE BATTLE OF THE MENIN ROAD

MAP NO. 3

Sept. 20th. 1917

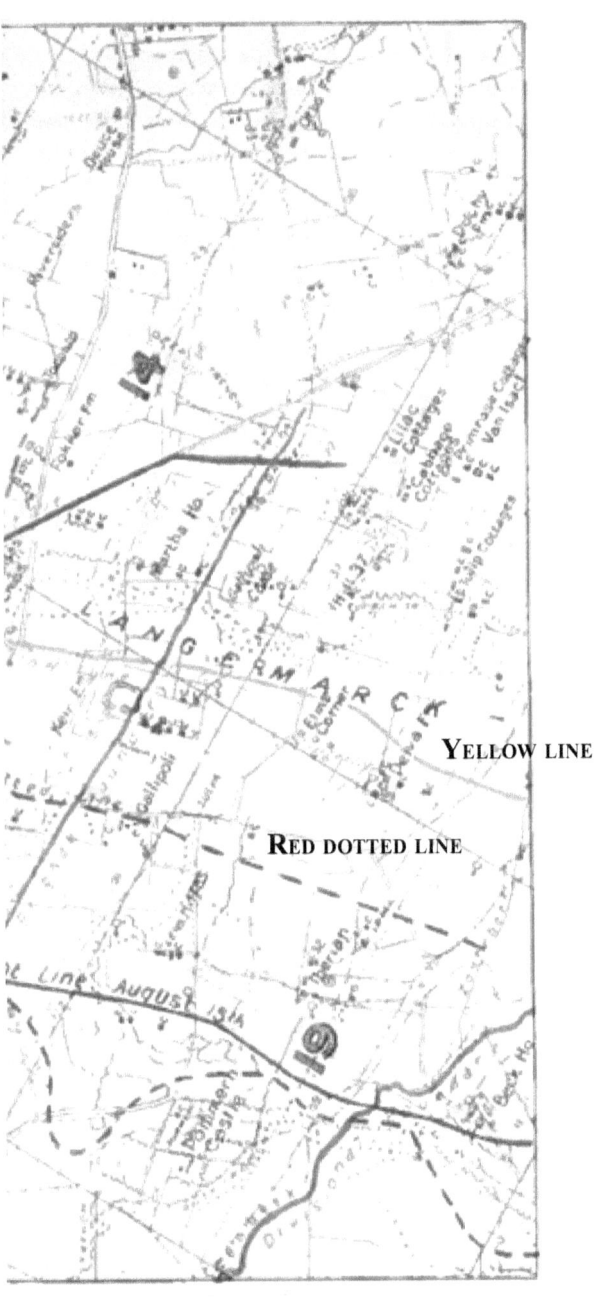

Dugouts at D 14 a 20 and Kansas House by A Company.

8. Unexpected concrete defences encountered during the advance will be garrisoned and consolidated, as soon as the final objective is taken, on the following principle: Each wave will be responsible for all ground between itself and the leading line of the wave in its rear. Should any pockets of the enemy still remain, they will be mopped up as this is taking place.

12. The reserve battalion (1/5th Royal Lancaster Regiment) will arrive in the area Aisne-Hindu Cot-Pond Farm about the time that the green line is taken.

The role of this battalion will be to deliver an immediate counter-stroke against any hostile counter-attack.

13. Prisoners' escorts, messengers, etc., when returning to their companies from the rear, will take back six bandoliers of S.A.A. from the forward dumps.

14. Dress:—Fighting order, with packs instead of haversacks. Every N.C.O. and man will carry:—

1 No. 23 rifle grenade.
2 Aeroplane flares.
4 Sandbags.
1 Bandolier extra S.A.A.—Carried in the pack.
1 Lewis gun magazine

Parties of men specially selected to deal with dugouts will carry two No. 23 rifle grenades.

Every rifle grenadier will carry six Hales No. 24 rifle grenades.

Shovels will be carried by every man, less runners, signallers, stretcher bearers, and Nos. 1 and 2 of Lewis gun teams.

Men carrying shovels will not carry the entrenching tool.

Bayonets will not be fixed until immediately before leaving the assembly line,

15. The battalion will be fitted out on the early morning of Y day. Bombs and S.A.A. will be drawn from the St. Jean dump by small parties from each company. At the same time parties will draw shovels and sandbags from the Divisional R.E. dump, St. Jean Wieltje Road, 600 yards west of Wieltje. These carrying parties must have returned to Congreve Walk-Liverpool Line by 5.30 a.m. on Y day. After that hour there must be no movement over the open.

16. The brigade main dump is at C 23 c 31 (old German front line). Advanced brigade dumps are established at Spree Farm (C 18 d

53) and at dugouts C 18 d 75.

17. All ranks will carry during the attack the iron ration and the unexpended portion of Z day's rations.

Rations for Z plus 1 day will be dumped as far forward as possible. Water bottles will be filled from the water-carts on the evening of Y day.

18. Barrage map will be issued later.

19. Points for Liaison:

With 2/5th Lancashire Fusiliers	Kansas House.
	D 14 a 02.
With 1/6th Liverpool Regiment	D 14 c 54.
	D 14 c 95 40.

20. Headquarters 164th and 165th Infantry Brigades will be the Wieltje dugout. Battalion Headquarters will be at the commencement Capricorn Keep and dugouts C 18 d 86; subsequent moves will be notified.

21. Aid Post: Pond Farm, C 18 b 80.

22. Zero Hour will be 5.40 a.m.

Watches will be synchronised.

23. Communication between companies and Battalion Headquarters will be by runner and visual.

All messages will be duplicated by a second means of transmission. Two pigeons will be carried by D Company and two by A Company, moving in the leading wave.

Second Lieutenant Whitehurst will be responsible for:—

(a) Laying a wire from Battalion Headquarters to brigade forward station at Pond Farm, and from Battalion Headquarters to battalion forward command post.

(b) Establishing visual between Battalion Headquarters and battalion forward command post about D 13 central, if practicable.

(c) Establishing relay runner posts about D 13 c 26, D 13 d 16, and Keir Farm.

Contact 'plane can be recognised by a rectangular attachment on both lower planes and a white dumb-bell on either side of the body.

Whenever the 'plane calls for signals by sounding the klaxon horn or firing a white Verey light, the most advanced lines of infantry will:—

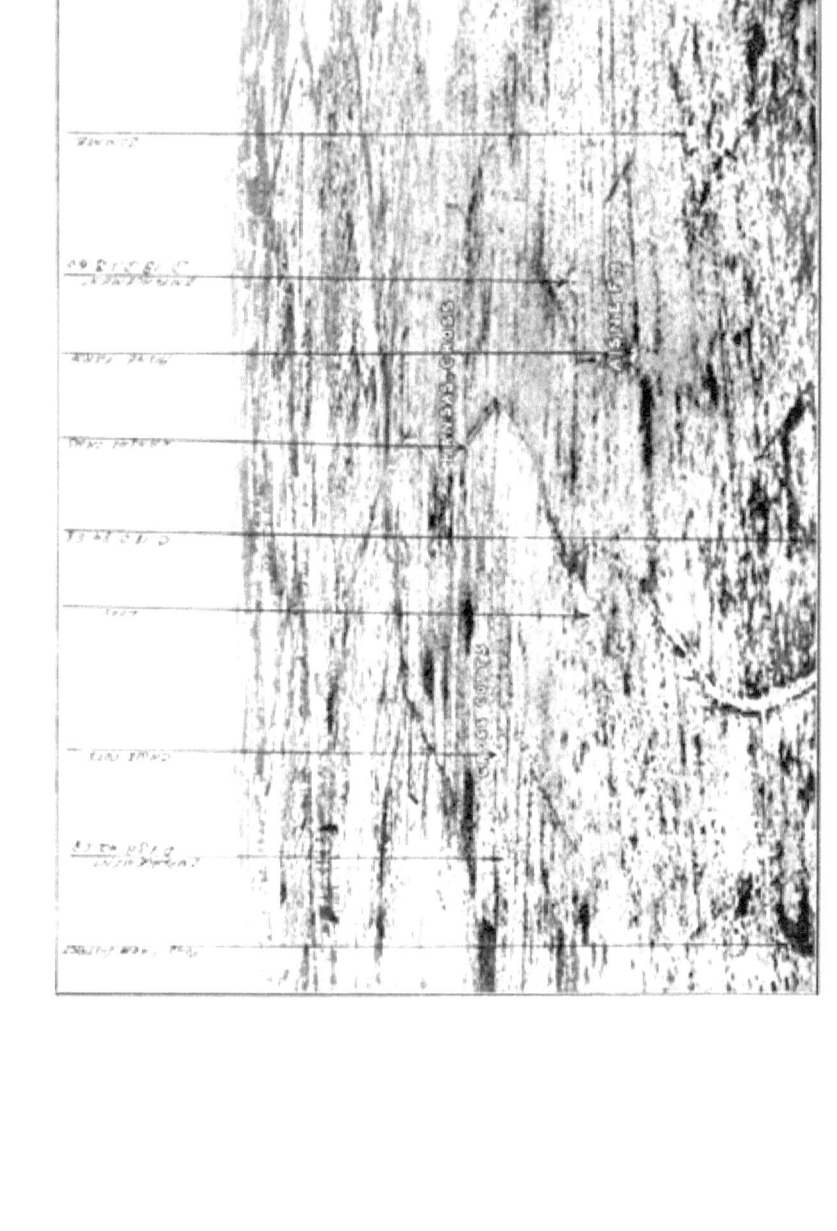

(a) Light flares in the bottom of a shell hole.

(b) Show Watson fans white and coloured sides alternately 30 seconds.

The 'plane will call for signals at Zero plus 1 hour.

Zero plus 2 hours.
Zero plus 2½ hours,

and at such other times as may be necessary.

S.O.S. signal is a rifle grenade bursting into two red and two green lights.

24. Second Lieutenant Brooke will be responsible for:—

(a) Keeping liaison with 1/4th Royal Lancaster Regiment during their advance to the Yellow Line.

(b) Establishing a battalion forward command post about D 13 central and keeping the whole front under close observation.

25. Acknowledge in writing.

(Signed)	R. N. L. Buckmaster,
18th September, 1917.	Captain and Adjutant,
Issued at 8 a.m.	1/4th Loyal North Lancashire Regiment.

EXTRACTED FROM WAR DIARY.

Ypres.

15th September. Fairly quiet day.

One other rank reinforcement. One other rank to Field Ambulance sick.

16th September. About 10.45 a.m. 10 enemy aeroplanes dropped bombs in the vicinity of the camp, causing one casualty. Road near camp heavily shelled at dusk.

Two other ranks wounded.

17th September. Situation normal. Reconnaissance of forward area carried out. W day in connection with forthcoming operations.

One other rank killed in Vlamertinghe.

18th September (X day). Day spent in fitting out, etc. On the evening of this day the battalion moved forward to the Congreve Walk-Liverpool Trench line, running through the village of St. Jean. Our artillery were very active throughout the night.

Two other ranks wounded. One other rank died of wounds.

St. Jean (Trenches!.

19th September. Commencing at dawn, our artillery opened the

24 hours' bombardment preparatory to the attack. The enemy's reply during the day was exceedingly feeble.

Commencing 9.30 p.m., the battalion moved off from St. Jean by platoons at 200 yards' distance, *via* the Wieltje-Gravenstafel road. The night was quiet, and there was practically no hostile shelling.

Battalion Headquarters were established at Capricorn Keep (C 18 d 55 65) at 11 p.m. The Keep consisted of six very strong dugouts of reinforced concrete. Three were taken over as headquarters by this unit and three by the 1/4th Royal Lancaster Regiment.

Casualties: Two other ranks killed; three other ranks wounded.

20th September. The battalion was reported in position of assembly at I a.m. The lines to be taken up by the various waves were marked by tape, which had been laid as soon as darkness permitted. When once in position the assaulting troops lay in shell holes until zero hour. A continuous drizzling rain made the ground sticky and the going bad. The line of assembly was a north south line running through Somme (D 13 c 50 25). During the night things were fairly quiet, though lively artillery fire developed on our right soon after 3 a.m.

Zero hour was at 5.40 a.m., at which time the artillery barrage opened.

The 1/4th Loyal North Lancashire Regiment moved forward from the assembly position in rear of the 1/4th Royal Lancaster Regiment. The 1/4th Royal Lancaster Regiment had for its objective (1) the Red Dotted Line and (2) the Yellow Line, and it was intended that the 1/4th Loyal North Lancashire Regiment should "leapfrog" at the Yellow Line and capture and consolidate the Green Line.

The enemy barrage was promptly opened on the approximate line of our assembly position a proof that the enemy were fully prepared for the attack. This caused the three rear waves, i.e., the four companies of the 1/4th Loyal North Lancashire Regiment, to close well up on to the 1/4th Royal Lancaster Regiment, and it appears that in a good many cases this was overdone, causing the two units to be intermingled and considerably undermining the principles of organisation.

The creeping barrage was being governed by two new principles, tried for the first time and designed to combat and counteract the enemy's new system of defence:—(1) there were two definite pauses in the barrage, during which it was intended that companies should replace casualties from the rear and generally reorganise; (2) the barrage started to move forward at the rate of six minutes every hundred yards and later at the rate of eight minutes every hundred yards.

The attack to commence with went well, though a great many casualties were inflicted by enemy machine gun fire, which from the start was very well directed. Aisne Farm was reported taken at 6.5 a.m., though a platoon of the 1/4th Loyal North Lancashires had to give assistance in the attack on this strong point. A message timed 8.17 a.m. stated:

Attack appears to be going well.

The first pause was made on the red dotted line, though apparently very little re-organisation was found practicable. Soon after moving forward again considerable trouble was caused by hostile machine guns on the flanks bringing enfilade fire to bear on our advancing troops. According to reports received, this was particularly the case on the right, where the left battalion of the 105th Infantry Brigade was held up before Gallipoli, as a result of which an enemy machine gun on Hill 37 was playing havoc with the waves in the valley through which we were advancing.

The result of these obstructions on either flank was that the men of this battalion in many cases inclined outwards, leaving an exceedingly thin line facing the original objective. In some cases whole platoons found themselves attacking strong points on the frontage of other battalions. Particularly was this so in the case of Gallipoli, in the ultimate capture of which men of this battalion very materially assisted.

Very few of our men reached the yellow line, though a message from the Battalion O.P., timed 8.45 a.m., stated that it appeared to be taken and consolidation commenced. Finally, therefore, a line of resistance was sited and consolidated about mid-day between the red dotted and yellow line, with posts of Lewis gun teams thrown out 50 to 100 yards to the front.

The enemy was not finally dislodged from the vicinity of Gallipoli and the adjoining Suvla until after 10 a.m., by which time the barrage was of no further assistance.

20th September. At 10.50 a.m. the enemy was reported massing for a counterattack in the vicinity of Nile and Fokker Farms, but nothing except heavy shelling materialised on our front. Soon after 1 p.m. various S.O.S.'s were sent up, and apparently local counter-attacks, without any success, were launched on both our flanks.

In the afternoon an effort was made to reorganise the battalion, which was now reported to consist of only four officers and 60 rifles in the firing line. The right battalion frontage was now being held by a mixed line of the 1/4th Royal Lancaster Regiment and the 1/4th Loyal North Lancashire Regiment, stiffened by two companies of the 1/5th Royal Lancaster Regiment, who, as battalion in brigade reserve, and detailed to assist in the capture of the objective and to deal with any hostile counter-attack, had dug themselves in on a line in rear of our consolidated positions.

About 7 p.m. an officers' patrol went forward to reconnoitre Keir Farm And discover whether it was held by the enemy. This patrol, however, did not succeed in its objective and lost its way, and the project had to be postponed till the following morning.

As soon as darkness allowed, an effort was made to examine our positions and to find out whether measures for defence were complete. They were found to be held by at least six Lewis guns, while there were in all four machine guns, two of which were German, and proved very useful against the enemy.

During the night patrols were sent out, and a further effort made to find the defences of Keir Farm. Keir Farm was not identified, and it was therefore assumed that it no longer existed as a concrete defence. No signs' of the enemy were seen. The night passed without incident, though shelling on both sides was maintained fairly consistently.

Casualties:—

Officers:—Killed—Captain F. W. S. Baker (Commanding B Company), Second Lieutenant A. B. Fergie.

Wounded—Captain R. H. Tautz, M.C. (Commanding C Company), Second Lieutenant E. G. Baker (Commanding A Company), Second Lieutenant A. P. Smith, Second Lieutenant H. Dance, Second Lieutenant J. Oldham, Second Lieutenant R. Grisedale, Second Lieutenant A. Martin, Second Lieutenant B. Myers, Second Lieutenant C. B. Holmes (died of wounds, 28th September, 1917).

Other Ranks:—Killed 23, Wounded 161, Missing 11; Total 195.

Four other ranks reinforcements from base.

The following notes by an officer who was present are added to complete the account:

At about 10 p.m. the battalion began to arrive by platoons, each platoon coming up in silence, knowing we were close up to the enemy outposts, winding in single file over the uneven ground, being shown its tape, filing along it and lying down to wait for the dawn; the assembly was completed by 1 a.m. the hour fixed, and apparently unknown to the enemy.

At this hour, to add to the discomfort, a steady drizzle set in, but a tot of rum was served out and most of the men were soon asleep, to be waked at dawn by the crash of our opening barrage.

Battalion Headquarters retired to Capricorn Keep, while the medical officer and his men settled in Pond Galleries. Both these blockhouses had been built of concrete by the Boche to shelter his reserves from our shelling in earlier days during the days that followed they were severely tested, but never failed us.

At Zero, 5.40 a.m., while it was still dark, down came our creeping barrage, and the King's Own began to advance. Our men had been told to give them a good start and, full of eagerness as they were, would have done so had the answering enemy barrage not come down on their tails; this had been foreseen and its position judged from previous registration, and the assembly position was just in front but only just and the "shorts" got some of our men, causing the rest to hurry and close up on the King's Own, who were already passing Aisne Farm. We had to complete the capture of this, and lost heavily in the process.

Under terrific machine gun fire from the front and both flanks, causing casualties at every step, the two battalions struggled forward to get to grips with their unseen enemies, and soon arrived at the two groups of blockhouses, Loos and Gallipoli, with four others lying between them.

These two groups, though the latter was off the allotted front, at once became the immediate objectives the left hand companies took the Loos blockhouses one by one, nine in all, with bomb and bayonet; the companies on the right swung round and joined the King's Liverpool Regiment in storming Gallipoli; in the centre small parties of men, their officers having been hit, took the other four and so reached the red line.

Lieutenant Brooke went forward, and, with a few signallers, established a forward command post near Loos; our machine gunners came up and turned five of the newly-taken Hun machine guns round on the enemy, and things seemed to be going well, but the hour-long pause of the barrage was too long, the hail of cross-fire from more distant machine guns still continued, and the men, who had sought cover in shell holes, were out of sight and scattered, though strenuous efforts to reorganise were made by the few leaders who remained, and with a certain amount of success. But the line had lost its cohesion, and when the barrage went on only a portion of the line saw it and attempted to follow.

Lieutenant Brooke had notified the capture of the red line to Battalion Headquarters, but no further message coming through, the second in command went forward to clear up the situation; on reaching the red line he could at first see no one, but soon stumbled into a shell hole full of men, and was able, running from one hole to another, to locate the whole line up to the flanks of the adjoining battalions, and to estimate the casualties.

The barrage had already passed the green line and the machine guns in the blockhouses were active. Their crews could see every movement, and the troops on both flanks were stationary, so that at the moment no further advance was likely to succeed—moreover, everyone had had time to feel the reaction. So the order was given to dig in and to send out small patrols to try to occupy the ground immediately in front, and by this means the line was advanced still further.

Lieutenant Holden took charge of one of these, while Second Lieutenant Pruden supervised consolidation.

About this time the Hun seems to have realised the position, for he opened out with every gun he had, shelling the captured pillboxes and putting a very heavy barrage all round the aid post and Battalion Headquarters, but his attempt at counter-attack was beaten off by machine gun, Lewis gun, and rifle fire.

We afterwards found out that Suvla and The Capitol had not been taken, nor had Cross Cots—had they been the cross-machine gun fire on us would have been much less intense.

No praise is too high for our stretcher bearers, who all through that day and the succeeding days toiled without intermission bringing in wounded; the aid post was in the line of the Hun barrage, a concrete structure, with a passage two feet wide on the enemy side with chambers opening off it; the stretcher cases had to be dressed out in the open, while the passage was crowded with walking wounded, some of them Huns—the look of utter weariness and dejection on the faces of the latter was a thing not easily forgotten.

The runners did splendid work; a few were killed as they made their way over the shell-tossed ground-the wonder is that any escaped.

For five days the battalion remained in those shell holes, beating off one counter-attack after another with the help of our gunners, who were truly magnificent. At first it was impossible to reorganise properly owing to the mixing of battalions, but ultimately a definite frontage was allotted to us by brigade, and that night we sorted ourselves out from the King's Own and companies were picked out and given a definite bit of line—A and B in front, C and D in close support. At the same time the line was advanced considerably, especially on the right, the posts on Hill 37 having been taken by the right brigade.

Getting rations up to the line was a terrible business—runners and guides kept losing their way, and more than one party nearly entered Hun territory; but guide wires were laid to companies, the C.Q.M.S.'s did their work splendidly, and the men were fed and kept going.

About 25th September we were relieved by the 59th Division, a genial lot—full strength—who seemed to expect to find trenches and dugouts! Thanks to the tapes and wires which had been laid, relief was quick, and we all dribbled back to St. Jean, where companies assembled by the cookers and had hot tea and rum served out. They were actually singing the revulsion, I suppose.

After a lot of delay we got into trucks on the Decauville railway (a metre gauge affair). The commanding officer was balanced on the back of the little engine, and as we started, some wit shouted out, "Don't move, sir! You might upset her!"

Additional light is thrown on the course of the battle by the platoon narratives:—

Lieutenant E. G. Baker, Commanding A Company, was hit in the head during the advance. No. 1 Platoon Commander, Lieutenant Smith, was badly wounded in the thigh before the first strong point was reached. Private Wyre fired some rifle grenades into it, after which the platoon rushed it with men of other units, and bombed and bayoneted the enemy out. Sergeant

Beaumont then led them towards Schuler Galleries, when he was shot through the head about 50 yards behind the red line. About 16 men under Private Wyre found their way to the red line; others, with an officer of the King's Own, went forward on the left. He said he would take them to the yellow line, but was killed by a sniper. They were willing to go on, but had no leader till Sergeant Knowles of No. 3 came up and took a small party out under heavy cross machine gun fire to the domed strong point on the road.

No. 2 got on all right till Lieutenant Dance was hit in the arm. They took a small strong point on the right with others helping, and also helped to take Aisne Farm, where one Hun officer and eight men were taken.

Sergeant Knowles took eight men to the left to take the strong point in the road, but there were about 30 enemy in a trench in front of it, and he was compelled to fall back again for lack of support. Two sections helped to take the strong point in front of Loos.

Captain Baker, Commanding B Company, was wounded at 6.30 a.m., but continued to advance; he was killed at 7 a.m. at a strong point about 150 yards to the right of Loos. At this same point five out of the Lewis gun team of seven were put out of action (one killed and four wounded). Sergeant-Major Roberts bombed the strong point.

Sergeant Pitcher, of No. 6, with five men, assisted in the attack on the strong points at Loos and was severely wounded. Second Lieutenant Fazackerley, during the pause in the barrage, advanced with Lance-Corporal Clayton and four men to a point on a ridge to find a possible position for Lewis gun. Here they were subject to intense enfilade machine gun fire from the right flank in the direction of Gallipoli, which made it impossible to advance further until the right flank had advanced.

Second Lieutenant Martin, Commanding No. 11, was badly wounded immediately after zero, and Sergeant Murphy assumed command. This platoon assisted in the capture of Aisne House; at least 20 Germans were taken there.

In No. 10 Lance-Corporal Charnley was wounded immediately after zero, and during the pause Mr. Myers and one or two others were sniped, and when they moved forward again only one bomber remained.

In No. 9, at nightfall, Mr. Fergie, Mr. Holmes, and two sergeants went forward to reconnoitre a forward position. The two officers were struck by a shell and were both very badly wounded. Lance-Corporal Anderton took over command. Private Pendlebury was wounded on the afternoon of the 23rd for the third time. C Company Commander (Captain Tautz) was wounded at the first pause.

No. 13, owing to the darkness, got mixed up with the 1/4th King's Own on the left flank, and helped the Lancashire Fusiliers to carry Schuler Galleries.

D Company Headquarters Lewis gun team, when near Gallipoli, was shot down by machine gun fire, but Corporal Prescott retrieved the gun. Visual communication with the battalion forward signalling post was opened from behind a dugout at D 13 b 10 by Private Roocroft, company signaller, and Private Parkinson, of B Company, and was maintained by shutter and lamp until the night of the 21st.

On the morning of the 21st, Corporal Prescott and Private Goodwin, Company Runner, went forward of the line and shot some enemy snipers who had been annoying the troops in the line. On the evening of the 23rd, during an intensely heavy bombardment. Corporal Prescott volunteered and kept observation all the time, though wounded in the shoulder by shrapnel, and refused to go to the aid post until the troops were relieved.

No. 14 attacked the strong point at D 13 d 26 in conjunction with a party of the 1/4th King's Own, then Second Lieutenant Holden and the remaining men of his party moved to attack Gallipoli, which was holding up the advance. This fight lasted about an hour.

On the 21st September, Second Lieutenant Holden, who was patrolling to Keir Farm, was writing a message to send by pigeon when he was killed. There were four other casualties, and the pigeons were killed.

No. 15. At 10 a.m. on 21st September, Second Lieutenant Pruden took a small patrol to Keir Farm. During the night an advanced post held by Lance-Corporal Gorton and five men with two Lewis guns was buried. One gun was in action again immediately, and the other after six hours.

EXTRACTED FROM WAR DIARY.

Trenches

21st September. There was fairly lively shelling at dawn, but the situation was reported quiet at 7.30 a.m. The front was continually patrolled before daylight and no signs of the enemy found. During the morning a further officers' patrol worked forward to Keir Farm and confirmed the previous report that it was practically non-existent. On the afternoon of this day the strength of the companies in the line was reported at 90, though it was known there were still many more men of this unit who had become merged in the battalions on either flank.

At about 4.40 p.m. the 1/8th King's Liverpool Regiment, on the left of the 2/5th Lancashire Fusiliers, attacked and occupied Schuler Farm. Owing to the small amount of resistance encountered it was decided that the 2/5th Lancashire Fusiliers should take Cross Cotts and that then the 1/4th Loyal North Lancashire Regiment should conform by moving forward to the new alignment. The attack on Cross Cotts, however, never materialised, as at 6.30 p.m. heavy enemy counterattacks were launched on Hill 37 on our right, and on the London Division on our left, the front held by this unit simply being subjected to an intense bombardment. Our artillery promptly replied to the S.O.S., and no enemy succeeded in reaching our lines.

During the ensuing night a further effort was made to complete the reorganisation by separating the 1/4th Royal Lancaster Regiment and the 1/4th Loyal North Lancashire Regiment. This unit took over the south, *viz.*, 200 yards of the Keir sector, extending approximately from D 13 d 23 32 to D 13 d 23 75. By this means a few more men were collected together. The battalion was then organised on a two-company frontage with two companies in support, and the whole line was straightened and pushed forward an average depth of 50 yards. It was found that the only practicable way of doing this was by arranging a system of guide wires of a fixed length, which were taken out by posts in advance and, after their direction, etc., had been checked, the rear wave advanced along them by platoons and took up the new alignment. It was intended that this process should be repeated by leapfrogging the two waves until the yellow line was reached, but owing to the still imperfect state of organisation, it was decided to postpone this movement until the following night.

During this night, however, guide wires were laid from the main line to the isolated Lewis gun posts 100 yards in front. This ensured cohesion and gave the most forward men confidence. Guide wires were also made from the main line of resistance to Battalion Headquarters to facilitate the work during the night of carrying parties bringing up S.A.A and food.

The enemy's artillery was quiet during the night, but our own was very busy, apparently with gas shells, upon the enemy's batteries.

Killed: Second Lieutenant H. Holden and two other ranks.

Wounded:—Two other ranks.

22nd September. There was a certain amount of shelling about dawn, otherwise the day was quiet.

As soon as it was dark, the right of the battalion was advanced 150 yards and connected with a machine gun in a shell hole near Keir Farm about D 13 d 60 55. This movement, which was successfully carried out with the help of guide wires, brought our line round in such a way as to face the enemy, whose position now ran approximately north-west south-east. Connection was also maintained with the 165th Brigade on our right, but in view of the fact that the latter were being relieved, it was not considered advisable to carry out any further advance, so as to avoid any possibility of bringing down an enemy S.O.S. barrage.

The usual posts were pushed out in advance of the new line.

Owing to the exhaustion of several officers in the line, two were brought down for a rest to Battalion Headquarters, and the signalling and intelligence officers took over control of the companies. The night was quiet. Two companies of the 2/6th North Staffordshires came into support to our brigade.

Casualties: Two other ranks wounded.

23rd September. The day passed without incident. Patrols before dawn saw nothing of the enemy. An S.O.S. was sent up on our right at 3.50 p.m., but nothing materialised.

At 5 p.m. the enemy heavily bombarded our positions, and on front line system and the vicinity of Battalion Headquarters were heavily bombarded for three hours. By 8.15 p.m. all was quiet again and the relief was begun. The relieving unit was the 2/6th North Staffordshires (59th Division), who took over our frontage with one company. Relief was completed without casualties about 11 p.m.

A special effort was made to secure identifications before being relieved, and a patrol that went out with this object in view returned with two prisoners, who were encountered in No Man's Land. The capture of these prisoners proved the presence of the third German

Division opposite this part of the line since the attack was launched on the 20th.

Upon relief. Companies concentrated at St. Jean, where, after hot tea had been supplied from the cookers, a train was provided to take the battalion to Vlamertinghe.

24th September. The battalion arrived at camp south of Vlamertinghe at 430 a.m. Morning was spent in resting, etc. At 3 p.m. the brigade entrained and travelled from Vlamertinghe to Poperinghe, detrained at Poperinghe, and boarded 'buses at a point about one mile south-west of the town. By this means we went to Watou area, and were accommodated in tents at Hill Camp (K 12 d 78).

143 other ranks from reinforcement camp
11 other ranks from base.

Telegrams:

Please convey to all ranks 55th Division the Army Commander's congratulations on the fine record of the Division during the hard fighting of the past two months. The Army Commander wishes specially to thank all ranks for their splendid efforts, which have contributed greatly to the success of the last attack and to wish them all good luck and success in the future. Despite their long period in the line prior to commencement of operations they have well maintained and increased their high reputation.

Fifth Army.

Brigadier-General Stuart and all ranks West Lancashire Reserve Brigade send heartiest congratulations to West Lancashire Division on their splendid success.

Well done, 35th West Lancashire Division! Accept my most hearty congratulations. I sincerely trust your losses are not heavy.

Derby.

To all ranks of the 55th (West Lancashire) Division.
I regret that owing to the move of the division I have not been able to see all units since the fight on 20th September. I hope to do so later as opportunity offers.

The messages received from higher commanders and others since the battle have been published from time to time as received and have no doubt been read by all ranks, who will see from these messages how well the higher commanders have appreciated the work of the division.

In addition, I have recently been allowed to see the reports on the division rendered to General Headquarters by the army and the corps in which we served. In these reports the division is spoken of as "a good fighting division possessing the right spirit" and as "a first-rate division." I know that all ranks throughout the division will share the pride that I feel myself in reading those opinions of the commanders under whom we have served.

I have also had the advantage of reading scores of stories of individual courage, determination, endurance, and self-sacrifice, narrated by commanding officers in bringing the services of individuals of all ranks to notice for recognition. These stories increase my pride in the division and my confidence in it.

The West Lancashire Division had a good reputation before the recent fighting in front of Ypres. You have now won for it a reputation second to none in the Expeditionary Force, and every soldier in the division may well be proud of belonging to it. That reputation I feel confident you will cherish and maintain. We are now in an easy part of the line, but ordinary trench duties demand constant alertness, endurance, and conscientious observance of orders; besides it is up to us at all times to take advantage of any opportunities for aggressive action which will cause loss or damage to the enemy. It is by such action, as well as by smartness and good discipline when out of the line, that the great reputation of the West Lancashire Division can, and I am sure will, be kept up by each soldier in it, of every rank.

H. S. Jeudwine,
55th Division Headquarters, Major-General,
10th October, 1917 Commanding 55th Division.

The following decorations were awarded in respect of the battle and announced 11th November:—

Military Cross	Captain A. T. Houghton.
	Second Lieutenant S. A. H. Pruden.
	Second Lieutenant L. Brooke.
D.C.M.	200051 C.S.M. Roberts, H.
	200077 Corporal Prescott, S.

Military Medal	200782 Private Parks, T.
201197 Corporal Thompson, J.
200682 Private Coupe, F.
200895 Lance-Sergeant Knowles, R.
 12154 Lance-Corporal Cayton, R.
290665.S Private Pendlebury, T.
202967 Private Yates, W.
291178 Private Goodwin, H.
201350 Corporal Robinson, J.
29679 Private Parkinson, T.
 34304 Private Jones, T.
16940 Private Cunningham, D.
202099 Private Wyre, F.
200756 Lance-Corporal Gorton, F.
201542 Sergeant Bell, H.
 6693 Lance-Sergeant Murphey,
200352 J. Private Thistleton, T.
238002 Private Roocroft, W.

CHAPTER 8

Cambrai, 25th September, 1917 to 6th December, 1917

At Watou we began once more to pull the battalion together and bring it up to strength, and reinforcements began to come in. Captain Duggan, M.C., from the 10th Battalion, joined us here, also Second Lieutenants J.O. Firth, J. H. Livesey, H. Ramsbottom, and P. Adamson, and 18 other ranks.

On the 26th we marched to Hopoutre, where we entrained and moved out at 9.30 a.m., travelling in cattle trucks *via* Arras to Bapaume, where we arrived about 7 p.m. Thence we marched through desolate and ruined country to a pile of ruins labelled Ytres, where we shared a canvas camp with a battalion of the Buffs for the night; they left the following morning.

Major Crump rejoined us from England on the 30th.

We stayed at Ytres resting, bathing, reorganising, and training, till 3rd October, when we left the 4th Corps area and marched to a canvas camp at Aizecourt-le-Bas in the 3rd Corps area; the camp was on a hill top, and it was bitterly cold. From here reconnaissances of the new forward area were carried out, the 164th Brigade being in divisional reserve.

Second Lieutenant Easterby came back on the 5th, and on the 10th Second Lieutenants J. L., W. H. F., and F. C. Smith, D. Carmichael, J. E. F. Nicholson, R. B. Wilkinson, and C. Taylor joined us as officer reinforcements, followed by Second Lieutenants L. Frost, F. G. Green, and C. Milne on the 13th.

On the 12th we marched to Villers Faucon into billets; the following day companies moved forward to Lempire, where we became support battalion to the right brigade.

The country in which we now found ourselves was a pleasant change from Flanders; the soil was chalk like the south-east of England, and the scenery was, or had been, similar; but the Germans in their retirement had systematically destroyed everything—cut down every tree, blown up every house and structure down to the very telegraph poles, and poisoned the wells—it was a desolate and dead country. Curiously enough, he had left the cellars intact, and as these, even under wattle-and-daub houses, were solidly built of brick, with arched brick roofs, they made excellent, if rather dark, hiding-places and billets.

We never quite understood these cellars, so much better than the houses to which they belonged; some said they were specially built as wine cellars, that being once a wine country; others favoured the theory that they were specially designed as refuges in war time.

From Lempire, which corresponded to Ypres in this sector, we sent working parties up the line every night. A Company had four posts, known as Lempire Central, Lempire East, Yak and Zebra Posts, which were manned day and night, the garrisons showing no movement during the daytime.

On the 18th we relieved the 1/4th King's Own in the right battalion subsector of the brigade front. The line was in truth no line, but a string of posts connected by trenches apparently freshly dug in the stiff clay which here overlay the chalk; each post provided with a mined dugout for the garrison rather a pleasant place, we thought, on first acquaintance, as we were told that horses could be ridden (and were, just at first) right up to the front line!

On this occasion companies were disposed as follows:

Gillemont Post, the only place which showed signs of wear, was held by D Company, with one platoon of A, as Left Front Company; Cat Post by C as Right Front Company: Duncan and Doleful Posts by A as Support Company; and Ken Lane, a sunken road lined with dugouts, by B, the Reserve Company, and Battalion Headquarters.

Of course, previous to our taking over the sector, the divisional artillery had begun to wake up the Hun by concentration shoots, which were continued at intervals —the retaliation was mostly in the shape of *minenwerfer* on Gillemont Post, which reminded us on that account, of Railway Wood.

During the five days we had plenty to do in becoming acclimatised and establishing the old trench routine again with a new set of officers and men; very few were left now of the June lot, and many of the

N.C.O.'s had never seen a trench before. Here Second Lieutenants W. G. E. Taylor, C. A. Rush, Hornby, and 12 other ranks reinforced us. A perpetual source of joy to the old ones these drafts were; first they had to be taken down and "put through it," and then taught how to behave, if they didn't know, but somehow or other at the end of a fortnight, they seemed to have settled down and become part of us.

The 1/4th King's Own relieved us on the 23rd, and we went back to St. Emilie, whence, during the next few days, we provided working parties for the front line, going into the line again on the 29th, when we relieved the 1/5th South Lancashires in the Birdcage sector the relief was completed without casualties by 8.30 p.m. The medical officer, who had had a pretty stiff time on 20th September, went sick that night, and Captain E. Watson Williams, R.A.M.C, took over his duties.

On the 30th October the enemy trench-mortared our front line, killing three and wounding nine men otherwise the tour was quiet, and on 1st December we were relieved by the 1/9th King's Liverpool Regiment and went by light railway to Hamel or Tincourt it was a double village, and usually known by this latter name. It was stated above that every village in the area had been destroyed—this place was an exception, as some of the civil population had been left there by the Hun, so that we found it almost intact. The companies' billets had wire beds in them, and we added to these while we were there. Our total strength at this time was 39 officers and 777 other ranks the fighting strength being 24 officers and 546 other ranks, so that in numbers, at any rate, we had partly recovered from our losses in the Salient.

We had a very pleasant time at Hamel till the 16th, when we returned to St. Emilie; during the period Captain Buckmaster assumed command of B Company and Second Lieutenant Pruden became adjutant of the battalion, a position he retained till the Armistice. Lieutenant-Colonel Hindle had been at brigade since the 13th, commanding the 164th Brigade during the absence of Brigadier-General Stockwell on leave, afterwards going on leave himself, and Major Crump had been in command of the battalion.

On the 16th we moved back to St. Emilie, and on the 17th we relieved the 1/5th King's Liverpool Regiment in the Gillemont sector.

On the morning of the 18th November, the battalion was disposed as follows (see map):—

GILLEMONT FARM SECTOR

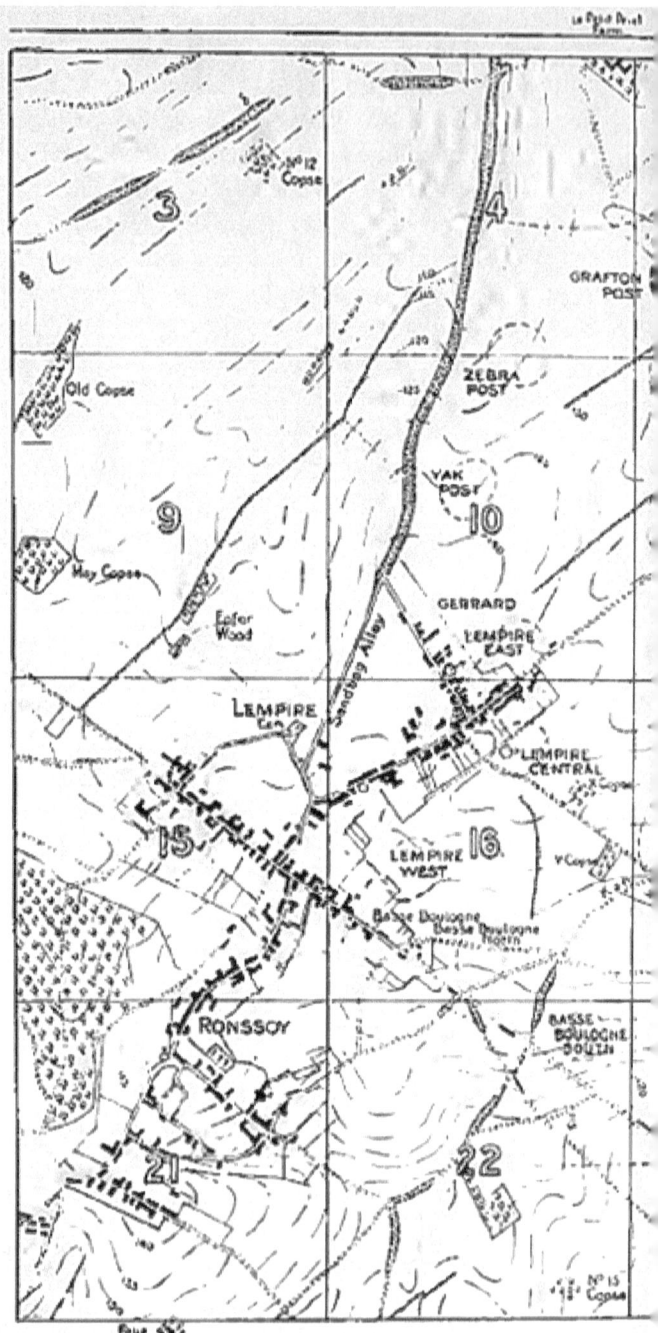

Map No. 4

NOVEMBER, 1917

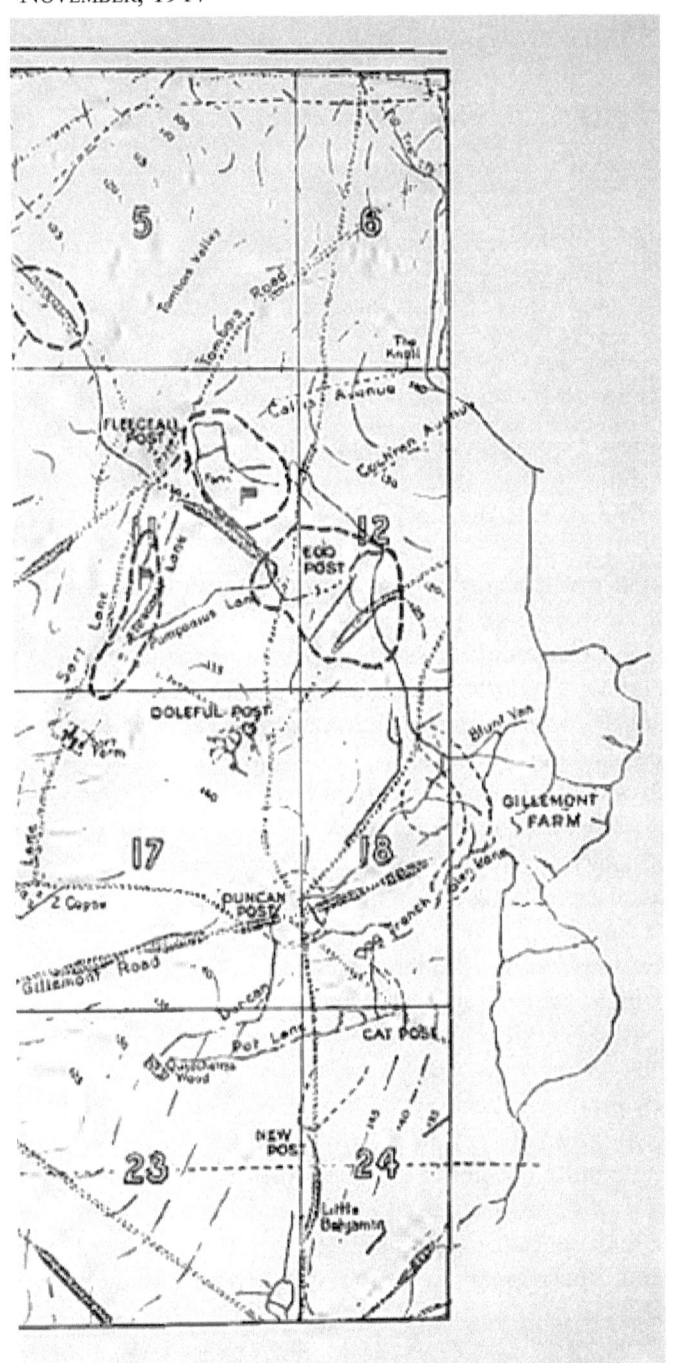

Front line—
> D Company, under Lieutenant Shippobottom, in Cat Post.
>
> C Company, under Lieutenant Lonsdale, in Gillemont Farm sector.

Supports—
> B Company, under Captain Buckmaster, in Duncan and Doleful Posts.

Reserve—
> A Company, under Captain Houghton, in Ken Lane with Battalion Headquarters.

Major Crump was in command of the battalion, and attached to A Company was a raiding party of 19 in training for a raid, under Lieutenant Adamson. At 5.30 a.m. the Boche opened a hurricane bombardment on the Gillemont Farm sector with trench mortars, including 80 heavy *minenwerfer* brought up the night before, and reduced the front trench to a shapeless mass of craters: out of 12 posts[1] only Sergeants Hartley and Hogg and half-a-dozen men were left alive; all the rest, with the officer (Lieutenant Firth) and sergeant on duty, who were found at the head of the communication trench under two feet of earth, were killed and buried.

About 200 Huns entered our line in three places, equipped with spades and rations, and worked forward bombing, and things looked serious; but Lieutenant Lonsdale, though badly shaken, kept his head, organised his headquarters details into a firing line who held up the enemy advance, and managed to telephone to Battalion Headquarters, and A Company was ordered to counter-attack.

The barrage which had been put down on Ken Lane was by this time falling off, and, as the men were standing to, Lieutenant Adamson was able to push off at once with his raiders and one platoon of A, followed by the rest of A under Captain Houghton, with very few casualties. As soon as the enemy saw the first wave come over the hill he began to retreat rapidly, but not before the counter-attackers and the gallant remnant of C had bayoneted a score or so. Some of the Huns had entered D Company's line and caused a few casualties there, among others Lieutenant Shippobottom, a very promising young of-

---

1. A post normally consisted of an N.C.O. and 6 men.

ficer, who was caught by a bomb as he came out of Company Headquarters.

This affair was reported in *The Times* as follows:—

9.30 p.m.—At dawn this morning a strong hostile raiding party attacked our trenches in the neighbourhood of Guillemont Farm, south-east of Epehy north-west of St. Quentin), and effected an entry at certain points. Our troops counter-attacked across the open, and after sharp fighting, in which we captured a few prisoners, ejected the enemy.

Lieutenant Adamson received the M.C. for his excellent leadership—the way he worked round the flanks of the hill was pretty to watch, and Sergeants Hartley and Hogg also received the M.M. for their stout fight with a few men against overwhelming odds.

It fell to A Company to clear up the mess, and they took over the sector that night; the men were dead beat, the front line blown to bits, and lateral communication interrupted to such an extent that four officers were on duty simultaneously the whole night through.

The following day was spent in making further clearance, and special parties from Battalion Headquarters and pioneers carried on through the night.

The raiders who went to Cat Post did not enter our trenches, but bombed them from the parapet, doing some damage and causing a few casualties. They then returned to their own lines.

The enemy left two unwounded prisoners in our hands, two wounded prisoners, and about ten dead were left in our trenches.

Our casualties were: Second Lieutenant J. A. Firth, killed; Second Lieutenant F. Shippobottom, wounded, died of wounds in hospital; Second Lieutenant R. Hornby, slightly wounded, remained at duty; 11 other ranks killed, 21 other ranks wounded, 48 other ranks missing—many of these being buried in the destruction of the trench.

The following extracts from the *War Diary* refer to our share in the Cambrai attack:—

19th November. The work of reorganisation was completed, and the repairing of the trenches went on. At 1 p.m. orders were received that it was Y day, and the preparation for the attack to be made on Z day started at once. Our artillery and trench mortars completed their wire cutting programme. Enemy shelled our supports with 5.9's and 4.2's during the day.

D Company, who were holding Cat Post sector, were ordered to remain there and to push posts into the Gillemont sector when the assaulting troops moved forward.

At 2.30 p.m. A Company sent 50 other ranks to the 164th Trench Mortar Battery as carrying parties for guns moving forward, and 20 Other Ranks to the 164th Machine Gun Company as carriers to their guns moving forward. Between 11 p.m. and 12 midnight the remainder of A and C Companies, who were holding the Gillemont sector, were relieved by the 1/4th Royal Lancaster Regiment, who were to assault the Gillemont defences of the enemy in the morning. On relief these companies proceeded to Ken Lane and were held in Battalion reserve.

B Company, who were in support at Duncan and Doleful posts, took up dispositions as follows during the night:—

One platoon as permanent garrison Fleeceall Post.

One platoon as permanent garrison Grafton Post.

One platoon as permanent garrison Island Traverse.

Owing to our losses in Lewis gun personnel, sustained in the raid on the 18th, we were unable to carry out a programme of Lewis gun fire for barrage purposes that had been allotted to us. This was taken over by the 1/5th King's Liverpool Regiment, with the assistance of two Lewis gunners from the platoon of B Company in Fleeceall Post.

The evening and night was very quiet; there was no enemy activity whatever.

Two other ranks to Field Ambulance sick.

20th November. Z day. At 2 a.m. the battalion was disposed as follows:—

Headquarters	Ken Lane.
D Company	Cat Post Sector.
B Company	Headquarters and one platoon, Fleeceall Post; one platoon, Grafton Post; one platoon, Island Traverse.
A and C Companies	70 other ranks detached as carrying parties; remainder at Ken Lane, with one platoon organised to occupy Doleful Post if required.
Aid Post	Duncan Post.

Zero hour was at 6.20 a.m.

The duty allotted to us was permanently to hold the brigade front and on no account to move forward in support of the assaulting battalions.

The attack on Gillemont was at first successful, but by 1 p.m. all our troops were driven back to our original front line. The attack on the Knoll was unsuccessful owing to the wire not having been cut.

Our garrison in the original line stood fast all through.

The enemy heavily shelled our front and support lines, especially Duncan Post, throughout the day and succeeding night.

Our casualties were:—One other rank killed, eight other ranks wounded, three other ranks missing.

At 8 p.m. the posts at Fleeceall, Grafton, and Island Traverse were relieved by the 1/8th King's Liverpool Regiment and 2/5th Lancashire Fusiliers, and on relief proceeded to Duncan Post. At midnight the entire Company (B) was organised into a wiring party, and commenced wiring in front of the Gillemont sector.

The carrying parties attached to the Trench Mortars and Machine Guns were returned to A Company at Ken Lane by 10 p.m., except one party of 20 other ranks which did not arrive till the 22nd. At 10 p.m. A and C Companies commenced to relieve the 1/4th Royal Lancaster Regiment in the Gillemont sector.

Two other ranks to Field Ambulance sick.

21st November. At 1 p.m. the relief of the 1/4th Royal Lancaster Regiment was completed. The 1/4th Royal Lancaster Regiment proceeded to Ken Lane and Sart Farm. The day was quiet; the work of clearing the trenches and reorganising was continued. At 2 p.m. one Platoon B Company relieved a Company of the 1/5th King's Liverpool Regiment in Doleful Post.

*22nd Novembe*r. The day was abnormally quiet. Three daylight patrols were sent out to discover any signs of an enemy retirement. Enemy front line was found to be held in force. At 8 p.m. the battalion was relieved by the 1/7th King's Liverpool Regiment, and on relief proceeded to Vaucellette Camp X 13 c, and came under command of the B.G.C. 166th Infantry Brigade. C Company did not go to Vaucellette, but proceeded to billets in St. Emilie.

The battalion was present in billets at Vaucellette Camp by 11 p.m.

Three other ranks to Field Ambulance sick.

The next few days were spent in repairing billets and replacing equipment lost in the recent battle, and on the 28th we marched back to billets at Villers Faucon; Major Crump left the battalion to take over

Map No. 5

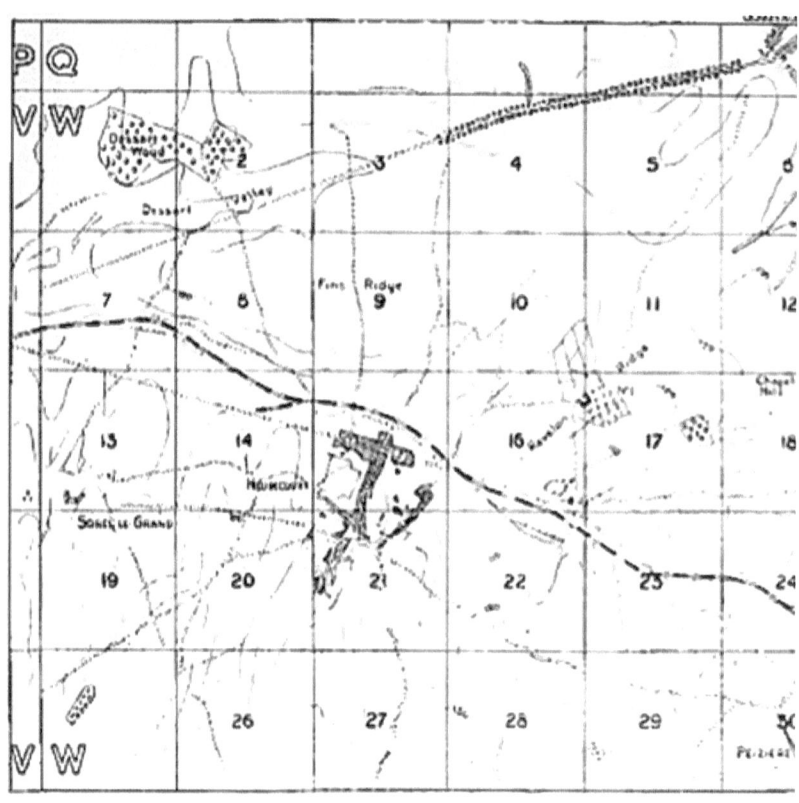

The Vaucellette Farm Area

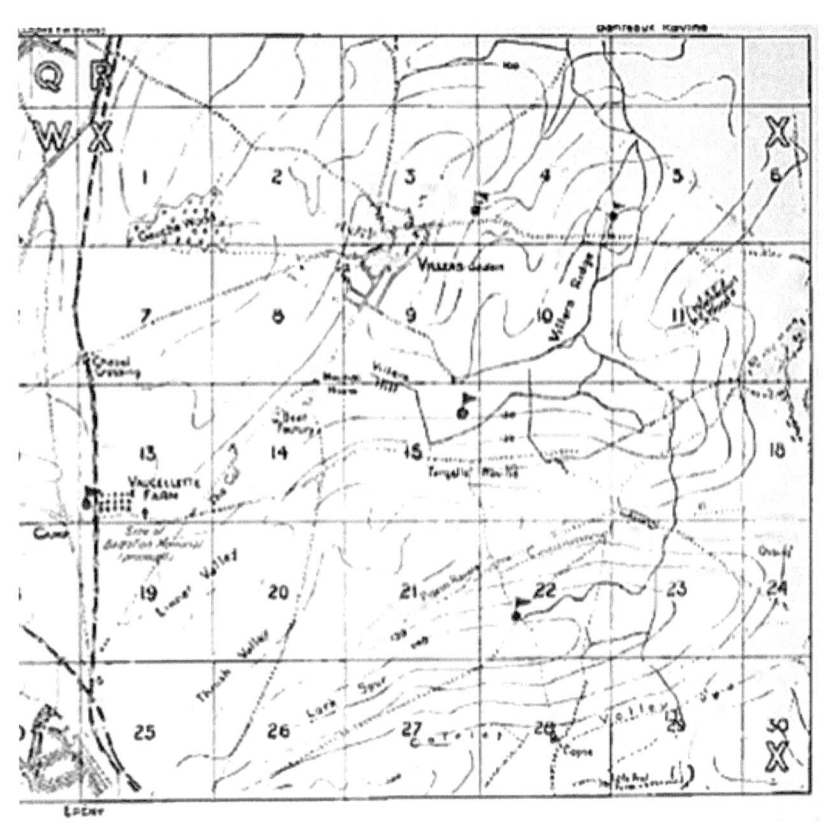

Nov. 30th, 1917

command of the 1/10th King's Liverpool Regiment.

On the 29th, after a warning order, which was afterwards cancelled, we marched to Vaucellette Camp, just behind the ruins of a farm of that name. Apparently the divisional commander had noticed, while making a tour of the forward area on the 28th, that the enemy was reconnoitring with low-flying aircraft as well as registering targets with his artillery, and knowing that movement behind the enemy's lines was above normal, he suspected an attack on our front, hence our move.

In order to make clear the events that followed, which were by no means clear to us at the time, it is necessary to quote *in extenso* from the *History of the 55th Division*:—

> The division was at this time holding a front of 13,000 yards, supported only by two brigades of field artillery!
>
> This wide frontage could not of course be continuously held; it consisted of platoon posts, connected by travel trenches, and distributed in depth so far as circumstances allowed. But with such a wide front an effective distribution in depth was impossible with the troops available. On the morning of the attack, the portion of the line extending from Banteaux Ravine to Wood Road was held by the 1/5th South Lancashires. South of them in the Honnecourt sector were the l/5th North Lancashire Regiment, and in the Ossus sector the 1/10th King's Liverpool Regiment. The 1/5th King's Own were in support. The 165th Infantry Brigade on the right was disposed as follows:— 1/6th King's Liverpool Regiment from Ossus Wood to Heythrop Post; 1/5th King's Liverpool Regiment from Grafton Post to Ego Post; and 1/7th King's Liverpool Regiment southwards from this point to Cat Post and New Post. The 1/9th King's Liverpool Regiment were in support. The 164th Infantry Brigade were in divisional reserve.
>
> At seven o'clock on the morning of the 30th, in thick fog, a very heavy bombardment broke out upon the whole divisional front, and all tracks and roads were heavily shelled. Almost simultaneously a message was received at the Headquarters of the 166th Brigade in Epehy, from the 35th Brigade, which was on our immediate left, stating that the l/5th South Lancashires were being heavily trench mortared and that the S.O.S. had gone up. Communication with this battalion was at once at-

tempted, but without result, and save for a visual signal message received at 7.43 a.m. stating, 'We know nothing yet, O.K.,' nothing further was heard from the 1/5th South Lancashires, nor did a man of that battalion return.

It was presently, however, to be made clear that the enemy had broken through somewhere on the left of the l/5th South Lancashires, and was pushing forward in large numbers and with great rapidity on Villers Guislain. Between 7.38 a.m. and 7.45 a.m., Germans in considerable force were seen on Villers Ridge, and a few moments later large numbers of British troops, not of our division, were seen to be falling back from the direction of Gonnelieu just north-west of Villers Guislain. Very shortly after eight o'clock enemy machine guns were firing on our batteries from the high ground south of Gauche Wood, and enemy aeroplanes, flying as low as 100 feet, were subjecting Villers Guislain and the ground in its vicinity to heavy machine gun fire.

At 8.15 a.m. the enemy were seen to be advancing in strong force southwards from the north of the cemetery—*i.e.*, on the western side of Villers Guislain. The position of the village was precarious.

Meantime, as late as 7.57 a.m., the 1/5th North Lancashire Regiment had reported: 'No Infantry action,' but at 8.15 a.m. a message was received from the Liverpool Scottish on their right, stating that the enemy was advancing from his trenches at Ossus 2. A quarter of an hour later an indistinct message from the 1/5th North Lancashire Regiment was received at the Headquarters of the 166th Brigade, to the effect that the enemy was through on the left—the line was then cut.

By 8.20 a.m. the enemy were reported to have penetrated our lines at Holt's Bank, and a few moments after large bodies of the enemy were seen in Pigeon Quarry—north of the Liverpool Scottish and between them and the 1/5th North Lancashire Regiment. Almost simultaneously the enemy were reported to be coming over in extended order and in large numbers, wave after wave, to Eagle Quarry, on the 165th Brigade front, and also to be advancing on Fleeceall Post on the south. By 9.15 a.m. the enemy had penetrated the divisional front from the Birdcage northwards for about 800 yards, and were even reported to have been seen in Gloucester Road. Villers Guislain, turned from the north and eventually surrounded, was reported at 9.30 a.m. to be in enemy hands, and a little over half-an-hour later the enemy had succeeded in progressing to within a few hundred yards of Vaucellette Farm. He got no further, for there he met the 1/4th Loyal North Lancashires.

All Press accounts are strangely silent about the work the battalion did at Vaucellette Farm on the 30th November, 1917.

The scene of the action was the col or ridge at the head of the valley which runs along the northern edge of Villers Guislain and up towards the south-east (see map); this ridge commanded the railway for a considerable distance, and by holding on to it we were able to keep the Hun off Chapel Hill; had he occupied this feature and mounted machine guns there, most of the area of open grass land between Heudecourt and Peiziere would have been under direct fire, with obvious consequences, whereas its retention by us kept this covered, and also covered the flank of the Guards when they counter-attacked and drove the Boche back out of Gouzeaucourt.

The front had been very quiet and the possibility of trouble seemed to most of us very remote, but all precautions were taken, and before we turned in on the night of the 29th, Colonel Hindle's orders as to the issue of bombs, extra bandoliers, haversack rations, and filling of water-bottles were carried out to the letter. At the same time company boxes, gramophones, etc., were with us, and we spent a cheery evening, with little thought for the morrow.

At dawn the next day heavy firing was heard to the north, but at first we put this down to the aftermath of the Cambrai push and paid little attention to it; by degrees it increased in violence, and the commanding officer gave the order to stand-to, but carry on with breakfasts, which were just ready—this was at 7.50 a.m. Soon after he sent Lieutenant Fazackerley (intelligence officer) forward to find out what was going on, and Lieutenant Johnson to 166th Brigade for orders, our own Brigade Headquarters and three battalions being still back at Hamel resting.

About 8.30 a.m. information was brought by Lieutenant Fazackerley that the enemy was advancing all along our immediate front, and the commanding officer at once sent for company commanders at the double; one of us, who knew him well, afterwards said it was the first time the commanding officer had ever been in a hurry. In a few words he made his dispositions: A company to hold the left under Captain Houghton; B Company, under Captain Buckmaster, the centre in front of the farm; and D Company, under Captain Matthew, to the right at the head of the Linnet Valley. By this time straggling remnants of the division on our left were to be seen crossing the railway; a few were collected and taken forward by A Company.

The companies standing in readiness were at once led forward by their commanders, and took up positions as shown on the map, gaining the crest at the moment when a party of Huns was in the act of crossing the railway just south of chapel crossing; A Company caught them before they reached dead ground and wiped them out, while a Lewis gun mounted on the railway and a platoon beyond it secured the approach up the valley. It is difficult to estimate the number of Huns shot down by this company alone in the first five minutes—the countryside was alive with them, advancing in small patrols with light machine guns.

The enemy had also stationed heavy machine guns in various buildings, especially a Beet Factory to our front, and during the whole action our troops were subjected to continuous and accurate traversing fire from these, and to a certain amount of shelling.

From this point our *War Diary* will speak for itself:—

30th November, 7.40 a.m. "Stand-to" order received from 166th Infantry Brigade. Intelligence Officer and scouts sent forward to reconnoitre.

9 a.m. Our infantry and artillery observed retiring on our left in the direction of Heudecourt. Artillery reported they had abandoned guns in Villers Guislain. Battalion Headquarters, under R.S.M., sent forward to form line on north-east side of Vaucellette Farm, where they immediately came under machine gun fire from the enemy advancing from Villers Guislain.

A Company were ordered up on their left, and had to fight hard to reach their position; the enemy had already seized Chapel Crossing, All the officers of this company eventually became casualties.

B and D Companies were ordered to continue the line on the right of Headquarters on the east side of Vaucellette Farm. All Companies were quickly in position; fire was opened, and the enemy ceased to advance and took up a position on a line running from the Beet Factory to Chapel Crossing. At the time there were no troops in position on our right or left flanks. This state of things prevailed until dusk, when the Canadian Mounted Brigade arrived.

11 a.m. Orders were received from the 166th Infantry Brigade to clear enemy from Villers Guislain. Battalion ordered to advance in extended order to clear enemy from Villers Hill. This they proceeded to do, led by Lieutenant-Colonel R. Hindle, D.S.O.

The men were firing from the hip as they advanced, and the foremost line of the enemy began to retire. The advance was successful until the centre of the line reached a point about 200 yards from the crest of the hill, when ammunition ran short. At this time fresh enemy troops advanced over the hill in considerable strength.

The colonel was killed, and all three company commanders became casualties. The adjutant took command of the battalion and ordered a withdrawal to Vaucellette Farm. This was carried out slowly, under covering fire from the left flank.

A defensive line was established on the east side of Vaucellette Farm, and the men commenced to dig themselves in with their entrenching tools, under cover of Lewis gun fire. A supply of ammunition was brought up by stretcher bearers returning from the Aid Post.

11.30 a.m. At this time Major Crump, who was reconnoitring under orders from the G.O.C. (166th Infantry Brigade) established a post on the Epehy-Villers Guislain Road, consisting of one Vickers gun and team, one officer and 30 other ranks of various units. The gun in this post did great execution amongst the enemy in Leith Walk, and effectually prevented him from advancing further.

12 15 p.m. A composite battalion of the 12th Division arrived as reinforcements, one company being sent to strengthen our garrison in front of the farm, two companies continued our line northwards, and one company was kept in the camp as local reserve. Touch was obtained on the left with the 9th Essex Regiment.

12 55 p.m. Major Crump having completed reconnaissance and reported to 166th Infantry Brigade, was ordered by the G.O.C. to assume command of the battalion and to take with him two Vickers guns and teams and supply of ammunition for Lone Tree Post (Epehy-Villers-Guislain Road). One gun was sent to right flank of the post to command the Linnet Valley, the other to Vaucellette Farm. Soon afterwards touch was obtained with l/4th Royal Lancaster Regiment on our right.

1.30 p.m. C Company arrived as reinforcements and were sent into the trench south of the farm, in front of the railway. After this the consolidation of the line was carried on by the men with the entrenching tool, only a few picks and shovels being available. This was eventually remedied by the arrival of the battalion mobile reserve of S.A.A. and tools, so that, with the help of the composite battalion (12th Division), a fire trench was dug across the whole front of the farm, and a considerable amount of wire put out soon after dark.

5 *p.m.* The Canadian Cavalry Brigade, under Brigadier-General Seeley, arrived at rear line of Vaucellette Camp. One regiment dismounted and reinforced our line. One regiment dug a support line west of the farm. C Company were relieved at 11 p.m. by the 1/8th King's Liverpool Regiment, and went into the line east of the farm to assist in the consolidation of the position.

Our casualties were:—

Killed: Lieutenant-Colonel R. Hindle, D.S.O.; Second Lieutenant J. H. Livesey.

Wounded and Missing (afterwards reported killed):—

Captain R. N. L. Buckmaster.

Wounded:—

Captain A. T. Houghton, M.C.; Captain F. K. Matthew, Second Lieutenant E. M. Easterby, Second Lieutenant R. B. Wilkinson, Second Lieutenant P. Adamson, Second Lieutenant F. G. Green, Second Lieutenant J. E. P. Nicholson.

Other Ranks: Killed 11, Wounded 84, Missing 15.

Writing to express his sympathy with Alderman R. Hindle, Chorley, on the loss of his son, the late Lieutenant-Colonel Hindle, D.S.O., Major-General H. S. Jeudwine said:

> Lieutenant-Colonel Hindle's death was a great blow to all of us. To his battalion it seemed irreparable. His never-failing keenness, his courage and determination, were of inestimable value, and had made his battalion one of the finest, if not the finest, in the division. His cheerfulness and modesty endeared him to everybody. His battalion did splendid work under his leadership in the attack in front of Ypres. There he came safely through great dangers, though he never spared himself.
> The last action was quite unforeseen. When the German attack appeared probable it fell to him and his battalion to occupy a position of great importance. I saw him on the day preceding

the attack and gave him orders which he carried out most loyally, as I had the utmost confidence he would. He was killed almost instantaneously at the head of his men, where he always was when there was danger.... It will, I am sure, be some consolation to you to know that the fine fight he made with his battalion was the means of definitely checking the German advance in that part of the field, and of preventing their reaching a position which would have endangered large forces.

Vaucellette Camp.

1st December. At 1 a.m. the battalion was relieved by the composite battalion of the 12th Division, and on relief went into brigade reserve at the railway dugouts (W 23 b) 57 c S E. The day was spent in reorganising the battalion. At 11 p.m. the battalion was relieved by the King's Own Yorkshire Light Infantry, and proceeded by route march to billets at Hamel, arriving at 3 a.m.

Second Lieutenant J. Johnson wounded. One other rank to Field Ambulance sick.

Extract from a letter received by the G.O.C. 164th Infantry Brigade from the G.O.C. 55th Division:—

> I saw the corps commander today, and he said that they (*i.e.,* the 1/4th Loyal North Lancashire Regiment) had saved the situation. He had seen the commander-in-chief, and he had agreed.

CHAPTER 9

The Givenchy Period, 7th December, 1917, to 3rd September, 1918

On the 6th December, 1917, the remnant of the battalion marched back from Tincourt to Canvas Camp, Flanicourt, arriving there at 12 30 p.m. The next day we spent in putting up more tents and cleaning up. Captain Duggan, M.C., and Captain Hore, M.C., rejoined us from England and 22 other ranks from the reinforcement camp.

On the 8th we entrained at 10 a.m. and were taken to Maroeuil, and marched in pouring rain to billets at Lattre St. Quentin, arriving there at 2 30 a.m., where we rested all the following day.

On the 10th we marched to Tincques, and the following day to Bryas. On the 11th we marched to Henchin, and the following day to Delette, where 11 other ranks reported as reinforcements. Here we entered on a long course of training. On the 22nd news came that Lieutenant-Colonel J. A. Crump had been mentioned in despatches.

On Christmas Day, after Church Parade, we had a splendid battalion dinner in the local hall and a concert in the evening.

Snow fell on the 26th and interfered with training.

Our total casualties for the year 1917 are recorded in the *War Diary* as follows:

	Killed	Wounded	Missing	Wounded & Missing	Gassed	Died of Wounds	Sick to F.A.
Officers	14	31	2	2	0	1	19
Other Ranks	137	627	159	0	11	1	520
Totals	151	658	161	2	11	2	539

January, 1918.

On New Year's Day we found ourselves still at Delette, where we had an excellent dinner. Congratulations were received from the king, the commander-in-chief, the army commander, and the divisional commander. The following days were spent in company training and bathing. There was a snowstorm on the 8th. There were good ranges here, and one of the companies was on the range every day.

On the 14th the New Year's Honours List came out. The Military Cross for Captain Matthew; Captain Buckmaster, Corporal J. Collier, Lance-Corporal J. Baker, and Private J. Maher being mentioned in despatches. Second Lieutenant Ramsbottom joined us as a reinforcement.

On the 19th the brigade was inspected at Coyaque by the Army Commander, General Horne, who took the opportunity of welcoming the brigade to his army. The following officers joined for duty:— Captain T. D. Collett, Second Lieutenants H. A. Latham, J. Dawson, W. Hughes, N. Smith, and T. Stanley.

On the 20th the award of a Bar to the Military Cross to Captain Pruden and the Military Cross itself to Second Lieutenant H. Fazackerley were announced.

There were regular lectures during the period on a variety of subjects, and many keen football matches were played.

On the 25th another batch of officers—Lieutenant G. B. Wardle and Second Lieutenants O. R. Cooper, R. Hodgson, G. H. Frost, E. H. Studdard, and L. O. Halliwell joined us, followed, on the 30th, by a draft from the 1/5th North Lancashires, consisting of:—Captains R. W. B. Sparkes, M.C., and B. J. Phillips, Second Lieutenants J. S. Hampson, T. H. Scott, W. E. Pasley, J. H. Friar, F. Greaves, A. James, T. McLachlan, M.C., J. T. Taylor, and 163 other ranks.

On the 31st the total strength of the battalion was 56 officers (including the medical officer and the *padre*) and 942 other ranks, there being actually 43 officers and 631 other ranks serving with the battalion.

Two more officers, Second Lieutenants Beresford and Horsfall, and two other ranks arrived on the 2nd February, and Second Lieutenants Symes and G. Haworth came on the 3rd, Second Lieutenant R. Smith on the 4th, and Second Lieutenants G. Kirkby and H. Bailey on the 6th.

We had never been so strong in numbers since the Battle of Festubert, and the rest and daily training had improved our morale, so that

W.O.s AND N.C.O.s DELETTES, 1918

when we moved away from Delette on the 7th February we presented a very different spectacle to the handful of survivors who had mustered after the Vaucellette Farm affair at the end of November, 1917.

Esprit-de-corps is a wonderful thing, and has been noticed by many people during the war. Officers and men rejoining their companies after perhaps two years' absence would find awaiting them the same company they had left, although perhaps no officer and only half-a-dozen men remained of it, and though on this date the commanding officer was the only officer still present who had left England with the battalion, and there were probably not more than 20 of the originals with him, yet in some indefinable way the battalion was the same one. Not perhaps so thoroughly grounded in some ways as it originally had been, but with all the cumulative experience of three years of war governing its every move.

On the 7th February, escorted by the divisional band (which was generally considered an ominous sign), we marched to Estree-Blanche, and arrived there very wet about 12 noon. Six men were sent to Field Ambulance sick.

The following day we marched on to Cantrainne, arriving there at 3 p.m., again very wet, and on the 9th on to Fonguieres, where all were present and billeted by 1 p.m.

Sunday was devoted to Church Parade and cleaning up, the strength of the battalion being recorded as 51 officers and 708 other ranks. Second Lieutenant P. Adamson, M.C., rejoined us here.

The next three days were spent in training and preparations for the trenches and reconnaissance of the forward area, in this case the La Bassée Canal sector.

On the 14th we relieved the 1/8th Lancashire Fusiliers by daylight. Companies marching *via* Bethune and the canal bank. Relief was completed by 4 30 p.m.

Here we found civilians living in the "village line," and small shops! Our dispositions were on a different principle to those which obtained at Ypres, all companies being in the front line, in the order, from right to left—C, B, A, and D, each company being disposed in depth. C Company was on the south of the canal, the remainder on the north. Battalion Headquarters was at Kingscleare.

Here we took up again the old trench routine, nightly patrols, working on the trenches, and so forth.

The position itself was a curious one. Givenchy, the scene of so much desperate fighting in 1914, was a village completely destroyed, some few remnants of walls and a mass of bricks, the remains of a large church, being all that remained of a fair-sized village; it lay on the western slopes of a small knoll, which formed the southern and western extremity of the Fromelles Aubers ridge. The opposing trenches had been dug in 1914, so that the actual crest of the knoll was in No Man's Land, and the opposing trench lines were out of sight of one another.

In the intervening years of warfare, Givenchy had been one of the most active mining centres on the British front, with the result that by the time the 55th Division took over, the front line on the crest of the knoll consisted of a continuous line of craters 800 yards long.

Both sides occupied the high tops of the craters, but the view was practically limited by the top of the crater opposite. The position was one of great importance—if the Germans gained possession of the whole of Givenchy Hill they would command the whole of La Bassée Canal from where it passed through our lines to Bethune, as well as a large area in close proximity to what remained to France of its great northern coalfield.

The country to the north of the spur was dead flat for miles, and the roads were all overlooked from the crest of the hill. Every effort had been made to strengthen the position by the construction of a series of tunnels for shelter during bombardments, but the exits from these were not of the best. A certain amount of cementing had also been done. By April 9th the Givenchy—Festubert area was a mass of apron fencing stretching back in depth for several thousand yards.

The dangers of this tunnel system and the difficulties of negotiating the mass of wire in this area necessitated careful practice in the action of the troops holding it. Posts were manned daily from the tunnel system, this action being timed and every officer, N.C.O., and man thus learnt his way about the whole system of defence.

The action of the battalion in support was definitely laid down. No counterattack across the open was to be made on account of the number of apron fences; in the event of the enemy penetrating at any point into the line, further penetration was to be stopped by the supports, and when the enemy was pocketed he was to be cut off by movement along the trench system against his flanks and rear. All posts and strong points were wired in all round, and had orders to fight to the last even if surrounded. All this careful preparation bore fruit later, on April 9th, which was, as a battle, a most remarkable example of the value of taking the British soldier into your confidence and making

Map No. 6

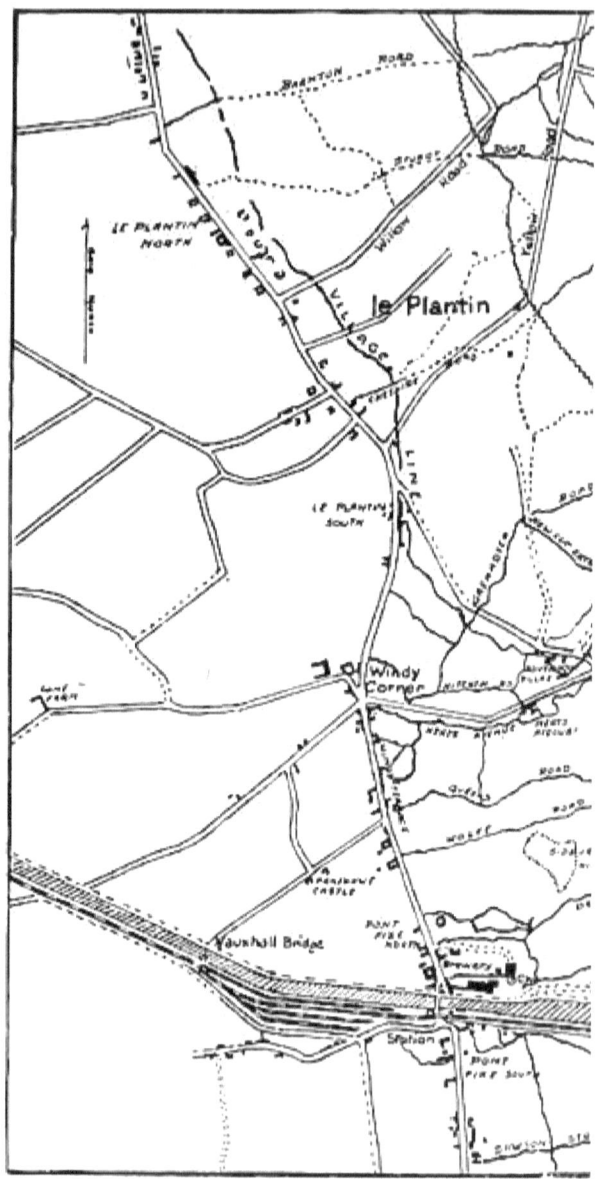

Givenchy Area

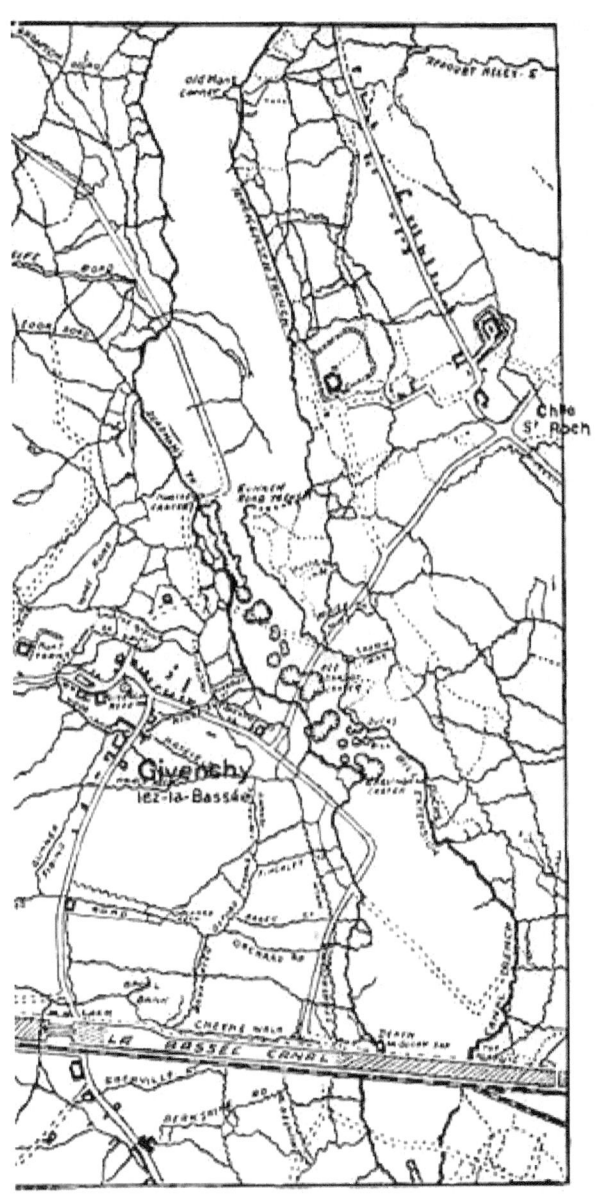

April, 1918

him understand why he was ordered to do something.

On the 15th, seven other ranks joined us as reinforcements.

On the 17th, at 3.15 a.m., a silent raiding party of enemy rushed the crater post of D Company, under cover of smoke bombs. The enemy were quickly ejected, and left two dead in our lines. Our casualties were:—Second Lieutenant Westwood and two other ranks wounded, three other ranks missing.

The next day we hit back, sending a patrol into the enemy's front line, who searched it for 200 yards without finding anybody. The attempt was repeated on the following day, and an enemy wiring party was rushed.

On the 20th the 1/4th King's Own relieved us by daylight, and we moved into support. Headquarters and A, B, and C Companies being in the village line and D Company in Le Preol. The following days were quiet, and we were busy repairing the defences. Seven men went sick.

On the 25th we relieved the 2/5th Lancashire Fusiliers in the right sector, by daylight, the dispositions being similar but companies from right to left being—D, B, C, and A. Our patrols found enemy machine gun fire very active. Second Lieutenant W. H. F. Smith went to Field Ambulance sick.

The following day was quiet, and at night our patrols were very active trying to get into the enemy's lines to secure a prisoner. Ultimately the enemy got so "windy" that they sent up their S.O.S., and their barrage came down on our support lines. After 40 minutes' retaliation by our guns everything became normal. Second Lieutenant James-Alfred was wounded. Thirty-two other ranks reinforcements joined us.

The next day was quiet, but the night was lively, four patrols being in No Man's Land searching for enemy all night. From enemy machine gun fire we had the misfortune to lose Second Lieutenant Adamson, M.C.. who was killed. Second Lieutenant Hulme was sent to Field Ambulance sick.

On the 28th there was the usual amount of artillery activity during the day. At 7.30 p.m. a raiding party, consisting of Second Lieutenants Taylor and Cooper and 28 other ranks, raided an enemy machine gun post but found it empty, and could not penetrate further owing to machine gun fire.

On March 21st the long-expected attack against the Allied front commenced. The 5th Army, on the right of the 3rd Army, were driven back, and the enemy almost reached Amiens. In order to fill the hole thus made, the 1st and 2nd Armies were denuded of reserves, and as a direct result of this the 164th Brigade, which was in divisional reserve, was constantly being rushed up to points of concentration at night in case the Boche attacked, and all ranks learnt thoroughly to dislike the code word "Bustle." On about April 1st, at the Corps Headquarters, it was decided that the division must risk all on the line Givenchy-Festubert, supporting battalions of brigades being close up behind their battle line. The establishment of the main line of defence on the line of Festubert Village made the position of Givenchy difficult, as the line of defence of the right brigade holding the position was 800 yards in front of the left brigade.

The Battle of Givenchy.

At about 7 a.m. on the 9th April, in thick fog which made observation impossible, the enemy appears to have attacked the left brigade of the 2nd Portuguese Division in strength and to have broken into their trenches.

Shortly after 7 a.m. an attack had developed on the right Brigade of the 40th Division, and soon afterwards the attack opened on our front. Map No. 7 is a copy of the German map which was captured by us in the course of the battle, from which the German plan can be clearly gathered.

The 164th Infantry Brigade was holding Givenchy, with the 1/4th Royal Lancaster Regiment on the right and the 1/4th North Lancashire Regiment on the left, 2/5th Lancashire Fusiliers in support with three companies in the village line (a continuation of the Festubert line) and one company and headquarters at Gorre, some distance back. On the left of the 164th Infantry Brigade, the 165th Infantry Brigade held the village line (Festubert) in strength; north of the 55th Division were the Portuguese; the 166th Infantry Brigade was in divisional reserve; south of the canal the 1st Division held the line. The 164th Infantry Brigade and the 165th Infantry Brigade were covered by the 276th and the 275th Artillery Brigades, or rather groups.

The amount of artillery available was not great for the frontage to be covered. At 4.15 a.m. the enemy opened a heavy bombardment, reaching as far back as Gorre; this was largely a gas bombardment, but all reports showed that no mustard gas was being used, which was suspicious, as previous experiences further south had shown that, when the enemy really intended to attack, he did not use mustard gas for

MAP NO. 7

FACSIMILE OF GERMAN MAP SHOWING PLAN OF ATTACK.

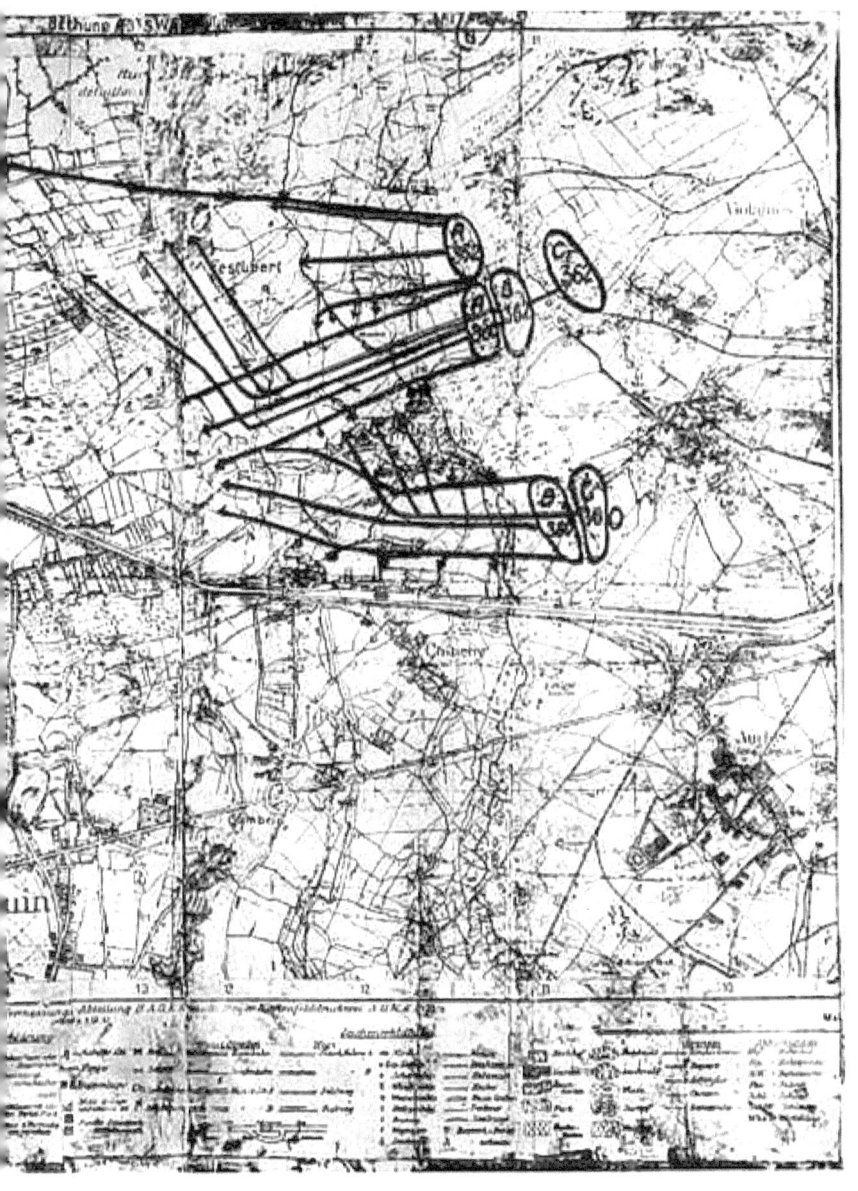

Captured April 9th, 1918

fear of getting into it himself.

At this time the front line companies reported by wire that the situation was normal, but that all ranks were standing to. The morning was extremely foggy, the limit of vision being about 30 yards at the best. About 5 a.m. the code word "Bustle" was received from brigade, and at 6 a.m. a very heavy bombardment of our front line system commenced—some of the heaviest shelling ever experienced by the battalion.

The enemy's procedure so far had been exactly the same as that used against the 5th Army on March 21st. The shelling of the front line system increased in intensity, many trench mortars being in action.

At 8.45 a.m. the front line companies reported that the enemy was advancing, and the S.O.S. went up from the companies and Battalion Headquarters (Southmoor Villa), though doubts were freely expressed as to the rockets being seen on account of the thick fog, which was accentuated by the smoke and dust of the bombardment; they were seen, however, and the artillery and machine gun barrages opened promptly. From this time onwards till midnight savage fighting went on in the front line system.

The German Divisional orders, captured during the course of the day, showed that the 4th Ersatz Division, which had been made up to strength and re-equipped, had been brought into the line for the purpose of making this attack. This division had been specially selected for this attack, as it had for many months held the Givenchy Festubert front and was supposed to know the ground well. It was strengthened with storm-troops and heavy machine guns. The general plan was to attack the Givenchy salient on the flanks, striking towards Windy Corner on the north, and forwards and through Spoil Bank to Pont Fixe on the south; each of these attacks was to be carried out by one regiment of three battalions, strengthened with storm-troops and heavy machine guns.

On reaching the objectives Windy Corner and Pont Fixe, these two attacks were to join hands, and thus cut off the main Givenchy position.

No direct frontal attack was to be made across the craters, but machine guns were to be mounted on the commanding crests which were to engage the garrison while the encircling attacks were in progress.

One battalion of the northern attack had orders on gaining the position Windy Corner-Le Plantin South to turn north along the Festubert Village line and clean up in co-operation with an attack by one battalion of the reserve regiment.

As soon as these actions had been successful, a general advance was to be made on Gorre.

The attacking Boche had been carefully instructed that "the 55th Division is a tired division, only fit to hold a quiet section of the line." Before nightfall he found out his mistake. Owing to the thick fog and the amount of wire, the fighting from the commencement of the Boche attack until the afternoon consisted of isolated fights carried on all over the area by small parties of officers and men, but all acting on a preconceived plan.

The garrisons of the strong points located the enemy by means of patrols, so that when the fog lifted at about 11 a.m. they instantly opened heavy fire with rifles and machine guns.

The enemy succeeded in getting into one half of the concrete pill box in Cavan Lane, but the crew fought him through the gas curtain while the machine gun continued its fire northwards with excellent results, until a counterattack, led by Captain Lonsdale, M.C., from Bunny Hutch tunnel entrance, freed the crew.

The enemy actually entered our lines at several places, notably Givenchy Keep, Piccadilly Trench, Ware Road, Moat Farm, Battalion Headquarters, Kitchen Road, and Windy Corner, but he was very quickly driven out, except at Givenchy Keep, Battalion Headquarters, and Windy Corner; the situation at these three points was not really satisfactory until after mid-day.

The enemy's northern attack failed to take any strong points covering the north flank of the Givenchy salient; it did succeed in taking Le Plantin South and in penetrating into Windy Corner, but was then held up by the garrison and Battalion Headquarters details in Herts Redoubt and Southmoor Villa.

The enemy looted the divisional canteen and established his Battalion Headquarters there, thus being immediately in rear of the Battalion sector. A counter-attack by the 165th Infantry Brigade re-took Le Plantin South, and a local counter-attack organised by Battalion Headquarters, restored the situation at Windy Corner, but not before the enemy had captured our Aid Post and some 50 prisoners, including the *padre*, and had sent small patrols forward toward Lone Farm, who, however, were destroyed by our advanced 18-pounders, which blew them to pieces at close range, bits of Boche being scattered on the trees and hedges in the vicinity.

Ultimately the German Battalion commander and 120 Boches were captured in Kitchen Road. These men were all found to be loaded with the contents of our divisional canteen; needless to say, they were quickly relieved of their loot.

The Boche continued to press his troops forward into the angle between Givenchy Kill and the Le Plantin Festubert Line, suffering very severe losses from our heavy and continuous fire on his flanks; in many instances his own machine guns, manned by our Lewis gunners, were turned against him with excellent results. He could get no further and was completely disorganised by the fog and wire, and the situation on this flank became stabilised for the moment. The l/4th King's Own, who were holding the right sector of the brigade front, had suffered very heavy losses from the preliminary bombardment, owing to the lack of shell-proof cover, the trench system having been practically destroyed.

The enemy, advancing over the flat between the southern crater and the canal, overran the main line of defence, but failed to take the most advanced sap, "Death or Glory," situated on the bank of the canal. The garrison of this sap, consisting of one platoon, about 18 strong (of the l/4th King's Own), maintained a heavy enfilade fire on the advancing enemy, causing him very heavy casualties. Though cut off for five hours, this garrison most gallantly held its position, and later in the day sallying forth, captured a machine gun and crew.

Despite the losses incurred from "Death or Glory" sap, the Boche pushed on and captured Orchard Keep, the garrison of which had been destroyed by shell fire, and penetrated into Gunners' Siding, at its junction with the main . communication trench, Orchard Road. He, however, failed to take either Marie Keep to the north or Spoil Bank Keep to the south. His further progress beyond Gunners' Siding was checked by supports pushed up by the 2/5th Lancashire Fusiliers. His endeavours to push north of Gunners' Siding were checked by the few men of the garrison and the anti-tank 18-pounder gun in the trench. This gun, though damaged by shell fire to such an extent that the breach had to be opened with a pick, fired no fewer than 150 rounds at a range of 200 yards at the enemy. Time after time the enemy tried to rush it across the open or along the trench, but were beaten off by the infantry covering the gun.

At about 10.45 a.m. the situation had stabilised on the front of our brigade, and was as follows:—

A large number of the enemy were in the low ground in the angle between the north face of the Givenchy salient and the Le Plantin South—Festubert line. Another large force were on the flat plateau between Marie Keep, Gunners' Siding, Spoil Bank Keep, and Death And Glory Sap. In other words, the enemy were divided into two, and contained in two deep pockets. At 11 a.m. the fog cleared, and there was a very marked increase in the rifle and machine gun fire, as all along the front small parties of troops, acting on their own initiative, began at once to attack the nearest Boche in flank and rear, forcing him to maintain his position in the pockets.

Orders were then issued to push every available man up to close the mouths of the two pockets. The forces available were divided into two parties, the northern of which was to seize Grenadier Road, thereby closing the mouth of the northern pocket and cutting off all the enemy in it.

This force acted with great vigour, and not only gained Grenadier Road, but also re-took the commanding saps on the northern craters, giving valuable observation over the flat ground to the north and the approaches to the Portuguese front.

The southern force ("King's Own" and Lancashire Fusiliers) was ordered to move up Cheyne Walk, regain the front line, and then move northwards, closing the mouth of the southern pocket.

This force succeeded in freeing Death and Glory Sap and regaining the main line of defence, but could not regain its crater posts owing to the complete destruction of the trenches leading to them.

These movements commenced at 11.30 a.m., and were covered by a concentrated barrage fire by our artillery on Canal Reserve, in which the enemy were believed to have their reserves massed. During the progress of the operations no enemy supports came up, and direct evidence is now available that this was due to the artillery barrage.

It will be remembered that early in the morning about 50 officers and men were captured by the enemy round the First Aid Post at Windy Corner, among them being the Rev. L. N. Forse, chaplain to the 4th Loyal North Lancashire Regiment. This officer was many weeks in Germany, and on his return to the brigade on release stated that he and ten other prisoners were taken off by the Boche to one of the trenches north of the craters. The ground in this area was covered with enemy dead, and our rifle and machine gun fire was very heavy. Later the party were moved southwards behind the craters, making for Canal Reserve trench. At about 11.30 a.m. the party were thirty yards or so from the trench, which was packed with about 500 enemy massed three deep. Our barrage opened and fell right in the trench, doing tremendous execution, unfortunately knocking out 23 of the chaplain's party. After half an hour the barrage ceased, and the remnants of the party made for the trench, but found it quite impossible to move along it owing to the Boche dead in it. The massed enemy reserves appeared to have been completely destroyed by our artillery fire.

The mouths of the pockets being closed and the enemy surrounded, it was only a matter of time before he was forced to surrender in groups.

There were many acts of bravery on the part of individual officers and men, and many honours were won.

The outstanding features of the action were:—(*a*) absolute preparedness for action, (*b*) the sending out of scouts to locate the enemy, (*c*) the prompt initiative shown by all ranks, which was responsible for the breaking up of the enemy's attack and his complete defeat.

By 3.45 p.m. we had regained the whole of our defensive system, with the exception of the saps on the southern craters. As soon as darkness came on, an attack was organised by the Royal Lancaster Regiment to recover the crater saps in their area. This was very successful, a large number of prisoners being taken

At 2.45 a.m. on April 10th, the brigadier was able to inform the division that the brigade held its line intact, including the forward saps, as it had been held on April 8th.

During the afternoon of April 9th two companies of the South Lancashire Regiment came up, one being allotted to each battalion in the line. The company allotted to the 4th Loyal North Lancashire Regiment was posted in Grenadier Road, with one platoon at Le Plantin South, and they did yeoman service in relieving our tired men.

Throughout April 9th the action of our artillery had been admirable. Two 18-pounder batteries of the 11th Division which could fire on our front were handed over to the brigade, and two heavy batteries belonging to the corps placed themselves under the orders of the brigade.

As soon as darkness permitted, all guns north of the canal were withdrawn south of the canal, and the guns came out of their emplacements and took up positions in the open.

The 165th Infantry Brigade had maintained its main line intact, but had given up its advanced posts. No touch could be obtained with the Portuguese on the left, and early in the morning of April 10th the enemy were pushing through clear of and north of the 165th Infantry Brigade.

The 165th threw back its left flank at right angles, the defensive flank being continued by all units of the division.

After 4 p.m. the rest of the day was spent in reorganising the posts and mopping up the few remaining enemy left in the sector. Our communication trenches were continuously shelled. At about 4 p.m. B Company, 1/5th South Lancashires, came up as reinforcements and manned our left flank from New Cut to Windy Corner.

Our casualties were:—

Officers—
    Killed: Second Lieutenant L. Brooke, M.C.
    Wounded: Second Lieutenant R. E. Horsfall, G. C. Horner, C. Haworth, and P. B. Beresford.
    Missing: Chaplain L. N. Forse (prisoner of war) and Lieutenant W. H. Jenkins, medical officer.

Other Ranks—
    Killed 43, Wounded 100, Missing 50.

No further attacks were made on our front.

On the 10th, although enemy guns and aeroplanes were very active, an attempt was made to clear out the trenches and bury the dead.

Captain A. A. Turner, R.A.M.C, reported for duty as medical officer.

Captain Collett was wounded on the 11th by enemy shelling, which was heavy, especially on headquarters in the afternoon and a barrage on our lines at 6 p.m.

Second Lieutenant Vincent, M.C, was wounded by artillery fire on the 12th.

During the 10th and subsequent days, the artillery with the 164th Infantry Brigade played a big role in breaking up many enemy concentrations against the thrown-back flank. The enemy was unable to move his men forward without coming under the observation, and very often the close fire of, our northern posts and flanks.

Thus ended a highly-successful action, in which the battalion played an important part. Had the day gone against the division, the Allies might have had to abandon the Pas de Calais. A glance at the map will show the seriousness of such a step.

The brigade continued, despite heavy artillery bombardment, to hold the line until the division was relieved by the 1st Division.

THE REMNANT OF GIVENCHY KEEP, 1920.

During the action of the 9th of April, and the night of the 9th and 10th, the following casualties were incurred by the brigade:—Killed, wounded, and missing: 35 officers, 659 other ranks.

The enemy lost about 600 killed in our lines and No Man's Land. No estimate can, however, be made of his casualties in his own lines, but, judging from the reports of returned prisoners of war, these were exceptionally heavy.

The following captures were made: Prisoners: 641, including many officers and two battalion commanders; 100 light and heavy machine guns, and one regimental band. In addition, on April 11th, an Austrian artillery officer was killed on the Red Dragon Crater, and the identifications obtained from him were the first direct evidence of the presence of Austrians on the Western Front. A very fine range-finding instrument was captured at the same time. This instrument was presented by the battalion to the West Lancashire Field Artillery.

On the 13th the communication trenches were practically cleared of blocks. The keeps were heavily shelled in the afternoon. Fourteen men arrived from the reinforcement camp.

On the 14th enemy artillery was still very active, and all preparations were made to meet further attacks.

On the 15th the enemy annoyed us by persistent harassing fire throughout the day.

Second Lieutenant Westwood was killed and one other rank wounded. The new *padre*, Captain R. R. Schofield, arrived.

On the 16th, amidst active enemy artillery fire, the 1st Black Watch relieved us, the relief being completed with three casualties. We marched back to Beuvry, where we em'bussed and were taken to Lozingham.

Captain Hore, M.C., went to England sick, and Second Lieutenant E. M. Studdart to Field Ambulance.

127 other ranks arrived from reinforcement camp.

The battalion was not billeted until 4 a.m.

The next few days were spent in reorganising and training. Captain Carmichael and Second Lieutenants Greaves and Taylor and five other ranks going sick.

On the 22nd we went *en masse* to the Divisional Theatre.

On the 23rd we em'bussed at 7 a.m. for Vaudricourt, where we arrived at 9 30 a.m.

An advance party was sent to take over the Support Battalion area of the Givenchy sector. A "B team" of seven officers and 110 other ranks went to Vurbure. We em'bussed again at 8 p.m. and went to Armeguin, whence we marched to relieve the 1st Northamptons in support.

C Company were at Windy Corner and D Company at Pont Fixe, A, B, and Headquarters being on the canal bank. We had one man killed and one man wounded.

The next day on the whole was quiet. There was some shelling at Windy Corner with 4.2's One other rank was killed.

The 25th was quiet up to 9 p.m., when a heavy barrage was placed on our support lines. The whole battalion was on working parties by night. Our support lines were again bombarded at 2.20 p.m. on the 26th.

Platoons were detached and sent to the Lancashire Fusiliers and the King's Own in case of need, and A Company remained in the Village Line all night.

Eight other ranks were wounded on this and the following day.

The following are extracts from various telegrams, letters, and Press cuttings referring to the Battle of Givenchy:—

(SPECIAL SUPPLEMENTARY DESPATCH.)

THE 55TH DIVISION AT GIVENCHY.

Headquarters, France, Monday, 1.15 p.m.
On the morning of the German attack on April 9th, 1918, the 55th (West Lancashire) Division (Territorial) was holding a front of about 6,000 yards, extending from the La Bassée Canal to just south of Richebourg l'Avoue, where its line joined that held by the Portuguese. The enemy's attack on the southern portion of this front was delivered by all three Regiments of the 4th Ersatz Division, which was well up to strength. A captured divisional order issued by the General Staff of this German division, and dated April 6th, 1918, shows that its objectives were "the ground and the British position in the triangle formed by Givenchy-Festubert-Gorre." The following passages from this captured order are of special interest:—

In our attack our three regiments will be opposed by at most six companies in front and at most two reserve battalions in Festubert and Givenchy. One battalion in divisional reserve is south of the La Bassée Canal in Le Preol. It will be prevented by our powerful artillery fire from taking part in the fight for Festubert and Givenchy. The troops are elements of the English

55th Division, which, after being engaged on the Somme, has suffered heavy losses in Flanders and at Cambrai, and was described by prisoners in March, 1918, as a division fit to hold a quiet sector, that is below the average quality.

The order containing the passages quoted above was distributed among all officers and under-officers of the 4th Ersatz Division down to platoon commanders, presumably with a view to encouraging the troops prior to their attack, and in the belief that the opposition met with would not be very serious. If this was his expectation the enemy was most signally disappointed.

Throughout the early part of the morning of April 9th, the 55th Division beat off all attacks on its forward zone, and maintained its line intact. Later, when the German infantry had broken through the Portuguese positions on its left, the division formed a defensive flank facing north-east on the line Givenchy-Festubert to the neighbourhood of Le Touret. This line it maintained practically unchanged until relief, through six days of almost continual fighting, in the course of which it beat off repeated German attacks with the heaviest losses to the enemy, and took nearly 1,000 prisoners.

At one time, on the first day of his attack, the enemy's troops forced their way into Givenchy and Festubert. Both villages were shortly afterwards regained by the 55th Division as the result of a highly-successful counter-attack, in which several hundred Germans were captured. All further attempts on the part of the enemy to carry these positions broke down before the resolute defence of the 55th Division. Though he succeeded on April 11th in entering a post north of Festubert, he was thrown out again by a counter-attack, and on the night of April 12th the 55th Division improved its position in this neighbourhood, capturing a German post and taking several prisoners.

Next day, during the afternoon, the enemy heavily bombarded the whole front held by the division between Gorre and the Lawe Canal, and subsequently attacked in strength. He was once more repulsed with heavy loss by the most gallant and successful defence of a division which he had been pleased to describe as consisting of second-class troops.

Telegrams Received.

From Field Marshal Sir Douglas Haig, K.T., G.C.B., G.C.V.O., K.C.I.E.,
April 10th, 1918:—

Please convey to General Jeudwine and to all officers and men of the 55th Division my congratulations on their splendid fighting yesterday, especially at Festubert and Givenchy.

From General Sir H. Plumer, G.C.B., G.C.M.G., G.C.V.O., Commanding 2nd Army, April 9th, 1918:—
Many congratulations on your success at Givenchy from the 2nd Army.

From Lieutenant-General Sir H. S. Home, K.C.B., K.C.M.G., Commanding 1st Army, April 9th, 1918:—
Sincere congratulations to you and all ranks of the 55th Division on your splendid defence today.

From Lieutenant-General Sir R. Haking, K.C.B., K.C.M.G., Commanding XI. Corps, April 10th, 1918:—
I wish to thank you, your brigade, battalion, and company commanders, for the splendid manner in which you have repelled the enemy's attack along your whole front and formed a very wide flank on your left when the division there was driven back.

The fine offensive spirit displayed by officers and men on this occasion reflects the highest credit upon the whole division. Although heavily attacked along your whole front and your left flank turned, you have been successful in maintaining your original line and even gaining some ground and capturing over 700 prisoners.

The co-operation of the artillery, engineers, and pioneer battalion was excellent throughout, and it will be a great pleasure to me to report the matter to the Army Commander.

From the Earl of Derby, K.G., Secretary of State for War, April 10th, 1918:—
Well done, 55th! You have done splendidly, as you always do.

From the XI. Corps, April 11th, 1918:—
The Corps Commander wishes his congratulations conveyed to all ranks of the 55th Division on again beating off German attacks.

From G.O.C. 1st Division, April 11th, 1918:—
On behalf of the 1st Division I wish to convey to you and all ranks of the 55th Division our admiration of your stout fight at

Givenchy and Festubert.

From the 42nd Division, April 20th, 1918:—
All ranks of the 42nd East Lancashire Division most heartily congratulate the 55th West Lancashire Division on their magnificent defence of Givenchy. They are glad to be able to think that the work and plans commenced by them stood their Lancashire brothers in good stead.

From the 51st Division, April 10th, 1918:—
Heartiest congratulations from all ranks 51st (Highland) Division on the fine victory won by you yesterday.

From the 57th Division:—
All ranks 57th Division congratulate 55th Division on their fine fight.

From the Mayor of Preston, April 13th, 1918:—
I have heard with greatest admiration of the splendid work of the officers and men of your division. We are very proud of them.

EXTRACTS FROM NEWSPAPERS.

The Times, April 11th, 1918:—

55TH DIVISION'S FINE FIGHTING.
(From our Special Correspondent.)

The breach made by the Portuguese retirement threw an enormous strain on the British 55th Division on the extreme right, which held the positions about Givenchy. The Lancashire men threw back their left to make a flank on that side, and then began the defence of Givenchy, which will be remembered as one of the brilliant incidents of this war. The ground here was of some importance, as being almost the only exception to the general flatness of the battle area. Three times, it is said, at least, the German masses succeeded in breaking a way into Givenchy, once during the course of the day, and twice during the evening and night, only to be thrown out again by the most dashing counter-attacks. This morning Givenchy and all our original line remained in our hands, and I believe it still remains, and, out of the prisoners taken, over 700 were captured by the Lancashire men.

(Note. Of these, 560 were taken by the 1/4th North Lancashire Regiment.)

The Times, April 12th, 1918:—
The section of attack was delivered in great strength, some eleven or twelve divisions being used on not more than 17,000 yards, and the weight of the impact drove back the Portuguese front at the centre. It was the magnificent stand of the 55th Lancashire Division at Givenchy which prevented what might have been a rather serious disaster. Of the behaviour of our men in this fighting round Givenchy nothing could be said in too high praise. This morning the Germans were still attacking here, and in vain."

Daily Mail, April 15th, 1918:—
For the work of such divisions as the 9th, 51st, and 55th no praise can be too high, no words of laudation extravagant. With their backs to the wall they have shown that they are capable of reaching new heights of heroism, as great as any the glorious past has known.

Daily Mail, April 16th, 1918:
They have fought with a gallantry and endurance worthy of their race, and the heroism of the 55th (Lancashire Territorial) Division is worthily celebrated by Sir Douglas Haig in a special despatch. Their country may indeed be proud of these men who are so lavishly giving their blood on her behalf, and she will follow their efforts with her love and prayers.

Le Petit Parisien, April 12th, 1918:—
At the beginning of the attack, after the Portuguese had been forced back, the plan of the German High Command was checked thanks to the indomitable resistance which was offered by the British right flank. There the enemy found established a Lancashire Division the 55th which will certainly be mentioned in the *communiqué*. It is the least that can be done for this division. For ten hours three German divisions tried in vain to dislodge it.

Le Matin, April 13th, 1918:—
It was there that the 55th Division as I have already told you— held on and triumphed. I wanted to see with my own eyes some of these bravest of the brave. But before seeing them I had

already seen their prisoners. . . .

'One should be almost proud to have been beaten by such men,' said one prisoner who belonged to the German nobility. An officer of the highest rank said to them (the 55th):

'You have accomplished one of the finest feats-of-arms—perhaps the finest of the whole war.'

It is true. They had fought to the limit of the impossible.

On the 28th we moved into the right sector and relieved the 1/4th King's Own A Company to Mairie Redoubt, B Company to Death or Glory Sap, C and D to Gunners' Siding. The sap had been heavily trench-mortared before we took over, and parts of it were blown in. One other rank was killed and four wounded. The award of the French *Croix de Guerre* to Sergeant J. Cookson was announced.

On the 29th, Death or Glory Sap was heavily "minnied." Two other ranks were killed and three wounded. On the 30th, there was some heavy shelling, though only one man was wounded, but we lost one man killed and one wounded from *minenwerfer* the following day. On the 2nd we were relieved by the 1/5th King's Liverpool Regiment, 12 men being wounded in the course of the day, and went back to rest.

This rest was thoroughly enjoyed by the whole battalion, being the first real rest since the Battle of Givenchy. The billets were good, and the canteen well stocked.

On the 8th, we moved back to the line, Major Duggan, M.C., being in command, and relieved the l/7th King's Liverpool Regiment in the right sector.

Wiring and working under difficult conditions continued until the 12th, three men being killed and eight wounded, two missing, and seven sick during the tour. We were relieved on the night of the 12th by the 2/5th Lancashire Fusiliers, and moved back to support.

On the 14th, A Company carried out an operation against the enemy's front line post in Willow Drain, penetrating his line at one point and establishing a block which they held till about 10.30 p.m., being then obliged to withdraw by strong counter-attack. The front and support lines were heavily bombarded from 6.15 p.m. till about 11 p.m., harassing fire being kept up until 2 a.m.

The raiding party sustained heavy casualties. Going across No Man's Land—a mass of shell holes—Second Lieutenant Ibbotson was wounded and then killed by a shell; Second Lieutenant Milne was killed by a bomb while passing through the enemy wire; and Second

Lieutenant Cooper was wounded by a bullet in the throat, causing the loss of his voice, but gallantly went on writing his orders in his pocket book and carrying on until killed by a second bullet.[1] There is no record of the other casualties, but they numbered about 50.

This raid was supported by a creeping barrage, the ground in the neighbourhood being blanketed throughout by artillery and Stokes' mortars.

On the 1/7th we relieved the 1/4th King's Own in the left Givenchy sector, A Company at Plantain South, B Company left front Company, C Company right front Company, D Company holding the Keeps. Four other ranks were killed and Second Lieutenant Chapman and 19 other ranks wounded during the tour, which came to an end on the 20th, when the 1/6th King's Liverpool Regiment relieved us at 2.10 a.m.

The battalion then moved back to rest billets.

The period now under review was known as the "bustle" period, as that was the code word on receipt of which all kinds of moves were to take place which cannot here be detailed.

In our rest billets at Vaudricourt we went through the usual training and bathing routine until the 26th, when we relieved the 1/7th King's Liverpool Regiment in the Givenchy left sector. During the rest Second Lieutenant Hampson was killed and four men wounded.

At this time a stringent order was issued that anyone damaging crops was to be court-martialled (rather a contrast to the same period in the previous year, when the fields which formed our training grounds being covered with young corn, we had been ordered to disregard the crops entirely. Obeying this order went literally against the grain!).

On the 25th May the following honours were announced:—

Bar to Military Medal:—Corporal Pendlebury, M.M., and Lance-Corporal P. Wyre, M.M.

Military Medal:—Sergeants R. Parkinson and A. Lowe, Corporal J. Gradwell, Privates A. Hommans, G. Rotherham, T. Marsh, W. Goodram, J. Meadows, R. Williams, F. Lloyd, J. Read, L. Cunliffe, and T.

---

1. Two years afterwards his parents received this pocket book. The last entries are as follow:—"Remainder of section to follow L C. Price Tell Sergeant."
"You have done damn well, but you aren't finished yet! Read this to him."
"Bomb the Boche out. See that gap in the parapet? I want to get the whole section there." Can we get a message back to Capt. Swaine? I suggest let one man take Farnworth back and also message. Tell O. C. A Co. . . . . "
So it ends.

Farnworth.

We had five men wounded on the 27th.

On the 28th, described in the *War Diary* as "a quiet day," a small party of the enemy entered one of our posts in Piccadilly at 12.30 a.m. It was immediately bombed out without casualties to us. The attempt was repeated the following day, but frustrated by our Lewis gunners and rifle grenadiers. Thirteen men were wounded in the next three days.

On the 1st June, the enemy bombarded us heavily with mustard gas shells and shrapnel for two hours, killing Second Lieutenant Greaves and wounding Captain Lonsdale and 10 other ranks.

On the 2nd, also described as "a quiet day," six other ranks were killed and Second Lieutenant Dawson and 23 other ranks were wounded, and on the following day two killed and 15 wounded. The Battalion was relieved in the evening by the 1/4th King's Own, when we went back to support. Working parties occupied us for the next few days, three men being killed, one missing, and five wounded during the period.

On the 8th, on relief by the 1/6th King's Liverpool Regiment, we moved back to rest billets at Vaudricourt.

The following appeared in the King's Birthday Honour List:—

Mentioned in Despatches:—Lieutenant-Colonel J. A. Crump, Privates R. Worden and J. Bates.

Distinguished Service Order:—Lieutenant-Colonel J. A. Crump.

Bars to Military Cross:— Major Duggan, M.C., Captain Lonsdale, M.C., Second Lieutenant H. Fazackerley, M.C.

Military Cross:—Captain D. Carmichael, Lieutenant A. Bardsley, Second Lieutenants H. Bailey and C. Milne.

Distinguished Conduct Medal:—Company Sergeant-Major Ireland, Sergeants J. Miller, M.M., and A. Atkinson, Privates F. Reddish, J. Livesey, and T. Parkes, M.M.

Companies were thoroughly reorganised. Training was carried out and sports were held.

On the 14th June, Major T. G. Williams, M.C, 1/7th King's Liverpool Regiment, took over command of the battalion. On the same day the battalion relieved the 1/7th King's Liverpool Regiment in the right Givenchy sector. The usual routine was carried out during the tour. The enemy bombarded the sector on the 19th and again on the 20th at 3 a.m., when he put down a severe barrage of 4.2's and some mustard gas. We were relieved on the night of the 23rd by the 1/4th

King's Own. During the tour our casualties were:—Second Lieutenant Pasley and eight other ranks killed, and 17 other ranks wounded, Lieutenants Hyndson and Pierce, Second Lieutenant Boddington, and 16 other ranks going sick to hospital.

Our bombing post in Half-Moon Trench was not more than 20 yards distant from a bombing post in the enemy's sector, and after a careful reconnaissance had been made under the supervision of the officer commanding B Company (Captain R. H. Smith, M.C), Second Lieutenant Weatherhill volunteered to take out a patrol the following night and raid the enemy's trenches. The night was a particularly dark one, but, unfortunately, the enemy discovered the patrol getting out of the trenches, and the attacking party was subjected to a heavy fire from machine guns and bombs. The patrol remained out for about an hour, but finally they returned to the trenches, and it was found that Second Lieutenant Weatherhill was missing and two other ranks wounded. Another patrol was immediately sent out by the officer commanding B Company to find out what had happened to Second Lieutenant Weatherhill, but this and other subsequent patrols met with no success.

On the 27th, on relief, we went back into support, and at 5 a.m. on the following day to rest billets at Vaudricourt. Here the G.O.C presented medals and ribbons to officers and men of the battalion on the 30th.

On the 1st July, at the Brigade Horse Show, the battalion did very well, carrying off the Championship Cup and six first prizes, which in itself was sufficient reward to the officer commanding Transport (Lieutenant A. Bardsley, M.C.) and all other ranks. It might here be mentioned that, under the supervision of Lieutenant A. Bardsley, the Battalion Transport did very well in the Division Show and later on obtained first prize at the Corps Transport Show.

On the 3rd we moved up in position to the line and relieved the 1/7th King's Liverpool Regiment in support in the Givenchy sector, one man being killed and four wounded, and two more wounded the following day.

On the evening of the 7th we relieved the 2/5th Lancashire Fusiliers on the left sector a very difficult relief, Companies having to move up their sectors through a heavy bombardment of 4.2's, 5.9's, whizzbangs, and *minenwerfers*. This was the enemy's retaliation for our bombardment in connection with a raid carried out on our flank by the 1st Cameronians. One other rank was killed and six wounded. The next few days were spent in the usual routine and working and wiring parties, and were fairly quiet, our casualties for the tour being: Seven other ranks killed and eight wounded.

On the Kith we were relieved by the 1/6th King's Liverpool Regiment, and moved back to Le Preol, where we stood-to for the night, moving back to Vaudricourt the following morning.

On the 20th a dance for officers and men took place in the Recreation Hut.

On the 22nd we relieved the 1/5th King's Liverpool Regiment in the right Givenchy sector.

No prisoners having been captured by the corps for about a fortnight, the divisional commander was very anxious that prisoners should be obtained for the purpose of identification, and with this end in view, on the 27th, two reconnaissances by Second Lieutenant Archibald on the old British Line opposite Orchard Road during the morning, and by Second Lieutenant Dawson opposite Finchley Road Sap in the afternoon, found both enemy posts unoccupied. It was therefore decided that these two officers should take part in a silent daylight raid, and on the following day both officers took over patrols. Second Lieutenant Dawson's patrol met with no success, but Second Lieutenant Archibald's patrol succeeded in capturing three of the enemy and one machine gun and returned to our trenches with no casualties and without a single shot having been fired by either side.

Congratulatory telegrams were received by the officer commanding and Second Lieutenant Archibald was awarded for his gallantry the Military Cross and the non-commissioned officer who accompanied him was awarded the Military Medal.

On the 29th, at his own request. Second Lieutenant Dawson again tried to effect an entry into the enemy's line, and was successful in finding three men and a strong working party, which the patrol promptly bombed. Our casualties were nil, and from documents subsequently captured from the enemy it would appear that these raids had a depressing effect on the enemy's morale.

On the 30th, Second Lieutenant Archibald and two other ranks again entered the post and reconnoitred the trench, finding quantities of bombs. Later in the day they returned to the enemy's trench, collected all explosives in a dugout, and blew it up. We were relieved that night by the l/4th King's Own, and went back into support. The casualties during the tour were eight other ranks wounded.

On the 1st August we found ourselves in the Givenchy Village

Lines.

On the 3rd we tried to select a shooting team for the Army competition, but had to give it up owing to hostile shelling. That night we moved back to rest billets at Vaudricourt. Boxing, cricket, dances, and Divisional Horse Shows were the chief events of the next few days.

The battalion relieved the 1/6th King's Liverpool Regiment in the left Givenchy sector on the 9th. All ranks of the battalion, with the exception of those actually on sentry posts, were employed during the day on wire carrying and making "concertinas" with a view to strengthening the defences, and during this tour the battalion accomplished a great improvement in the wire defences.

Things were quiet, except for wire-cutting by our artillery, up till the 15th, when we had two hours' shelling by yellow cross gas shells, projected from trench mortars. We moved back to support in the evening, being relieved by the 2/5th Lancashire Fusiliers. During the tour. Second Lieutenants Archibald, Cowan, and Shell were wounded, and four other ranks were wounded and 14 other ranks were gassed. The next few days in support were occupied by bathing, working and carrying parties, the casualties being: Three other ranks killed, 18 wounded, and Second Lieutenants Dixon, Dawson, and 61 other ranks gassed.

On the 23rd, we moved in to hold the right and left sub-sectors during the capture of the craters by the 1/4th King's Own and the 2/5th Lancashire Fusiliers, which operation was successfully accomplished.

There was a good deal of shelling during these days, Second Lieutenant Fazackerley, M.C., and one other rank being killed, one other rank gassed, and Second Lieutenant Pride and 10 other ranks wounded. The loss of Second Lieutenant Fazackerley, M.C., was keenly felt by all ranks of the battalion.

On the 27th we went back to rest billets at Vaudricourt.

On the 3rd September we relieved the 1/6th King's Liverpool Regiment in the Givenchy left sub-sector. The craters were heavily shelled between 4 and 6 p.m. with 5.9's and blue and yellow cross gas. Reconnoitring patrols pushed out at daylight and established posts on the west edge of Chappelle St. Roche. Second Lieutenants Tennant, Kershaw, and Scott, and 21 other ranks were gassed, 1 killed, and 1 wounded.

The change of mental attitude in this chapter and in the next is very noticeable. No longer do we take part in costly attacks on a wide front or beat off similar attacks by the enemy, nor do we sit still and merely harass him. We feel ourselves winning at last—the game becomes more exciting as we begin to press, and then to follow, a beaten enemy.

Chapter 10

The Advance

On the 1st September, 1918, orders were received that infantry brigades in the line must be prepared to follow up the enemy rapidly should he commence to withdraw on the divisional front, fighting patrols to make good what ground they could; this was consequent upon reports of fires and explosions behind the enemy's line and information from enemy prisoners.

On the 4th, patrols having reported the evacuation of the enemy's front line trenches. Battalion Headquarters moved up from Windy Corner to Givenchy Keep Tunnel. D Company secured a prisoner. One of our night patrols encountered enemy at Roche Alley, and a sharp fight ensued; we left one man severely wounded, who was brought in by a daylight patrol. Lieutenant King and 38 other ranks were gassed, one other rank killed, and Second Lieutenant Davies and two other ranks wounded.

The following day, daylight patrols continued to push up Roche Alley and Cupola Alley, and established outposts, our own line being in advance of the right battalion. The enthusiasm of all ranks to push forward was much marked, and the respective companies vied with each other in their endeavour to establish posts farthest east of any in the battalion or in the division. Four other ranks were wounded and 12 other ranks gassed.

On the 6th there was a little scattered shelling; we were relieved in daylight by the 1/4th King's Own, and went into support. The next two days were occupied with carrying parties, which involved hard and continuous work owing to the state of the trenches and the increasing distance between the front line posts and the reserves. We had one other rank killed, seven wounded, and three gassed.

On the 9th we relieved the King's Own again, and patrols located the enemy at Apse House. The following night a patrol attacked him, but without success.

The 11th was very wet, and on the 12th we were relieved by the 2/5th Lancashire Fusiliers and moved back to support. The casualties during the tour were: 5 other ranks killed, Second Lieutenants Jones, Daniels, Marsden and Thomas and 18 other ranks wounded, 1 other rank gassed.

The weather began to improve. The enemy carried out as usual the daily strafe on the craters on the 13th. Two other ranks were killed, one wounded, and two gassed.

On the 14th, four platoons from A and C Companies were detailed for carrying parties to the 2/5th Lancashire Fusiliers, who were attacking Canteleux Trench at 1.30 p.m. The operation was classed as unsuccessful owing to strong counter-attack and heavy shelling, but they secured 10 prisoners. Second Lieutenant L. B. Smith was killed whilst assisting the attack of the Fusiliers, and six other ranks were wounded. The 1/7th King's Liverpool Regiment relieved us, and we were taken back by 'buses to Vaudricourt, where we rested, trained, and carried out the usual recreational programme.

On the 20th, Lieutenant-Colonel T. G. Williams, M.C., went on leave, and the battalion was then under the command of Major A. E. Entwistle.

On the 21st, the divisional boundaries having been altered, we relieved the 18th Gloucesters on the canal, A Company taking over the outpost line north of the canal, B Company the outpost line south of the canal. The relief passed off without incident.

On the 22nd, B Company pushed their forward posts out about 400 yards. Much enemy harassing fire on this and the following days. The weather broke on the 23rd. On the 25th, companies changed over.

On the 28th, we were relieved by the 1/4th King's Own, and went into support at Barge House. The casualties during the tour were: 5 other ranks killed. Second Lieutenant Kirkby and 10 other ranks wounded.

On the 30th, B and D Companies attacked the distillery, capturing 58 prisoners, but were forced back to their original line later in the day. Second Lieutenant Bryne and three other ranks were killed. Second Lieutenant Cairns and 46 other ranks were wounded, and two other ranks missing.

On the 1st October, Major H. J. G. Duggan returned from the Senior Officers' Course, Aldershot, and took over command from Major Entwistle. On the same day, at 6 15 a.m., B and D Companies, each reinforced by two platoons of C Company, attacked and captured the distillery and machine gun posts on the right and left of it; 23 prisoners and four machine guns were taken; Second Lieutenant Griffiths, Parkinson, Haworth, and Bowler and six other ranks were wounded and 13 other ranks killed. At night we were relieved by six platoons of the King's Own, and moved back into support.

On the 2nd, early morning patrols having reported that the enemy was retiring along his whole front, we moved forward, Headquarters being in Marie Keep. The movement was continued on the following day, 2 other ranks being killed and 5 Other ranks wounded and missing.

On the 4th, we went back to positions of assembly in La Bassée, going into reserve billets on the 5th.

On the 5th, Lieutenant-Colonel T. G. Williams returned from leave and resumed his command.

On the 8th, we marched to billets at Bethune, and were comfortably billeted by 4 p.m. Here Second Lieutenant W. E. Crossley, M.C., M.M., Captain R. J. Cross (Chaplain), and Second Lieutenants Blount, Towers, and Kennett joined for duty.

On the 12th, we went up in lorries and relieved the 1/5th King's Own as outpost battalion on the left brigade front, Battalion Headquarters being at Lattre.

On the 14th, our patrols at dawn found the enemy very alert, and located several machine gun posts west of the Haute Deule Canal. Some harassing fire on our forward posts during the day. Two other ranks were killed. Second Lieutenant Taylor and nine other ranks missing, and Second Lieutenant Crossley and one other rank wounded.

On the 14th, the enemy artillery became more active, and our patrols were heavily engaged by machine guns. The marshes were found almost impassable, the water being eight feet deep in places. Our sentry posts located in the marshes were unremitting in their attempts to push forward, and the spirit of all ranks, despite the conditions, was excellent. Seven other ranks were killed and

11 other ranks wounded. Second Lieutenant R. G. Latham joined for duty.

On the 15th the harassing fire continued. Our patrols were very active, but did not advance. Captain W. L. Price and five other ranks were wounded. Second Lieutenant H. C. Saville joined for duty.

On the 16th, patrols reported some of the enemy posts unoccupied. At 12 noon D Company and two platoons of B Company crossed the Haute Deule Canal at Les Anscruilles, and proceeded to attack from the flank the strongly-held bridgehead at Bac de Wavrin, A and C Companies attacking frontally at the same time. The attack was under the personal supervision of Major H. J. G. Duggan, M.C. The bridgehead was taken at 9 p.m., and patrols pushed on to the Seclin Canal. Pontoon bridges were thrown across the canals. Lieutenant Bury and Second Lieutenant Taylor and one other rank were wounded.

On the 17th, the 25th Lancashire Fusiliers and the 1/4th King's Own passed through our outposts at 5 a.m. The battalion reorganised and assembled at Wavrin. At 4 p.m. we moved to Noyelles, and were billeted by 11 p.m. Second Lieutenant Taylor died of wounds. Second Lieutenant Hailwood and two other ranks were killed and seven other ranks were wounded.

On the 18th, at 3 a.m., we moved into the main outpost line of resistance east of D'Enchemont.

On the 19th, at 7 a.m., the battalion passed through the outpost line held by the King's Own on the Lamarq River, and advanced—A and C Companies in front and B and D in support. The enemy resistance was practically nil, and the villages of Cysoing, Bourghelles and Wannehain and Esplechin were captured. At night we took up outpost positions, with B and D Companies along the line of resistance, on the high ground east of Wannehain; A Company found the outposts to the east. One other rank was wounded.

On the 20th, the 25th Lancashire Fusiliers marched through our outpost lines and we moved into brigade reserve. One other rank was wounded.

On the 21st, in the afternoon, we moved into billets at Froidmont. At 2 a.m. on the 22nd, we relieved the 1/4th King's Own in the outpost line—C Company on the right, D on the left, A and B Companies in support. We attempted to advance, but were unable to do so owing to heavy machine gun and artillery fire, five other ranks being killed, 14 wounded, and one missing. Our daylight patrols found the enemy was holding a strong line with many machine guns. At the time of relief it was understood that the enemy had been cleared out of the wood in O 33 b and d, but when the officer commanding D Company (Captain Montague Smith) attempted to enter the wood he was met by strong machine gun fire.

The officer commanding D Company planned two attacks on the

wood, but the enemy were so strong as to make these unsuccessful. Artillery assistance was asked for, and at 4.30 p.m., under an artillery barrage, D Company attacked and was completely successful in capturing the wood, taking 18 prisoners and four machine guns. Outposts were pushed up in front of the wood, and at dusk the company was relieved by B Company (Captain R. H. Smith, M.C.).

At 2 a.m. on the 23rd, we drove off an enemy counter-attack, but at 4 30 a.m. a strong counter-attack delivered from the flank with the strength of about two companies forced our posts to withdraw from the wood. There was a thick fog at the time of the attack, and, communications having broken down, no assistance was forthcoming from our artillery. The officer commanding B Company, however, immediately organised Company Headquarters and a platoon of A Company and delivered a quick counter-attack, which, whilst it was not successful in regaining the wood, effectually managed to establish us some little distance our side of the wood. We were relieved by the 2/5th Lancashire Fusiliers about midnight. Second Lieutenants Chambers and Blount and 33 other ranks were missing, one other rank killed, and 25 other ranks wounded. We moved into billets at Froidmont, where Battalion Headquarters had to change their location, being shelled with mustard gas. Seven other ranks were wounded.

On the 25th, we relieved the 1/4th King's Own in the main line of resistance, Battalion Headquarters being at Ferme du Baron, C Company on the right, D Company in the centre, A Company on the left, and B Company in support. Lieutenant King rejoined us here. The next two days were occupied in working parties.

On the 28th, we were relieved by the l/7th King's Liverpool Regiment, and moved to billets at Wannehain, where we bathed and rested. Two officers and 59 other ranks had gone sick during the month. A divisional paper chase was attended by the mounted officers on the 1st November.

On the 9th, the enemy having retired further, we moved on to Esplechin, and on the 10th to Barry, marching to Villiers St. Amand on the 11th.

The Armistice at 11 o'clock on that day put a stop to further operations. Whilst nobody could be sorry that the war had come to an end, it was annoying to be stopped when we had at last really got going and the fox was in sight.

Many of us thought at the time, and still think, that we might have gone on a little further, and that it was a mistake not to push the advance and really rout the enemy.

At eight o'clock on Armistice night the Battalion Band attended a dance given by the brigadier, General C. B. Stockwell, C.B., C.M.G., D.S.O., and the first social function after the Armistice at which the officers of the battalion were represented was a great success.

Captain M. Smith was awarded the Military Cross for his gallantry and initiative displayed in the successful attack on the wood O 33 b and d. Captain R. H. Smith was awarded a Bar to his Military Cross for his personal bravery and initiative in organising a prompt counter-attack after we had lost the wood O 33 b and d. Major H. J. G. Duggan, M.C., was awarded the D.S.O. for personal bravery and leadership displayed at Bac de Wavrin and the attack on the wood O 33 b and d.

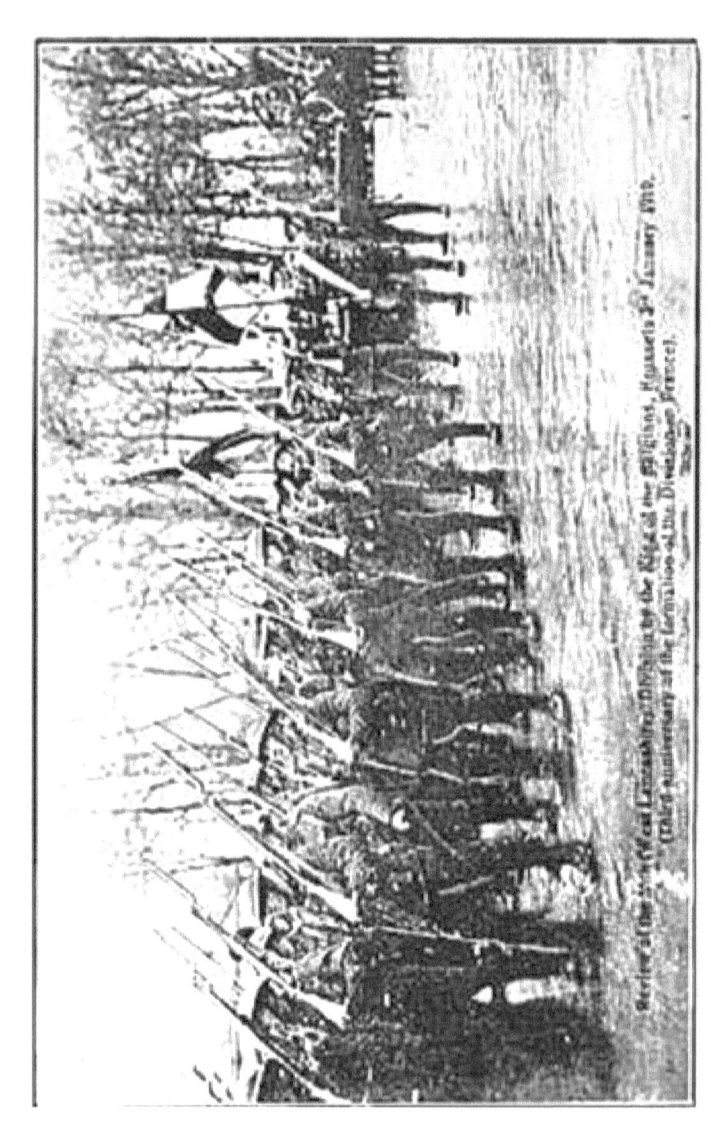

The Colours marching past the King of the Belgians, Brussels, 3rd Jan, 1919

Chapter 11

After the Armistice

Although fighting was now over, the "War" was not. Working parties and training still continued at Leuze, whither we marched on the 14th, and on the 25th the "Education Period" commenced. We moved to Wattine (Chappelle) on the 26th, and on the 2nd December sent an escort, consisting of Captain S. H. Pruden, M.C., and Lieutenant Bulling, Company Sergeant-Major Roberts, and two sergeants, to England to bring out the Colours, which were handed to them on the 7th in Preston by the mayor. The same day the battalion lined the main road on the occasion of the king's visit to Leuze.

The Colour Party rejoined us on the 10th, and the Colours paraded with the battalion for the first time on the 13th. On the 15th we moved to Ath. On the following days we moved to Eugheheim, Lembecq, and Uccle, where we prepared for a long stay in good billets. Second Lieutenant A. Livesey was awarded the Military Cross.

The total casualties for the year 1918 were as follows:—

	Killed	Wounded	Missing	Gassed	D. of W.	W. & M.
Officers	10	31	6	4	1	25
Other Ranks	140	514	101	154	0	595
Totals	150	545	107	158	1	620

Officers 77.   Other Ranks 1,504.

The battalion marched past the King of the Belgians in Brussels. The total casualties of the battalion for the whole of the war are set out in the *War Diary* as follows:—

	Killed	Wounded	Missing	W. & M.	M. believed Killed	Died of Wounds	Gassed	Dwnd.	Sick to F.A.
Officers	37	95	11	2	2	4	4	0	65
Other Ranks	376	1846	596	10	0	165	1	1	1496
Totals	413	1941	607	12	2	169	5	0	1561

Officers 220.   Other Ranks 4,301.

Most of those entered as "Missing" were afterwards reported "Killed in Action;" many were reported "Prisoners of War," and it is a matter of history now these were kept alive by the weekly parcels which reached them from the Prisoners of War Committee in Preston, to which our grateful thanks are due.

The process of demobilisation and disintegration of the battalion now set in, and our numbers steadily dwindled until nothing but the Cadre was left. The Cadre returned to Preston on the 12th June, 1919. Only short notice was received, but there was a good turnout of officers and men who had served with the battalion, and an entertainment was given by the corporation.

With this function the War History of the unit comes to an end. Practically all of us are now back in civil life, a few not much the worse for wear, others maimed or with impaired faculties, but 870 officers and other ranks rest in France and Belgium, and to their memory it is hoped to erect a memorial over there.

As the 55th Division Memorial is to be put on Givenchy Hill, the scene of the battalion's best-known exploit, another site has had to be fixed upon. This has been found on the crest of the ridge on which Vaucellette Farm stood, where the battalion on 30th November, standing alone, stemmed the advancing tide of Huns. To the *maire* of Villers Guislain and to M.M Henri and Leon Nolin, the owners of the ground, we owe the gift of a small square plot by the roadside there, on which to erect a memorial to our comrades.

> *These gave up the years to be*
> *Of joy and work, and that unhoped serene*
> *That men call age; and those who would have been*
> *Their sons, they gave, their immortality."*

Although many graves have been marked and identified, there are countless others which never can be; hence the necessity of a single monument to include all.

Those graves which can be identified have been marked with the Divisional Cocarde, a representation (about six inches in diameter) in colour, on enamelled iron, of the 55th Division badge.

The telegraph post at which the *padre* is standing marks the site of the Battalion Memorial, with the broken trees surrounding Vaucellette Farm about 200 yards behind

Appendixes

Appendix A

1/4th LOYAL NORTH LANCASHIRE REGIMENT

A LIST OF HONOURS AND DISTINCTIONS EARNED BY THE BATTALION.

DISTINGUISHED SERVICE ORDER.

Lieutenant-Colonel R. Hindle, D.S.O., June, 1917. Bar to D.S.O., September, 1917.
Lieutenant-Colonel J. A. Crump, D.S.O., June, 1918.
Major H. J. G. Duggan, D.S.O., January, 1919.
Lieutenant-Colonel T. G. Williams, D.S.O., June, 1919.
Major H. Parker, D.S.O., June, 1919 (Brigade Major, 42nd Division).

MILITARY CROSS

2nd Lieut. P. Parker	1915	2nd Lieut. S. B. Westwood	1918
Capt. J. O. Widdows	1915	2nd Lieut. H. Bailey	1918
2nd Lieut. H. Lindsay	1915	2nd Lieut. C. L. Hore	1916
2nd Lieut. H. Lonsdale	1917	2nd Lieut. E. Fairclough	1916
2nd Lieut. S. A. H. Pruden	1917	2nd Lieut. D. Archibald	1918
Capt. A. T. Houghton	1917	Capt. J. A. Burnside	1918
Capt. D. Carmichael	1918	2nd Lieut. H. Brown	1918
2nd Lieut. J. Adamson	1917	2nd Lieut. J. M. Caie	1918
2nd Lieut. H. Vincent	1917	2nd Lieut. J. Cairns	1918
2nd Lieut. L. Brooke	1917	2nd Lieut. J. Levesley	1918
2nd Lieut. R. H. Tautz	1917	2nd Lieut. J. Dawson	1918
Capt. F. K. Matthew	1917	2nd Lieut. R. S. Hulme	1918
Lieut. A. Bardsley	1918	Capt. H. H. Smith	1918
2nd Lieut. H. Fazackerley	1917	Capt. H. S. P. Walmsley R.F.C.	1917
2nd Lieut. C. Milne	1918		

BAR TO MILITARY CROSS.

Capt. D. Carmichael	1918	Capt. H. Lonsdale	1918
Capt. S. A. H. Pruden	1917	Major H. J. G. Duggan	1918
2nd Lieut. H. Fazackerley	1918		

MENTIONED IN DESPATCHES OFFICERS.

Lieut.-Col. R. Hindle (twice)
Major J. A. Crump (3 times)
Major H. Parker
Capt. R. N. L. Buckmaster
Lieut. F. W. S. Baker
2nd Lieut. F. K. Matthew

Capt. L. Duckworth
Lieut. W. March
Capt. E. M. Rennard
Lieut. H. Whitehurst
Lieut. H. Lindsay

MENTIONED IN DESPATCHES OTHER RANKS.

1846	Pte. Clarkson, W. A.	January, 1917
2411	Pte. Foley, T.	January, 1917
200158	Pte. Cookson, J.	January, 1917
1689	Lance-Cpl. Parkinson, T.	January, 1917
200182	R.Q.M.S. Corns, R.	June, 1917
200128	C.S.M. Dudley, J.	June, 1917
202826	Pte. Tyldesley, W.	June, 1917
200379	Pte. Maher, J.	November 7th, 1917
200048	Pte. Worden, R.	April 7th, 1918
201078	Cpl. Collier, J.	November 7th, 1917
206088	Pte. Yates, J.	November 7th, 1918
200367	Sgt. Dunn, R.	June, 1919
	Lance-Cpl. Baker, J.	1917

DISTINGUISHED CONDUCT MEDAL.

266716	Pte. Cowburn, W.	January 14th, 1916
200012	Sgt. Lester, E.	January 14th, 1916
200204	Pte. Moore, W.	January 14th, 1916
1330	Sgt. Pye, J. R.	January 14th, 1916
200002	C.S.M. Lindsay, C.	January 14th, 1916
3975	R.S.M. Farnworth, J. E.	January 14th, 1916
804	C.S.M. Edwards, T. J.	January 14th, 1916
200388	Sgt. Fletcher, J.	January 14th, 1916
200450	Pte. Ward, T.	July 30th, 1916
200392	Sgt. Hogg, J.	July 30th, 1916
201697	Sgt. Farnworth. H.	January 19th, 1917
24980	Sgt. Ashton, E.	September 17th, 1917
200081	C.S.M. Roberts, H.	October 3rd, 1917
200077	Sgt. Prescott, S.	October, 1917
202703	Sgt. Atkinson, A.	September 3rd, 1918
28064	Pte. Reddish, F.	September 3rd, 1918
201336	Pte. Livesey, J.	September 3rd, 1918
200293	Sgt. Miller, J.	September 3rd, 1918
200575	C.S.M. Ireland, J.	October 3rd, 1918
241584	Pte. Harris, W.	November 2nd, 1918
201260	Lance-Cpl. Butcher, T.	July 31st, 1917
	Pte. Parkes, T.	1918

MILITARY MEDAL AND MERITORIOUS SERVICE MEDAL.

8	Sgt. Entwistle, T.	M.M.	August 23rd, 1916
1984	Sgt. Lancaster, J.	M.M.	August 23rd, 1916
301	Cpl. Bettley, B.	M.M.	September, 1916
2859	Cpl. Osbaddeston, J.	M.M.	November 16th, 1916
34325	Sgt. Goodridge, D.	M.M.	January, 1917
200293	Pte. Miller, J.	M.M.	November, 1916
200875	Pte. Seed, T.	M.M.	November, 1916
200090	Sgt. Yates, R. T.	M.M.	July, 1917
34979	Sgt. Cosgrove, J.	M.M.	September, 1917
202761	Pte. Spencer, J.	M.M.	September, 1917

MILITARY MEDAL AND MERITORIOUS SERVICE MEDAL Continued.

200489	Cpl. Homer, A.	M.S.M.	September, 1917
31987	Cpl. Walmsley, J.	M.M.	September, 1917
201390	Lance-Sgt. Robinson, J.	M.M.	October, 1917
200682	Pte. Coupe, F.	M.M.	October, 1917
200352	Pte. Thistleton, T.	M.M.	October, 1917
201197	Cpl. Thompson, J.	M.M.	October, 1917
200756	Lance-Cpl. Gorton, F.	M.M.	October, 1917
200895	Sgt. Knowles, R.	M.M.	October, 1917
291178	Pte. Goodwin, C. J. H.	M.M.	October, 1917
16940	Pte. Cunningham, J.	M.M.	October, 1917
34304	Pte. Jones, T. E.	M.M.	October, 1917
238001	Pte. Roocroft, W.	M.M.	October, 1917
6693	Sgt. Murphy, J.	M.M.	October, 1917
202099	Pte. Wyre, P.	M.M.	October, 1917
201683	Cpl. Dring, A.	M.M.	August 11th, 1918
200541	Sgt. Turner, F.	M.S.M.	August 29th, 1918
240966	Lance-Cpl. Davenport, T.	M.M.	September 9th, 1918
202467	Lance-Sgt. Holt, A.	M.M.	October 26th, 1918
30479	Lance-Cpl. Bamford, W.	M.M.	October 26th, 1918
40834	Pte. Lee, S. N.	M.M.	October 26th, 1918
30471	Lance-Cpl. Davies, G. J.	M.M.	October 26th, 1918
202640	Pte. Cunliffe, L.	M.M.	October 26th, 1918
29405	Pte. Goldstraw, J.	M.M.	October 26th, 1918
26006	Cpl. Summers, E. M.	M.M.	November 29th, 1918
200056	R.Q.M.S. Aspden, J.	M.S.M.	December, 1918
200568	Sgt. Ryan, T.	M.S.M.	1918
20540	Sgt. Birch, R.	M.S.M.	1918
290177	C.S.M. Porter, R.	M.S.M.	1918
200864	Cpl. Bell, W.	M.M.	
240412	Pte. Farnworth, T.	M.M.	October, 1918
2046	Sgt. Leach, J.	M.M.	July, 1916
184	Pte. Gent, C.	M.M.	July, 1916
200081	C.Q.M.S. Roberts, H.	M.M.	July, 1916
200222	C.Q.M.S. Heywood, J. W.	M.M.	July, 1916
2553	Pte. Latham, E.	M.M.	July, 1916
200174	Lance-Cpl. Bamber, J.	M.M.	July, 1916
274	Sgt. Bates, A.	M.M.	July, 1916
165	Sgt. Board, J. H.	M.M.	July, 1916
4948	Pte. Gent, F.	M.M.	July, 1916
200240	Pte. Ainscough, T.	M.M.	January, 1917
29679	Pte. Parkinson, T.	M.M.	September, 1917
200057	Sgt. Heaps, J.	M.M.	September, 1917
200357	Pte. Parkinson, J. H.	M.M.	September, 1917
200143	Cpl. Finnerty, T.	M.M.	September, 1917
200782	Pte. Park, T.	M.M.	September, 1917
201356	Lance-Cpl. Norris, P.	M.M.	September, 1917
12154	Lance-Sgt. Cayton, T.	M.M.	September, 1917
201542	Sgt. Bell, H.	M.M.	October, 1917
202967	Pte. Yates, W.	M.M.	October, 1917
200541	Sgt. Turner, F.	M.M.	January, 1918

MILITARY MEDAL AND MERITORIOUS SERVICE MEDAL Continued.

200218	Sgt. Parkinson, T. R.	...	M.M.	September 3rd, 1918
200643	Sgt. Cookson, J. E.	...	M.M.	September, 1917
36204	Pte. Read, J. ...	...	M.M.	October 7th, 1918
202072	Pte. Meadows, J. ...	...	M.M.	October 7th, 1918
202814	Pte. Rotherham, G.	...	M.M.	October 7th, 1918
200661	Cpl. Gradwell, J. ...	...	M.M.	October 7th, 1918
32211	Pte. Williams, R. ...	...	M.M.	October 7th, 1918
240239	Sgt. Lowe, J. ...	...	M.M.	October 7th, 1918
200809	Cpl. Pitcher, F. ...	...	M.M.	August, 1917
200237	Lance-Sgt. Sharples, W.	...	M.M.	October 7th, 1918
243878	Sgt. Threadgold, W.	...	M.M.	October 7th, 1918
36729	Pte. Goodram, W.	...	M.M.	October 7th, 1918
202702	Sgt. Kelly, H. ...	...	M.M.	October, 1918
202881	Sgt. Aspden, J. ...	...	M.M.	October, 1918
29342	Sgt. Payne, W. ...	...	M.M.	October, 1918
34075	Lance-Cpl. Norris, H.	...	M.M.	October, 1918
290665	Pte. Pendlebury, T. ...	...	M.M.	October, 1917
12910	Pte. Rathbone ...	...	M.M.	August, 1917
200146	Pte. Bates, J. ...	...	M.M.	August, 1917
200414	Pte. Clarkson, W. H.	...	M.M.	August, 1917
	Pte. Hornmans, A. ...	...	M.M.	1918
	Pte. Marsh, T. ...	...	M.M.	1918
	Pte. Lloyd, F. ...	...	M.M.	1918
	Sgt. Hartley ...	...	M.M.	1917
	Sgt. Hogg ...	...	M.M.	1917

BAR TO MILITARY MEDAL.

12154	Sgt. Cayton, T.	...	...	January, 1918
290665	Cpl. Pendlebury, T.	...	...	June, 1918
202099	Cpl. Wyre, P. ...	...	...	October 7th, 1918
201683	Cpl. Dring, A. ...	...	...	October 26th, 1918
202640	Pte. Cunliffe, L.	...	...	October 26th, 1918
200293	Sgt. Miller, J. ...	...	...	October 26th, 1918
202647	Sgt. Holt, A. ...	...	...	October, 1918

CROIX DE GUERRE (FRENCH).

230	Sgt. Lester, E. ...	...		June, 1915
200158	Sgt. Cookson, J.	...	...	August 17th, 1918
201683	Cpl. Wilkinson, J. S. ...		...	January, 1919

MEDAILLE MILITAIRE (FRENCH).

301	Cpl. Bettley, B.	...	...	September, 1916
202752	Cpl. Wilkinson, J.	...	...	August 29th, 1918

MEDAILLE MILITAIRE (BELGIAN).

200077	Sgt. Prescott, S.	...	...	January, 1919

Appendix B

The Casualty Lists

These lists originally compiled in Battalion Orderly Room as the casualties were reported, have now been checked with Records. It is too much to hope that they are absolutely correct, but the compilers have done all they can to correct mistakes.

The following signs and abbreviations have been used :

✠ K. in A.   Killed in Action.
✠ D. of W.   Died of wounds received in action the first date that of the wounds ; the second the death.
R.P. of W.   Prisoner of war returned the date being that of capture.
W.   Wounded.
N.T.   An entry in the Battalion Roll which the Record Office cannot trace probably owing to the number being that by which a man was known in another Battalion.

1/4th LOYAL NORTH LANCASHIRE REGIMENT.

A list of all casualties sustained by the Battalion between April, 1915, and November, 1918.

Rank and Name.	No.	Coy.	Nature of Casualty.	Date.
Pte. Abraham, T.	28206	A	W.	18 11 17 and 2 6 18 N.T. 8 8 16
Pte. Abram, P.	3636	D	W.	22 6 16
2nd Lieut. Absolom, W.			W.	9 4 18
Pte. Acult	27904	B	R.P. of W.	15 8 15
Pte. Adams, E.	2813	A	W.	9 9 18
Pte. Adams, F.	30915	B	W.	30 11 17
✝ 2nd Lieut. Adamson, J.			K. in A.	27 2 18
Pte. Addison, A.	1945	A	W.	8 8 16
Pte. Addison, E.	1465	D	W.	15 6 15
Pte. Affleck, G. H.	203598	A	W.	31 4 17
2nd Lieut. Agostini, H. F. S.			W.	7 6 17
Pte. Ainscough, G.	200444	C	W.	20 9 17
Pte. Ainscough, J. R.	25789	B	W.	16 7 17
Pte. Ainsworth, A.	203142	B	W. N.T.	9 4 18
✝ Pte. Ainsworth, J.	2055	D	K. in A.	15 6 15
Pte. Ainsworth, T.	4554	B	W. N.T.	9 9 16
✝ Lance-Cpl. Alcock, T	28201	A	D. of W.	11 5 18 ; 24 5 18
Lance-Cpl. Alcock, T.	30477	B	W.	1 6 18
Lance-Cpl. Aldridge, T. F.	3444	C	W.	8 8 16
✝ Pte. Alexander, J.	17912	B	K. in A. N.T	3 7 18
Pte. Alker, T.	4328	B	W.	9 9 16
Pte. Allan, W.	3356	C	W.	15 6 15
✝ Pte. Allen, J.	202880	D	D. of W.	15 7 17 ; 15 9 17
Cpl. Allen, M.	2501	B	W.	28 6 16
Pte. Allen, P.	34829	C	R.P. of W.	20 9 17
Pte. Allen, R.	5640	B	W.	31 7 17
✝ Lance-Cpl. Allen, R.	202611	B	K. in A	31 7 17
✝ Lance-Cpl. Allen, S.	202890	D	K. in A. N.T.	16 9 17

297

Lance-Cpl. Allen, T.	202829		W.	10 18 3 7 14
Pte. Allcock, U. F.	27895	B	W.	3 8 12
Sgt. Allen, W.	5694	B	W.	30 7 17
Sgt. Allen, W.	202665	A	W.	31 7 12
Pte. Allison, G.	2819	A	K. in A.	15 6 15
✝ Pte. Allison, H.	37257	B	W.	27 9 18
✝ Pte. Almond, E.	41616	A	K. in A.	8 7 18
Pte. Almond, J.	3046	D	K. in A.	31 10 15
Lance-Cpl. Almond, R.	27895	B	W.	N.T. 9 7 18
✝ Pte. Almond, T.	201200	C	K. in A.	18 11 17
Pte. Alker, T.	4832	C	W.	N.T. 9 6 16
Pte. Alsopp, A	4858	B	W.	8 8 18
✝ Pte. Alty, T.	202135	A	K. in A.	31 7 17
Pte. Amatt, J.	235052	B	W.	31 7 17
✝ Pte. Amers, J.	30751	A	W.	30 9 18
✝ Sgt. Anderson, A.	18387	A	K. in A.	1 10 18
Srt. Anderson, J. T.	41695	A	W.	15 5 18
✝ Lance-Cpl. Anderton, J.	23156	C	K. in A.	18 11 17
Pte. Anderton, J. H.	305563	C	W.	6 9 18
Pte. Anderton, W.	169088	B	W.	31 7 18
Pte. Andrew, J.	306507	B	W.	19 8 18
Sgt. Anglezarke, J.	1334	D	W.	15 8 15
Lance-Cpl. Anyon, T.	306	C	W.	28 10 15 and 9 9 16
✝ Pte. Anyon, W.	3959		D. of W.	17 11 15
✝ Pte. Annes, W.	28202		D. of W.	19 11 17
✝ Pte. Archer, E. H.	202234	B	D. of W.	17 6 18
✝ Pte. Archer, J.	41611	D	K. in A.	8 7 17
Pte. Archer, W.	28203	A	W.	30 10 18
2nd Lieut. Archibald, D.	—		W.	5 8 18
✝ Pte. Arkwright, F.	24074	C	K. in A.	20 9 17
✝ Lance-Cpl. Armer, E.	201750		K. in A.	31 7 17
✝ Pte. Armiage, E	202833	B	K. in A.	18 11 17
Pte. Armstead, J.	201574	D	R.P. of W.	9 4 18

298

Pte. Armstrong, H.	2451		D	R.P. of W.	9 4 18
†Pte. Armstrong, W. F.	3232		C	K. in A.	15 6 15
Lance-Cpl. Arstall, J. H.	288005		A	K. in A.	9 9 18
†Pte. 2nd Lieut. Ashcroft, G.	202575		A	K. in A.	19 9 17
				K. in A.	31 7 17
Pte. Ashes, H.	20505		B	W.	9 4 18
Sgt. Ashton, A.	24980		B	W.	6 11 15
Pte. Ashton, E.	2937		B	W.	16 4 18
Cpl. Ashton, J.	238011		C	W.	24 8 18
Lance-Cpl. Ashton, T. J.	36384		D	W.	30 7 17
Pte. Ashton, W.	4569		B	W.	30 7 17
Pte. Ashton, W.	20237		B	D. of W.	20 4 17
†Cpl. Ashton, W.	202704		C	W.	5 9 18
Lance-Cpl. Ashworth, A.	41696		C	W.	3 9 18
Pte. Ashworth, A.	200552		C	W.	24 10 18
†Pte. Ashworth, J.	2622		B	K. in A.	15 6 15
†Pte. Ashworth, J.	4035		B	K. in A.	29 5 16
†Pte. Ashworth, J. R.	28205		A	K. in A.	29 5 18
Pte. Ashworth, R.	6210		A	W.	9 9 16
Pte. Ashworth, T.	2556		A	W.	15 6 15
Pte. Ashworth, W.	202792		C	K. in A.	20 9 17
†Cpl. Askew, A.	7244		D	W.	9 9 18
Pte. Aspden, J.	202881		D	W.	31 7 17
Pte. Aspden, J.	6267		B	W.	31 7 17
Pte. Aspinall, A.	6322		B	W.	30 8 16
Lance-Cpl. Aspinall, J.	202681		D	W.	11 6 17
Pte. Aspinall, J.	5710		A	W.	11 6 17
Pte. Astin, J.	6265		C	W.	15 7 17
Lance-Cpl. Astley, F.	242524		B	W.	14 5 18
Pte. Astley, H.	7627		B	W.	8 8 16
Lance-Cpl. Astley, J.	146		D	W.	9 9 16
Pte. Astwood, G. W.	6231				

†Pte. Allison, G.	2819	B	K. in A.	15 6 15
Pte. Allison, H.	37257	A	W.	27 9 18
†Pte. Almond, E.	41616	D	K. in A.	8 7 18
Pte. Almond, J.	3016	B	W.	31 10 15
Lance-Cpl. Almond, R.	27805	C	W.	N.T. 9 7 18
†Pte. Almond, T.	201200	C	K. in A.	18 11 17
Pte. Alker, T.	4832	B	W.	N.T. 9 9 16
Pte. Alsopp, A.	4858	A	W.	8 8 16
†Pte. Alty, T.	202135	B	K. in A.	31 7 17
Pte. Aniatt, J.	235052	A	W.	31 7 17
Pte. Amers, J.	50751	B	W.	30 9 18
Sgt. Anderson, A.	18387	A	K. in A.	1 10 18
Sgt. Anderson, J. T.	41695	A	W.	15 8 18
†Lance-Cpl. Anderton, J.	231136	C	K. in A.	18 11 17
Pte. Anderton, J. H.	300653	C	W.	6 9 18
Pte. Anderton, W.	169088	B	W.	31 7 17
Pte. Andrew, J.	300607	B	W.	19 8 18
Sgt. Anglezarke, J.	1334	D	W.	15 8 15
Lance-Cpl. Anyon, T.	306	C	W.	28 10 15 and 9 9 16
†Pte. Anyon, W.	38959	C	D. of W.	17 11 15
†Pte. Annes, W.	28202		D. of W.	19 11 17
Pte. Archer, E. H.	201234	B	D. of W.	17 6 18
Pte. Archer, J.	41611	D	K. in A.	8 7 17
Pte. Archer, W.	28203	A	W.	30 10 18
2nd Lieut. Archibald, D.			W.	5 9 18
†Pte. Arkwright, F.	24074	C	K. in A.	20 9 17
†Lance-Cpl. Armer, E.	201750		K. in A.	31 7 17
†Pte. Armitage, E.	202831	B	K. in A.	18 11 17
Pte. Armitstead, J.	201371	D	R.P. of W.	9 4 18
Pte. Armstrong, H.	2451	D	R.P. of W.	9 4 18
†Pte. Armstrong, W. F.	3232	C	K. in A.	15 6 15
†Lance-Cpl. Arnold, F. G.	238005	A	K. in A.	9 4 18
Pte. Arstall, J. H.	202575	A	K. in A.	19 9 17
†2nd Lieut. Ashcroft, G.			K. in A.	31 7 17

300

✠Pte. Ashes, H.	20505		B	K. in A.	9. 4.18
Sgt. Ashton, A.	24980		B	W.	9. 4.18
Pte. Ashton, E.	2937		B	W.	6.11.15
Cpl. Ashton, J.	238011		D	W.	16. 4.19
Lance-Cpl. Ashton, T. J.	36384		B	W.	24. 8.18
Pte. Ashton, W.	4569		B	W.	31. 7.17
Pte. Ashton, W.	20237		B	W.	31. 7.17
✠Cpl. Ashton, W.	202704			D. of W.	20. 4.17
Lance-Cpl. Ashworth, A.	41696		C	W.	5. 9.18
Pte. Ashworth, A.	41696		C	W.	3. 9.18
Pte. Ashworth, A.	205552		A	W.	24.10.18
✠Pte. Ashworth, J.	7622		C	K. in A.	15. 6.15
✠Pte. Ashworth, J.	4035			K. in A.	29. 5.16
Pte. Ashworth, J. R	28205		B	K. in A.	29. 9.16
Pte. Ashworth, R	6210		B	W.	9. 9.16
Pte. Ashworth, T.	2556		A	W.	15. 6.15
Pte. Ashworth, W.	202792		A	W.	20. 9.17
✠Cpl. Askew, A.	7244		C	K. in A.	9. 9.16
Pte. Aspden, J.	202881		D	W.	31. 7.17
Pte. Aspden, J.	6267		D	W.	31. 7.17
Pte. Aspinall, A.	6322		D	W.	8. 8.16
Lance-Cpl. Aspinall, J.	202681		B	W.	11. 6.17
Pte. Aspinall, J.	5710		B	W.	11. 6.17
Pte. Astin, J.	6265		D	W.	15. 7.17
Lance-Cpl. Astley, F.	242524		A	W.	14. 5.18
Pte. Astley, H.	7627		C	W.	8. 8.18
Lance-Cpl. Astley, J.	146		B	W.	8. 8.18
Pte. Astwood, G. W.	6231		D	W.	9. 9.16
✠Pte. Atherton, W.	201744		B	D. of W.	3.12.17
Pte. Atherton, W.	2685		A	W.	31. 7.15
Pte. Atherton, W.	4483		B	W.	9. 9.16
Sgt. Atkinson, A.	202703		A	W.	10. 4.18 and 23.10.18
✠Pte. Atkinson, F.	2615		C	K. in A	15. 6.15

301

Pte. Atkinson, G. W.	3159		W.		9 6 15
Pte. Atkinson, H.	4449	B	W.		9 6 15
Pte. Atkinson, J.	2065	D	W.		15 6 15
Pte. Atkinson, L.	28204	D	W.		30 11 17
Pte. Atkinson, T.	10701	A	W.		19 7 17
		B			
Pte. Baxendale, W.	2032	C	W.		15 6 15
Pte. Battersby, A.	2273	B	W.		15 6 15
Pte. Baker, A.	2407	B			30 5 15
✠Pte. Ball, S. J	2312		K. in A.		15 6 15
✠Pte. Baldwin, J.	1731		K. in A.		21 11 15
✠Pte. Bamber, A. J.	2806		K. in A.		15 6 15
✠Pte. Banister, R.	202637		K. in A.		31 7 17
Pte. Bamber, J.	3	B			15 6 15
Pte. Banks, S. E.	3321	C	R.P. of W.		18 11 17
✠Lance-Cpl. Baker, J. T	23493	D	K. in A.		22 10 18
✠Lance-Cpl. Baron, J. E.	18520	B	K. in A.		1 10 18
Pte. Barrett, J. R.	29087	A	W.		30 9 18
Pte. Bassett, C.	35677		W.		1 10 18
Pte. Barry, J.	242209	D	W.		1 10 18
Sgt. Bamford, M. S.	203018	B	W.	N.T.13	
✠Pte. Barnes, F.	30608	D	D. of W.		10 11 18
Lance-Cpl. Bates, F. W.	202793	A	W.		23 10 18
Pte. Bailey, H.	24818	B	W.		23 10 18
Pte. Ball. H.	1412	D	W.	and 1 4 16	15 6 15
✠Lance-Cpl. Bamber, E. H.	1648	B	K. in A.		15 6 15
Pte. Bamber, R. H.	1653	A	W.		15 6 15
Lance-Cpl. Ball. F.	1775	A	W.		15 6 15
Pte. Baines, J. G.	2250	B	W.		30 5 15
Pte. Bamford, J.	3592	C	W.		20 5 16
Pte. Barlow, F.	4860	B	W.		30 7 16
Sgt. Bates, A. E.	271	A	W.		3 8 16
Pte. Bamford, T.	3074	A	W.		5 8 16
Cpl. Batty, F.	248	B	W.		8 8 16

302

	Name			Number		Status		Date
Pte.	Banks, J.			3938		W.		8 8 16
Pte.	Barton, A.			3971		W.		8 8 16
✠Pte	Baxendale, G.			3914		K. in A.		8 8 16
Pte	Barnes, J.			4523		W.		9 8 16
✠Pte.	Baines, L.			4000		K. in A.	N.T.	9 9 16
✠Pte.	Ball, E.			4439		K. in A.		9 9 16
Pte.	Baines, T.			4029		W.		9 9 16
Pte.	Barnes, T.			4828		W.		28 8 16
Pte.	Barlow, W. H.			2267		K. in A.		15 6 15
✠Pte.	Barnish, W.			4002		K. in A.		15 6 15
✠Pte.	Barlow, F.			1055		K. in A.		15 6 15
✠Pte.	Barnett, H. L.			3321		K. in A.		20 9 15
✠Pte.	Bateson, W.			2624		K. in A.	N.T.	15 6 15
✠Pte.	Bath, F.			16896		W.		29 8 16
	Baxendale, J.			141		W.		13 9 17
Pte.	Barton, A.		B	3231		W.		23 7 17
Pte.	Baxendale, R.		C	201726		W.		12 7 17
Pte.	Bamber, W.		A	2005306		W.		14 7 17
Pte.	Battersby, W.		D	202658		W.		40 7 17
Pte.	Bamber, W.		D	201251		W.		31 7 17
Pte.	Barron, H.		C	36907		W.		31 7 17
Pte.	Barton, A.		B	200993		W.		31 7 17
Pte.	Bancroft, L.		D	202884		R.P. of W.		27 5 17
Lance-Sgt.	Batty, F.		B	200116		W.		3 6 18
Lance-Cpl.	Barnes, A.		B	202115		W.		7 7 18
Pte.	Backhouse, L.		C	202970		W.		16 8 18
Pte.	Bates, G. W.		B	36159		W.		5 9 18
Pte.	Barrow, J.		R	201121		W.		8 9 18
Pte.	Barrett, W.		A	38678		W.		13 9 18
Pte.	Barnes, F.		D	306908		W.		13 6 18
Pte.	Balmer, R. W.		H	28220		W.		
Pte.	Baron, H.		A	30921		W.		
Pte.	Baron, J. W.			24769		W.		23 9 18
✠Pte.	Barlow, A.		A	16898		K. in A.		

Rank	Name	Number			Status		Date
Pte.	Barker, W.	304358			W.		29 7 17
2nd Lieut.	Baker, E. G.				W.		20 9 17
†Capt.	Baker, F. S.				K. in A.		20 9 17
Pte.	Barton, R.	200191			W.		20 9 17
†Pte.	Baines, A.	202200			K. in A.		4 4 18
†Lance-Cpl.	Ball, R.	13057		B	W.		20 9 17
Pte.	Barker, W.	202971		C	K. in A.		20 9 17
Pte.	Baxendale, J.	202807		A	K. in A.		30 10 18
Pte.	Balding, B. J.	200650		C	R.P. of W.		18 11 17
†Pte.	Baxter, C. E.	34907		C	K. in A.		20 11 17
Pte.	Bamber, W.	201299		B	W.		20 11 17
Pte.	Burscough, A.	200646		D	W.		30 11 17
Pte.	Battersby, J. W.	202658		D	W.		30 11 17
†Pte.	Ball, J.	201506		B	K. in A.		9 4 18
†Cpl.	Bamber, J.	200174		A	K. in A.		11 4 18
Pte.	Barlow, S.	13618		D	W.		9 4 18
Pte.	Barnish, J.	201147		D	K. in A		12 4 18
†Pte.	Baines, A.	202200		D	R.P. of W.		12 4 18
Pte.	Bailey, J.	27910		D	W.		15 4 18
Pte.	Balmforth, C.	200631		C	K. in A.		14 5 18
†Cpl.	Bailey, J.	30159		A	K. in A.		15 5 18
†Pte.	Bamford, H.	24675		D	W.		19 5 18
Pte.	Bates, J.	200146		C	W.		19 5 18
Lance-Cpl.	Bates, J.	30172		C	W.	N.T.	27 5 15
Cpl.	Bateson, F.	196222		B	W.		15 6 15
Pte.	Bennett, R.	200153		A	Died		15 6 15
Cpl.	Bennett, J.	261		C	W.		27 10 18
†Pte.	Bentham, J.	278		D	D. of W.		15 6 15
Pte.	Bennett, J.	318		A	W.		8 8 16
†Pte.	Beaver, D.	2299		B	W.		30 9 18
Cpl.	Bennett, E.	202620		D			15 6 15
Pte.	Beardsworth, A.	1139				and	9 9 16

Name	No.	Coy	Status	Date
Sgt. Bell, T. B.	1003		W.	30 5 15 and 7 9 16
†Lieut. Best, F. R.			K. in A.	1 6 16
†Pte. Benson, H.	2130	B	K. in A.	4 6 16
Pte. Berry, E.	4864	B	W.	2 8 16
Pte. Bell, R.	4853	B	W.	4 8 16
Pte. Bennitt, J.	2006	B	W.	8 8 16
†Cpl. Beesley, R. H.	200189		K. in A.	31 7 17
†Pte. Berry, W.	2901		D. of W.	19 9 15
†Sgt. Bent, A.	3053		Died	27 1 15
Cpl. Be field, J.	261		W.	9 9 16
†Sgt. Bettley, W. B.	301	B	D. of W. 26 9 16	12 10 16
Pte. Beetham, A.	3221	B	W.	26 9 16
Lance-Sgt. Bell, T.	5601	B	W.	3 11 16
Pte. Bevins, G. S.	2023506	C	W.	1 6 17
Pte. Bennett, C. H.	2022623	C	W.	4 6 17
Pte. Berry, B.	202885	R	W.	31 7 17
Pte. Beck, W.	29401	C	W.	1 6 18
†Pte. Beardwell, W. H.	30215	D	K. in A.	16 6 18
Pte. Berrington, J.	26392	B	W.	5 9 18 N.T.
Pte. Beardsworth, A.	200276	D	W.	7 9 18
†Pte. Berry, W. E.	32681	A	K. in A.	11 9 18
Pte. Berry, E.	2020 10	B	W. of W.	23 9 18
†Pte. Bennett, W.	21342	C	D. of W.	17 9 17
†Pte. Bennett, J. T. R.	200392	B	W.	21 9 17
Pte. Berrington, E.	24949	A	W.	20 9 17
†Lance-Sgt. Beaumont, W.	265289	C	K. in A.	20 9 17
Pte. Beardwood, H.	200011	C	W.	20 9 17
Pte. Bean, H.	202614	D	R.P. of W.	18 11 17
†Pte. Belgin, F.	28217	B	K. in A.	18 11 17
†Pte. Best, J.	37714	D	W.	9 4 18
Pte. Bennett, H.	35300	C	D. of W. 11 4 18	17 4 18
†Sgt. Beechey, T. J. D	2023333		W.	9 4 18
2nd Lieut. Beresford, G. G.		B	W.	9 4 18
Pte. Beaman, G. E.	34332			

Pte.	Billington, S.	2029	A	W.	15 6 15
Pte.	Birch, R.	2235	A	W.	15 6 15
Sgt.	Birtwistle, H.	38023	A	R.P. of W.	15 10 18
✝Pte.	Billington, R.	3169	B	K. in A.	15 6 15
Pte.	Bibby, J.	784	B	W.	30 10 15
✝Pte.	Bilsborough, R.	4400	A	K. in A.	2 8 16
Sgt.	Billington, W	3190	A	W.	8 8 16
Pte.	Bibby, J.	208	C	W.	8 8 16
Pte.	Billington, E.	3351	B	W.	8 8 16
2nd Lieut.	Bigger, T. A			W.	8 8 16
✝Pte.	Bingham, H.	200600	A	D. of W.	8 4 17
Pte.	Binks, W.	235019	C	W.	13 4 17
Lance-Cpl.	Billington, T.	201622	B	W.	12 7 17
Pte.	Birmingham, J.	202466	D	W.	14 7 17
Pte.	Bickerstaffe, R.	200695	B	W.	31 7 17 N.T.
✝Pte.	Bishop, A.	202794	A	K. in A.	31 7 17
✝Pte.	Bibby, R.	202705	B	K. in A.	31 7 17
✝Pte.	Bibby, T.	200271	D	K. in A.	31 7 17
Pte.	Birch, L.	201814	D	W.	3 6 18
✝Pte.	Bibby, J. W.	23691	A	K. in A.	20 9 17
Pte.	Birchenough, H. E.	292904	C	W.	18 11 17
Sgt.	Bishop	200190	A	W.	30 11 17
Pte.	Bibby, J.	28065	B	W.	30 11 17
Pte.	Bibby, C.	200606	B	W.	30 11 17
Lance-Sgt.	Bingham, J.	238012	D	W.	21 3 18 N.T.
✝Pte.	Bibby, J.	29078	B	K. in A.	13 4 18
✝Pte.	Billington, R. G.	28212	D	W.	12 4 18
✝Pte.	Birch, A.	37572	B	W.	20 9 17
✝Pte.	Birch, F.			D. of W.	10 5 18
Pte.	Birmingham, J	244766	D	W.	25 5 18
Pte.	Bleasdale, C.	200576	A	W.	15 6 15
Pte.	Blackshaw, J.	262	C	W.	15 6 15
2nd Lieut.	Blount, G. A.			Missing	23 10 18

†Cpl. Blackledge, H.	1469	D		K. in A.	15 6 15
†Pte. Bland, R.	1453	C		K. in A.	15 6 15
Pte. Blundell, J.	13434	C		W.	13 7 16
Pte. Blakeley, W.	4558	B	N.T.	W.	13 8 16
Lance-Cpl. Bloom, H.	20257-1			W.	31 7 17
†Lance-Cpl. Blackledge, A.	1393			K. in A.	13 6 15
Pte. Blaylock, G. F.	202883	D		W.	17 8 18
Lance-Cpl. Bland, W.	210531	C		W.	1 9 18
†Pte. Blackledge, M.	22904	C		K. in A.	31 7 17
Pte. Blackhurst, J.	203012	D		W.	20 9 17
Pte. Blackburn, R.	202345	A	N.T.	W.	20 9 17
†Pte. Bleasdale, J.	203865	D		K. in A.	30 11 17
Pte. Blackborough, W.	235004	B	N.T.30	11 17
†Pte. Bloy, A.	35565	B		W.	9 4 18
†Pte. Blakeley, W.	201784	C		K. in A.	9 4 18
†Pte. Blackborough, W. H. S.	28218	D		K. in A.	18 5 18
Pte. Bowling, J.	2076	D		W.	15 6 15
Pte. Bond, F.	2531	B		W.	15 6 15
Pte. Bolan, J.	2741	C		W.	13 6 16
Pte. Boardman, J.	23504-8	C	N.T.	W.	23 7 18
Capt. Bolingbroke, C. B.			N.T.	W.	9 9 16
Pte. Bolton, C. A.	29402	D		W.	30 9 18
Sgt. Bolton, W.	392	A		W.	15 6 15
Cpl. Booth, R.	1362	D		W.	15 6 15
Lance-Cpl. Boardman, G.	1427	D		W.	15 6 15
Sgt. Boardman, G.	1427	D		W.	26 9 16
†Pte. Bonny, J. C.	2012	C		K. in A.	31 5 18
Pte. Bowker, T.	2784	B		W.	9 9 15
Pte. Bolton, J.	1760	A		W.	21 10 15
Sgt. Board, A.	165	D		W.	5 8 16
Pte. Booth, J.	1498	A		W.	4 8 16
Pte. Bootle, S.	3867	C		W.	8 8 16
Pte. Bowes, T.	4586	C		R.P. of W.	8 8 16
Lance-Cpl. Boyle, W.	2403	B		W.	9 9 16

Pte.	Bond, G.	265051	D		W.	17 5 17
†Sgt.	Boothroyd, F.	202730	D		K. in A.	18 5 17
†Pte.	Booth, W.	203791	A		K. in A.	31 7 17
†Pte.	Boast, W. R.	19			K. in A.	15 6 15
†Pte.	Bolton, C.	1381			K. in A.	15 6 15
†Pte.	Bond, H.	201614			K. in A.	31 7 17
†Pte.	Bone, W.	1616			Died	25 1 16
	Braithwaite, F. J.	2557	A		K. in A.	15 6 15
†Pte.	Briggs, J.	2225	A		K. in A.	18 8 16
†Pte.	Booth, W. H.	203564	C		K. in A.	31 7 17
Pte.	Bond, R.	245139	B		W.	31 7 17
Pte.	Bottoms, F.	203610	A		W.	3 6 18
Pte.	Booth, H.	49947			W.	N.T. 16 6 18
Pte.	Bourne, W.	34878			W.	11 9 18
2nd Lieut.	Bowler, F. C.				W.	30 9 18
Pte.	Booth, S. G.	202577	D		W.	20 9 17
†Pte.	Bolton, J. T.	31907	A		K. in A.	20 9 17
†Pte.	Boyle, J.	35575	C		K. in A.	20 9 17
†Pte.	Bond, J.	37599	A		K. in A.	30 11 17
Pte.	Bostock, E.	28203	B		W.	30 11 17
Pte.	Bott, A. J.	12175	D		W.	30 11 17
Pte.	Bond, A.	28208	D		R.P. of W.	17 2 18
†Pte.	Bolan, J.	200712	C		K. in A.	9 4 18
Pte.	Boon, T.	34868	C		W.	9 1 18
Pte.	Bounds, J. H.	28214	B		W.	13 4 18
†Pte.	Booth, F.	36387	C		K. in A.	10 5 18
Pte.	Bolton, J.	240906	C		W.	11 5 18
Pte.	Brindle, G.	1996	A		W.	29 5 15
Pte.	Brooks, E.	2824	C		W.	31 5 15
Pte.	Bnerley, T.	48	B		W.	15 6 15
Pte.	Bretherton, E.	89	B		W.	15 6 15
2nd Lieut.	Brindle, J. L.				Died at Home	13 3 18
†Capt.	Brindle, J. L.					
Pte.	Brandwood, G.	201626	A		W.	2 8 17

✠Pte. Brooks, C.	28215			K. in A.	30 11 17
Pte. Brindle, W.	13291			W.	30 9 18
✠Pte. Bradshaw, E.	30923	A		K. in A.	13 10 18
Pte. Bronilow, J.	30913	A B		W.	13 10 18
Pte. Brown, A.	23498	B		W.	N.T. 17 10 18
✠Pte. Bury, R.	2857			K. in A.	15 6 15
Pte. Bretherton, E.	1675	B		W.	15 6 15
Pte. Brindle, G.	1906	A		W.	29 5 15
Pte. Brooks, E.	2821	C		W.	30 5 15
2nd Lieut. Bryce Smith, H.				W.	5 11 15
Lance-Cpl. Brennan, J.	1292	C		W.	28 6 16
Pte. Brown, J.	4852	C		K. in A.	28 6 16
✠Pte. Brierley, W.	1946	B		W.	6 8 16
Pte. Bradley, A	3436	C		K. in A.	8 8 16
✠Pte. Brierley, H.	3913	A		K. in A.	8 8 16
✠Cpl. Bridge, H.	1449	C		W.	7 7 16
Pte. Bradshaw, H.	164	B		W.	9 9 16
Sgt. Brown, B.	2292	C		W.	9 9 16
Pte. Brooks, F.	4859	B		W.	6 11 16
Pte. Briggs, F.	4862	A		W.	21 11 16
Lance-Sgt. Brown, A.	5600	B		W.	2 6 17
Pte. Briggs, J.	202071	B		W.	N.T. 8 6 17
Pte. Brierley, J. H.	31937	D		W.	N.T. 8 6 17
Pte. Briggs, E.	202834	B		W.	4 6 16
Pte. Brooks, F.	202035	B		W.	7 6 17
Cpl. Brooks, B.	202630	C		K. in A.	18 7 17
✠Pte. Brown, G.	202601	A		W.	18 7 17
Pte. Brewin, M.	202849	B		W.	31 7 17
Pte. Bradbury, J.	203770	B		W.	31 7 17
Pte. Broad, J.	201576	A		W.	31 7 17
✠Pte. Bradley, J.	235031	A		K. in A.	31 7 17
Lance-Cpl. Bradley, C.	201218	B		W.	31 7 17
Cpl. Brennand, F.	200740	B		W.	31 7 17
✠Pte. Breakell, R.	203145	B		K. in A.	31 7 17
✠Pte. Breckon, G.	242983	D		K. in A.	2 6 18

Pte. Bradnum, H.		41621	D	W.		16 8 18
Pte. Bridge, J.		32993	D	W.		16 8 18
Pte. Bradley, J.		41622	B	W.	N.T.	19 8 14
Pte. Breakell, S.		201271	D	W.	N.T.	4 9 15
2nd Lieut. Bratton				W.	30 10 15	
Pte. Brown, C.		306503	C	W.		5 9 18
Pte. Brown, J.		30957	B	W.		14 9 18
Pte. Bromley, C.		27110	C	W.		20 9 18
Cpl. Briggs, F.		202038	A	W.		20 9 18
Pte. Brooks, B.		202650	C	K. in A.		20 9 18
Pte. Bramall, J.		244993	C	W.		20 9 18
Pte. Brown, L.		28222	B	R.P. of W.		17 11 17
†Pte. Bramwell, T.		37632	A	K. in A.		18 11 17
Pte. Brierley, H.		25538	A	W.		30 11 17
‡Pte. Brown, R.		15103	D	K. in A.		30 11 17
‡Pte. Bradley, E.		201211	D	K. in A.		30 11 17
Pte. Briggs, W.		31589	D	K. in A.		30 11 17
‡Pte. Brown, H		37313	D	W.		26 3 18
Pte. Brown, H.		28224	A	K. in A.		28 3 18
'2nd Lieut. Brooke, L.				R.P. of W.		9 4 18
Pte. Bradburn, B.		10712	B	W.		9 4 18
Cpl. Brindle, A.		202037	B	K. in A.		9 4 18
‡Pte. Brown, E.		28155	C	W.		9 4 18
Pte. Brown, T.		231573	C	Missing	N.T.	9 4 18
Sgt. Brough, R.		247009	D	W.		15 6 18
Pte. Burgh, H.		2057	D	W.		15 6 18
Pte. Burns, W.		2617	C	K. in A.		21 7 18
‡Pte. Bushles, J.		200920	D	K. in A.		30 11 17
Capt. Buckmaster, R. N. L.				W.	N.T.	30 9 18
Pte. Butler, L. O.		10601	B	W.		9 9 18
Lieut. Bury, W. H.				W.	and 16 10 17	
Pte. Burke, T.		29134	B	W.		23 10 18
C.S.M. Burke, J.		2209	B	W.		15 6 18

Pte. Butcher, R.	775	B	W.		15.6.15
✠Pte. Burns, F.	2886	B	K. in A.		15.6.15
✠Pte. Ball, R.	3520	D	K. in A		3.11.15
Pte. Ball, H.	1412	D	W.		1.4.16
Pte. Butler, S.	2503	A	W.		31.7.16
Pte. Burt, H.	243188	D	W.		5.8.16
Pte. Burt, J.	5081	C	W.		8.8.16
Pte. Burscough, A.	4293	C	W.		8.8.16
Pte. Bunting, W.	3919	C	W.		8.8.16
Pte. Burke, W.	246	B	W.		8.8.16
Pte. Buttry, R.	1790		W.		8.8.16
2nd Lieut. Bury, W. H.			W.		9.9.16
Pte. Burrows, E.	4425	B	W.		9.9.16
Pte. Bickell, H.	2018	B	W.		9.9.16
Pte. Buckingham, F.	6213	C	Missing		9.5.17
Pte. Baker, J.	19738	B	W.		19.5.17
Pte. Butterworth, H.	200821		W.		13.7.17
Pte. Bastin, E.	202758	B	W.		31.7.17
Lance-Cpl. Butcher, T.	202760		W.		31.7.17
Pte. Buckley, A.	29718	D	W.		31.7.17
Lance-Cpl. Buckley, F.	238013	B	R.P. of W.		31.7.17
Pte. Bulgar, P.	203806	D	W.		31.7.17
Lance-Cpl. Buck, J.	18287	B	W.		17.8.18
Pte. Burke, S.	31560	C	W.		21.8.18
Pte. Butterworth, J.	25558		W.		3.9.18
Lieut. Bulling, A. E.			W.		1.10.18
Pte. Buth, F.	16896	D	W.		20.9.17
✠Pte. Bullough, C	202168	C	K. in A.		31.7.17
Pte. Burke, E.	32155	C	W.		18.11.17
Pte. Burrows, H.	202616	C	W.		18.11.17
✠Pte. Butler, F.	24536	A	K. in A.		20.11.17
✠Pte. Budd, W.	28209	C	K. in A.	N.T.	18.11.17
Pte. Buckley, L.	28223	A	W.		30.11.17
Lance-Col. Buck, J.	18287	D	W.		21.3.18
Pte. Burns, T. H.	30925	D	Missing	N.T.	12.4.18

311

Pte. Butler, A.	25219		D	W.		12 4 18	
Pte. Burns, H.	21757		B	W.		28 4 18	
†Pte. Butler, S.	200597		A	D. of W.	14 5 18 ;	19 5 18	N.T.
Pte. Bythell, C. T.	243876		A	W.		24 3 18	
Pte. Byrom, L.	202784		B	W.		31 7 17	
†2nd Lieut. Byrne, W.				K. in A.		30 9/18	
Pte. Byrom, S.	41623		A	W.		14 5 18	
Pte. Cardwell, T.	4612		B	W.		9 9 16	
Pte. Cartmell, E. G.	305		C	W.		15 6 15	
Pte. Cartmell, W.	336		A	W.	and	26 9 16	
						15 6 16	
Sgt. Cash, S.	6174		A	W.	and	26 9/16	
Lance-Cpl. Caffery, J.	2106		C	W.		28 9 16	
Pte. Caine, F.	26841		D	W.		28 6 17	
Rev Caley, W. L. B.		Chaplain		W.		4 6 17	
Pte. Cawham, H	3395		A	W.		31 7 17	
Pte. Callon, W.	3902		D	W.		31 7 17	
†Pte. Castle, J.	4539		A	K. in A.		5 8 16	
Pte. Calligan, R	4614		C	W.		8 8 16	
Sgt. Carter, T.	322		C	W.		8 8 16	
Pte. Cavies, T.	3250		C	W.		13 8 16	
Pte. Caddich, J.	4308		C	W.		9 9 16	
†Pte. Carter, G. T	2953		B	K. in A.		14 6 15	N.T.
Pte. Catterall, J.	4303		A	W.		26 3 16	
†Pte. Catterall, P.	1442		D	K. in A.	and	8 8 16	
†Pte. Carter, W.	1909		C	K. in A.		1 4 16	
Pte. Cain, E.	30		B	W.		23 4 16	
Lance-Cpl. Caton, J. C.	42		B	W.		26 5 16	
†Pte. Calder, J. H.	2995		C	K. in A.		28 6 16	
Pte. Caffery, T. J.	1095		C	W.		26 6 16	
Lance-Cpl. Calderbank, H.	1645		A	W.		3 8 16	

Lance-Cpl. Caffery, J.	...	2106	...	C	W.	5.8.16
Lance-Cpl. Cartmell, W.	...	200173	...	A	W.	2.8.17
Pte. Carrington, G.	...	202157	...	C	W.	31.7.17
✠Pte. Calvert, W.	...	235007	...	D	D. of W.	26.8.18
✠Pte. Catterall, M.	...	9244	...		K. in A.	20.11.17
Pte. Cavanagh, J. W.	...	204880	...	B	Died	10.7.17
Pte. Calvert, W. H.	...	28229	...	A	W.	20.11.17
Lance-Cpl. Caton, R.	...	200545	...	A	W.	20.11.17
Pte. Catterall, G.	...	28233	...	B	W.	20.11.17
Pte. Calvert, J.	...	2654	...	D	W.	15.6.15
✠Pte. Cashmore, H. W.	...	2917	...	A	K. in A.	15.6.15
✠Pte. Catterall, L.	...	2665	...	D	K. in A.	15.6.15
✠Pte. Calder, J. H.	...	2995	...	A	K. in A.	28.6.18
✠Pte. Carney, F. R. J.	...	28246	...	A	K. in A.	30.11.17
Pte. Cadd, W.	...	29263	...	A	R.P. of W.	23.10.18
Pte. Cass, T. ...	...	38883	...	A	W.	N.T. 11.9.18
2nd Lieut. Cairns, J.	...		...		W.	30.9.18
✠Pte. Carter, H.	...	38666	...	B	K. in A.	1.10.18
Sgt. Cayton, T.	...	12154	...	B	W.	30.9.18
Pte. Carroll, E. S.	...	30959	...	C	W.	1.10.18
✠Pte. Carlill, A.	...	31006	...	B	K. in A.	4.11.18
Pte. Cartwright, G.	...	10274	...	A	W.	N.T. 23.5.18 and 29.10.18
✠Pte. Carr, S. ...	...	201436	...	C	D. of W.	24.5.18
Pte. Cartwright, J.	...	2320	...	B	W.	16.6.18
Pte. Carrodus, R.	...	31874	...	B	W.	3.7.18
Pte. Cardwell, A.	...	28225	...	D	W.	9.7.18
Pte. Carroll, J.	...	29405	...	D	W.	16.8.18
Pte. Cartmell, J.	...	27958	...	D	W.	17.8.18
✠Sgt. Calvert, W.	...	235007	...	B	D. of W.	25.8.18
Pte. Cardwell, A.	...	28225	...	D	W.	21.8.18
Pte. Carr, C.	...	3685	...	B	W.	4.9.18
Lance-Cpl. Cavies, T.	...	201009	...	B	W.	31.7.17
Cpl. Cavies, T.	...	201009	...	B	W.	4.9.18

†Pte. Capley, C.	9024		B	K. in A.	15 4 18
Capt. Collett, C. G.				W.	15 4 18
†Cpl. Carson, W.	240177		A	K. in A.	9 4 18
Pte. Carroll, J.	29405		D	W.	25 4 18
Pte. Catterall, J.	201653		A	W.	26 4 18
Capt. Carmichael, D.				W.	20 4 18
Pte. Carpenter, G.	34323		D	W.	30 11 17
Pte. Casson, J.	28227		A	W.	2 5 18
Pte. Chapman, J.	6149		C	W.	26 9 16
Pte. Churm, F. L.	200232		C	W.	21 7 17
Pte. Chapman, R.	3844		D	W.	N.T.
†Pte. Charnley, T. A.	4017		D	K. in A.	8 8 16
†Pte. Chapman, C.	3842		D	K. in A.	9 9 16
Pte. Chapman, J.	4746		C	W.	9 9 16
†Pte. Chadwick, J.	2052		D	W.	15 6 15
				D. of W.	31 7 16
Pte. Charnley, J.	1931		C	W.	5 8 16
†Pte. Charnley, F. C.	11186		B	K. in A.	31 7 17
Pte. Chipperfield, A. F.	34942		C	R.P. of W.	18 11 17
Pte. Chadderton, J.	202578		B	W.	21 11 17
†Pte. Child, J. J.	3604		A	K. in A.	15 6 15
†Pte. Chapple, G.	3360		D	K. in A.	16 6 15
Pte. Christian, J.	4202		A	W.	9 9 16
Pte. Charnley, J.	200422		B	W.	12 7 17
Pte. Chettleburgh, J. W.	29725		C	W.	31 7 17
Pte. Chambers, E. E.	11780		C	W.	5 9 18
Pte. Charlton, J.	34009		C	W.	1 10 18
2nd Lieut. Chambers, J.				Missing	23 10 18
2nd Lieut. Chapman, B. R. W.				W.	17 5 18
Cpl. Charlesworth, J.	25487		C	W.	19 5 18
†Pte. Carishem, T.	11086		D	K. in A.	2 6 08
Pte. Charnley, C.	36733		B	K. in A.	9 4 18
Pte. Chorley, J.	235163		B	Missing	N.T. 13 4 18
Pte. Chorlton, T. A.	29097		B	W.	9 4 18

314

Pte.	Clayton, G.	1324		W.	27/9/16
Pte.	Clayton, G.	200270		W.	13/7/17
					and 2/9/18
Pte.	Clayton, H.	4068	D	W.	8/8/16
Pte.	Clarke, E.	4680	B	W.	9/9/16
Lance-Cpl. Clarke, G.		2240	A	W. N.T.	9/9/16
†Pte.	Clough, J.	2575	C	K. in A.	9/9/16
Pte.	Clement, H.	4319	C	W. N.T.	9/9/16
Sgt.	Clayton, S. T.	1284	C	W.	15/6/15
Pte.	Clarkson, T.	2657	A	W.	26/4/16
†Pte.	Clarke, J.	35	C	K. in A.	28/6/16
†Sgt.	Clarke, J. B.	24008	C	K. in A. N.T.	28/6/16
Lance-Cpl. Clough, J.		2575	C	W.	1/8/16
Pte.	Clarkson, J. R.	3080	A	W.	5/8/16
Pte.	Clark, W.	3297	C	Missing	2/8/17
Pte.	Clarkson, R.	200571		W. N.T.	31/7/17
Pte.	Clay, J.	200660		W.	20/9/17
†Pte.	Clayton, S.	2059	D	K. in A.	15/6/15
†Pte.	Clark, W.	41709		K. in A.	30/9/18
†Cpl.	Clarkson, L.	4419	D	W.	15/6/15
Pte.	Clarkson, W. H.	1916	A	K. in A.	28/6/16
Pte.	Clarke, J.	28458	C	W.	15/6/15
†Pte.	Clarke, L. G.	28232	B	Presumed Killed	4/9/18
Pte.	Clarke, J.	240241	B	W.	9/4/18
Pte.	Clarke, J.	201441	D	R.P. of W.	9/4/18
†Pte.	Clarke, R. T.	28231	D	K. in A.	13/4/18
†Pte.	Clayton, E. H.	28228	B	W.	14/9/18
Pte.	Clare, P.	20549	C	W.	9/4/18
†Pte.	Clarkson, H.	120	C	K. in A.	27/4/18
†Cpl.	Collier, J.	201978	A	K. in A.	15/6/15
†Pte.	Collier, S.	202740		K. in A.	1/12/17
†Pte.	Commons, E.	140		K. in A.	9/9/16
Pte.	Cotton, W.	3912	C	Missing	16/6/15
					9/9/16

315

†Pte.	Corless, H.	3398		C	D. of W.		2/10/16
Pte.	Cooper, G.	3046		D	W.		26/9/16
Pte.	Corcorn, T.	202013		A	W.		2/6/17
Pte.	Collins, A.	202621		B	W.		5/6/17
Pte.	Counsell, J.	18740		A	W.		10/7/17
Pte.	Cooper, G.	200875		B	W.		15/7/17
Pte.	Coey, T.	34396		A	W.		15/7/17
Pte.	Coote, W.	200595		D	W.		18/7/17
R.S.M.	Corns, R	200182		C	W.	N.T.	18/7/17
†Pte.	Coe, S. C	260005		C	K. in A.		21/7/17
Sgt.	Cookson, J.	200158			W.		21/7/17
Pte.	Coulton, L.	200966		A	W.	N.T.	31/7/17
Lance-Sgt.	Collins, W.	2239		C	W.		8/8/16
Pte.	Cox, T.	4871		C	W.		8/8/16
Pte.	Cocker, T.	4629		C	W.		x/x/16
Pte.	Collier, T.	5538		C	W.	N.T.	x/x/16
Lance-Cpl.	Corner, H	4179		D	W.		x/x/16
Pte.	Comber, T.	3664		C	W.		x/x/16
Pte.	Cookson, J.	39303		C	W.		x/x/16
Pte.	Coxhead, R.	3530		C	W.		x/9/16
Pte.	Cowley, C.	5011		B	W.		9/9/16
Pte.	Corless, H.	3398		C	W.		9/9/16
Pte.	Cocker, W.	3774		C	W.		9/9/16
†Pte.	Costello, E. G.	1873		A	K. in A.	N.T	9/9/16
Pte.	Collins, W.	3790		B	W.		9/9/16
Pte.	Cowell, C.	1487		D	W.		14/6/15
Pte.	Cowell, R.	3056		B	W.		14/6/15
Pte.	Collinson, W. E	1373		C	W.		15/6/15
Pte.	Cookson, J	314			W.	and N.I.	30/5/18
Pte.	Compton, T.	129		D	W.		20/4/16
†Pte.	Connolly, W.	1462			K. in A.		15/6/15
†Pte.	Connor, C. J.	32142			D. of W.		26/3/18
†Cpl.	Coupe, R.	2525			K. in A.		14/7/16
†Pte.	Coupe, T.	6			K. in A.		11/9/15

316

†Pte. Croston, A.		28		K. in A.	16 10 14
Pte. Coxhead, R.		3530		W.	3 7 16
Pte. Corless, H.		3398		W.	17 16
Pte. Cox, T.		4871		W.	5 7 16
Cpl. Cowburn, W.		783		W.	N.T. 5 8 16
Pte. Cottom, R.		200751		W.	N.T. 31 7 17 and 20 9 17
Pte. Coulton, L.		202966	A	W.	31 7 17 and 20 9 17
Lance-Cpl. Cooper, J. C.		202104	D	W.	20 9 17
Lance-Cpl. Conway, J.		26812	A	W.	30 10 17
†Pte. Coupe, T.		4119	C	K. in A.	11 9 15
Pte. Collins, R.		28045	C	W.	N.T. 18 11 17
Pte. Cornwell, J. A.		202631	A	W.	20 11 17
Pte. Conlon, R.		28226	A	W.	30 11 17
Pte. Corrie, T.		3061	B	W.	N.T. 30 11 17
Pte. Colvin, J.		2400	C	W.	15 6 15
Pte. Coupe, F.		2678	A	W.	15 6 15
Pte. Corry, J.		144	B	W.	15 6 15
†Pte. Cortman, F.		1429	D	K. in A.	15 6 15
†Pte. Cocker, E.		2088	D	K. in A.	15 6 15
Pte. Cookson, J.		3038	C	Missing	15 6 15
Pte. Corfield, J. E.		29403	D	K. in A.	17 6 18
Pte. Cocking, E.		3967	A	W.	9 9 16
Pte. Cockran, A.		30612	B	W.	3 9 18
Lance-Cpl. Coleman, R.		26009	A	W.	30 9 18
Pte. Connolly, J.		11711	B	R.P. of W.	30 9 18
Pte. Commins, A. S. G.		303362	A	W.	23 10 18
Pte. Cones, G. E.		24455	A	D. of W. 24 10 18; 27 10 18
†Pte. Cookson, T.		202541	B	W.	15 6 15
Sgt. Corns, E.		1435	D	W.	15 6 15
Pte. Cowell, C.		1487	A	W.	15 6 15
Lance-Cpl. Collins. W.		2239	A	W.	14 5 18
Pte. Connors, J.		28238	A	K. in A.	14 5 18
★2nd Lieut. Cooper. W. R.					

Pte. Corry, J.	202061		D	W.	N.T. 14/5/18
C.Q.M.S. Cosgrove, J.	34979		B	W.	14/5/18
Pte. Coop, F.	61215		A	W.	N.T. 29/5/18
Sgt. Cookson, J.	200158		C	W.	30/5/18
Pte. Coleman, E. A.	299912		A	W.	1/6/18
Cpl. Collier, F. W.	202905		C	W.	2/6/18
Pte. Coleman, W.	238027		D	W.	2/6/18
Pte. Coyle, W.	416630		D	W.	2/6/18
2nd Lieut. Cowan, C. B.				W.	3/9/18
Pte. Cox, E.	26224		C	W.	30/11/17
Pte. Coley, T.	34336		B	W.	30/11/17
Pte. Cook, H. J.	28230		B	W.	5/12/17
†Pte. Colleney, T.	14568		B	D. of W.	13/4/18
Pte. Cooper, G.	290769		C	W.	11/4/18
Pte. Colquhoun, C. W.	35673		D	W.	16/4/18
Pte. Cox, J.	240515		B	W.	1/5/18
Pte. Cox, J.	29404		C	W.	29/9/16
Pte. Crook, G.	3859		A	W.	10/1/17
Pte. Crompton. B	4672		B	W.	19/5/17
Pte. Crompton, S.	31605		C	W.	27/5/17
Pte. Crook, W.	25634		D	W.	6/5/17
Pte. Craig, J.	2350032		A	K. in A.	31/7/17
†Pte. Crook, R.	202530		A	W.	8/8/16
Pte. Crook, P.	4874		C	W.	1/8/16
Pte. Cross, W.	3890		D	W.	and 9/9/16
Pte. Crane, J.	2829		B	W.	9/9/16
Pte. Croasdale, A.	586		D	W.	28/5/16
Pte. Cross, H.	4854		B	W.	3/7/16
Pte. Crabtree, J.	15		B	K. in A. Shock	31/7/16
2nd Lieut. Crone, J.			A	W. in A.	21/8/16
Pte. Cross, T.	1746		A	K. in A.	31/7/16
Pte. Critchley, J.	202666		A	D. of W.	3/8/16
†Pte. Cross, J.	202628				4/8/17

318

✠Pte. Crook, R.	...	202530	...	A	...	K. in A.	31 7 17
Pte. Cross, E. S.	...	261166	...	C	...	W.	20 9 17
✠Pte. Croft, J.	...	36961	...	B	...	K. in A.	20 9 17
Pte. Crook, P.	...	201014	...	C	...	D. of W.	30 11 17
Pte. Crane, J.	...	2829	...	B	...	W.	15 6 15
Pte. Craven, E.	...	2872	...	B	...	W.	15 6 15
Sgt. Cross, E.	...	735	...	A	...	K. in A.	15 6 15
2nd Lieut. Craven, N. J.					...	W.	15 6 15
Pte. Cross, S.	...	26161	...	C	...	W.	3 9 18
Pte. Crank, R. A.	...	30611	...	B	...	W.	4 9 18
Pte. Crowther, R.	...	30691	...		...	W.	9 9 18
✠Pte. Crerar, J.	...	290092	...	C	...	K. in A.	9 9 18
2nd Lieut Crossley. W. E.		28886	...	D	...	W.	30 9 18
					...	W.	13 10 18
✠Pte. Crook, G.	...	201495	...	B	...	K. in A.	16 8 18
							14 10 18
Pte. Cryer, H.	...	202563	...	C	...	W.	24 10 18
✠Pte. Cross, T.	...	200384	...	A	...	Killed in Brussels	25 4 19
Pte. Crossen, J.	...	1625	...	C	...	W.	15 6 15
Pte. Croft, J. A.	...	290282	...	A	...	W.	14 5 18
Pte. Crossley, A.	...	201635	...	A	...	W.	23 5 18
Pte. Crook, S.	...	205045	...	B	...	W. N.T.	15 8 18
Sgt. Crabtree, H.	...	243857	...	D	...	W.	16 8 16
Lance-Sgt. Crougham, J.	...	201446	...	B	...	W.	25 3 18
						and	9 4 18
Pte. Croasdale, E.	...	200211	...	D	...	Missing N.T.	9 4 18
Lance-Cpl. Crompton, J.	...	265149	...	D	...	W.	13 4 18
✠Pte. Crossley, A.	...	28235	...	C	...	K. in A.	9 4 18
Pte. Crossley, W.	...	204945	...	A	...	W.	9 4 18
✠Pte. Crowe, A. J.	...	265105	...	B	...	K. in A.	25 4 18
✠Pte. Crabtree, E.	...	243857	...	A	...	K. in A.	14 5 18
Pte. Cumming, J.	...	4980	...	B	...	W.	9 9 16
Pte. Cunliffe, J.	...	14318	...	D	...	W.	1 6 17
Pte. Curwen, C.	...	4429	...	B	...	W.	2 8 16
Pte. Curly, J.	...	243651	...	D	...	W.	31 7 17

Pte. Curry, J.	202905	C	W.		31 7 17
				and	18 11 17
Pte. Cunningham, D.	16940	D	W.		30 10 17
Pte. Cuthbert, H.	202579	D	K. in A.		18 11 17
Pte. Culshaw, J. H.	280753	D	D. of W.		10 12 17
Pte. Curl, A. J.	242856	D	K. in A.		1 – 10 18
Pte. Cunningham, W.	1615	C	W.		15 6 18
Pte. Cunliffe, S.	28243	A	W.		25 5 18
Pte. Culshaw, J. H.	3281	A	W.	N.T.	9 4 18
Pte. Curtis, T. S.	416632	B	W.		11 5 18
Pte. Cutler, J.	23207	B	W.		9 5 18
Sgt. Cyr, D.		B	W.	N.T.	30 11 17
Capt. Crump, J. A.			Shock		15 6 18
Pte. Dainty, G.	1886	D	W.		15, 6, 15
Sgt. Davenport, J. E.	1545	B	W.	N.T.	26 5 15
Pte. Darwen, J.	2956	B	W.		15 6 15
Pte. Davidson, C.	3896	D	W.	N.T.	28 6 16
Pte. Daisy, T.	7042	C	W.		7 8 16
Pte. Davies, W.	1905	A	W.	N.T.	8 8 16
Pte. Davies, C.	3981	C	W.		8 8 16
Pte. Daley, J. B.	5927	C	W.		8 8 16
Pte. Dalton, A.	1726	C	W.		9 9 16
Pte. Daggers, R.	1518	B	W.	N.T.	9 9 16
Pte. Dale, W.	202567	B	W.		6 6 17
Pte. Davies, G. A.	34317	A	W.		5 6 17
Pte. Davies, H.	202567	D	W.		30 7 17
Pte. Davenport, S. R.	235010	C	W.		31 7 17
Pte. Dawson, R.	202483	B	W.		31 7 17
Lance-Cpl. Davies, W. J.	34301		W.		31 7 17
2nd Lieut. Dance, H.			W.		20 9 17
Pte. Dandy, J.	18235	B	W.		29 9 19
Pte. Davies, S.	21465	A	W.		20 9 17
Pte. Davies, A. E.	290644	B	W.		20 9 17
Pte. Davies, S	202048	A	W.		20 9 17

320

Pte. Daggers, G.	...	200210		C	W.	20 9 17
Pte. Davies, W.	...	28248		B	W.	30 11 17
Lance-Cpl. Davey, F.	...	203380		B	W.	9 4 18
Pte. Davies, O.	...	39878			D. of W. 26 6 18 and 17 10 18	
†Pte. Davies, R.	...	24124			K. in A.	23 4 18
†Pte. Davies, T.	...	202513			K. in A.	20 9 17
Pte. Davenport, S.	...	29105		A	K. in A.	31 7 17
2nd Lieut. Dawson, J.					W.	20 5 18
Pte. Davies, D. M.	...	41170		D	W.	2 6 18
Pte. Dawson, R.	...	202483		B	W.	18 8 18
Pte. Davenport, H. C.	...	37837		C	W.	3 7 18
2nd Lieut. Davies, H.					W.	11 7 18
2nd Lieut. Daniels, H.					W. N.T.	5 9 18
Pte. Davies, E.	...	41075		A	W.	11 9 18
Cpl. Dandy, J.	...	18235		D	W.	14 9 18
Pte. Davies, E. C	...	28420		D	W.	27 9 18
Pte. Davies, W. J.	...	34501		B	W.	30 9 19
Pte. Dand, M.	...	41634		D	W.	14 10 18
2nd Lieut. Davies, W. A.					K. in A.	16 8 18
Sgt. Daggers, H.	...	16440		C	W.	15 6 18
Pte. Davies, G.	...	29108		A	W.	9 4 18
Pte. Davies, E. G.	...	29388		B	W.	14 5 18
†Lieut. De Blaby, R.					D. of W.	14 10 18
†Sgt. Devey, F.	...	1592		B	K. in A.	8 8 18
Pte. Dennison, R.	...	1058		C	W.	9 8 16
†Pte. Dewhurst, J.	...	2554		A	K. in A.	15 6 15
Pte. Dewhurst, F.	...	4567		B	W.	16 5 15
						8 10 16
Pte. Dewhurst, F.	...	6248		B	W.	9 9 16
Pte. Dempsey, J.	...	6249		B	W.	9 9 16
†Pte. Dempsey, J.	...	202838		B	K. in A.	7 6 17
Pte. Dean, C. H.	...	201599		B	W.	46 5 17
Pte. Delaney, J.	...	200050		B	W.	16 7 17
Pte. Dewhurst, F.	...	202837			W.	31 7 17

321

Pte.	Dean, J. W.	242152	D	W.	20 9 17
†Pte.	Derbyshire, S.	203653		Died	6 4 17
†Pte.	Dewhurst, H.	203406		K. in A.	7 6 17
Cpl.	Dinwoodie, D.	28074	C	K. in A.	18 11 17
†Pte.	Dearden, W.	202449	A	W.	N.T.30 11 17
Pte.	Dench, G.	235009	B	D. of W.	17 12 17
Pte.	Demain, E. H. C.	28251	B	W.	9 4 18
Sgt.	Dean, J.	201094	D	W.	N.T. 13 4 18
†Pte.	Dexter, F. G.	41403	D	K. in A.	16 8 18
Pte.	Deardon, W.	202049	B	W.	16 8 18
Lance-Cpl.	Dewhurst, J.	25799	D	W.	13 7 17
Cpl.	Dewhurst, J.	25799	A	W.	12 4 18
Lance-Cpl.	Dickenson, A.	2567	B	K. in A.	3 8 16
Pte.	Dixon, R.	2658	B	W.	15 9 16
Pte.	Dixon, T.	3982	D	W.	31 7 16
Pte.	Dixon, R.	4541	D	W.	9 9 16
Pte.	Diggle, W. T.	3027	C	W.	26 9 16
Pte.	Dingsdale, T.	202405	B	W.	31 7 17
†Lance-Cpl.	Dickinson, D.	200626		D. of W.	7 4 17
Pte.	Dickenson, R. M.	202634	B	W.	31 7 17
Pte.	Dilworth, A.	22552	C	Missing	20 9 17
Pte.	Digby, H. L.	282407	B	K. in A.	N.T.18 11 17
†Pte.	Dixon, W.	376537	C	D. of W.	8 11 17
Pte.	Dickenson, T.	290509	D	W.	19 2 18
Pte.	Dickenson, T.	23741		W.	16 8 18
2nd Lieut.	Dixon, J. G. H.			W.	17 8 18
†Pte.	Downing, J.	2981	A	K. in A.	16 6 15
Pte.	Dowding, H.	1559	C	W.	8 8 16
Pte.	Dobson, H. G.	1535	B	W.	8 8 16
Pte.	Doble, F.	203237	B	W.	8 9 16
Pte.	Dodgson, J.	2851	C	W.	9 9 16
Capt.	Donald, S. R.			W.	9 9 16
Pte.	Doyne, W.	6125	C	K. in A.	9 9 16
†Pte.	Dobson, S. B.	202122	A	K. in A.	8 8 16
†Sgt.	Donnelly, J.	202900	D	K. in A.	19 5 17

†Cpl.	Doran, J.	240607			K. in A.	2/3/18
†Pte.	Duncan, A. G.	243033			K. in A.	20/9/17
Pte.	Dodgson, J.	200773	A		W.	9/9/18
Pte.	Doult, H.	203334	B		K. in A.	7/9/18
†Pte.	Donkin, A.	30999	C		W.	21/9/18
Pte.	Dobson, G.	30964	B		K. in A.	17/10/18
Pte.	Draper, F.	6273	D		W.	9/9/16
Pte.	Draper, G.	28148	A		K. in A.	30/10/17
Pte.	Drew, W.	204911	D		W.	12/4/18
Pte.	Drury, A.	201683	A		W.	30/9/18
Pte.	Durham, R.	2618	D		W.	15/6/15
Pte.	Duckworth, A.	3403	A		W.	12/7/15
†Pte.	Dunn, S.	302	A		K. in A.	20/8/15
Pte.	Dugdale, W.	2922	B		W.	28/6/16
Pte.	Dunderdale, E.	203346	B		K. in A.	8/8/16
2nd Lieut. Duckebury, O. H.					W. R.P. of W.	8/8/16 N.T.
Pte.	Dudley, J.	3338	C		W.	9/9/16
Pte.	Duerdon, J.	4673	A		W.	9/9/16 N.T.
Pte.	Duckworth, H.	6276	D		K. in A.	9/9/16
Pte.	Duckworth, S.	6235	C		W.	26/9/16
Pte.	Duckworth, E.	6217	B		W.	26/6/16
2nd Lieut. Duerden, W.					W.	26/9/16
Pte.	Duggan, J.	6175	A		W.	29/9/16
†Pte.	Duerden, T.	6176	A		K. in A	23/12/16
C.Q.M.S. Dudley, J.		200128	B		W.	21/5/17
C.S.M. Dudley, J.		200128	A		R.P. of W.	31/7/17
†Pte.	Duckworth, A.	201111	D		D. of W.	8/6/16
†Pte.	Duggan, J.	202796	D		D. of W.	8/6/17
Pte.	Dunne, G.	235025			W.	31/1/17
Pte.	Dunn, J.	28252	C		W.	18/11/17
Pte.	Dunnigan, J.	202123	B		W.	30/7/17
Pte.	Duckworth, H.	28249	D		W.	17/2/18
Pte.	Duckworth, A.	243501	A		K. in A.	20/5/18
†Cpl.	Dutton, T.	30465	D		K. in A.	2/6/18

Pte. Duxbury, B.	201781	B	W.		3 6 18
Cpl. Durose, F.	39576	C	W.	and 10 9 18	
Pte. Dunn, J.	32285	D	W.	N.T. 27 7 18	
Pte. Duddie, T.	30330	B	K. in A.	17 8 18	
Cpl. Duxbury, W. T.	202699	A	K. in A.	2 10 18	
Pte. Duckworth, A.	243501	A	W.	31 7 17	
Pte. Dyson, J.	202580		W.	30 11 17	
				5 6 18	
Pte. Eaves, J.	1098	C	W.	15 6 15	
Pte. Eastham, J.	3912	D	W.	8 8 16	
Pte. Eastham, T.	3018	B	W.	8 8 16	
Pte. Eastham, R.	3139	C	W.	9 9 16	
Pte. Eaves, T.	200698	B	K. in A.	31 7 17	
Pte. Eaves, R.	200225	C	K. in A.	31 7 17	
Pte. Eastham, R.	200937	C	W.	31 7 17	
Pte. Eastwood, J. A.	41637	A	K. in A.	14 5 18	
Pte. Easton, G. H.	28255	B	W.	3 7 18	
Pte. Easthorpe, C. A.	35186	B	K. in A.	11 10 18	
Pte. Eales, J.	41638	D	W.	4 9 18	
2nd Lieut. Eccles, W.			K. in A.	30 5 18	
Pte. Eckton, J.	2302	A	W.	15 6 15	
Pte. Eckersley, A.	243224	A	W.	8 8 16	
Pte. Eccles, F.	4546	B	K. in A.	9 9 16	
Pte. Eckersley, J.	6170	D	W.	21 12 16	
			K. in A.	10 1 17	
Pte. Eckersley, J. H.	202389	D	W.	31 7 17	
Pte. Eccles, T.	201288	A	W.	20 9 17	
Pte. Eccleston, I.	341506	R.A.M.C.	W.	N.T. 30 11 17	
Pte. Ecceston, J.	201102	B	W.	30 11 17	
Pte. Eckersley, J	202389	D	W.	10 4 18	
				and 16 8 12	
C.S.M. Edwards, T. J.	804	C	W.	15 6 15	
Pte. Edwards, C.	1617	C	W.	15 6 15	
Pte. Edwards, F. D.	4946	C	W.	23 12 16	

324

Rank	Name	Number	Coy	Status	Date
Pte.	Edge, J.	202622	A	W.	31 7 17
Cpl.	Edgar, K. V.	201616	B	W.	31 7 17
Pte.	Edwards, F. D.	202107	A	W.	23 12 16 and 20 10 17
Pte.	Edge, F.	28275	B	W.	9 4 18
Pte.	Edwards, J. W.	235496	B	W.	5 9 18
Pte.	Edwards, T.	14541	B	W.	30 9 18
†Pte.	Egan, J.	4397	B	D. of W.	26 9 16
†Pte.	Egan, L.	242017	C	K. in A.	25 4 18
Pte.	Ellison, E.	2991	B	W.	8 8 16
Pte.	Elliott, R.	3508		W.	10 1 18
Pte.	Ellis, F. C.	26574	C	D. of W.	16 6 18
†Pte.	Ellemont, E. S.	28453	B	W.	4 9 18
Pte.	Ellis, B.	96018	B	W.	N.T.
Pte.	Ellison, R.	30962	B	W.	17 10 18
Pte.	Elgar, H.	260108	C	K. in A.	23 10 18
†Pte.	Ellerby, W.	243867	B	W.	30 9 18
Pte.	Emmet, J.	3954	C	W.	N.T. 9 9 16
Pte.	Entwistle, J.	3538	A	W.	9 9 16
Sgt.	Entwistle, T.	200025		W.	and 31 7 17
†Pte.	Enderby, W.	201642	C	K. in A.	18 11 17
Pte.	Entwistle, T.	243828	D	W.	11 9 18
Pte.	Entwistle, R.	243340	B	W.	NT. 30 9 18
Pte.	Evans, A.	2079	D	W.	15 6 15
Pte.	Evans, A.	4607	D	W.	8 8 16
Lieut.	Evans, A. J. D.			W.	8 8 16
Pte.	Evans, C.	202051	C	W.	9 6 17
†Sgt.	Evans, R.	201790	C	K. in A.	31 7 17
Pte.	Evans, G. F.	362201	A	W.	31 7 17
Pte.	Evans, A.	293389	B	W.	3 6 18
2nd Lieut.	Easterby, E. M.	4879		W.	9 9 16 and 30 11 17

325

Pte. Farmer, J.	844		C		W.	15 6 15
Pte. Fairclough, C.	1063		C		W.	15 6 15
2nd Lieut. Fairclough, E. L.					W.	8 8 16
†Pte. Farrell, T.	2686		B		K. in A.	15 6 15
Pte. Fallown, W.	1994		B		W.	28 6 16
‡Cpl. Farrell, W. A.	202030				K. in A.	8 8 16
‡2nd Lieut. Falby, E. F.					K. in A.	9 9 16
Pte. Fazackerley, W.	3484		B		W.	9 9 16
†Pte. Fairclough, W.	4420		B		W.	9 9 16
Lance-Cpl. Farnworth, H.	201637		C		W.	21 5 17
Pte. Fairbrother, W.	203550		C		W.	31 7 17
†Pte. Farrer, L.	19005		B		D. of W.	18 11 17
Pte. Farrer, G.	202798		A		W.	13 1 18
Cpl. Faraday, W.	202889		D		W.	30 11 17
Pte. Faulkner, W.	38259		D		W.	30 11 17
Pte. Fazackerley, T.	201364		D		W.	N.T. 23 3 18
Lance-Cpl. Fazackerley, T.	201364		D		W.	15 4 18
Pte. Farnell, D.	11645		A		W.	25 4 18
Pte. Fairbrother, A.	20694		B		W.	30 4 18
Pte. Farnworth, T.	240412		A		W.	14 5 18
Pte. Faragher, W.	11642		D		W.	and 2 6 18 17 8 18
†2nd Lieut. Fazackerley, H.			C		K. in A.	25 8 18
Pte. Fayen, W.	32080		A		W.	20 7 18
Pte. Fenton, J.	2580		B		W.	15 6 15
Lance-Cpl. Fenton, T.	24		D		W.	1 7 16
Pte. Fearnley, E.	202651				K. in A.	15 5 17
‡2nd Lieut. Fergie, A. B.			B		W.	20 9 17
Cpl. Fenton, T.	200012				K. in A.	14 4 18
‡Pte. Folown, J.	200458		D		D. of W.	11 9 18 28 8 16
‡Pte. Farrey, J.	11644		D		W.	12 9 18
†Pte. Fell, H.	30645		C		K. in A.	24 9 18
‡Pte. Fell, W.	265331		C		W.	18 4 17
Pte. Fielding, R	3311		C		K. in A.	15 6 15

Pte. Fishwick, W.		186	D	W.	14 9 15
2nd Lieut. Firth, E. S.			A	W.	8 8 16
†Pte. Finch, R. J.		2303	D	K. in A.	15 6 16
Pte. Fishwick, H.		3555	D	W.	8 8 16
Pte. Finney, J.		1299		W.	9 9 16 N.T.
Lieut. Fisher, G. J.		200098	R.A.M.C.	W.	31 7 17
Pte. Finney, H.		235167	C	R.P. of W.	2 8 17
Pte. Fisher, W.		13386	C	R.P. of W.	18 11 17
†2nd Lieut. Firth, J. O.				K. in A.	18 11 17
Pte. Finney, J.		202744	D	W.	30 11 17
Pte. Fitzgerald, T.		376349	B	W.	10 4 18
†Pte. Fielding, J. B.		41302	D	K. in A.	29 4 18
Pte. Fiddler, J. N.		389985	C	W.	8 11 N.T.
Pte. Fitzgerald, E.		81015	C	W.	6 6 18
Lance-Cpl. Fisher, W.		28454	B	W.	16 8 18
Sgt. Fisher, W.		28454	B	W.	30 9 18
Pte. Fiori, G.		406688	B	W.	4 9 18
†Sgt. Fisher, J. V.		22768	D	K. in A.	22 10 18
Pte. Fitzgerald, A.		10185	A	W.	25 10 18
Pte. Finney, F.		29275	A	W.	7 7 18
Pte. Finch, T.		30645	C	W.	8 8 18
Lance-Cpl. Fisher, E. E.		13881	C	W.	4 9 18
†Cpl. Fletcher, J.		1987	B	K. in A.	10 4 16
Lance-Cpl. Fletcher, J.		1755	D	W.	15 6 15
†C.Q.M.S. Fletcher, J.		1755	D	K. in A.	31 7 17
Pte. Flowers, T.		84	A	W.	30 5 15
†Pte. Fletcher, W.		2691	C	K. in A.	15 6 15
†Pte. Forrest, J.		37598		K. in A.	15 6 15
Pte. Flannery, L.		3165	A	W.	15 6 15
†Pte. Fletcher, J.		200419	C	K. in A.	31 7 17
†Pte. Flockhart, D.		202566	B	K. in A.	31 7 17
Pte. Fletcher, U.		37668	A	W.	20 9 17
†Pte. Fletcher, H.		200499	B	K. in A.	20 9 17
†Pte. Flanagan, L. E.		28264		W.	25 4 18

Pte. Flaherty, T.	29117		D	W.	26 4 18 and 25 8 18
†2nd Lieut. Fullerton, F.				K. in A.	31 7 17
Pte. Fleming, J. W.	28075		A	W.	9 9 18
Sgt. Fowler, E.	1349		D	W.	15 6 15
Pte. Fowler, E.	1571		D	W.	15 6 15 and 8 8 16
Pte. Fowler, H.	155		D	W.	15 6 15
Pte. Forrest, J. F.	3185		D	W.	5 9 15
‡Pte. Foster, E.	1445		D	D. of W.	5 8 16
‡Pte. Forshaw, R.	2574		B	K. in A.	15 6 15
‡Pte. Fowler, J.	2773		C	K. in A.	15 6 15
2nd Lieut. Forshaw, C. H.				W.	9 9 16
†2nd Lieut. Forrest, R.				K. in A.	27 9 18
Pte. Forrest, J.	200968		D	W.	4 6 17
Pte. Foreman, R.	200743		B	W.	7 6 17
‡Pte. Forsyth J.	201038		D	K. in A.	31 7 17
Sgt. Foley, W.	200097		D	W.	20 9 17
Pte. Forrest,	202839		B	D. of W.	23 9 17
Pte. Fox, W. H.	282.58		C	R.P. of W.	9 4 18
‡Pte. Ford, W.	235141		C	Missing	8 4 18 N.T.
‡Pte. Fowler, J.	31681		D	K. in A.	13 4 17
Cpl. Foy, J.	200058		B	K. of A.	18 5 17
Cpl. Foulkes, C.	18989		A	W.	4 6 17
Pte. Foster, G.	28758		D	W.	26 5 18
Sgt. Fryer, W.	6074		D	W.	3 6 18
Rev. Forse, L. N.				R.P. of W.	28 6 16 N.T.
†Lance-Cpl. Frazer, A.	2690		A	K. in A.	15 6 15
Pte. Freebury, A.	2875		C	Missing	13 6 15
2nd Lieut. Francis, J. E.				W.	18 5 17
Pte. Frame, A.	202584		D	W.	N.T. 18 11 17
Pte. Frame, J.	203453		B	W.	9 4 18
Pte. France, A.	202548		D	Missing	13 4 18
2nd Lieut. Frost, L.				W.	2 5 18

2nd Lieut. Fryer, T. H.				W.	25/5/18
Lance-Cpl. Fryer, G.	200618		A	W.	27/5/18
Pte. Francis, W. H.	241708		D	W.	22/8/18
Pte. French, T. W.	28269		A	W.	22/9/18
Pte. Frost, F. H.	35036		D	W.	22/10/18
Pte. Francombe, W.	28268		B	W.	23/7/18
Pte. Frodsham, J.	37684		D	W.	14/5/18
Pte. Fyles, E.	207		D	W.	3/8/16
†Pte. Gardner, J.	1091		D	K. in A.	15/6/15
Pte. Galloway, T.	36200		B	W.	20/11/17
†Pte. Garlinge, C. J.	8912		A	K. in A.	23/11/17
Pte. Gartshore, R.	30363		B	W.	28/3/18
Pte. Garrett, F.	28271		D	R.P. of W.	9/4/18
Pte. Gaskin, S.	28300		D	W.	29/4/18
†Pte. Gale, A. G.	19000		B	K. in A.	8/6/18
Pte. Gaunt, R.	282039		B	W.	21/6/18 N.T.
Pte. Gardner, R.	2249		B	W.	28/9/16
Pte. Gallagher, J.	1716		B	W.	15/6/15
Pte. Gaskell, J	7406		A	W.	3/8/16
Pte. Garside, R. C.	4881			W.	8/8/16
†Pte. Geldeard, R.	2061		A	K. in A.	15/6/15
Pte. German, A.	29411			W.	29/5/18
Pte. Gent, D. A.	1468		A	K. in A.	15/6/15
Pte. Gent, F.	36888		B	W.	2/6/18
Pte. Gerber, C.	41303		B	W.	8/6/16
†Pte. Gerrard, L.	201739		B	K. in A.	31/7/17
†Pte. Gent, F.	4849		B	K. in A.	28/6/16
†Pte. Gerrish, J.	29282		D	K. in A.	3/9/18
Lance-Sgt. German, G. H.	13393		D	W.	4/9/18
Lance-Sgt. Gerrard, W.	38681		B	W.	13/4/18
†Lance-Sgt. George, T.	42040		B	K. in A.	14/10/18
†Pte. Gill, H.	28274		C	K. in A.	29/10/18

Lance-Sgt. Giddens, H.	202772		W.	D	30/11/17
Cpl. Gibson, J.	162200		W.	B	9/4/18
✠Pte. Gisby, S.	303368		K. in A.	C	10/4/18
Pte. Gibson, D.	202800		W.	B	13/5/18
✠Pte. Gilbertson, R.	29127		K. in A.	A.	8/7/18
✠Pte. Gidlow, A.	2246		K. in A.	A	9/9/16
Pte. Gibson, T.	202773		W.	D	9/9/16
Pte. Gillibrand, J	4278		W.	D	29/5/16 and 9/9/16
Pte. Gilmaur, W. H.	5284		W.	B	20/9/16
✠Pte. Ginger, F.	353972		K. in A.	A	31/7/17
✠Lance-Cpl. Gillett, N.	210		K. in A.	D	28/6/16
Sgt. Gillett, C.	330		W.	B	28/6/15
Sgt. Gillett, T. E.	175		W.	D	15/6/15
Pte. Gill, G. A.	290		W.	D	15/6/15
✠Pte. Gillibrand,	152		K. in A.		3/5/15
Pte. Gill, I.	6686		W.	A	3/8/16
✠Pte. Gilbertson, R.	29127		K. in A.	A	8/7/18
✠Lance-Cpl. Gillabrand	2960		W.	B	9/9/16
			K. in A.		25/9/17
Pte. Gillett, J.	25301		W.	A	9/6/17
✠Pte. Gidman, A.	29123		K. in A.	B	9/4/18
Pte. Gledhill, W.	242322		W.	C	20/9/17
✠Lance-Cpl. Glover, T.	779		K. in A.	D	28/5/15
Lance-Cpl. Gorton, F.	200756		W.	D	30/11/17
Pte. Goddard, E.	27761		W.		9/4/18
Pte. Gore, T. H.	23657		W.	C	3/6/18
Pte. Gore, T. W.	41088		W.	D	8/7/18 N.T.
Pte. Godfrey, R.	3289		W.	D	9/9/16
Pte. Gorton, H. V	12235		W.	A	18/5/17
✠Pte. Gordon, A.	202754		K. in A.	C	18/7/17
Pte. Goodram, G.	288003		W.		21/7/17 and 20/9/17
Pte. Gore, J. A.	2773		W.	A	15/6/15
Pte. Gorton, J.	195		W.	D	5/9/15

†Pte. Gorton, J.	202853			K. in A.		31/7/17
Pte. Gough, R.	105		B	W.		31/7/17
†Pte. Gorst, T. H.	1944		A	K. in A.		15/6/16
Pte. Gorse, W.	4433		A	K. in A.		30/7/16
Pte. Goodier, L.	28270		D	W.		9/4/18
Pte. Gough, G.	41647		A	W.		14/5/18
†Pte. Goodram, W.	36729		B	K. in A.		1/10/18
Pte. Gornall, E.	36877		B	P.R. of W.		23/10/18
Pte. Goodier, R.	201280		B	Missing		23/10/18
†Pte. Greenhalgh, J.	37290		B	K. in A.		18/11/17
2nd Lieut. Green, A.				W.		30/11/17
Pte. Griffiths, J.	37259		A	W.		9/4/18
Col. Grant, W.	36559		C	W.		9/4/18
Pte. Graham, E.	29118		A	W.	N.I.	9/4/18
Pte. Gregson, J.	29124			W.		9/4/18
Pte. Gray, J.	235011		A	R.P. of W.		9/4/18
†Pte. Greenwood, H.	201568		D	K. in A.	N.I.	9/4/18
Pte. Greenwood, R.	29409		D	K. in A.		29/4/18
†Pte. Gresty, O. F.	39617		B	W.		28/4/18
Pte. Grimshaw, H.	29410		C	K. in A.		16/5/18
2nd Lieut. Greaves, F.				K. in A.		1/6/18
†Pte. Grinter, W.	27177		D	K. in A.		2/6/18
†Pte. Grayson, W.	25592		B	W.		19/9/16
2nd Lieut. Gray, W.				W.		9/9/16
Pte. Green, F.	2420		D	W.	N.I.	9/9/16
Pte. Greenwood, G.	4650		D	W.	N.I.	9/9/16
Pte. Gradwell, J.	200661		A	W.		6/5/17
Pte. Greenwood, W. R.	202640		B	W.	N.I.	11/6/17
Pte. Grey, W. H.	202642		B	W.		12/7/17
Pte. Gregory, G.	26662		B	W.		31/7/17
Pte. Grey, I. W.	235011		A	W.		31/7/17
†Pte. Green, J.	244966		A	K. in A.		31/7/17
Pte. Green, H.	200841		A	W.		2/8/17
Pte. Gregson, E.	200412		A	W.		31/7/17
Pte. Gregory, G.	26662		A	W.		2/8/17

†Pte. Gregson, W.	2955			Died	25 7 15
2nd Lieut. Gresdale, R.	—		C	W.	20 9 17
†Lance-Cpl. Greenhalgh, G.	202475		D	K. in A.	20 9 17
Pte. Grimshaw, A.	10721		A	W.	N.T. 20 9 17
Pte. Griffiths, J.	7259		C	W.	20 9 17
Pte. Grinse, T.	25503		C	W.	12 4 15
╪Pte. Gregson, H.	200715			Died	28 6 16
╪Capt. Gregson, E. M.	—			K. in A.	15 6 15
Cpl. Green, J.	56		B	W.	15 6 15
Pte. Grungy, T.	70		A	W.	15 6 15
Pte. Greenwood, R.	1009		C	W.	15 6 15
Pte. Gregory, W.	1343		B	W.	15 6 15
Cpl. Green, W.	1593		B	W.	15 6 15
Pte. Gregson, C.	1943		A	W.	15 6 15
Pte. Greenwood, C.	3265		B	W.	and 8 8 16
Pte. Grime, J.	3342		D	W.	15 6 15
Pte. Greenwood, J.	2585		B	W.	15 6 16
Pte. Green, H.	2900		A	W.	1 8 16
Pte. Gregson, E.	1914		A	K. in A.	15 6 15
†Pte. Griffin, W.	200953		A	W.	2 8 16
Pte. Green, H.	2900		C	W.	5 8 16
Pte. Green, J.	4996		C	W.	8 8 16
Pte. Grimes, F.	3604		D	W.	8 8 16
Pte. Gregson, A.	3402		B	W.	8 8 16
Pte. Grime, T.	7775		B	W.	13 7 16
Pte. Greenwood, C.	2265		C	W.	9 7 16
Pte. Greenhalch, J.	202953		B	W.	9 8 18
Pte. Greenwood, J. W.	28275		D	W.	15 8 18
Pte. Green, C.	240729		D	W.	16 8 18
Pte. Green, C.	30614		A	W.	31 7 17
Cpl. Graham, E.	200686		A	W.	2 8 17
╪Pte. Green, J.	241896		D	K. in A.	5 9 18
Cpl. Grimshaw, T.	12324		A	W.	9 9 18
Pte. Griffiths, T.	29412				

332

2nd Lieut. Griffiths, H. W. C.			W.	1/10/18
Pte. Graham, R.	41723	B	W.	30/9/18
Pte. Gregory, H.	240549	B	W.	23/10/18
†Pte. Grimshaw, J.	3375		K. in A.	15/4/15
Sgt. Gunn, A.	202498	B	K. in A.	21/4/18
Pte. Gulloway, E.	28272	D	W.	4/9/18
Pte. Gunn, F.	38667	C	W.	17/10/18
Pte. Guffogg, J.	241216		W.	9/4/18
Pte. Gynes, W.	201404	D	W.	8/6/17
Pte. Hankinson, W.	16150	B	W.	9/4/18 and 7/7/18
†Pte. Haworth, W.	291340	C	K. in A.	9/4/18
Pte. Harris, H. L.	246588	D	W.	9/4/18
Pte. Haner, T.	202962	B	W.	18/11/17
				9/4/18 and 17/8/18
Pte. Harold, T. R.	282958	A	W.	10/4/18
†Pte. Haslam, L.	203757	A	K. in A.	9/4/18
Cpl. Hanley, L.	241169		W.	9/4/18
Cpl. Hawkins, T. H.	243083		W.	9/4/18
Cpl. Harvey, M.	241723		W.	9/4/18
†Cpl. Haslam, H.	242279	A	Died	18/10/18
Cpl. Haworth, D.	41654	D	W.	2/5/18
†Cpl. Hampson, W.	29415	A	K. in A.	14/5/18
Lance-Cpl. Hancox, W.	201562	A	W. & Missing	14/5/18
Pte. Hampson, F.	202961	D	W.	14/5/18
Lance-Cpl. Hankinson, J.	202466	A	W.	15/5/18
†2nd Lieut. Hampson, J.			K. in A.	21/5/18
Pte. Hacking, J.	236655	A	W.	1/6/18
Cpl. Harwell, E. J.	38839	D	W.	3/6/18
Pte. Hartley, H.	205006	B	W.	18/6/18
Pte. Hayes, J.	202561	A	W.	20/6/18
Pte. Hall, J.	299729	D	W.	15/8/18
Pte. Haighton, F.	4136676	D	W.	15/8/18
Pte. Hayes, F.	235500	D	W.	15/8/18

✠Pte. Hargreaves, F.	202803	A		K. in A.		9.9.16
✠Cpl. Hartley, A.	1135	A		K. in A.		9.9.16
Pte. Hardy, J. R.	37799	A		W.		9.9.16
Pte. Harrison, J.	5054	A		W.		9.9.16
Pte. Hartley, J. W.	4678	D		W.	N.T.	9.9.16
Pte. Haslam, R.	202059	D		W.		9.9.16
Pte. Hacking, T.	4259	D		W.	N.T.	9.9.16
Pte. Halley, H.	6103	D		W.		9.9.16
Pte. Hankinson, J.	3175	B		W.		9.9.16
Pte. Hamer, J.	4802	B		W.		9.9.16
✠Pte. Hargreaves, J. H.	4895	C		K. in A.		25.9.16
Pte. Harvey, A.	6301	B		W.	N.T.	26.9.16
Pte. Harrison, J.	14592	A		W.		6.4.17
Pte. Hargreaves, H.	202564	C		W.		21.6.17
2nd Lieut. Hall, R. A.	202939			W.		4.5.17
Pte. Halliwell, W.	202725	D		W.		12.7.17
✠Pte. Harrison, T. C.	240645	A		K. in A.	N.T.	21.7.17
Lance-Cpl. Haworth, H	238931	C		W.		20.7.17
Lance-Cpl. Haworth, J.	15384	C		W.		21.7.17
Pte. Hardacre, J.	201796	C		W.		21.7.17
✠Capt. Harris, A. L.	—			K. in A.		31.7.17
Sgt. Hall, A	200587	C		W.		31.7.17
Pte. Hall, C.	202627	D		W.		31.7.17
Pte. Harrison, W.	201588	B		W.		31.7.17
Pte. Hardman, T.	201349			W.		31.7.17
Pte. Hargreaves, G.	368222	C		W.		31.7.17
✠Pte. Hatton, R.	202525	B		K. in A.		31.7.17
✠Pte. Haworth, J. H.	202610	B		K. in A.		31.7.17
✠Pte. Halsall, P.	202734	D		K. in A.		31.7.17
✠Sgt. Hurley, J.	147	D		Died		8.8.16
Pte. Hall	138	D		W.		8.8.16
✠Cpl. Hall, H.	200604	D		K. in A.		8.8.16
Pte. Harrison, W. A.	4955	D		W.		8.8.16
Pte. Hart, F.	4885	C		W.		8.8.16

†Sgt. Harling, W.	161	B	K. in A.		15 6 15
†Pte. Harrison, P.	2198	(R.A.M.C.)	K. in A.	N.T.	8 8 16
Pte. Hart, E.	1404	D	W.		15 6 15
Pte. Hague, A. E.	2123	B	W.		15 6 15
Pte. Hayes, W.	2279	B	W.		15 6 15
Pte. Hargreaves, P.	2677	A	W.		15 6 15
†Pte. Hall, G. H.	28092	C	K. in A.		18 11 15
†Pte. Hart, G. F.	28292	B	K. in A.		18 11 17
Pte. Hannah, J.	28291	B	R.P. of W.		18 11 17
Pte. Harvey, W.	28067	A	W.		20 11 17
†Pte. Hardacre, J.	202140	A	D. of W. 9 12 17	.30 11 17
Pte. Harrison, G. S.	28282	A	W.		.30 11 17
Pte. Hankinson, W.	16150	B	W.		.30 11 17
Pte. Hart, J.	202230	D	R.P. of W.		.30 11 17
Pte. Harrop, W.	16238	D	W.		.30 11 17
Pte. Hardman, F.	28289	D	W.		.30 11 17
Pte. Halliwell, W.	202725	D	W.		.30 11 17
Lance-Cpl. Halsall. W. H.	241351	C	W.		9 4 18
Pte. Hampson, J. P.	28281	B	W.		9 4 18
Pte. Haslam, L.	19372	B	W.		9 4 18
†Pte. Hammond, L.	202979	B	K. in A.		31 7 18
Pte. Hawkland, H.	202168	B	W.		31 7 18
Pte. Hatch, W.	18600	B	Missing		31 7 18
Pte. Hargreaves, A.	13411	D	Missing		31 7 18
Pte. Hardman, E.	200280	D	W.		20 9 17
Pte. Hamer, W.	37637	D	W.		20 9 17
Pte. Hardman, W.	32015	D	W.	and	21 9 17
Pte. Hackett, F.	14785	D	W.		30 8 18
Pte. Hankinson, W.	64.50	B	W.	N.T.	20 9 17
Pte. Harrobin, W.	202989	C	W.	N.T. 18	11 15
Pte. Haighton, J.	238017	C	W.		28 3 18
Pte. Hartley, T.	30029	C	W.	and	18 11 16
Pte. Hayhurst, J. T.	1463	B	W.	N.T.	8 8 16

335

Name	No.	Coy	Status	Date
C.S.M. Harwood, J.	81	D	W.	9 9 16
†Cpl. Hawkhurst, C.	1618	C	K. in A.	9 9 16
Cpl. Hartley, J.	1661	C	W.	9 9 16
Pte. Halliwell, H.	3986	A	W.	9 9 16
Sgt. Hall, A.	2402	C	W.	13 9 16
†Pte. Harrison, G.	1289	C	K. in A.	6 6 15
Pte. Hall, T. V.	2083	D	W.	6 6 15
Pte. Harrison, W.	4195	A	W.	8 7 16
†Pte. Hardacre, J.	5004	A	D. of W.	31 7 17 9 12 17
Pte. Hamer, H.	88883	B	W.	N.T. 31 7 16
Pte. Hamer, A.	2004489	A	Missing	2 8 16
2nd Lieut. Haque, A. E.			W.	5 8 16
Pte. Harrison, F.	2964	C	W.	15 6 15
Pte. Hankinson, J.	3175	B	W.	15 6 15
Pte. Harrison, J.	2919	D	W.	15 6 15
Pte. Hartley, T.	3029	C	W.	21 10 15
Pte. Hartley, H.	2558	B	W.	29 10 15
Pte. Hargreaves, A.	1616	A	W.	29 10 15
Pte. Hall, H.	138	D	W.	30 10 15
Pte. Hart, J.	143	D	W.	26 4 16
Pte. Hartley, H.	2558	B	W.	26 5 16
Cpl. Harrison, F.	2964	D	W.	28 6 16
†Pte. Haslam, G.	2558	B	K. in A.	14 6 15
†Pte. Hayes, J.	2771	A	K. in A.	15 6 15
†Pte. Hardickey, M.	2842	B	W.	15 6 15
	255		Died	23 6 15
†Pte. Haley, J. W.	200604		D. of W.	11 9 16
†Cpl. Hall, H.	200058		K. in A.	8 8 16
†Pte. Hartley, H.	203330	D	K. in A.	8 8 16
Pte. Heyes, J. B.	30948	D	W.	16 8 18
Pte. Hazeldine, J.	202760	C	W.	11 9 18
†Pte. Horrobin, W.	29571		D. of W.	12 9 18
†Lance-Cpl. Hawitt, W.	29413		K. in A.	24 9 18
Pte. Hardacre, A. N.	30492	A	W.	30 9 18

Pte. Harmer, W.	309966		B	R.P. of W.	23/10/18
Pte. Hardman, W.	222628		A	W.	23/10/18
Pte. Hadwin, W. B.	248863		A	W.	24/10/18
Pte. Harrison, T.	29130		D	R.P. of W.	22/10/18
Pte. Hamer, W.	28766		A	W.	29/10/18
Pte. Hall, A. W. W.	416650		D	W.	8/6/18
Pte. Hancox, J.	30497		A	W.	16/8/18
Sgt. Hall, A.	2402		C	W.	8/8/16
Pte. Hayes, A.	2026659		A	W.	31/7/17
✠Pte. Hartley, J. F.	28052		B	K. in A.	30/11/17
✠Lance-Cpl. Hackett, T. K.	202528		A	K. in A.	9/4/18
Lance-Cpl. Halton, A.	1709			R.P. of W.	8/8/16
Pte. Hayes, J.	202561		A	W.	16/6/18
Pte. Harvey, T. G.	309965		B	W.	14/10/18
✠Pte. Heap, E.	28171		D	K. in A.	9/4/18 N.T.
Pte. Henthorne, S.	240906		A	W.	9/4/18
✠Pte. Heeney, W.	28276			K. in A.	10/4/18
✠Pte. Herd, J.	9609		B	K. in A.	25/4/18
✠Pte. Hallows, E.	202656			K. in A.	31/7/17
✠Pte. Hanson, F.	202687			D. of W.	31/7/17
✠Pte. Hargreaves, J. H.	62222			D. of W.	3/10/16
✠Pte. Harrison, J.	16558			D. of W.	2/8/17
✠Lance-Cpl. Harwood, J.	200558			K. in A.	14/5/18
Pte. Heaps, E.	240270		A	W.	2/6/18
Pte. Heaps, J.	201465		A	W.	2/6/18
Pte. Heywood, T.	30496		D	K. in A.	16/8/18
✠Pte. Heath, E. W.	27487		B	W.	16/8/18
Pte. Heather, B.	235047		D	W.	9/9/16 N.T.
Pte. Heap, L. H.	3554		B	W.	9/9/16
Pte. Hestmondhalgh, H.	4143		B	W.	27/6/16
Pte. Hewarth, W. A.	2319		A	W.	15/6/15
Sgt. Heaney, C.	1704		D	W.	and 8/1/17
Pte. Henitt, F.	2001/16		C	W.	5/8/17
Pte. Heaps, R.	202527		A	R.P. of W.	31/7/17

†Cpl. Heaps, R.	200567		K. in A.	31 7 17
Pte. Heald, D.	3539		W.	8 8 16
Lance-Cpl. Henderson, J. H. A.	2789	D	W.	9 9 16
Pte. Horn, W.	3968	C	W.	22 9 16 and 7 10 18
Pte. Heskith, H.	2606	C	W.	9 9 16
†Pte. Hey, S.	202856	C	K. in A.	9 9 16
Pte. Heeley, J.	253	A	W.	11 9 16
Cpl. Heywood, E.	199	B	W.	9 9 16
†Pte. Heaps, J.	1788	C	K. in A.	15 6 15
†Pte. Helm, F.	2768	C	K. in A.	16 6 15
†Pte. Hewitt, H.	2863	B	K. in A.	15 6 15
†Pte. Helm, H.	2927	A	W.	16 6 15
Pte. Hewitt, A. E.	2049	B	W.	31 7 16
Pte. Helme, T.	104	D	W.	15 6 15
Pte. Hesketh, J.	3287	C	W.	15 6 15
Pte. Hesketh, P.	2007	D	W.	15 6 15
Pte. Heaton, A. E.	2074	A	W.	31 7 16
Pte. Hewitt, J.	4141	C	K. in A.	8 8 16
†Pte. Heyes, V.	2743	D	W.	1 7 16
Sgt. Heaney, C.	1704		Died	15 6 15
Pte. Henderson, T. O	202554		K. in A.	20 2 17
†Pte. Henley, W.	289	A	K. in A.	15 6 15
†Lance-Cpl. Hesketh, H.	22717	D	W.	31 7 17
Pte. Hewitt, A. E.	2049	B	W.	8 8 16
Pte. Hendy, W.	200488	D	W.	N.T.18 11 17
Pte. Heaton, C.	200294	A	K. in A.	30 11 17
†Pte. Heaps, J.	200557	D	W.	20 9 17
Pte. Heywood, W. H.	290554	A	W.	16 8 18
Pte. Heywood, J. W.	255501	B	W.	14 10 18
Pte. Higginbotham, F.	30097	D	W.	22 10 18
Pte. Heron, S. C.	244871	B	R.P. of W.	23 10 18
Pte. Helm, E.	29128	D	W.	24 10 18
A.R.S.M. Heywood, H.	200222	D	W.	
Pte. Heald, A.	201313	A	W.	9 7 18

Pte. Helme, J. E.	29137		W.		4.9.18
†Pte. Heath, L.	40395	D	D. of W.		9.9.18
†Capt. Hibbert, C. G. R.		B	Presumed Killed		15.9.18
†Pte. Higgins, R.	29132	B	K. in A.		9.4/18
Sgt. Hindey, F.	240268	A	W.		25.4.18
Pte. Higgins, L.	4787	B	W.	N.T.	9.4.18
†Lance-Cpl. Higham, E.	2611	B	K. in A.		9.4.18
†Pte. Hill, H.	28288		K. in A.		11.3.18
†Lance-Cpl. Higgins, J.	240083	B	K. in A.		8.7.18
Pte. Hibbert, W.	241553	A	W.		7.7.18
Pte. Hickson, T.	30491	A	W.		7.7.18
Pte. Hilton, W.	28295	D	W.		16.8.18
†Sgt. Hills, H. L.	3783	B	K. in A.		9.9.18
†Pte. Hitchon, H.	6223	B	D. of W.	9.9.16	13.9.16
2nd Lieut. Higson, F.			W.	N.T.	13.11.16
Pte. Higham, W.	200877	B	W.		31.5.17
†Pte. Hilton, J. R.	17102		D. of W.		15.6.17
Pte. Highfield, J.	200457	B	W.		7.6.17
Pte. Higham, H.	201022	C	D. of W.		9.7.17
Pte. Hill, H.	11513	A	W.		16.7.17
†Pte. Hinsley, A.	202891		K. in A.		30.9.16
†Pte. Hirst, E.	30193		D. of W.		30.5.18
Pte. Hodson, G. A.	258041		K. in A.		2.6.18
†Pte. Holden, S.	4886		D. of W.		29.6.16
†Pte. Horan, C.	4382	A	Died		24.2.17
Pte. Higham, A.	203728	C	W.		31.7.17
Pte. Hilton, T.	242181	C	W.		5.8.16
Pte. Higham, F.	202136	B	W.		9.8.16
Pte. Highfield, J.	1993	C	W.		8.8.18
Pte. Higham, H.	3273	C	W.		5.8.16
Lance-Cpl. Hill, J.	304	U	D. of W.		15.6.15
†Lance-Cpl. Hill, E.	780	B	K. in A.		25.8.16
†Pte. Higgenson, F.	2936		W.		14.6.15
Pte. Hicks, F.	1291	C	W.		15.6.15

339

Name		No.			Coy.		Casualty		Date
Pte. Huntsley, A.	...	6281	...	...	D	...	W.		9 9 16
†Capt. Hibbert, C. G. R.	...		...	...		...	Presumed Killed		15 6 15
Sgt. Hogg, J.	...	200092	...	...	C	...	W.	... N.T.	9 4 18
Cpl. Hodson, R.	...	240653	...	...	D	...	Missing		9 4 18
Pte. Howard, C.	...	240240	...	...	A	...	W.	... N.T.	9 4 18
Pte. Holden, W.	...	25388	...	...	A	...	W.		14 5 18
Pte. Hopwood, T.	...	304480	...	...	D	...	W.		11 5 18
†Pte. Holwill, R. H.	...	27963	...	...	A	...	W.		23 8 18
†Pte. Howard, W.	...	36702	...	...		...	K. in A.		20 5 18
†Lance-Cpl. Horribin, W.	...	29574	...	...		...	D. of W.		24 9 17
†Pte. Hough, J. W.	...	23246	...	...		...	K. in A.		31 7 17
†Pte. Howarth, H.	...	5247	...	...		...	K. in A.		27 8 16
†Pte. Howarth, W. J.	...	29140	...	...		...	K. in A.		9 4 18
Pte. Howson, L.	...	202057	...	...	D	...	W.		31 7 17
Pte. Hobbs, W. A. E.	...	38840	...	...	C	...	W.		20 5 18
Pte. Houghton, W. J.	...	28030	...	...	A	...	W.		29 5 15
†Pte. Hodson, J. A.	...	30195	...	...	D	...	Missing	... N.T.	2 6 18
†Pte. Holland, L.	...	28284	...	...	D	...	K. in A.		3 6 18
†Pte. Holmes, J.	...	240065	...	...	B	...	K. in A.		5 6 18
Pte. Holt, H.	...	201786	...	...	D	...	W.		25 6 18
Pte. Howard, W.	...	28031	...	...	C	...	W.		27 6 18
Pte. Hopwood, F.	...	30489	...	...	A	...	W.		7 7 18
Pte. Hope, F.	...	243548	...	...	D	...	W.		16 8 18
†Pte. Howarth, J. R.	...	6279	...	...	D	...	K. in A.		9 9 16
Pte. Howson, R.	...	6101	...	...	D	...	W.		9 9 16
Lance-Cpl. Holland, W.	...	1584	...	...	B	...	W.		9 9 16
†Lance-Cpl. Hope, J. H.	...	4899	...	...	B	...	K. in A.		9 9 16
†Lance-Sgt. Horsefield, T.	...	3396	...	...	B	...	K. in A.		30 6 16
†Pte. Hollingworth, P.	...	200558	...	...	C	...	Missing		31 7 17
Pte. Hopkins, E.	...	235013	...	...	C	...	K. in A.		29 5 17
2nd Lieut. Holden, H. S.	...	3283	...	...	B	...	R.P. of W.	... N.T.	3 5 17
Pte. Hodgkiss, H	...	31981	...	...	A	...	W.		31 7 17
†Pte. Horner, A. E.	...	200646	...	...	A	...	K. in A.		9 6 17
Pte. Holt, A.	...	202698	...	...	B	...	K. in A.		12 7 17

Pte. Hodson, E.	203265		B		W.		13 7 17
†Pte. Horsefield, R. A.	20280		A		K. in A.		21 7 17
Pte. Homans, A.	36178		D		W.		31 7 17
Pte. Hornby, W.	202060		B		W.	N.T.	31 7 17
Pte. Houghton, J.	200777				W.		31 7 17
Pte. Holden, W. A.	31834		A		W.		31 7 17
Pte. Howarth, W. L.	202491		B		W.		31 7 17
†Pte. Howlding, W.	203812		A		K. in A.		31 7 17
†Pte. Hoyle, R.	1681		A		K. in A.		8 8 16
Cpl. Houghton, F.	54		B		W.		8 8 16
Pte. Hodgson, F.	1691		D		W.		8 8 16
Pte. Hodgson, J.	4427		D		W.		8 8 16
Pte. Hornby, E. R.	4454		C		W.		8 8 16
Pte. Hogg, J.	4027		D		W.		8 8 16
Pte. Holcroft, G.	6430		B		W.		8 8 16
2nd Lieut. Holden, J. A.	—				W. & R.P. of W.		9 8 16
†Pte. Howe, W. D.	4635		A		W.		9 9 16
Pte. Homer, A.	2044		B		W.		9 9 16
Lance-Cpl. Holland, W.	1584		C		K. in A.		9 9 16
†Pte. Holden, W.	3450		C		W.	N.T.	9 9 16
Pte. Holgate, H.	4460		D		W.		8 8 16
Pte. Hodgson, J.	1418		B		W.		8 8 16
Pte. Hosker, T.	2962		B		W.		8 8 16
†Pte. Hollinghurst, J.	1646		B		K. in A.		16 6 16
Pte. Hodgkinson, D. R.	1789		B		K. in A.		16 6 15
†Pte. Hogg, J.	2219		B		W.		15 6 15
†Pte. Howard, J.	2513		B		K. in A.		16 6 15
†Pte. Howarth, J.	2597		C		K. in A.		16 6 15
†Pte. Hoiker, J.	2753		B		K. in A.		16 6 15
†Pte. Holt, W.	300		D		K. in A.		16 6 15
†Pte. Henley, W.	289		C		K. in A.		16 6 15
Pte. Hoggorth, M.	4888		A		W.		14 7 16
Pte. Howson, L.	4887		D		W.		16 7 16
Pte. Holt, T.	4524						3 8 16

Pte.	Holden, C.	...	53		...	W.	29 5 15
Pte.	Hodgson, J.	...	204	B	...	W.	15 6 15
Pte.	Howarth, F.	...	2093	D	...	W.	16 6 16
Pte.	Horsfield, T.	...	3396	D	...	W.	16 6 15
Pte.	Houlding, J. C.	...	78	B	...	K. in A.	15 6 15
Pte.	Holmes, T.	...	2843	B	...	K. in A.	6 11 15
✠Pte.	Hoyle, R.	...	1681	A	...	K. in A.	8 8 16
Pte.	Hood, D.	...	200253	D	...	W.	15 6 15
Pte.	Hodson, W.	...	1567	D	...	W.	15 6 15
Pte.	Holland, R.	...	1579	A	...	W.	15 6 15
Pte.	Holland, W.	...	1584	B	...	W.	15 6 15
Pte.	Hoyle, R.	...	1681	A	...	W.	15 6 15
Pte.	Hodgson, F.	...	1691	D	...	W.	15 6 15
Lance-Cpl. Holden, R.		...	1740	B	...	W.	15 6 15
Pte.	Howarth, R.	...	2653	C	...	W.	15 6 15
Pte.	Hodson, E.	...	2825	B	...	W.	13 6 15
2nd Lieut. Houghton, A. T.		...	—		...	W.	30 11 17
Capt. Houghton, A. T.		...	202435	B	...	R.P. of W.	18 11 17
✠Pte.	Houghton, W. H.	...	28285	B	...	K. in A.	18 11 17
Pte.	Houghton, A. F.	...	—		...	W.	18 11 17
2nd Lieut. Hornby, R.		...	—		...	W.	30 11 17
Pte.	Holland, H.	...	13644	B	...	K. in A.	18 11 17
✠Pte.	Horarth, W.	...	36077	D	...	W.	9 4 18
Pte.	Holland, W. H.	...	28286	D	...	W.	9 4 18
2nd Lieut. Horsfall, R. E.		...	—		...	W.	9 4 18
2nd Lieut. Howarth, J.		...	—		...	W.	9 4 18
2nd Lieut. Horner, G. S.		...	—		...	Missing	31 7 17
Pte.	Hopkins, E.	...	32183	B	...	Missing	31 7 17
Pte.	Holgate, H.	...	200288	D	N.T.	W.	18 9 17
Pte.	Holland, H.	...	17484	D	...	W.	20 9 17
Pte.	Holden, G. B.	...	37656	D	...	W.	20 9 17
✠2nd Lieut. Holden, H.		...	13644	B	...	K. in A.	21 9 17
✠2nd Lieut. Holmes, C.		...	—		...	D. of W.	20 9 17

Lance-Cpl. Hough, R.	202930	B	W.		20 9 17
Lance-Cpl. Hoggett, A.	201272	B	W.		20 9 17
†Pte. Hodson, R.	36086	D	K. in A.		20 9 17
Pte. Horan, J.	201740	A	W.		20 9 17
†Pte. Howarth, A.	42059		K. in A.		20 9 17
†Pte. Howarth, T.	202804	A	K. in A.		20 9 17
Pte. Holt, A.	202647	D	W.		30 10 17
Lance-Sgt. Holt, A.	202647	D	W.		18 5 18
Sgt. Holt. A.	202647	D	W.		15 10 18
Pte. Holmes, T.	306520	D	W.		4 9 18
Cpl. Hoole, R.	202982	C	W.		10 9 18
Pte. Horrocks, J.	201986	B	W.		14 9 18
Pte. Howard, T.	28296	B	W.		23 9 18
2nd Lieut. Howarth, G.			W.		1 10 18
†Pte. Honey, C.	36017	D	K. in A.	N.T.	30 9 18
Pte. Holt, H.	20176	B	W.		14 10 18
Pte. Horsley, J.	40964	D	W.		22 10 18
Pte. Howarth, R.	33924		W.		31 7 17
2nd Lieut. Howarth, L.			W.		17 10 18
†Pte. Hockey, F.	202626	D	K. in A.		30 11 17
Pte. Hoodless, L.	28277	A	W.	N.T.	30 11 17
Lance-Cpl. Hough, R.	202430	B	W.	N.T.	9 4 18
Sgt. Hogg, J.	200092	C	W.		13 5 18
Pte. Hodgson, H. O.	240348	B	W.		9 4 18
†Cpl. Hutchinson, J.	240067	D	W.		9 4 18
Pte. Hughes, F.	28280	D	K. in A.		10 4 18
†Cpl. Hunt, G. N.	202608	A	K. in A.		9 4 18
†Pte. Hutchinson, T.	28299	B	W.		11 4 18
Cpl. Huddart, W. P.	290794	A	R.P. of W.		9 4 18
Pte. Hunt, J. W.	235026	A	D. of W.	2 5 18	5 5 18
†Pte. Hubbard, H.	39396	D	K. in A.		10 5 18
†Pte. Hunt, W.	29414	C	W.		14 5 18
Lance-Cpl. Hutchinson, J.	202553	A	W.		14 5 18
Pte. Hulme, W. E.	240092	A	W.	N.T.	30 5 18
Pte. Hurst, C.	34173	A	W.		

Rank	Name	Number	Coy	Status	Date
Pte.	Hutchinson, W.	4465	B	W.	9, 9, 16
Pte.	Hubbersty, T.	4575	B	W.	9, 9, 16
Pte.	Hudson, G.	6241	C	W.	25, 9, 16
Cpl.	Hubbersty, J.	200544	A	W.	21, 7, 17
Pte.	Humphries, H.	4891	C	W.	9, 9, 16
Pte.	Hunter, J.	171	D	W.	15, 6, 15
Cpl.	Hunter, J.	171	D	W.	8, 8, 16
Pte.	Hudson, E.	1963	B	W.	16, 5, 15
†Pte.	Hutton, A. H.	1083	C	K. in A.	14, 7, 16
Cpl.	Hall, H.	2522	D	W.	2, 8/16
Pte.	Hurley, J.	200054	D	W.	15, 6, 15
Pte.	Hudson, J.	244	C	W.	1 - 4, 16
Pte.	Hall, H.	3983	D	W.	2, 8, 16
Pte.	Hurley, J.	2084	D	W.	3, 8, 16
2nd Lieut.	Hunt, J.	2300	A	K. in A.	4, 6, 15
†Pte.	Hunt, R.	4273		K. in A.	29, 5, 16
Pte.	Hunt, D.	2241	B	W.	15, 6, 15
Pte.	Hubbersty, J.	28287	C	R.P. of W.	18, 11/17
Pte.	Hughes, J. G.	202500	B	W.	30, 11, 17
Pte.	Hulme, S.	4891	C	W.	30, 7, 17
†Pte.	Humphries, H.			D. of W.	28, 9, 17
Pte.	Hulme, W.	235134	D	W.	20, 9, 17 N.T.
Pte.	Hunter, T. D. J. L.	244867	A	W.	20, 9, 17 N.T.
†Pte.	Huddleston, E.	290729	C	K. in A.	20, 9, 17
Pte.	Hurst, O. H.	243111	D	W.	16, 8, 18
Pte.	Hubbick, A.	26691	C	W.	1, 10, 18
†Pte.	Hudson, F.	34112	D	K. in A.	22, 10, 18
†Pte.	Hull, F.	240113	B	R.P. of W.	23, 10, 18
†Pte.	Harrison, J.	16538		D. of W.	2, 8, 17
†Pte.	Hunter, W.	201472		K. in A.	22, 4, 17
†Sgt.	Hurley, J.	200063		K. in A.	8, 8, 16
†Pte.	Ianson, K.	201678	D	K. in A.	34, 7, 17 N.T.
†2nd Lieut.	Ibbotson, G. S.	235162		K. in A.	14, 5, 18

344

Pte. Ikin, J.	25270	C	W.		3/6/18
✠Dr. Inglis, W.	1555	B	K. in A.		15/6/15
Pte. Ince, R.	132	D	W.		15/6/15
✠Pte. Ingram, J.	3275	C	K. in A.		8/8/16
✠Lance-Cpl. Ingle, H.	202762	C	K. in A.		9/9/16
Sgt. Innes, A.	202937	B	W.		31/7/17
Pte. Ince, W.	203633	D	W.	N.T.	9/4/18
Pte. Ince, J.	3695	D	W.		4/8/16
Pte. Ince, J.	39955	D	W.		16/8/18
✠Pte. Irving, G.	219	D	K. in A.		15/6/15
Pte. Irving, A.	4573	D	W.		8/8/16
Lance-Cpl. Isherwood, J.	6263	D	W.		9/9/16
Sgt. Isles, R.	993	C	W.		15/6/15
✠C.S.M. Isles, R.	200195	C	K. in A.		21/7/17
Pte. Isherwood, A.	202858	C	W.		30/11/17
✠Pte. Isherwood, R.	290916	B	K. in A.		25/4/18
✠Pte. Jackson, S.	1622	B	K. in A.		15/6/15
✠Pte. Jackman, J.	217	B	K. in A.		15/6/15
Pte. Jackson, T.	1464	D	W.		15/6/15
Pte. Jackson, W.	1694	A	W.		15/6/15
✠Lance-Cpl. Jameson, A.	1069	C	K. in A.		16/6/15
✠Pte. Jackson, J.	3419	B	K. in A.		8/8/16
Pte. Jackson, W.	6226	B	W.		9/9/16
Pte. Jackson, J.	202582	B	W.		12/7/17
Pte. Jackson, W.	3183	D	W.	N.T.	21/7/17
Pte. James, W. J.	202147		W.		31/7/17
✠Pte. Jagger, A.	202449	B	K. in A.		31/7/17
✠Cpl. Jackson, W.	202651	C	K. in A.		31/7/17
✠Cpl. Jackson, H.	202701	C	K. in A.		31/7/17
Pte. Jackson, J. J.	2713	B	R.P. of W.		9/4/18
Pte. Jamieson, H.	28076	D	W.		25/4/18
Pte. Jackson, R. S.	41534	D	W.		14/5/18
✠Cpl. Jackson, W.	27792	C	K. in A.		8/6/18
✠Pte. Jackson, J.	41738	B	K. in A.		22/6/18

Name	Number				
☩Pte. Jackson	300596		K. in A.		11 8 18
Pte. James, L. M.	42001	A	W.		16 8 18
Pte. Johnson, L.	305920	D	W.		4 9 18
Pte. Jackson, H.	305919	D	W.		4 9 18
Pte. Jones, A.	214364	C	W.	N.T.	3 9 18
Pte. Jacobs, M.	245144	C	W.		3 9 18
Pte. Jameson, T.	305967	B	W.		30 9 18
Pte. Jackson, W.	3183	D	W.		28 2 18
2nd Lieut. Jenkinson, T. C.			W.		31 7 17
Sgt. Jeffries, W.	34300	A	W.		14 5 18
Pte. Jeffrey, E. H.	5280	B	W.	N.T.	14 5 18
☩Pte. Johnson, R. L.	2406	B	K. in A.		15 6 15
2nd Lieut. James-Alfred			W.		26 2 18
Lieut. Jenkins, W. H.		Medical Officer	W.		9 1 18
Pte. Jolly, J.	1035	A	W.	and 8 1 17	15 6 15
Pte. Jones, E. J.	1288	C	W.		15 6 15
Pte. Jolly, J.	1969	B	W.		15 6 15
Pte. Joyce, V.	2547	B	W.		15 6 15
Pte. Jones, M.	107	B	W.		15 6 15
☩Lance-Cpl. Johnson, W.	2264	A	K. in A.		1 8 16
Pte. Johnson, W.	3568	B	W.		8 8 16
Pte. Jones, J.	4189	A	W.		9 9 16
Pte. Jordan, J.	5342	C	W.		14 11 16
☩Pte. Johnston, W.	202583	B	K. in A.		2 6 17
Pte. Jones, W.	202509	B	W.		2 6 17
2nd Lieut. Johnston, W. H.			W.		1 6 17
Pte. Jordan, J.	202391	C	W.		18 7 17
Pte. Jones, I. O.	205361	B	W.	N.T.	31 7 17
Pte. Jones, W.	202509	B	W.		31 7 17
Pte. Johnson, J.	232255	A	W.		30 11 17
Pte. Jones, C.	200797	A	W.	and 30 11 17	20 9 17
Pte. Jolly, J.	201003	D	W.		20 9 17
Pte. Johnson, F.	37575	B	W.		20 9 17

346

†Pte. Jones, W.	19741	B	K. in A.		20 9 17
Pte. Jones, G. H.	27571	B	W.		20 9 17
Lance-Cpl. Johnson, J. E.	203780	C	W.	N.T. 18	11 17
Pte. Jones, P.	36191	A	W.		30 11 17
†Pte. Johnson, J.	23253	A	K. in A.		30 11 17
Pte. Jones, J.	202581	C	W.		28 2 18
†Lance-Cpl. Jones, W. E.	29057	A	K. in A.		9 4 18
†Pte. Jones, T. E	54304	B	K. in A.		14 5 18
Pte. Jones, A.	36191	A	W.		3 6 18
Pte. John, D. T.	41200	D	W.		28 7 18
Pte. Jones, C. M.	50649	C	W.		4 9 18
Pte. Jones, H.	29417	C	W.		11 9 18
2nd Lieut. Jones, H.			W.	N.T. 30	9 18
Lance-Cpl. Jones, F.	6765	D	W.		13 10 18
Pte. Jones, J.	30655	A	Missing		16 10 18
Pte. Jones, A.	242875	D	W.		22 10 18
†Cpl. Johnson, H. C.	40329	B	K. in A.	N.T.	1 18
Lance-Cpl. Jones, F.	6756	D	W.		18 7 18
Pte. Jump, J.	202975		W.		30 7 17
Pte. Jump, R. W.	36848	C	W.		
Pte. Kay, C.	2221	D	W.		15 6 15
†Pte. Kay, E.	3040	C	K. in A.		15 6 15
Pte. Kay, F.	4916	D	Missing		8 8 16
Pte. Kay, G.	202063	A	W.		9 9 16
				and	18 7 17
†Pte. Kay, G.	8311	B	K. in A.	N.T	20 9 17
Pte. Kay, J.	37664	B	W.		20 9 17
†Lance-Cpl. Kay, J.	203523	C	K. in A.		14 5 18
†Pte. Kellett, W.	3438	A	W.		15 6 15
			Died		30 6 16
Pte. Kellett, W.	1476	D	W.	N.T.	15 6 15
Pte. Kempster, J.	1297	C	W.		15 6 15
Pte. Kellett, F.	2808	A	W.		15 6 15
✠Lance-Col. Kerfoot, I.	1204	D	K. in A.		15 6 15

†Pte. Kell, T. W.	2630		K. in A.		15 6 15
Pte. Kelly, J.	2040		W.		2 8 16
Pte. Kelly, P.	5356		W.		8 8 16
Pte. Kellett, A. J.	3929		W.		9 9 16
Pte. Kent, G.	233		W.		9 9 16
Pte. Kelly, W.	4897		W.		9 9 16
Pte. Kenyon, F.	6116		K. in A.		31 7 17
Pte. Kenyon, T. W.	202972		W.		9 9 16
†Lance-Cpl. Kellgariff, J.	2068		W.		29 9 16
Pte. Kenyon, W. R.	6185	N.T.	W.		29 9 16
Pte. Kershaw, W.	4619		W.		9 6 17
Pte. Kenyon, F. H.	361192		W.		8 6 17
Sgt. Kelly, A.	202202		W.		31 7 17
Pte. Kellaway, A. A.	26185		W.		20 9 17
Pte. Kershaw, W.	202893		W.		7 7 17
Pte. Kelton, A. G.	243920		W.		
Pte. Kershaw, F.	202788		W.		30 11 17
Sgt. Kelly, A.	202702		W.		30 11 17
Lance-Cpl. Kent, A. E.	29144		W.		9 4 18
Pte. Kelsall, A.	202661		W.		10 4 18
Pte. Kennedy, N.	293391		W.		10 4 18
Pte. Kettley, C.	18841		W.		25 4 18
Pte. Kerridge, A. D.	293390		W.		2 6 18
Pte. Kerfoot, W.	37248		W.		16 8 18
Sgt. Kelly, W.	202702		W.		17 8 18
Pte. Kendrick, C. G.	30992		W.		16 8 18
Cpl. Keith, D.	30460		W.		23 9 18
2nd Lieut. Kershaw, E.			W.		26 5 18
Cpl. Kent, G.	200113		W.		3 9 18
Pte. Killgarriffe, J.	2068		W.		27 7 49
Pte. Kirkham, M.	30889		W.		15 6 15
†Pte. Kirby, R.	3962		W.		15 6 15
Pte. Kippax, J.	4949		K. in A.		3 8 16
Lance-Cpl. Killgarriffe, E.	2007		W.		8 8 16
†Pte. Kirk, J.	202859	N.T.	K. in A.		9 9 16
†Pte. Kippax, J.	202108		W.		9 9 16

†Pte. Kirk, J.	...	2028.59	...		K. in A.	9 9 16
†Pte. Kippax, J.	...	202108	...	B	W.	9 9 16
†Lance-Cpl. Kippax, R.	...	202108	...	C	K. in A.	4 6 17
Pte. Kilby, I.	...	16878	...	C	D. of W.	5 6 17
Pte. King, T.	...	200534	...	A	W.	31 7 17
Pte. Kilshaw, W.	...	320.37	...	A	W.	31 7 17
Pte. Kilby, W.	...	2030.63	...	D	W.	31 7 17
Cpl Kirkham, A.	...	200559	...	A	W.	20 9 17 N.T.
Pte. Kirkman, J.	...	2429.76	...	A	W.	13 4 18
Pte. Killick, E. V.	...	42004	...	D	W.	22 8 18
Pte. King, C.	...	309.46	...	D	W.	30 9 18
Pte. Kirkham, C.	...	306.81	...	A	W.	20 10 18
Pte. Kimberley, A.	...	320.92	...	A	W.	8 7 18
Lieut. King, E.	...		...		W.	3 9 18
Pte. Kirkman, J. W.	...	2274	...	C	W.	8 8 17
†Pte. Kirkman, J. W.	...	7721	...	D	K. in A.	8 8 16
Pte. King, T.	...	2213	...	A	W.	31 9 17
Pte. Kirkham, A.	...	200.599	...	A	W.	31 7 17
Pte. King, J. A.	...	2030.83	...	B	Missing	23 4 18
2nd Lieut. Kirkby, G.	...		...		W.	25 9 18
Pte. Knott, A.	...	202757	...	C	K. in A.	9 9 16
†Pte. Knight, J.	...	203594	...	A	K. in A.	31 7 17
Pte. Knox, A.	...	5632	...	A	W.	30 11 17
†Sgt. Knowles, R.	...	200895	...	A	K. in A.	9 4 18
Pte. Knapper, J.	...	306.22	...	C	W.	16 8 18
Pte. Knight, W.	...	235502	...	B	W.	30 9 18
Pte. Knight, C.	...	201.599	...	B	W.	14 10 18
†Pte. Knowles, A.	...	201454	...	A	K. in A.	31 7 17
Pte. Knight, W.	...	235502	...	B	W.	23 10 18
†Pte. Knowles, F. G.	...	35176	...		K. in A.	31 7 17
†Pte. Large, H.	...	265663	...	—	Died	9 7 17
Pte. Lapping, G.	...	28090	...	C	W.	18 11 17

Pte.	Lawrenson, J.	37682	D		W.	20 11 17
✝Pte.	Lawrenson, W.	201213	A		K. in A.	30 11 15
✝Pte.	Lawson, F.	27232	B		K. in A.	30 11 15
Pte.	Latimer, E. M.	244818	D		W.	16 8 18
Pte.	Lawson, T. S.	51638	C		W.	25 9 18
Pte.	Laithwaits, W.	6106	D		W.	9 9 16
Pte.	Lawson, M.	4061	B		W.	9 9 16
Pte.	Lawson, T.	4091	B		W.	9 9 16
Pte.	Larmour, T.	201760	B		W.	31 7 16
Pte.	Larkin, F.	1348	D		W.	26 6 15
Cpl.	Lancaster, I.	1984	B		W.	15 6 15
Sgt.	Lancaster, J.	1981			W.	1 8 16
Pte.	Lambert, S	2588	B		W.	15 6 15
Pte.	Larmour, J.	231	B		W.	28 7 16
Lance-Cpl.	Latham. E.	2553	D		W.	3 8 16
Pte.	Larkin, C.	4865	D		W.	8 8 16
Pte.	Latham, T.	4301	D		W.	8 8 16
Pte.	Lambert, H.	4369	B		W.	8 8 16
Pte.	Latimer, J.	4689	C		W.	9 9 16
Pte.	Landston, F.	192432	D		W.	30 9 18
Pte.	Lake, R. C	260129	C		W.	28 6 18
Pte.	Law, A.	3252	C		W.	8 8 16
✝Pte.	Latham, C. W.	30624	B		K. in A	1 10 18
Pte.	Leyland, P.	37254	B		W.	20 9 17
Pte.	Lees, R. E.	298875	C		R.P. of W.	18 11 17
Pte.	Lewis, P.	202749	C		Missing	18 11 17
✝Pte.	Leach, H. J.	27967	A		K. in A	30 11 17
Pte.	Lennon, J.	243771	D		W.	11 4 18
✝Pte.	Leary, A.	17549			K. in A.	9 4 18
✝Pte.	Lewtas, J.	4900	B		K. in A.	29 9 16
Pte.	Lee. J. T.	309969	D		W.	30 9 18
Pte.	Lewis, W. T.	30625	D		R.P. of W.	15 8 18
Pte.	Levitt, F. J.	35647	B		W.	9 9 16
Pte.	Leach, F	2401			W.	
Pte.	Linness. E.	41669	C		W.	2 5 18

✝Sgt. Lightbowne, J.	24061		B	K. in A.	18/11/17
✝2nd Lieut. Livesey, J. A				K. in A.	30/11/17
Pte. Lilburn, W. J.	33725		B	W.	9/4/18
Pte. Lipman, S.	29152		C	W.	9/4/18
✝Pte. Lightfoot, H.	29154		C	K. in A.	23/9/18
Pte. Lingard, S.	4500		D	W.	N.T. 9/9/16
Pte. Livingstone, J.	245		C	W.	9/9/46
Pte. Livesey, R.	202968		B	W.	14/4/17
Pte. Lightfoot, W. B.	36194		C	R.P. of W.	31/7/17
Pte. Livesey, J.	5439		A	W.	20/9/17
Pte. Liddell, W.	243511		B	W.	20/9/17
✝Pte. Lister, F.	202938		A	K. in A.	15/6/15
Pte. Livesey, J.	2805		D	W.	31/8/15
Lance-Cpl. Lister, A.	1385			W.	
✝Capt. Lindsay, H				K. in A.	8/8/16
Pte. Liptrot, J.	202421		D	W.	9/4/18
Pte. Lloyd, F.	202973		B	W.	14/6/18
✝Pte. Lloyd, L.	18335			K. in A.	9/4/18
Pte. Lloyd, J. G.	41216		D	W.	4/9/18
Pte. Lloyd, W. S.	203832		A	W.	23/10/18
✝Pte. Longworth, W.	17838		B	K. in A.	30/11/17
Sgt. Lowe, A.	240239		B	W.	9/4/18
Capt. Lonsdale, H				W.	1/8/18
Pte. Loud, J.	13866		C	W.	16/5/18
Pte. Lomas, S. W.	29392		B	W.	9/4/18
Pte. Loud, A.	204976		C	W.	5/9/18
✝Pte. Lowe, B.	235049			K. in A.	31/7/17
Pte. Lofthouse, J.	2318		A	W.	15/6/15
✝Cpl. Lofthouse, J.	200583		A	K. in A.	29/5/17
✝Pte. Lord, T. E.	203014		C	K. in A.	1/6/17
✝Cpl. Lomax, J.			R.A.M.C.	K. in A.	31/7/17
Pte. Lowe, W.	203599		A	W.	31/7/17
Pte. Loftus, J.	4356		C	W.	9/9/16
Pte. Lowe, J. H	30623		D	W.	30/9/18
Pte. Legan, S.	27552		C	R.P. of W.	22/10/18

†Pte. Lowndes, T.	201532		K. in A.		31/7/17
Pte. Lowe, H.	30925		W.		22/10/18
Pte. Lund, J.	200688		W.		9/4/18
†Pte. Lupton, S.	201788		K. in A.		9/4/18
†Sgt. Lucas, E.	201091	A	Died while P. of W.		9/4/18
Pte. Lund, J.	2693	C	Missing		9/9/16
Pte. Lund, H.	4373	D	W.		9/9/16
†Pte. Lewtas, J.	4900	B	K. in A.		29/9/16
Pte. Lund, J.	285	C	W.		15/6/15
†Pte. Lucas, W.	2051	D	K. in A.		16/6/15
Pte. Lupton, W.	4090	B	W.		8/8/16
Pte. Lund, J.	4333	B	W.		9/9/16
Pte. Lucas, E.	3374	D	W.		9/4/18
†Pte. Lyons, C.	290060	C	K. in A.		7/6/17
Lance-Cpl. Lythgoe, R.	18346	D	W.		27/6/15
Pte. Lythgoe, S.	1611	C	W.		15/6/15
Pte. Lyon, G. E.	2281	C	W.		16/6/15
†Pte. Lynch, H.	2236	A	K. in A.		14/5/18
†Pte. Leitch, D. C.	36041	A	K. in A. N.T.		11/5/18
Pte. Lee, B.	27603	A	W.		9/9/18
Pte. Lewis, W. P.	306690	C	W.		30/9/18
Lance-Cpl. Leigh, W.	13306	B	Missing N.T.		9/9/16
Pte. Lewis, C.	4286	C	W.		9/9/16
Pte. Lees, C. J.	3132	C	W.		9/9/16
Lance-Cpl. Lewty, F.	3259	D	W.		9/9/16
Pte. Lee, G.	4939	B	D. of W.		9/9/16
Pte. Lever, E.	4186	A	W.		28/9/16
Pte. Leighton, E.	6187	A	W.		29/9/16
Pte. Leonard, J.	4606	A	W.		23/12/16
Pte. Lewis, J.	202065		W. and		30/12/16 / 15/4/17
Pte. Lee, H.	202437	B	W. M.		31/7/17
Pte. Levingstone, R.	202006	C	W.		31/7/17
†Pte. Leach, F.	202806	A	K. in A.		31/7/16

352

Lance-Cpl. Leeming, W.	260428	A	W.	N.T.	31 7 16
†Pte. Lewis, W.	203940	A	K. in A.		31 7 16
†Pte. Leadbetter, J.	32722	A	K. in A.		31 7 17
Pte. Lee, H. J.	2322	B	W.		15 6 15
Pte. Lees, C. J.	3132	C	W.		15 6 15
Sgt. Lester, E.	230	B	W.		29 6 15
Pte. Legard, E. R.	2112	D	W.		30 8 15
†Lance-Cpl. Leigh, J.	1387	C	K. in A.		16 6 15
†Pte. Leach, T. E.	1633	B	K. in A.		16 6 15
†Pte. Lee, G.	2641	C	K. in A.		16 6 15
Pte. Lee, J.	1295	A	W.	N.T.	1 8 16
Pte. Leeming, W.	1941	C	W.		2 8 16
Pte. Leach, J.	4415	B	W.		8 8 16
Pte. Lee, C. J.	4903	C	W.		8 8 16
Pte. Lees, C. J.	3132	C	W.		5 8 16
Pte. Lewis, J.	4899	B	W.		9 9 16
Pte. Lee, S. N.	40834		W.		30 9 18
†Pte. Makinson, T. E.	5260	A	Died		25 11 16
Pte. Madhill, T.	4408	A	W.	N.T.	9 9 16
Pte. Marsh, T.	4403	D	W.		9 9 16
Pte. Malley, J.	2612	C	W.		9 9 16
Pte. Martin, C. J.	3412	C	W.		9 9 16
Pte. Marsden, J.	4008	A	W.		9 9 16
Pte. May, A.	4662	D	W.	N.T.	9 9 16
Pte. Mather, T.	319533	C	W.	and 23 5 17	23 10 18
Pte. Magnall, E.	202862	C	W.		4 6 17
†2nd Lieut. Mather, V.			K. in A.		31 7 17
Pte. Makinson, J.	31989	B	W.		31 7 17
Pte. Massey, L.	201735	C	W.		31 7 17
Pte. Marchant, J.	12292	B	W.		31 7 17
Pte. Marsh, S.	202556	A	R.P. of W.		31 7 17
Pte. Marsden, F.	42370	C	Missing	N.T.	31 7 17

†Pte. Mannion, D. E.	36188		K. in A.		31/7/17
†Pte. Mair, J.	26419		K. in A.		31/7/17
2nd Lieut. Martin, A.			W.		20/9/17
Pte. Marsden, R.	202071		R.P. of W.		18/11/17
Pte. Marsh, P.	35254	C	W.		18/11/17
Pte. Mather, T.	290822	C	W.		30/11/17
Pte. Makin, R.	202106	A	W.		30/11/17
Cpl. Maher, J.	200379	B	Missing		9/4/18
†Pte. Matthews, T.	1043	D	K. in A.		15/6/15
†Pte. Mawsdley, T.	1486	C	K. in A.		2/4/16
2nd Lieut. Martin, A.	—	D	K. in A.		28/6/16
Pte. Marden, F.	761	B	W.		14/6/15
Pte. Marshall, H.	787	C	W.		25/5/16
Pte. Maymon, J. W.	2576	B	W.		15/6/15
Pte. Macheter, J.	2639	C	W.		15/6/15
Pte. Mather, W. H.	2969	C	W.		15/6/15
†Pte. Mansel, A. E.	35247		Died		21/5/18
†Pte. Marsden, J.	201473	C	K. in A.		9/9/16
†Pte. Matsell, J. H.	235012	D	K. in A.		31/7/17
Pte. Maden, S.	30069	D	W.		18/11/17
Pte. McGinnerty, W.	4124	A	W.		9/9/16
Pte. McHugh, J.	21482	C	W.		12/7/17
Pte. McNamara, P.	235410	C	W.	N.T.	13/7/17
†Pte. McCartney, H.	202584	B	K. in A.		21/7/17
Pte. McGreal, J.	201829	A	W.		21/7/17
Pte. McKerney, H.	201758		W.		31/7/17
2nd Lieut. McSweeney, D. A.	200354		W.		31/7/17
†Pte. McGerr, J.	17525	B	R.P. of W.		31/7/17
Pte. McMahon, J. J.	202494	B	K. in A.		31/7/17
Pte. McDerby, J.	241755	B	W.		31/7/17
Pte. McEwen, R.	34318	A	W.		20/11/17
†Pte. McDonald, R.	200205	C	Pres. K.		5/6/15
Pte. McKeown, J.	2736	B	W.		19/4/18
			D. of W.		9/7/15

Pte.	McGunnigle, P.	...	2269	W.	15/6/15
Pte.	McDougall, F.	...	1682	W.	19/9/15
Pte.	McCarthy, J.	...	4909	A	W.	8/8/16
Pte.	McGovern, J.	...	2634	D	W.	8/8/16
L-Cpl.	McWilliams, H.	...	4148	C	W.	8/8/16
Pte.	McCullough, R.	...	1985	D	K. in A.	8/8/16
Pte.	McMahon, J.	...	1999	D	W.	8/8/16
Pte.	McGaughrey, O.	...	29162	B	W.	10/4/18
Pte.	McLacklan, A.	...	29420	A	W.	26/4/18
Pte.	McClure, W.	...	8731	C	W.	N.T. 2/6/18
Pte.	McDonald, J. E.	...	29121	D	W.	30/9/18
†Pte.	McCann, J.	...	242713	A	K. in A.	2/10/18
Lance-Cpl. McNulty, J.		...	3150	B	W.	23/10/18
Pte.	McCormack, J.	...	203948	B	W.	4/9/18
Lance-Cpl. McDonald, R.		...	10053	D	W.	8/8/16
Pte.	McConnell, J.	...	3659852	C	R.P. of W.	18/11/17
Pte.	May, G., ...	...	2026679	C	K. in A.	31/7/17
†Pte.	Martin, T.	...	2028-16		K. in A.	8/9/16
Pte.	Marsden, H.	...	151	D	W.	15/6/15
Pte.	Makinson, N.	...	176	D	W.	1/6/15
Pte.	Harris, H.	...	218	D	W.	1/6/15 and 8/8/16
Pte.	Martin, J. T.	...	1129	A	W.	15/10/15
Pte.	Mayman, J.	...	25761	B	W.	19/10/15
Pte.	Martin, R.	...	181	D	W.	1/4/16
†Pte.	Harris, L.	...	1476	D	K. in A.	15/6/15
†Pte.	Martin, W.	...	3005	A	K. in A.	16/6/15
†Pte.	Marginson, A.	...	3368	C	K. in A.	16/6/15
Pte.	Maguire, J.	...	244	C	W.	16/6/15
Pte.	Maries, J.	...	311	B	K. in A.	16/6/15
†Pte.	Marsden, F.	...	761	C	W.	30/10/15
†Pte.	Madders, I.	...	2405	C	K. in A.	1/8/16
Pte.	Mayor, J.	...	4265	D	W.	8/8/16
Pte.	Marsh, S.	...	4428		W.	8/8/16
Pte.	Marshall, I.	...	194	D	W.	8/8/16

Pte. Mayor, R.		3477		W.		8 8 16
Pte. Mather, G.		37752		Missing	N.T.	8 4 18
Pte. Mayoh, I. P.		25569		W.		10 4 18
Pte. Marland, J.		19725		W.		2 5 18
Pte. Malpas, J. H.		41230		W.		2 6 18
Pte. Marsh, T.		243192	A	W.	and	11 5 18 24 9 18
Pte. Maude, A.		32254	C	W.		2 6 18
Pte. Massey, F.		306627	C	W.		20 7 18
Pte. Massey, E.		306628	D	W.		15 8 16
Pte. Malie, A.		30626	B	W.		4 9 18
Pte. Mansley, J.		223463	B	W.		4 9 18
† 2nd Lieut. Marsden				Killed		11 9 18
Sgt. Matthews, A. E.		41068	D	W.		22 10 18
† Cpl. Manson, T. M.		36014	A	K. in A.		22 10 18
† Pte. McHale, E.		292790	D	K. in A.		30 11 17
Pte. Mellis, J.		4242	C	W.		9 9 16
Pte. Metcalf, C. B.		292895	D	W.		19 5 17
Pte. Mellars, C. H.		255028	C	W.		31 7 17
† Sgt. Mercer, A.		1665	B	K. in A.		15 6 16
Sgt. Meredith, R.		4302	C	Missing	N.T.	4 8 16
Sgt. Melling, J.		1448	B	W.		8 8 18
Pte. Meadows, J.		202072	A	W.		27 5 18
Pte. Metcalfe, R.		309996	C	W.		2 10 18
Pte. Mellor, A.		340086	D	W.		14 5 18
Pte. Miller, J.		1181	D	W.		29 9 16
† Lance-Cpl. Middlehurst, A.		241745	C	K. in A.		5 6 17
Pte. Minion, A.		265750	B	W.		31 7 16
		200071	D	W.		9 8 16
Pte. Miller, G.		200815	B	W.	and	20 9 17 20 9 18
Pte. Mitchinson, D.		2073	D	W.		15 6 15
Pte. Miller, W. E.		2536	D	W.		15 6 15
Pte. Mills, J.		2569	B	W.		15 6 15
Pte. Minnion, A.		159	D	W.		15 6 15

†Pte. Middlehurst, W.		2026633		K. in A.	31 7 17
Pte. Milward, A.		42008	A	R.P. of W.	14 5 18
†2nd Lieut. Milne, C.				K. in A.	14 3 18
Sgt. Miller, J.		2002293	D	W.	1 10 18
Pte. Midgley, A. C.		29486	D	W.	30 9 18
Pte. Minors, S.		30927	B	R.P. of W.	23 10 18
Pte. Mitchell, R.		25152	A	W.	14 5 18
Pte. Morgan, J.		1797	B	W.	9 9 16
†Pte. Moncur, J.		2320	A	W.	15 6 15
				K. in A.	9 9 16
Pte. Molyneaux, J.		4267	A	W.	9 9 16
†Pte. Moore, E.		6286	D	Died	2 10 18
Pte. Moulding, F. N.		1466	B	W.	29 9 16
†Pte. Morris, H.		218	D	K. in A.	8 8 16
Capt. Matthew, F. K.				W.	30 11 17
†Pte. Moore, J.		3486		K. in A.	1 6 16
†Pte. Morris, L.		1476	B	K. in A.	15 6 15
Pte. Mort, N.		203801		Died	19 2 17
†Pte. Moscrop, S.		202621	C	D. of W.	14 7 17
†Pte. Morgan, E. J.		245080	C	K. in A.	19 9 17
Pte. Moss, R.		201386	B	W.	18 7 17
Pte. Molyneaux, A. E.		201734	C	W.	31 7 17
Pte. Monks, W		11723	A	W.	31 7 17
†Pte. Moulding, F.		2002286	B	W.	31 7 17
†Pte. Morley, W.		202495	B	K. in A.	31 7 17
Pte. Monen, M.		28078	A	W.	19 9 17
Pte. Moscrop. S.		202654	C	W.	18 11 17
Pte. Molloy, J.		2006654	C	W.	18 11 17
Pte. Moss, O.		2026638	A	R.P. of W.	9 4 18
Pte. Morgan, E. H		245115	B	W.	9 4 18
2nd Lieut. Moore, K.				K. in A.	15 6 15
†Pte. Monks, E.		1421	D	K. in A.	26 11 15
†Pte. Morris, R P.		5195	D	Drowned in Somme	28 7 16
Lance-Cpl. Moore, T		1350	D	W.	15 6 15

Pte. Morley, T.	1745	A	W.		15 6 15
Cpl. Moss, J. A.	1752	B	W.		30 5 15
Pte. Morey, S.	1784	B	W.		15 6 15
Lance-Cpl. Monks, J.	2003	D	W.		15 6 15
Pte. Montague, E.	2833	B	W.		20 4 16
Pte. Morris, F.	4456	A	K. in A.		15 6 15
✠Pte. Morris, J.	1294	C	K. in A.		16 6 15
✠Pte. Moss, J.	2652	B	K. in A.		4 8 16
✠Pte. Morley, S.	4237	C	K. in A.		5 8 16
✠Pte. Moss, R.	2972	B	Died		8 8 16
Pte. Mounsey, J.	4525	D	W.		8 8 16
Pte. Morgan, C.	4374	B	W.		8 8 16
Pte. Morris, T.	4962	B	W.	N.T.	10 1 18
Pte. Moreton, R. H. A.	2864	C	W.		6 7 18
Pte. Morton, T.	21344	D	W.		4 9 18
Pte. Molloy, J.	30926	B	W.	N.T.	4 9 18
Pte. Morgan, L.	4727		Missing		23 10 18
Pte. Morris, H.	30668	A	W.		8 9 18
✠Pte. Moss, B.	30679	A	K. in A.		23 10 18
Pte. Moss, J.	25243	B	W.		4 9 18
Cpl. Mooney, J.	25580	C	W.		23 10 18
Cpl. Murphy, J.	6692	C	W.		24 5 17
Pte. Muin, R. A. B.	361482	B	R.P. of W.		31 7 17
Pte. Murray, P.	2864	D	W.		20 9 17
Sgt. Murray, A. P.	284018	B	Missing W.	and	9 4 18 25 3 18
Pte. Mulliner, E. A.	1602	C	W.		4 9 18
Pte. Murray, W.	2285	B	W.		15 6 15
Pte. Murray, J.	2730	A	W.		15 6 15
Lance-Cpl. Muncaster, R.	200837	A	W.		31 7 16
Pte. Muse, J.	41508	A	W.		9 4 18
Pte. Murphy, J.	6693	C	W.		14 5 18
2nd Lieut Myers, B	—		W.		4 9 18
					20 9 17

2nd Lieut. Munroe, C. S.				W.		3. 8. 16
†Pte. Naylor, A.	2078	D	K. in A.		15 6. 15
†Sgt. Nabb, F.	202934	B	K. in A.		31 7. 17
Pte. Nelson, A.	2703	A	W.		15 6. 15
			D. of W.		20. 7. 17
Pte. Nelson, T.	4496	C	W.		8. 8. 16
Pte. Nelson, G. A.	29909	B	W.		8. 8. 16
Pte. Neville, J.	202778	D	R.P. of W.		9. 6. 17
Pte. Nelson, T.	201321	B	K. in A.		31 7. 17
†Pte. Newman, J. E.	35311	B			31 7. 17
Pte. Newsham, J	203321	C	W.		31 7. 17
†Pte. Nelson, J.	41668	D	K. in A.		29 4. 18
Pte. Needham, A.	20632	B	W.		16 8. 18
†Pte. Nelson, J.	14939		K. in A.		31 7. 17
Cpl. Nelson, G. H.	240856	D	W.		4 9. 18
†Pte. Netherwood, W.	39954	A	W.		9 9. 18
†Pte. Neilson, R. R.	110080	C	K. in A.		1 10. 18
†Pte. Nere, L.	29393	B	K. in A.		23 10. 18
†Pte. Newbery, H.	29164	C	K. in A.		17 6. 18
†Pte. Nickson, R.	2560	A	K. in A.		11 7. 15
Pte. Nixon, R.	1467	D	W.		15 6. 15
†Sgt. Nixon, R.	1467	B	D. of W.		23 8. 16
Pte. Nicholson, J.	2934	B	W.		28 6. 16
Pte. Neild, W.	345462	C	W.		27 2. 18
†Pte. Nightingale, J.	203589	A	K. in A.		9 4. 18
Pte. Nicolls, J. W.	37806	C	W.		2 5. 18
			K. in A.		1 10. 18
Pte. Nicholson, S. T.	35721	C	W.		3 9. 18
†Major Nickson			K. in A.	N.T.	30 10. 16
Pte. Nightingale, T.	203884	C	W.		3 9. 18
†Pte. Nichols, J. W.	37806	C	K. in A.	N.T.	1 10. 18
2nd Lieut. Nicholson, J. E. P.					30 11. 17
Pte. Nowell, M.	1417	A	W.		15 6. 15
Pte. Norwood, K.	2229	B	W.		15 6. 15

Name		Coy	Status	Date		
Pte. Norris, J. H.	1552	C	W.		29 8 15	
2nd Lieut. Nolan, M. W.			W.		30 10 15	
Pte. Norcross, J.	4036	A	W.		9 9 16	
Pte. Nowell, M.	200267	D	W.		6 5 17	
Pte. Norris, L.	2361	C	W.		20 9 17	
Lance-Cpl. Norris, P.	201356	B	W.		20 9 17	
Pte. Norris, T.	28165	B	W.	N.T.	25 4 18	
Cpl. Norris, J.	240026	B	W.		2 6 18	
Pte. Norris, A.	340475	B	W.		23 10 18	
Pte. Nolan, T.	41532	B	Missing		23 10 18	
Capt. and Adjt. Norman, C. C. (R.W.F.)						
Pte. Nutter, W.	4361	C	W.		15 6 15	
✝Sgt. Nuttall, J.	1666	A	W.	N.T.	9 9 16	
Lance-Cpl. Nutter, H.	20809	A	D. of W.	9 9 16	11 9 16	
Pte. Nuttall, H	29166	C	W.		30 11 17	
Pte. Nuttall, J.	30631	C	W.		9 4 18	
Lance-Cpl. Nugent, J. E.	29900	C	W.		1 8 18	
Pte. Nutter, W.	25397	B	W.		3 9 18	
Pte. Nuttall, J. H.	201995	B	W.		4 9 18	
					30 11 17	
✝Pte. Nuttall, T.	202690		K. in A.	and 9 4 18		
					31 7 17	
Pte. Oakley, C.	343333	A	W.		31 7 17	
✝Pte. Oates, P.	32251	C	D. of W.	20 9 17	21 9 17	
Pte. O'Brien, P.	56530	A	W.		5 8 16	
✝Pte. O'Brien, W. O.	4318	A	K. in A.		8 8 16	
Pte. O'Brian, S.	202810	C	W.		29 9 16	
Pte. O'Connor, J.	4817	D	W.		9 9 16	
✝Pte. O'Conner, J.	42142	B	D. of W.		26 3 18	
✝Pte. Oddie, G.	202826	B	K. in A.		9 4 18	
✝Pte. O'Flynn, C. E	203318	B	D. of W.	31 7 17	1 8 17	
Pte. O'Grady, C.	1970	C	W.		15 6 15	
Pte. Ogden, J.	202774		W.		9 9 16	
Pte. Ogden, B.	202585	D	W.		31 7 17	

Pte. O'Grady, C.	...	200045		B	W.	N.T. 16 8 18
Pte. Ogden, W.	...	42011		A	W.	7 9 18
†Pte. O'Heary, A.	...	17548		D	K. in A.	9 4 18
Pte. O'Keefe, T.	...	4912		R	W.	8 8 16
Pte. Oliver, C.	...	28508		B	W.	15 6 15
Pte. Oldnall, H.	...	2718		C	W.	and 3 8 16
						15 9 16
2nd Lieut. Oldham	...					20 9 17
Pte. Oldfield, A. E.	...	80516		C	W.	5 9 18
†Pte. Oldfield, J. T.	...	6261			D. of W.	20 9 16
Pte. O'Melia, W.	...	3870		C	W.	8 8 16
†Pte. O'Neill, T.	...	3122		C	K. in A.	15 6 15
†Pte. O'Neal, C. F.	...	6319		C	K. in A.	28 9 16
Pte. O'Neil, G.	...	201075		C	W.	21 7 17
Pte. Ormerod, G.	...	2558		B	W.	N.T. 29 10 15
2nd Lieut. Orrell, J. H.	...				W.	31 7 17
Pte. Ormerod, T.	...	4913		C	K. in A.	8 8 16
†Pte. Ormerod, O.	...	202739		C	K. in A.	9 9 16
†Pte. Ormerod, J. R.	...	6248		C	W.	25 9 16
Major Ord, R.	...				W.	31 7 17
2nd Lieut. Ordish, J. E.	...				W.	31 7 17
Pte. Ormerod, H.	...	200334		B	R.P. of W.	31 7 17
Pte. Orrell, F.	...	240710		B	R.P. of W.	9 4 18
Pte. Orr, C.	...	300672		B	W.	4 9 18
Pte. Orrell, R. J.	...	242868		B	W.	11 4 18
2nd Lieut. Ostrehan, R. A.	...				W.	1 1 16
Pte. Osbalderston, H.	...	201766		B	W.	12 7 17
†Lieut. Ostrehan, D. H.	...				Presumed K.	31 7 17
Lance-Cpl. Osgerby, H.	...	235003		B	W.	31 7 17
Sgt. Ouldcott, E.	...	251		D	W.	14 9 15
Pte. Ousey, S.	...	29393		B	K. in A.	8 8 16
†Lance-Cpl. Owen, E.	...	1900		A	W.	23 6 18
Pte. Owen, A.	...	3443		A	K. in A.	15 6 15
Sgt. Owen, C. F.	...	200199		C	W.	3 8 16
						27 4 18

361

†Pte. Owen, H. R.	...	238034		A	K. in A.	20 5 18
Pte. Owen, W.	...	40770		A	W.	23 10 18
Pte. Oxford, G.	...	6355		D	W.	8 8 16
†Pte. Oxford, N.	...	27722		D	D. of W.	12 1 18 ; 9 5 18
†2nd Lieut. Ogden, J. H.		3019			K. in A.	15 6 15
						22 10 16
						30 7 17
†Pte. Parkinson, R.	...	1085		A	K. in A.	2 11 14
Pte. Parkinson, I. A.	...	1690		D	Died at Home	15 6 15
Pte. Parkinson, C.	...	1926		B	W.	15 6 15
Pte. Park, L.	...	2663		D	W.	15 6 15
Pte. Park, T.	...	2877		B	W.	15 6 15
Pte. Parkinson, T.	...	2876		B	W.	15 6 15
Pte. Park, F.	...	86		B	W.	15 6 15
Cpl. Parkinson, J.	...	333		C	W.	9 10 15
Pte. Parkinson, R.	...	1079		B	W.	30 7 17
Lance-Cpl. Parkinson, R.		1079		B	W.	6 11 15
Pte. Parkinson, H.	...	2839		B	W.	15/6 15
†Pte. Parr, E.	...	2584		A	K. in A.	15 6 15
†Pte. Parkinson, J.	...	70		D	K. in A.	3 8 16 ; 7 8 16
†Pte. Palmer, J.	...	4101		B	D. of W.	8 8 16
C.S.M. Parkinson, E.	...	332		D	W.	8 8 16
Pte. Parkinson, H.	...	2839		B	W.	8 9/16
Lance-Sgt. Parkinson, A.		226		C	W.	9 9 16
†Pte. Park, W.	...	1586		A	K. in A.	9 9 16
Pte. Partington, J.	...	4915		B	W.	22 11 16
Pte. Parkinson, F.	...	2515		D	K. in A.	4 4 17
†Pte. Parkinson, W.	...	202132		A	W.	31 7 17
C.Q.M.S. Parkinson, W.		200178		B	W.	31 7 17
Pte. Parkinson, T. H.	...	202425		A	W.	31 7 17
Pte. Parkinson, W.	...	200818		B	W.	16 8 18
Lance-Cpl. Parkinson, W.		200259		B	W.	20 9 17
Lance-Cpl. Parkinson, T.		200782		B	W.	20 9 17
Pte. Park, T.	...	200167		C	W.	20 9 17

†Pte. Parker, R.	202606	D	K. in A.	20 9 17
Pte. Parkinson, J.	245161	D	W.	20 9 17
Major Parker, H.		A	W.	20 9 16
Pte. Parker, G.	31771	A	K. in A.	20 9 17
Pte. Parkinson, T.	200931	C	W.	30 10 17
†Pte. Parkinson, C.	25343	B	K. in A.	18 11 17
Cpl. Partington, J.	202079	C	W.	20 11 17
Cpl. Parkinson, A.	200111	D	W.	30 11 17
Pte. Paisley, D.	201557	D	W.	9 4 18
Pte. Payne, C. J.	36600	D	W.	9 4 18
Pte. Parkinson, J. S.	19100	D	R.P. of W.	12 4 18
†Pte. Parker, J.	38661	C	K. in A.	9 4 18
Pte. Patterson, H. C.	243807	C	W.	29 4 18
†Pte. Palmer, E.	39677	A	K. in A.	14 5 18
Pte. Parry, R.	13356	B	W.	27 5 and 30 9 18
†2nd Lieut. Pasley, W. E.			K. in A.	17 6 18
Pte. Parkinson, T.	296679	B	W.	4 9 18
Sgt. Parkinson, W.	200167	C	K. in A.	4 9 18
†Sgt. Parkinson, R.	200218	C	W.	7 9 18
2nd Lieut. Parkinson, H.			W.	1 10 18
Pte. Parker, R.	41252	A	W.	30 9 18
Lance-Cpl. Park, T.	200782	D	W.	30 9 18
†Sgt. Parkinson, R.	200218	C	K. in A.	13 10 18
†Pte. Parker T.	37647	B	K. in A.	23 10 18
†Lance-Cpl. Parkinson. J.	210117	B	K. in A.	16 8 18
Pte. Passy, J.	28091	A	W.	30 11 17
Pte. Parry, E.	290815	C	W.	9 1 18
Pte. Palmer, A.	241827	C	W.	9 4 18
†Lance-Cpl. Perry, A. J.	275	A	K. in A.	15 6 15
Pte. Pennington, A. E.	2737	B	W.	8 8 16
Pte. Perry, R.	5029	A	W.	9 9 16
Pte. Pearson, J.	3163	C	R.P. of W.	9 9 16
Pte. Pelzer, W.	6127	C	W.	27 9 16 and 15 11 16

363

Pte. Peel, W. E. M.	6250		C		W.	18 11 16
Pte. Pendlebury, J.	202602		A		W.	20 9 17
Pte. Pendlebury, T.	290665		C		W.	20 9 17
Pte. Perry, A.	16886		A		W.	20 11 18
Pte. Pearsley, A.	203369		B		W.	24 4 18
Cpl. Pendlebury, F.	290665		C		W.	28 7 18
Pte. Pemberton, C.	19993		C		W.	4 9 18
Pte. Perry, R.	202156		A		W.	15 9 18
✠Pte. Pearce, J.	14299		C		K. in A.	23 10 18
Pte. Perry, R.	200760		B		R.P. of W.	23 10 18
Pte. Pendlebury, W.	19894		B		W.	19 8 18
✠Capt. Peak, J. A.			—		Presumed Killed	15 6 15
Pte. Pendlebury, W.	19894		B		W.	9 4 18
Pte. Phillips, H.	12068		B		W.	20 9 17
Sgt. Pilkington, W.	200291		D		W.	15 6 15
Pte. Pickup, J.	2788		A		W.	15 6 15
Pte. Pickering, G. N.	3230		C		W.	15 6 15
✠Pte. Pilkington, G.	145		D		K. in A.	15 6 15
C.S.M. Pilkington, W.	1481		B		W.	8 8 16
Pte. Pickup, J.	2458		A		K. in A. N.T.	8 9 16
✠Pte. Pinner, E.	202730		C		W.	9 9 16
Pte. Pimley, R.	1925		B		W.	9 9 16
Pte. Pincock, J.	202969		C		W.	31 7 17
✠Pte. Pilkington, J.	36169		B		W. and	41 7 17, 20 9 17
✠Sgt. Pitcher, F.	208809		B		K. in A.	20 9 17
Pte. Pickles, F. S.	202619		D		D. of W. 20 9 17;	22 9 17
Sgt. Piper, F.	18001		A		W.	20 9 17
Cpl. Plummer, J.	1649		A		W.	14 9 18
Pte. Pollitt, J	212087		C		W.	9 9 16
Pte. Potter, R.	4319		B		W.	8 8 16
2nd Lieut. Pollard, P.					W.	9 8 16
Lance Cpl. Porter, T.	2537		C		W.	9 9 16

Name	Number	Coy		Date
Pte. Porter, W. G.	365906		W.	17 7 17 and 20 9 17
✠Pte. Potter, T.	32027	C	K. in A.	21 7 17
Sgt. Porter, J.	266047	C	W.	20 9 17
✠Pte. Poole, H.	200686	D	W.	30 11 17
			D. of W.	3 12 17
✠Pte. Pomfret, J.	202696	A	K. in A.	26 4 18
C.S.M. Porter, R.	290177	B	W.	20 5 18
Lance-Cpl. Porter, W.	32934	C	W.	2 6 18
✠Pte. Porteous, G.	265511	D	D. of W.	14 10 18
✠Pte. Power, C.	202429	C	K. in A.	21 7 17 N.T.
Pte. Price, H.	1690	B	W.	15 6 15
Pte. Preston, W.	2540	C	W.	9 9 16
Pte. Preston, A.	4515	C	Missing	9 9 16
✠Pte. Preston, J.	1914		W.	9 4 18 N.T.
	12760		K. in A.	9 9 16
✠Lance-Cpl. Procter, J.	4067	B	K. in A.	31 7 17
Lance-Cpl. Procter, A.	201663	A	W.	31 7 17 N.T.
✠Sgt. Price, T. R.	33176	A	K. in A.	31 7 17
Pte. Priebe, W. O.	35399	B	W.	31 7 17
Lance-Cpl. Procter, A.	202811	A	W.	20 9 17
✠Lance-Cpl. Preston, T	200621	D	K. in A.	23 9 17
Cpl. Prescott, S.	200077	D	W.	2 6 18
Sgt. Prescott, S.	200077	D	W.	14 5 18
Lance-Cpl Prince, F.	29172	A	Missing	4 9 18
Pte. Procter, J.	205071	B	W.	30 9 18 N.T.
Pte. Price, J.	30973	B	W.	15 10 18
Capt. Price, W. L.			W.	22 10 18
2nd Lieut. Pride, R.	31007	D	W.	27 8 18
✠Pte. Preston, J.	12760	C	K. in A.	9 4 18
Pte. Prestwich, D.	29423	B	W.	23 10 18
Pte. Purcell, R.	35788	C	W.	4 9 18
✠Pte. Pye, A.	2577	A	K. in A.	16 6 15
Pte. Pye, P.	2202	B	W.	15 6 15

365

Name	No.	Coy	Status	Date
Pte. Pye, F.	2571		W.	15 6 15
2nd Lieut. Pyke, W. E.			K. in A.	9 9 16
Pte. Pate, R.	27624		K. in A.	26 10 17
Pte. Quinn, J.	4349		W.	N.T. 9 9 16
Pte. Quirk, W.	203126		W.	31 7 17
Lance-Cpl. Ramsbottom, R.	17694	C	K. in A.	9 4 18
Pte. Rathbone, S. J	2108	C	K. in A.	15 6 15
Cpl. Rance, F.	1610	C	W.	15 6 15
Pte. Ranson, J. G.	2648	A	W.	15 6 15
Pte. Rankin, H.	2790	D	W.	15 6 15
Pte. Rathbone, J. T.	3474	A	W.	31 7 16
Pte. Rankin, H.	2790	B	W.	16 6 15
Pte. Ranson, H.	2651		K. in A.	15 6 15
2nd Lieut. Rawsthorn, A. E.			K. in A.	8 8 16
Pte. Ramsden, B.	1918	B	W.	9 9 16
Pte. Rayton, H.	3129	D	W.	9 9 16
Pte. Rapson, S.	6195	A	W.	9 9 16
Pte. Rawcliffe, A. E.	3370	B	W.	9 9 16
Pte. Rainford, C.	4997	B	W.	14 12 16
Pte. Ralphs, H.	4919	D	W.	1 4 17
Pte. Rapson, V.	202815	A	K. in A.	31 7 17
Pte. Ratcliffe, J.	202692	A	W.	31 7 17
Pte. Ramsden, C.	202695	B	K. in A.	26 9 18
Pte. Race, A. F.	235117	A	W.	20 9 17
Pte. Rathbone, D.	12910	C	K. in A.	19 9 17
Pte. Raby, G. A.	25872	C	K. in A.	18 11 17
Pte. Ratcliffe, G.	265897	A	W.	14 5 18
Pte. Ray, F.	202080		K. in A.	8 8 18
Pte. Ranson, A. E.	260119	D	W.	22 10 18
Pte. Rafferty, G.	30935	A	W.	23 10 18
Lance-Cpl. Reid, J.	52	A	K. in A.	15 6 15
Pte. Rees, J.	243123	C	W.	4 8 16

†Capt. Rennard, E. M.	...	—		K. in A.	8/8/16
Pte. Renwick, W.	...	4544		Missing ... N.T.	9/9/16
✠Pte. Read, J. R.	...	202433		K. in A.	1/3/17
Pte. Read, J.	...	36201	A	Missing	30/10/17
Pte. Rees, T.	...	35633	C	R.P. of W.	15/11/17
Pte. Read, R.	...	31785	B	Missing	9/4/18
Pte. Reddish, F.	...	28064	D	W.	12/4/18
Pte. Reeves, J. W.	...	42012	A	W. ... N.T	14/5/18
Pte. Reid, J. R.	...	290490	D	W. ... N.T.	16/8/18
Pte. Reid, A.	...	306635	B	W.	16/8/16
Pte. Relph, H.	...	23265	D	W.	30/9/18
Pte. Reid, A.	...	306635	D	W.	16/8/18
✠Pte. Redman, J. C.	...	29178		K. in A.	4/9/18
✠Pte. Riding, H.	...	2544		Died at Home	6/4/15
✠Pte. Riley, J.	...	1440	D	W.	15/6/15
Pte. Rigby, J.	...	1608	C	D. of W.	9/8/16
✠Pte. Richardson, H.	...	1952	A	W.	15/6/15
				K. in A.	8/8/16
Pte. Rigby, J. T.	...	2854	D	W.	15/6/15
Pte. Rigby, H.	...	3156	D	W.	28/6/15
Pte. Richardson, J.	...	4174	C	W.	14/7/16
Pte. Rigby, T.	...	1024	C	K. in A.	16/6/15
✠Pte. Riding, W.	...	2062	D	K. in A.	16/6/15
✠Lance-Cpl. Rigby, J. T.	...	2854	C	K. in A.	8/8/16
Pte. Riley, H.	...	200436	C	W.	8/8/16
✠Pte. Rigby, T.	...	241616		W.	8/8/16
				Died at Sea	4/5/17
Pte. Riley, R. S.	...	1614	C	W.	8/8/16
Pte. Richardson, J.	...	1951	A	W.	9/8/16
✠Pte. Riley, H.	...	1440	D	D. of W.	9/8/16
Pte. Rimmer, D.	...	2696	C	W.	9/9/16
Pte. Richardson, G.	...	27435	C	W.	14/4/17
Pte. Riley, J. E.	...	23269	A	W.	5/6/17
Pte. Ridehalgh. F.	...	202813	A	W.	16/7/17

367

†Pte. Rigby, J.	...	202726		K. in A.	21/7/18
2nd Lieut. Rigby, C.	...	—		Missing	31/7/17
Pte. Richmond, J.	...	201410	D	W.	20/9/17
Pte. Richardson, J. J.	...	23208	D	W.	20/9/17
Pte. Ridehough, G.	...	202689	A		and 30/11/17
Pte. Rigby, C.	...	208089	C	Missing	N.T. 18/11/17
Pte. Rigby, R.	...	202409	B	R.P. of W.	9/4/18
Pte. Ridsdell, J.	...	260131	D	W.	N.T. 9/4/18
Pte. Rigby, R.	...	24010	C	W.	12/4/18
Pte. Rigby, J. E.	...	25344	C	W.	10/5/18
‡Pte. Ridgard, J.	...	29181	A	K. in A.	14/5/18
Lance-Sgt. Ridgway, L.	...	210216	A	W.	18/5/18
Pte. Richardson, E. R.	...	29175	C	W.	2/6/18
Pte. Riley, J.	...	202868	C	W.	18/6/18
Pte. Rickard, H.	...	39205	D	W.	27/8/18
Pte. Rigby, J. E.	...	25333	C	W.	8/9/18
†Pte. Rigby, M.	...	29395	B	K. in A.	14/9/18
†Pte. Riding, G.	...	11904	B	K. in A.	28/9/18
Pte. Richardson, J.	...	203587	D	W. and R.P. of W.	30/9/18
Cpl. Richie, D.	...	200705	A	W.	23/10/18
Cpl. Riding, C.	...	29180	A	W.	23/10/18
Pte. Ripley, J.	...	30650	D	W.	16/8/18
Cpl. Robinson, R.	...	1109	C	W.	15/6/15
Pte. Round, W.	...	2516	C	W.	15/6/15
Pte. Robinson, T. E. W.	...	2582	B	W.	15/6/15
Pte. Robinson, H.	...	2850	C	W.	15/6/15
Pte. Robinson, A.	...	1569	A	W.	and 8/8/16
Pte. Roughsedge, G.	...	128	D	W.	3/11/15
2nd Lieut. Rogerson, H.	...	—		W.	1/11/15
Pte. Robinson, W.	...	2000	B	W.	1/1/16
‡Pte. Rogerson, G.	...	2414	C	K. in A.	27/3/16
‡Pte. Robinson, G.	...	4307	A	D. of W.	16/6/15
†‡Pte. Robinson, G. S.	...	265023		K. in A.	2/8/16
					20/9/17

368

Pte. Round, S.	2539		W.		8/8/16
†Pte. Robinson, H.	202637	C	K. in A.		28/8/16
Pte. Roberts, H.	1483	D	W.		8/8/16
Pte. Robinson, J.	243208	D	W.		8/8/16
Lance-Cpl. Rollins, F.	1447	D	D. of W.		8/8/16
†Pte. Robinson, P.	6252	C	K. in A.		12/9/16
†Lance-Cpl. Robinson, W.	3819	C	W.		9/9/16
Pte. Roberts, A.	4488	C	K. in A.		9/9/16
†Pte. Roberts, J.	477	D	W.		24/12/16
Pte. Roughsedge, H.	5578	A	K. in A.		9/1/17
†Pte. Rossall, J.	201554	B	W.		19/5/17
Pte. Rogers, W. B.	202504	B	W.		3/6/17
Pte. Robbins, E. H	33874	B	W.		2/7/17
Pte. Robinson, G.	200315	A	W.		15/7/17
Pte. Rollins, J.	200088	D	W.		30/7/17
Pte. Roscoe, J.	202273	B	W.		31/7/17
†Pte. Rowett, C.	201027	B	K. in A.		31/7/17
Pte. Rooney, W.	201208	B	K. in A.		31/7/17
†Pte. Robinson, C. W.	235043	B	K. in A.		31/7/17
†Pte. Robinson, F.	200637		K. in A.		15/6/15
Pte. Rossall, W.	203010	C	W.		31/7/17
Pte. Roberts, J. W.	37249	C	W.		20/9/17
Pte. Roberts, A. T.	290669	C	W.		20/9/17
Pte. Roberts, O.	36177	A	W.		21/9/17
Pte. Roach, F.	290214	D	R.P. of W.		18/11/17
Sgt. Robinson, H.	200577	B	W.		30/11/17
Lance-Sgt. Robinson, J.	201390	B	W.		30/11/17
Pte. Rourke, J.	25201	D	W.		9/4/18
†Pte. Roughly, A.	27663	B	K. in A.		9/4/18
Pte. Robinson, A.	245762		W.		9/4/18
C.S.M. Roberts, H.	200081	B	W.		7/6/17
Pte. Robbins, C. H.	33874	B	W.		9/4/18
†Lance-Cpl. Rooney, W.	201208	B	W.		25/4/18
			K. in A.		11/5/18
Pte. Roberts, J.	340038	A	W.		14/5/18

Pte.	Rose, B.	39681		A	W.	14/5/18
Sgt.	Roberts, G.	243767		C	W.	14/5/18
Lance-Cpl.	Rogerson, R.	200822		A	W.	8/9/18
†Pte.	Roberts, J.	203239		D	K. in A.	11/9/18
†Pte.	Robinson, J.	245202		A	K. in A.	1/10/18
Cpl.	Robinson, J.	243767		D	W.	N.T. 30/9/18
Pte.	Rose, J. E.	40469		D	W.	22/10/18
Pte.	Robinson, A.	265288		D	W.	N.T. 11/4/18
Pte.	Rukin, J.	1051		C	W.	15/6/15
†Pte.	Rutter, W.	1367		D	K. in A.	15/6/15
						1/4/16
Pte.	Rushton, J.	2578		C	W.	8/8/16
Pte.	Rushton, W.	202551		B	R.P. of W.	31/7/17
Pte.	Rudge, E. A.	306653		D	R.P. of W.	16/8/18
Pte.	Ryan, T. W.	2005568		A	W.	15/6/15
						and 18/7/17
Pte.	Ryan, J.	200409		B	W.	12/12/16
Pte.	Ryan, S.	202747		D	W.	13/6/17
Sgt.	Sanderson, F.	197		D	W.	15/6/15
Pte.	Sanderson, R.	201006		C	W.	8/8/16
Pte.	Samson, D.	5005		B	W.	9/9/16
						and 7/6/17
Pte.	Saul, T.	5298		B	W.	26/9/16
Pte.	Sandham, W.	201462		A	W.	29/5/17
Pte.	Savage, E.	202683		D	W.	10/7/17
†Pte.	Savery, F.	245109		C	K. in A.	31/7/17
Pte.	Sandham, J.	200398		C	W.	20/9/18
Sgt.	Saltmarsh, A.	29396		C	W.	29/9/18
Pte.	Sandford, H.	26647		D	W.	18/11/17
Pte.	Sandham, J.	202638		D	W.	13/4/18
Pte.	Salmon, H	202639		A	W.	11/5/18
Pte.	Salisbury, S.	202441		D	W.	31/7/17
†Pte.	Savage, G. F.	31909		A	K. in A.	20/9/17
Pte.	Salisbury, G.	241107		A	W.	20/9/17

370

Pte. Scudamore, R	21168		A	W.	14 5/17
Pte. Scott, J.	202784		D	W.	31 7/17 and 10 7/17
✠Pte. Scriven, A. H.	235039		A	K. in A.	31 7/17
2nd Lieut. Scott T. H. H.				W.	8 7/18
✠Pte. Scattergood, J.	30651		A	K. in A.	8 9/18
✠Pte. Scowcroft, W.	37227		D	K. in A.	20 9/17
Pte. Scowcroft, R.	202649		C	W.	21 9/17
Cpl. Scott, F.	201253		A	W.	20 9/17
✠Pte. Scott, J. H.	202388		D	K. in A.	23 10/18 and 18 11/17
Sgt. Scholes, H.	12176		B	W.	11 10/18
✠Cpl. Scott, F.	201253		A	K. in A.	23 10/18
2nd Lieut. Scott, T. H. H.				W.	3 9/18
Pte. Scholl, A. V.	35893		B	W.	9 4/18
Sgt. Seed, J.	473		A	W.	15 6/15
Lance-Cpl. Seed, Wm.	1137		A	W.	15 6/15
Cpl. Seed, A.	1663		A	W.	15 6/15
✠Sgt. Seed, A.	1663		A	K. in A.	9 9/16
Pte. Seddon, W.	2089		D	W.	15 6/15
Pte. Sergeant, E.	23		B	W.	15 6/15
Lance-Cpl. Seddon, J. W.	71		B	W.	15 6/15
Pte. Sewell, W. S.	4424		A	W.	21 6/16
✠Pte. Seed, J.	2722		B	K. in A.	15 6/15
✠Pte. Sellars, G.	3281		D	K. in A.	15 6/15
C.Q.M.S. Seed, W.	1660		A	W.	2 8/16
Pte. Selfe, H.	3918		D	W.	5 8/16
✠Cpl. Seed, H.	200344		A	K. in A.	13 6/16
Pte. Senior, B.	4557		C	W.	13 6/16
Pte. Settle. I.	7564		D	W.	13 6/16
✠Sgt. Seddon, G.	1434		D	K. in A.	8 8/16
Pte. Seddon, J.	2010		D	W.	8 8/16
Sgt. Seel, W.	2786			W.	8 8/16
✠Sgt. Sedgwick, T.	93		A	K. in A.	9 9/16

371

†Lance-Cpl. Sephton, H. V.	202462		A	D. of W	7 7 17
Pte. Sergeant, J.	41283		D	W.	8 7 18
Lance-Cpl. Seddon, R.	200066		D	W.	16 8 18
Pte. Sellar, W. L.	29190		C	W.	3 9 18
Pte. Seddon, H.	242031		B	W.	5 9 18
†Pte. Seddon, H.	201830		D	K. in A.	12 4 18
Pte. Sewell, E.	200466		A	W.	25 4 18
†Lance-Cpl. Seed, T.	200579		D	K. in A.	31 7 17
Cpl. Searle, W. C.	41058		D	W.	15 10 18
Lance-Cpl. Seddon, R.	200066		D	W.	22 10 18
†Sgt. Seed, A.	1663		B	K. in A.	9 9 16
†Sgt. Skingsley, W.	398		A	K. in A.	15 6 15
†Pte. Sharples, M.	1408		D	K. in A.	15 6 15
Lance-Cpl. Sharples, W.	1103		A	W.	15 6 15
Cpl. Sharples, J.	1140		B	W.	14 6 15
†Sgt. Sharples, J.	1140		B	K. in A.	2 8 16
Pte. Shipcott, W.	1793		A	W.	15 6 15
Pte. Shipcott, J.	1905		B	W.	15 6 15
Pte. Shipcott, W. J.	1930		B	W.	15 6 15
Lance-Cpl. Sherrington, B.	2004		D	W.	15 6 15
Lance-Cpl. Shuttleworth, F.	14		B	W.	29 5 16
Pte. Sharples, P.	334		A	W.	15 6 15
Pte. Shorrock, J.	3248		C	W.	15 6 15
Pte. Shorrock, A.	31120		C	W.	26 3 16
Pte. Sharples, W.	34456		A	W.	28 6 16
Pte. Sharples, T.	5785		A	W.	27 6 16
†Pte. Sharples, W. H.	2619		C	K. in A.	and 8 8 16
†Pte. Shuttleworth, T.	106		B	K. in A.	15 6 15
Pte. Shepherd, A.	182		D	W.	3 8 16
Pte. Shaw, R.	4530		B	W.	and 9 9 16
Pte. Shuttleworth, W.	4468		C	W.	8 8 16
Pte. Sharrocks, J.	201633		D	W.	8 8 16
Pte. Shenty, J.	5071		C	W.	9 9 16

Pte. Sharples, W.	...	1103	A	K. in A.	9 9 16
Pte. Shepherd, J.	...	5046	B	W.	29 9/16
Pte. Shepherd, F.	...	5629	A	W.	8 1 17
Pte. Sharples, W.	...	200237	R.A.M.C		21 7 17
✠Capt Shegog, R. W.	...		A	K. in A.	31 7 17
✠Pte. Shepherd, F.	...	202600	A	K. in A.	31 7 17
Pte. Sharples, H.	...	28129	C	W.	6 7 18 N.T
Lieut. Sholl, A. E.	...			W.	15 8 18
Pte. Shaw, D.	...	200497	D	W.	15 8 18
Pte. Sharples, H.	...	40871	B	W.	24 8 18
Pte. Shepherd, R.	...	306638	D	W.	4 9 18
Sgt. Sharples, W.	...	200423	D	W.	13 9 18
Pte. Sharpe, R.	...	29492	A	W.	13 9 18
✠Pte. Shutter, F.	...	306639	B	W.	14 9 18
Pte. Shipsides, W.	...	28084	D	K. in A.	6 12 17
C. S.-M. Sharples, H.	...	200043	D	W.	30 11 17
Pte. Shuker, A.	...	33158	C	W.	9 4 18
Pte. Shevlen, J.	...	201147	D	W.	13 4 18
✠Pte. Shackleton, H.	...	41679	B	K. in A.	25 4 18
Pte. Shillabeer, E. J.	...	41680	A	W.	14 5 18
✠Pte. Sharp, J.	...	203718	B	Missing	31 7 17
				Died	1 1 19
Pte. Shuttleworth, W	...	368615	D	W.	31 7 17
			C	W.	20 9 17
✠Pte. Shaw, G.	...	21776	A	K. in A.	20 9 17
✠2nd Lieut. Shippobottom. F.				D. of W.18 11 17; 20 11 17
✠Pte. Sharman, F.	...	309336	D	K. in A.	30/9/18
✠Pte. Sharples, R. N.	...	1144	A	W.	9/9/16
				D. of W.	11 9 18
Lance-Cpl. Simpson, W.	...	1026	B	W.	15 6 15
Pte. Silviera, C.	...	2113	B	W.	30 5 15 N.T.
Pte. Singleton, R.	...	2314	A	W.	15 6 15
Pte. Simpson, J.	...	2887	D	W.	15 6 15
Pte. Simpson, A.	...	3228	B	W.	15 6 15 and 8 8 16

373

Pte.	Silcock, T.	3911	A	W.	31/7/17
Pte.	Silcock, L.	2796	C	W.	16/6/15
Pte.	Simpson, J. J.	3147	C	W.	9/9/16
Pte.	Singleton, J.	2824	B	W.	9/9/16
Pte.	Simpson, J. E.	6255	C	W.	26/9/16
Pte.	Simpson, J.	200941	C	W.	27/9/16
Pte.	Silcock, W.	212669	A	W.	1/4/17
Pte.	Simpson, A.	202643	B	Died	3/5/17
Cpl.	Simpson, R.	201081		W.	4/6/17
Pte.	Simpson, T.	343309	C	W.	10/6/17
Pte.	Sidebottam, H.	326685	C	W.	23/6/17
Pte.	Simpson, J.	240843	C	W.	3/6/18
✝Pte.	Singleton, W.	241473	D	Missing (Pres. d.K.)	8/7/18
Lance-Cpl.	Simpson, J.	202870	C	W.	30/11/17
Pte.	Simmonite, W. E.	235005	C	W.	26/4/18
Pte.	Silvester, J.	27812	B	W.	28/4/18
Pte.	Simm, H.	25667	B	W.	28/4/18
Pte.	Silcock, T.	201414	A	W.	31/7/17
✝Pte.	Simm, W.	17261	B	K. in A.	20/9/17
✝Pte.	Simpkin, J.	309937	A	W.	30/10/17
Pte.	Slater, T.	200957	B	W.	24/10/18
✝Pte.	Slater, J.	1422		K. in A.	15/6/15
Pte.	Slater, J.	3323	D	W.	15/9/15
✝Pte.	Slater, F.	1578	A	K. in A.	15/6/15
✝Pte.	Slater, G.	1783	B	K. in A.	9/9/16
Pte.	Slater, A.	200732	B	K. in A.	15/6/15
Pte.	Slack, R.	3612	A	W.	8/8/16
Pte.	Slater, W.	42018	B	W.	31/7/17
✝Cpl.	Sleath, G. F.	23752	C	K. in A.	27/5/18
Pte.	Slater, D.	369929	A	W.	7/6/18
✝Sgt.	Slater, T.	202673	D	K. in A.	9/4/18
Pte.	Smith, J. J.	201631	C	W.	34/7/17
Pte.	Smith, J.	200290	D	K. in A.	9/9/16
				W.	15/6/15
				W.	15/6/15

374

Name	Number	Coy	Fate		Date
Sgt. Smart, J. E.	200333	B	W.		15/6/15
Pte. Smalley, C.	224	D	W.		15/6/15
†Lieut. Smith, W.	—	—	K. in A.	N.T.	15/6/15
Pte. Smith, J.	200290	D	W.		22/12/15
Pte. Smith, H.	201713	B	W.		8/8/16
Pte. Smith, R.	200873	C	W.		8/8/16
Pte. Smith, W.	242271	D	W.		8/8/16
Pte. Smith, J.	1474	D	W.		8/8/16
†Cpl. Smith, J.	200072	D	K. in A.		15/6/16
Pte. Smith, W.	4925	B	W.		8/8/16
Pte. Smith, E.	201780	B	W.		26/9/16
Pte. Smith, G.	202629	C	W.		7/6/17
Pte. Smethurst, J. R.	358868	A	W.	N.T.	31/7/17
Pte. Smith, G. F.	30361	A	W.		31/7/17
Pte. Smethurst, R.	202051	A	W.	N.T.	2/6/18
Cpl. Smith, H.	235036	B	W.		9/7/18
†Pte. Smith, J.	420019	D	K. in A.		16/8/18
†2nd Lieut. Smith, W. B	—	—	K. in A.		11/9/18
Pte. Smith, A.	40977	B	W.		14/9/18
Lance-Sgt. Smith, W.	202724	B	W.		30/11/17
Pte. Smith, H.	31577	B	W.		9/4/18
Pte. Smith, I.	265998	B	W.		9/4/18
Pte. Smith, A.	243755	D	W.		9/4/18
†Pte. Smith, D. H.	68097	A	K. in A.		2/5/18
Pte. Smith, W.	291915	D	Missing Pres'd D.		14/5/18
†Lance-Cpl. Smith, S.	242836	A	W.		31/7/17
Pte. Smith, A.	235017	C	K. in A.		31/7/17
†Pte. Smith, W.	201048	C	W.		20/9/17
2nd Lieut. Smith, A. P.	—	—	W.		20/9/17
Pte. Smith, H.	35243	C	K. in A.		20/9/17
†Pte. Smith, E.	201780	B	W.		20/9/17
Pte. Smith, S. F.	31951	A	K. in A.		30/10/17
†Pte. Smart, T.	319980	C	W.		18/11/17
Lance-Col. Smith, T.	8584	C			

†Pte. Smith, R.	200917		A	K. in A.	13 10 18
Lance-Cpl. Smith, A.	243755		D	W.	20 6 18
Pte. Smith, A.	235017		A	W.	30 11 17
Pte. Snape, W.	2965		C	W.	15 6 15
Pte. Snelgrove, J. C.	248		C	W.	15 6 15
Pte. Smithson, E. W.	5019		B	W.	9 9 16
†Pte. Snowling, G.	9934		C	K. in A.	18 11 17
Pte. Southworth, J.	2270		B	W.	15 6 15
Pte. Southworth, J.	160		D	W.	and 1 4 16, 15 6 15
Pte. Sowerby, W. C.	200329		C	R.P. of W	15 6 15
†Pte. Southworth, J.	2874		B	K. in A.	15 6 15
Pte. Southworth, D.	4920		B	W.	8 8 16
Pte. Southworth, A. M.	4499		B	W.	9 9 16
Pte. Southworth, D.	2026653		B	W.	31 7 17
Lance-Cpl. Southworth, D.	2026653		A	W.	18 11 17
†Pte. Southworth, W.	202542		A	K. in A.	5 8 17
Pte. Southam, J.	29182		C	W.	13 4 18
Pte. Southworth, C.	201420		B	W.	16 8 18
Pte. Somers, J.	375889		A	W.	31 7 17
Lance-Cpl. Springate, H.	131		D	W.	18 11 17
†Pte. Spencer, R.	2902		D	W.	15 6 15
Pte. Spivey, F.	1402		B	K. in A.	15 6 15
Pte. Speakman, W. J.	30664		D	W.	9 9 16
Pte. Speet, J. W.	30657		D	W.	4 9 16
Cpl. Spensen, R.	202899		B	W.	5 9 18
Pte. Spencer, J.	202761		D	W.	30 11 17
Pte. Squires, B. D.	1978		D	W.	31 7 17
Pte. Squires, A.	1492		D	W.	27 3 16
†Pte. Street, R.	2672		B	K. in A.	8 8 16
Pte. Stanton, J.	2979		A	W.	15 6 15
Pte. Stephenson, V.	119		B	W.	15 6 15
Pte. Stanton, P.	2924		A	W.	15 6 15
†Lance-Cpl. Stones, R.	1643		B	K. in A.	15 6 15

Pte. Stark, A. M.	3100		R.P. of W.	16/6/15
Pte. Starling, T.	210625		W.	1/8/16
✝Pte. Stevenson, R.	2554		Died	25/10/16
✝Cpl. Stephenson, L.	3151		K. in A.	28/6/16
Pte. Stott, E.	202986		W.	3/8/16
✝Pte. Shanley, H.	5007	B	W.	8/8/16
		C	D. of W.	13/8/16
Lieut. Strong, H. W.			W.	9/9/16
Lance-Cpl. Strettle, W.	2570	D	W.	9/9/16
Pte. Stubbs, F.	202775	B	W.	9/9/16
✝Pte. Strickland, T. A.	4053	A	K. in A.	29/5/17
Pte. Steam, D.	265015	A	W.	8/6/17
Pte. Stringer, A.	202088	B	W.	18/7/17
✝Sgt. Stephenson, V.	200052	C	K. in A.	18/7/17
✝Pte. Stephan, W. H.	368893	A	K. in A.	16/8/18
Pte. Stambridge, A.	10631	D	W.	16/8/18
Lance-Cpl. Stafford, J.	19564	A	W.	15/8/18
Lance-Cpl Stewart, T	203840	D	W.	30/11/17
✝Lance-Cpl. Stanford, H.	25775	A	K. in A.	30/11/17
Lance-Cpl. Stamper, J	280863	D	W.	30/11/17
Lance-Cpl. Stubbs, F	202775	D	W.	N.T. 25/4/18
Lance-Cpl. Stewart, T.	283040	D	W.	and 15/8/15
✝Sgt. Stansfield, A.	202767	D	K. in A.	31/7/17
✝Pte. Stearne, D.	235015	A	K. in A.	20/9/17
Pte. Stoddart, T.	30978	B	W.	30/9/18
✝Cpl. Stratton, S.	6333		K. in A.	20/9/17
Pte. Stroud, W. G.	405524	A	W.	19/10/18
Lance-Cpl. Stafford, J.	19564	A	W.	26/5/18
Pte. Sumner, J.	2650	B	W.	31/7/16
Pte. Sumner, R.	2600	B	W.	1/8/16
✝Pte. Sutcliffe, J.	6148	C	D. of W.	9/9/16 ; 16/8/18
Pte. Sumner, W.	32001	A	W.	3/5/17
✝Pte. Sutton, R.	200718	A	K. in A.	31/7/17
Pte. Sumner, J.	200848	A	W.	9/8/18

Pte. Sumner, W.	203638	C	W.		1 5 18
Pte. Sumner, T.	201017	B	R.P. of W.		31 7 17
†Pte. Swindlehurst, J.	4643	A	K. in A.		28 9 16
Pte. Swindells, J.	235041	B	W.		31 7 17
†Pte. Swift, G. T.	202667	A	K. in A.		31 7 17
Lance-Cpl. Swingler, E.	243201	B	W.		3 6 18
Pte. Swift, J.	32870	D	R.P. of W.		17 2 18
Pte. Swaine, A.	9014	B	W.	N.T.	18 11 17
Pte. Swann, D.	244630	D	W.		30 9 14
Pte. Syddal, A.	235165	B	W.	and	16 7 17
					30 11 17
Pte. Sykes, T.	37600	B	W.		30 11 15
†Pte. Singleton, R.	32832		K. in A.		31 7 17
†Pte. Swindlehurst, H.	202534		K. in A.		20 9 17
‡Lance-Cpl. Tattersall, W.	776	D	K. in A.		1 4 16
†Pte. Taylor, J.	2036	D	W.		15 6 15
					8 7 15
Pte. Taylor, A.	283	C	K. in A.		15 6 15
†Pte. Taylor, J. W.	2230	A	W.		13 6 15
†Pte. Tattersall, W.	3490	C	K. in A.		28 6 16
Pte. Taylor, R. A.	4513	A	K. in A.		31 7 16
Pte. Taylor, J.	4564	C	W.		8 8 16
Pte. Taylor, J. W	3306	C	W.		8 8 16
Pte. Taylor, J.	3541	D	W.		9 9 16
Pte. Tarbett, J. W.	4452	C	W.	N.T.	9 9 16
†Pte. Taylor, J.	200972	C	W.		9 9 16
Pte. Taylor, W.	4600	C	K. in A.		9 9 16
Pte. Taylor, T.	3538	D	W.		9 9 16
Pte. Tatler, W.	4991	B	W.		14 7 17
Pte. Taylor, W.	15055	B	K. in A.		31 7 17
†Pte. Taylor, T.	31905	A	W.		31 7 17
Lance-Cpl. Taylor, T.	202597	B	W.		20 9 17
2nd Lieut. Tautz, R. H.	—		W.		20 9 17
†Pte. Taylor, T.	201710	D	K. in A.		20 9 17

✠Pte. Taylor, J. E.	...	233016	...	A	K. in A.	17 9 17
Pte. Taysom, J.	...	2910886	...	C	W.	18 11 17
Pte. Taylor, T.	...	203544	...	C	R.P. of W.	18 11 17
✠Pte. Taylor, J. E.	...	200495	...	D	K. in A.	12 4 18
Pte. Taylor, G. C.	...	29197	...	D	W.	9 4 18
2nd Lieut. Taylor, W. G. E.	...	—	...		W.	1 6 18
Pte. Tabor, J. H.	...	202501	...	B	W.	2 6 18
Pte. Taylor, H. W.	...	322290	...	C	W.	3 6 18
✠Cpl. Tancock, E. J.	...	13601	...	D	D. of W. 18/6/18	22 6 18
✠Pte. Taylor, J	...	200495	...	D	K. in A.	7 7 18
Pte. Tarte, W.	...	36180	...	D	W.	16 8 18
Pte. Tabor, J.	...	202501	...	B	W.	4 9 18
Pte. Talbot, R.	...	309938	...	D	W.	4 9 18
Sgt. Taylor, J. W.	...	201044	...	C	W.	4 9 18
2nd Lieut. Taylor, W. G. E.	...		...		Missing	13 10 18
2nd Lieut. Taylor, J. T.	...		...		W.	16 10 18
Pte. Taylor, J.	...	309940	...	C	W.	23 10 18
Pte. Taylor, H.	...	376626	...	C	W.	9 4 18
✠Pte. Tennant, W.	...	6204	...	B	Missing (Pres'd K.)	26 9 16
✠Pte. Tebay, T.	...	160062	...	A	W.	10 4 18
2nd Lieut. Tennant, J.	...		...		K. in A.	14 5 18
Pte. Tew, A.	...	29398	...	B	W.	3 9 18
Pte. Thompson, A.	...	1637	...	C	W.	23 10 18
Pte. Thorpe, A.	...	2545	...	A	W.	15 6 15
✠Pte. Thorpe, A.	...	200614	...	A	K. in A.	15 6 15
Pte. Thomason, J. S.	...	260	...	C	W.	9 4 18
Pte. Thistleton, G.	...	338	...	A	W.	15 6 15
Pte. Thornley, H.	...	4926	...	B	W.	15 6 15
Pte. Threlfall, W.	...	3846	...	B	W.	8 8 16
Sgt. Thornber, A.	...	2316	...	D	W.	9 9 16
✠Pte. Thexton, S.	...	201041	...	D	K. in A.	9 9 16
Pte. Thomason, J. E.	...	21798	...	C	W.	24 5 17
✠Sgt. Thompson, J.	...	201350	...	A	K. in A.	3 6 17
Pte. Thistleton, T.	...	2003552	...	B	W.	10 6 17

Pte. Thompson, A.	290739		C	R.P. of W.	18 11 17
✠Pte. Threlfall, E.	32961		C	K. in A.	18 11 17
Pte. Thomas, J.	242697		D	D. of W.	18 ; 25 4 18
Sgt. Thompson, J.	201197		D	W.	9 4 18 ; 9 4 18
Sgt. Threadgould, W.	243878		A	W.	14 5 18
Pte. Thornton, F. J.	38221		A	W.	24 5 18 and 7 7 18
Lance-Cpl. Thompson, W.	201353		D	W.	23 5 18
Pte. Thomas, E.	29425		A	W.	29 5 18
Pte. Thompson, C. H.	29424		D	W.	16 6 18
2nd Lieut. Thomas, F.	—			W.	11 9 18
Pte. Thornycroft, A.	306640		B	W.	1 10 18
Pte. Thornley, E.	232228		A	W.	17 10 18
✠Cpl. Thomas, A. S.	29202		C	K. in A.	9 4 18
Pte. Timbrell, H.	2304		A	W.	30 5 15 and 9 9 16
Pte. Tipping, E.	2881		B	W.	15 6 15
Lance-Sgt. Tickle, H.	139		B	W.	1 1 16
Pte. Titterington, J.	3873		A	W.	8 8 16
Pte. Tinsley, T.	3057		C	W.	8 8 16
Pte. Timbrell, H.	2304		C	W.	9 9 16
Pte. Tilsley, W.	202926		A	W.	20 9 17
Pte. Tipping, F.	292203		C	W.	9 4 18
Pte. Tinsley, J. A.	30661		D	W.	17 8 18
Lance-Cpl. Tootle, E.	1185		B	W.	15 6 15
Cpl. Tomlinson, J. W.	1997			W.	15 6 15 and 18 9 15
Pte. Towers, W.	2673		A	W.	16 6 15
Pte. Tootell, J.	149		D	W.	3 9 15
✠Pte. Tomlinson, A.	76		B	K. in A.	15 6 15
✠Pte. Tootell, J.	2011		D	K. in A.	8 8 16
Pte. Tootell, J.	3240		D	W.	8 8 16
✠Pte. Todd, R.	4965		B	K. in A.	9 9 16
Pte. Tomlinson, F. J.	31771		A	W.	6 5 17

Pte. Tonge, H.	202998		B	R.P. of W.	31 7 17
Pte. Todd, F.	201059		D	W.	20 9 17
Lance-Cpl. Tootell, J.	200469		D	W.	20 9 17
Pte. Todhunter, J. L.	244867		A	W.	20 9 17
Pte. Todd, P. E.	26117		C	W.	18 11 17
Pte. Todd, W.	203248		A	W.	14 5 18
Pte. Todd, G. E.	30979		B	W.	13 10 18
†Pte. Tomlinson, A.	235044		A	K. in A.	31 7 17
Cpl. Travis, J.	1366		D	W.	15 6 15
Pte. Tracey, J.	201564		C	R.P. of W.	31 7 17
†Pte. Trafford, H. B.	203067		C	K. in A.	31 7 17
†Pte. Turner, F.	2311		A	K. in A.	15 6 15
Pte. Turner, V.	1919		A	K. in A.	15 6 15
Pte. Turner, W.	4943		B	W.	8 8 16
†Pte. Turner, W.	4563		C	K. in A.	9 9 16
Pte. Turner, J.	6207		B	W.	9 9 16
Pte. Turner, F.	4330		D	W.	29 9 16
Pte. Turner, E.	235042		B	R.P. of W.	31 7 17
Pte. Turner, J.	290171		C	W.	18 11 17
†Pte. Turnbull, T.	202648		A	K. in A.	30 11 17
Lance-Cpl. Tucker, A. C.	34261		A	W.	29 5 18
†Pte. Turvey, T.	42023		D	K. in A.	3 6 18
†Pte. Turner, G.	38808		B	K. in A.	11 10 18
†Pte. Turnbull, F. M.	42113		B	K. in A.	14 10 18
Pte. Tyldsley, P.	5082		C	W.	8 8 16
Pte. Tyson, H.	3387		D	W.	8 8 16
Lance-Cpl. Tyrer, F.	4540		D	W.	30 3 16
2nd Lieut. Tynell, R. F. L.				K. in A.	19 4 18
†Pte. Tyldsley, T.	29200		D	W.	16 6 18
Pte. Tyers, W.	41297		D	W.	31 7 17
Pte. Tyler, H	35474		B	W.	31 7 17
2nd Lieut. Tyldesley, H.	—				N.T.
Pte. Underwood, J. P.	2315		A	W.	15 6 15 and 30 10 15

381

†Pte. Unsworth, T.	29426		K. in A.		1 5 18
Pte. Underwood, T. W.	30942		W.		14 8 16
Pte. Urwin, H.	2866		W.		9 9 16
Pte. Urwin, H.	200779		W.		10 4 18
Pte. Utting, W.	2831		W.		15 6 15
Pte. Utting, W.	2880		W.		15 6 15
Pte. Vass, J.	4288	A	W.		31 7 16
Pte. Vaughan, D. W.	4655	C	W.		9 9 16
Pte. Vass, J.	4298	A	W.		9 9 16
Pte. Vause, J.	297	B	W.		10 12 16
Lance-Cpl. Valentine, G.	202513	C	W.		31 7 17
Pte. Vause, J.	31937	D	W.		12 7 17
Pte. Varey, W.	37652	D	W.		16 8 18
Pte. Vasey, J. W.	26511	B	W.		31 7 17
Pte. Valentine, G.	202573	B	W.		9 4 18
Pte. Vause, J.	31937	D	W.		9 7 18
Pte. Vickers, W.	148	B	W.		15 6 15
Pte. Vickerman, J.	1296	C	W.		and 9 9 16
2nd Lieut. Vipond, I. R.			W.		9 9 16
Pte. Vickers, A.	202922	C	W.		8 6 17
Pte. Vickers, A.	202922	C	W.		31 7 17
2nd Lieut. Vincent, H. C.			W.		and 9 4 18
†Pte. Waterworth, S.	4440	C	K. in A.		8 8 16
Pte. Walkden, F.	1621	C	W.		8 8 16
Pte. Waring, T.	2028	D	W.		8 8 16
†C.S.M. Waring, T.	1720	C	K. in A.		9 9 16
Pte. Walker, J.	202094	C	W.		9 9 16
†Pte. Walkden, J. H.	202755	C	K. in A.		9 9 16
Pte. Wallbank, J.	3024	A	W.	N.T.	9 9 16
Pte. Watkinson, H.	4045	A	W.	N.T.	9 9 16
Pte. Ward, C.	2912	B	W.		9 9 16

Pte. Walton, J. W.	2828		W.	15 5/15 and 9 9/16
†Pte. Waddicar, A.	202097	D	K. in A.	4 4/17
Lance-Cpl. Walton, J. W.	200761	C	W.	13 4/17
Pte. Ward, A.	31891	D	R.P. of W.	18 5/17
Pte. Wainwright, W.	202590	B	W.	14 7/17
Pte. Wall, J.	32166	A	W.	18 7/17
Pte. Watkinson, H.	201346	D	W.	20 9/17
Pte. Walker, L.	29914	C	W.	20 9/17
2nd Lieut. Walmsley, J. F.			W.	22 10/16
†Lance-Cpl. Walmsley, J.	201521	A	K. in A.	20 9/17
Pte. Watts, E. J.	31544	C	Missing	N.T.18 11/17
Pte. Waring, J.	200175	A	W.	N.T. 9 4/18
Pte. Walsh, J.	32964	C	W.	14 4/18
Pte. Walker, F.	29217	A	W.	9/4/18
‡Sgt. Ward, R. H.	200984	B	K. in A.	31 7/17
Cpl. Walmsley, J.	4992	C	W.	31 7/17
Pte. Walsh, W.	32085	B	W.	31 7/17
Pte. Welsh, S.	202921	B	W.	31 7/17
Pte. Ward, A.	202920		R.P. of W.	31 7/17
Pte. Walmsley, H.	31987	A	Died	6 11/16
†Pte. Walker, J.	1687		K. in A.	31 7/17
†Pte. Webb, S. G.	9226		D. of W.	22 9/17
†Pte. Wilbraham, T. E.	244686		D. of W.	23 8/16
†Pte. Wilkinson, R.	1149		D. of W.	22 5/18
Pte. Wilkinson, S.	29223	A	W.	31 7/17
†Pte. Warnes, P.	235040	A	W.	31 7/17
Pte. Watson, J. W.	202962	D	W.	31 7/17
Lance-Cpl. Walker, J. E. L.	34330	D	W.	31 7/17
Pte. Waite, E.	25576	A	W.	20 9/17
Pte. Waite, J.	37570	C	W.	20 9/17
Pte. Warren, R.	27361	C	W.	15 6/15
Pte. Wade, L.	1023		W.	15 6/15
‡Sgt. Waring, T.	1720	B	K. in A.	9 9/16

Pte. Waring, J.	2053	D		W.		15, 6, 15
Pte. Waters, E.	2978	A		W.		15, 6, 15
Pte. Walker, A.	3014	A		W.		15, 6, 15
Pte. Wainman, A.	3401	B		W.		30, 9, 16
Pte. Walton, T.	4108	D		W.		8, 8, 16
Pte. Walsh, A.	4938	D		W.		1, 7, 16
2nd Lieut. Walker, A. S.	—	C		W.		25, 4, 16
Pte. Wardley, J.	49352	A		W.		30, 6, 16
Lance-Cpl. Wade, R. W.	40069	A		W.		28, 6, 16
Pte. Ward, T.	1975	B		W.		29, 6, 16
Pte. Ward, A.	2787			W.		15, 6, 15
Pte. Walker, J.	4930			W.		31, 7, 16
Pte. Walsh, J.	4398	A		W.		?, 8, 16
Pte. Walmsley, C.	4167	B		W.		?, ?, 16
Pte. Watson, A.	376021	A		W.	N.T.	26, 4, 18
Pte. Walsh, J.	32495	A		K. in A.		14, 5, 18
†Sgt. Waine, W.	200357	A		W.		7, 5, 18
Pte. Walmsley, T.	376469	D		K. in A.		2, 6, 18
†Pte. Warrington, J. S.	41668			W.	N.T.	6, 5, 18
†Pte. Wallis, F. C.	243358			K. in A.		27, 6, 18
†Pte. Watkinson, H.	36793	D		W.		8, 7, 18
†Pte. Watson, M.	29427	D		W.		16, 8, 18
Pte. Walker, A.	30476	C		W.		16, 8, 18
Pte. Wadd, H.	40433	B		W.		4, 9, 18
Cpl. Warwick, W. A.	15554	B		W.		4, 9, 18
Lance-Cpl. Wainwright, W.	202590	B		W.		14, 9, 18
Pte. Walmsley, F.	41097	B		W.		14, 9, 18
Pte. Wandless, G. E.	30981	B		W.		24, 9, 18
Pte. Watts, J. A.	235513	C		W.		30, 9, 18
Pte. Ward, T.	343016	A		W.	N.T.	30, 9, 18
Pte. Warnes, H.				K. in A.		16, 11, 16
†2nd Lieut. Walton				K. in A.		2, 10, 18
†Pte. Walton, J.	30983	B				?, ?, ??

Pte. Watkinson, A.	25462		A	W.	23 10 18
Pte. Wafer, P.	22306		A	W.	14 5 18
Pte. Welley, L.	7526		C	W.	8 9 16
Pte. Webster, P. J.	6297		C	W.	9 9 16
Pte. Welsh, S.	6313		B	W.	25 6 16
✠Pte. West, J.	202155		C	K. in A.	15 7 17
✠Pte. Webster, P.	202907		A	K. in A.	21 7 17
✠Pte. Webster, W.	36175			W.	22 7 17
2nd Lieut. Westwood, S. B.				K. in A.	11 2 18
Pte. Webb, W.	35539		A	W.	17 2 18
Pte. Westhead, F.	203879		B	K. in A.	18 4 18
✠Pte. Weatherstone, J.	4470		D	R.P. of W.	31 7 17
Pte. Waston, W. A.	29429			K. in A.	31 7 17
2nd Lieut. Wetherill, W. B.				W.	3 8 16
Pte. West, H.	24664		D	Missing	20 5 18
✠Pte. Webster, S.	36175		A	K. in A.	16 8 18
✠Pte. Weaver, A.	24328		B	D. of W.	11 9 18
✠Cpl. West, G.	28195		A	K. in A.	2 10 18
Lance-Cpl. Whittle. R. H.	39539		C	W.	8 7 16
Pte. Whyte, J.	2870		C	D. of W.	25 9 16
✠Pte. Wharton, J.	3985		B	W. 8 8 16 ;	9 9 18
Pte. Whyte, P.	3762		C	W.	9 9 18
Pte. Whelan, G.	202924		C	W.	9 9 18
Pte. Whinney, C. T.	202785		A	W.	6 5 17
Pte. Whittaker, H.	202819		A	W.	6 5 17
Pte. Whitelegg, E.	202552		D	W.	7 6 17
Lance-Cpl. Whalley, W.	3211		C	K. in A.	18 2 17
✠Pte. Whiteside. J.	200673		D	K. in A.	30 7 17
Pte. Whittingham, H.	202657		A	W.	31 7 17
Pte. Whalley, R.	202170		A	R.P. of W.	20 9 17
Pte. Wharton, R.	37147		A	W.	30 11 17
Pte. Whittle, W.	201835		D	W.	30 11 17
Pte. Whalen, E.	201812			W.	

†Pte. Whalley, J.	23140		D	K. in A.	9/4/18
Pte. Whittaker, G.	203529		C	W.	31/7/17
Sgt. Whiteside, T.	200001		C	W.	31/7/17
Pte. Whalley, C.	200619		A	R.P. of W.	31/7/17
Pte. Whittle, J.	23759		B	Missing	N.T.
Pte. Whelan, G. E.	255168		C	R.P. of W.	31/7/17
	36676				
Pte. Whitley, B.	202677		D	W.	20/9/17
Lance-Sgt. Whiteside, J.	906		C	W.	15/6/15
Pte. Whittle, A.	1490		D	W.	15/6/15
Pte. Whiteside, J.	2135		B	W.	30/5/15
Pte. Whalley, C.	2552		A	W.	15/6/15
Lance-Cpl. Whiteside, T.	2		B	W.	and 8/8/16
Pte. Whittaker, W.	7		B	W.	11/8/15
Pte. Whewill, H.	80		B	W.	15/6/15
Pte. Whitehead, C.	3827		A	W.	9/7/16
Pte. Whittle, W.	415		A	K. in A.	15/6/15
†Pte. Wharton, A.	2024		A	K. in A.	15/6/15
†Pte. Whiteside, W.	2632		C	K. in A.	15/6/15
†Pte. Whalley, G. C.	3192		C	K. in A.	15/6/15
Pte. Whittaker, F.	242738		C	W.	4/8/16
Pte. Whiteside, J.	2138		B	W.	5/8/16
Pte. Whiteside, T.	242		C	W.	5/8/16
Pte. Whitehead, W. T.	29428		A	W.	04/5/18
Pte. Whittaker, R.	29220		B	W.	21/5/17
Pte. Whiteside, J.	15180		B	W.	18/6/18
Pte. Whitehead, C.	31516		A	W.	20/6/18
†Pte. White, F. H.	42030		C	D. of W.	25/6/18; 13/9/18
Pte. White, F.	19200		B	W.	N.T.
Pte. Whittaker, J.	25399		D	W.	25/6/18
Pte. Whitehead, W.	255306		B	W.	4/9/18
Lance-Cpl. Wharton, S.	201743		D	W.	5/9/18
Pte. Whittaker, J.	25399		B	W.	22/10/18

386

Name	Number	Coy	Status		Date
Pte. Whitfield, H.	30987	B	W.		23/10/18
†Capt. Whitfield, J. L.			K. in A.		15/6/15
Lance-Cpl. Wharton, S.	201743	D	W.		9/4/18
Pte. White, T. H.	27136	C	W.		8/8/16
Pte. Wilson, J.	1621	C	W.	N.T.	8/8/16
†Pte. Winrow, R.	7583	D	K. in A.		8/8/16
Pte. Wilson, J. H.	5442		W.		10/8/16
Capt. Widdows, J. O.	—		Shock		9/9/16
Pte. Wilkin, J.	1002	C	W.		9/9/16
Pte. Wilson, H.	4453	C	W.		9/9/16
†Pte. Wilson, J.	4384	C	K. in A.		9/9/16
Pte. Wilson, A.	201877	C	W.		9/9/16
†Pte. Williams, D. H.	202918		K. in A.		9/9/16
†Pte. Wicock, F. N.	13141		K. in A.		23/7/16
†Pte. Williams, J. B.	204811		Died at Home		30/12/17
†Pte. Worden, H.	202424		K. in A.		4/4/17
Pte. Winterbourne, W.	4997	C	W.	N.T.	9/9/16
Pte. Wilkinson, H.	4447	C	W.	N.T.	9/9/16
†Sgt. Williamson, M.	2002236	A	K. in A.		9/9/16
Pte. Wignall, W.	3771	A	W.		15/6/15
†Pte. Wilkinson, R.	5249	C	D. of W.		11/9/16
†Pte. Winstanley, J.	6113	D	K. in A.		28/9/16
†Pte. Williams, F.	2963	B	K. in A.		29/9/16
Lance-Cpl. Wilson, C. H.	6307	C	W.		18/11/18
Pte. Widdup, J.	202635	D	W.		4/4/17
Pte. Wilson, H. G.	36177	A	W.		2/6/17
Pte. Willett, W.	18618	B	W.		4/6/17
Pte. Wilson, R.	202993	B	W.		5/5/17
†Pte. Wignall, A.	201752	B	K. in A.		7/6/17
Pte. Willacy, H. P.	201439	C	R.P. of W.		15/7/17
†Pte. Wilson, R.	201225	C	K. in A.		31/7/17
Lance-Cpl. Wilson, C. H.	202916	C	W.		21/7/17
Pte. Willett, T. H.	202093	D	W.		21/9/17

Rank	Name	Number	Coy		Status	Date
Pte.	Wills, G. J.	25041	D		W.	20 9 17
Pte.	Williams, C. P.	28261	A		W.	18 11 17
Pte.	Wilson H.	24217	A		W.	18 11 17
†2nd	Lieut. Wilkinson, R. B.		A		K. in A.	30 11 17
Pte.	Willacy, E.	2003362	A		K. in A.	30 11 17
Pte.	Winstanley, W.	27807	A		W.	30 11 17
Pte.	Wickham, G. T. W.	2924	B		W.	19 3 18
Pte.	Williams, J.	34314	B		W.	9 4 18
†Pte.	Wilmore, H.	27666	B		K. in A.	25 7 17
†2nd	Lieut. Williams, B. H.				K. in A.	31 7 17
Pte.	Winstanley, E.	2002999	D		W.	31 7 17
Pte.	Wilson, T.	2017153	B		W.	31 7 17
Pte.	Wilcock, J.	2036629	D		W.	31 7 17
Pte.	Wilkinson, J.	2026688	D		W.	31 7 17
Pte.	Winnow, J.	27591	A		W.	17 9 17
†Pte.	Wignall, E.	3155			K. in A.	21 5 16
†Cpl.	Williamson, M.	1138	A		K. in A.	15 6 15
Pte.	Wilson, T.	1600	B		W.	9 9 16
Pte.	Williamson, P.	1699	A		W.	15 6 15
Pte.	Wilding, A.	2740	B		W.	15 6 15
Pte.	Wignall, E.	3155	C		W.	15 6 15
Pte.	Wilder, F.	33	B		W.	15 6 15
Pte.	Wilson, R.	255	C		W.	16 6 15
Pte.	Wilkinson, J.	2008863	C		W.	29 10 15
2nd	Lieut. Wilson, M.				W.	23 4 16
†Cpl.	Wilson, H.	1965	B		K. in A.	15 6 15
†Pte.	Windebank, T.	2499	C		K. in A.	15 6 15
Pte.	Wilson, H. S.	4634	C		W.	14 7 16
Pte.	Winrow, G.	4138	A		W.	5 8 16
†Pte.	Willan, G.	4501	A		K. in A.	8 8 16
†Pte.	Wilcock, J.	3935	B		W.	8 8 16
†Pte.	Williamson, H.	12024	A		W. Died	20 5 18 15 11 18

Pte.	Williams, J. D.	242028		A	W.	8/6/18
†Pte.	Wilding, J.	23501		D	W.	16/8/16
						14/10/18
Pte.	Wilson, H.	24217		A	W.	16/8/16
Pte.	Williams, E. B.	306-46		D	W.	-/9/18
Pte.	Winterbotton, J. A.	27111		D	W.	-/9/18
Pte.	Williams, F.	26826		D	W.	30/9/18
Pte.	Williamson, W.	30658		A	W.	30/9/18
Pte.	Wilson, H. W.	240713			W.	2/10/18
Pte.	Wiles, G.	309SS		B	W.	13/10/18
Pte.	Wiles, J.	306-13		B	W.	17/10/18
Pte.	Williamson, J.	30985		B	W.	23/10/18
Pte.	Winstanley, R.	23592		B	W.	23/10/18
Pte.	Wilby, G. H.	29069		B	W.	23/10/18
Pte.	Williams, G.	41530		B	W.	23/10/18
Pte.	Williams, R.	32211		A	W.	23/10/18
†Pte.	Wilkinson, A.	25945		A	K. in A.	16/8/16
Pte.	Wiles, J.	306-13		D	K. in A.	8/8/16
†Pte.	Wilson, J.	202098		B	K. in A.	2/6/17
†Pte.	Williams, H.	31977		A	K. in A.	9/4/18
Cpl.	Wilkinson, J. S.	202752		D	W.	23/10/18
Pte.	Williams, C. P.	28261		D	W.	8/8/16
†Pte.	Wilkinson, A.	25945		A	K. in A.	8/8/16
†Pte.	Woodruff, W.	3309		D	K. in A.	16/8/16
†Pte.	Woodhouse, E.	3978		D	K. in A.	8/9/16
†Pte.	Worthington, A.	2074		D	K. in A.	9/9/16
Pte.	Wood, E. L.	5095		C	K. in A.	9/9/16
†Pte.	Wootton, A.	6312		C	Missing	9/9/16
Pte.	Wood, J.	4309		B	W.	18/7/17
Pte.	Woodward, G.	5197		C	W.	20/9/17
Pte.	Worthington, G.	202589		B	W.	18/11/17
Pte.	Woods, J.	32177		C	K. in A.	
Pte.	Wood, F.	27078		C	K. in A.	
†Pte.	Worthington, J. S.	202644		C	W.	18/11/17
Pte.	Worthington, G.	202588		C		

389

Pte. Worthington, J.	37663	B	W.	30/11/17
Pte. Woodward, G.	202823	D	W.	9/4/18
Pte. Woods, J.	203593	B	W.	31/7/17
†Pte. Worsley, R.	200032	B	D. of W.	31/7/17 28/8/17
†Pte. Wood, W.	31518	B	K. in A.	31/7/17
†Pte. Woodcock, J.	17101	D	K. in A.	31/7/17
†Pte. Wood, F.	27078	C	K. in A.	19/9/17
Pte. Woods, J.	52177	B	W.	20/9/17
†Pte. Woodward, C. S.	250	B	K. in A.	29/6/16
C.S.M. Woods, J.	501	D	W.	15/6/15
Pte. Worthington, A.	2072	B	W.	30/5/15
Pte. Woods, J.	2586	A	W.	15/6/15
†Pte. Woodburn, A.	2669	A	W.	15/6/15
			D. of W.	3/11/15
Pte. Worswick, J.	2830	B	W.	15/6/15
Pte. Worthington, F.	2903	B	W.	15/6/15
Pte. Wood, H.	3082	C	W.	15/6/15
†Pte. Worsley, R.	73	B	W.	8/8/17
Pte. Woods, W. H.	235	C	D. of W.	15/6/15
Pte. Woods, J.	241	C	W.	15/6/15
Lance-Cpl. Woodward, C	250	B	W.	14/6/15
†Pte. Woodburn, A.	2669	A	D. of W.	8/11/15
†Sgt. Woods, R.	58	B	K. in A.	15/6/15
Pte. Worswick, J.	4933	A	W.	31/7/16
Pte. Woods, T.	4578	C	W.	3/8/16
†Pte. Worsley, F.	5001	B	K. in A.	8/8/16
Pte. Wood, H.	38971	C	W.	N.T. 28/7/18
Pte. Wood, E. C	41682	C	W.	12/5/18
Pte. Woodruff, F.	29204	B	W.	11/5/18
Lance-Cpl. Woods, D.	290208	A	W.	14/5/18
Pte. Woodward, G.	28250	B	W.	2/6/18
†Pte. Wood, H. E.	41085	D	K. in A.	N.T. 23/10/18
†Pte. Woodburn, W.	232037	A	K. in A.	9/9/16
†Sgt. Wrigley, W. H.	6201	A	K. in A.	

390

Pte.	Wrench, J.	11577	D	W.	2/7/17
Pte.	Wright, T. H.	205888	D	W.	30/11/17
Pte.	Wragg, W. H.	202915	C	W.	17/2/18
Pte.	Wright, T.	202588	D	W.	13/4/18
Pte.	Worden, M. C.	2643	A	W.	15/6/15
†Pte.	Wright, J.	202424		K. in A.	4/4/17
Pte.	Wright, W.	20638	B	W.	25/3/16
†Pte.	Wright, J.	1393	A	K. in A.	8/8/16
Pte.	Wright, J.	9216	B	W.	18/6/18
Cpl.	Winn, M.	3551	D	Died	4/10/16
Pte.	Wyre, P.	202990	A	W.	16/8/18
†Pte.	Winrow, J.	27591		D. of W.	18/9/17
Pte.	Yates, H.	201202	D	W.	16/8/16
Pte.	Yates, J.	241577	D	W.	15/8/18
†Pte.	Yates, J.	200888		K. in A.	9/4/18
Pte.	Yates, G.	2092	D	W.	15/6/15
Pte.	Yates, E.	1774	B	K. in A.	15/6/15
Pte.	Yates, F.	4774	C	W.	9/9/16
Pte.	Yates, H.	3561	D	W.	28/9/16
Sgt.	Yates, R. T.	200900	D	R.P. of W. N.T.	31/7/16
Pte.	Yates, W.	245883	D	W.	30/11/17
Pte.	Yates, J. R.	29224		W.	9/4/18
Pte.	Yates, F.	202913	C	W.	21/7/17
†Pte.	Yates, J.	201543	D	K. in A.	21/7/18
Pte.	Young, W. A.	29399	B	W.	30/9/18
Pte.	Young, W.	202676	B	W.	31/7/16
†Pte.	Younger, W.	30986	B	K. in A.	23/10/18
†Pte.	Yull, G. A.	3572	B	K. in A.	8/8/16

ALSO FROM LEONAUR
AVAILABLE IN SOFTCOVER OR HARDCOVER WITH DUST JACKET

THE ART OF WAR *by Antoine Henri Jomini*—Strategy & Tactics From the Age of Horse & Musket.

THE ART OF WAR *by Sun Tzu and Pierre G. T. Beauregard*—*The Art of War* by Sun Tzu and *Principles and Maxims of the Art of War* by Pierre G. T. Beauregard.

THE MILITARY RELIGIOUS ORDERS OF THE MIDDLE AGES *by F. C. Woodhouse*—The Knights Templar, Hospitaller and Others.

THE BENGAL NATIVE ARMY *by F. G. Cardew*—An Invaluable Reference Resource.

ARTILLERY THROUGH THE AGES—*by Albert Manucy*—A History of the DEvelopment and Use of Cannons, Mortars, Rockets & Projectiles from Earliest Times to the Nineteenth Century.

THE SWORD OF THE CROWN *by Eric W. Sheppard*—A History of the British Army to 1914.

THE 7TH (QUEEN'S OWN) HUSSARS: Volume 3—1818-1914 *by C. R. B. Barrett*—On Campaign During the Canadian Rebellion, the Indian Mutiny, the Sudan, Matabeleland, Mashonaland and the Boer War Volume 3: 1818-1914.

THE CAMPAIGN OF WATERLOO *by Antoine Henri Jomini*—A Political & Military History from the French perspective.

RIFLE & DRILL *by S. Bertram Browne*—The Enfield Rifle Musket, 1853 and the Drill of the British Soldier of the Mid-Victorian Period *A Companion to the New Rifle Musket* and *A Practical Guide to Squad and Setting-up Dtill*.

NAPOLEON'S MEN AND METHODS *by Alexander L. Kielland*—The Rise and Fall of the Emperor and His Men Who Fought by His Side.

THE WOMAN IN BATTLE *by Loreta Janeta Velazquez*—Soldier, Spy and Secret Service Agent for the Confederancy During the American Civil War.

THE BATTLE OF ORISKANY 1777 *by Ellis H. Roberts*—The Conflict for the Mowhawk Valley During the American War of Independenc.

PERSONAL RECOLLECTIONS OF JOAN OF ARC *by Mark Twain*.

CAESAR'S ARMY *by Harry Pratt Judson*—The Evolution, Composition, Tactics, Equipment & Battles of the Roman Army.

FREDERICK THE GREAT & THE SEVEN YEARS' WAR *by F. W. Longman*.

ALSO FROM LEONAUR
AVAILABLE IN SOFTCOVER OR HARDCOVER WITH DUST JACKET

THE 9TH—THE KING'S (LIVERPOOL REGIMENT) IN THE GREAT WAR 1914 - 1918 *by Enos H. G. Roberts*—Mersey to mud—war and Liverpool men.

THE GAMBARDIER *by Mark Severn*—The experiences of a battery of Heavy artillery on the Western Front during the First World War.

FROM MESSINES TO THIRD YPRES *by Thomas Floyd*—A personal account of the First World War on the Western front by a 2/5th Lancashire Fusilier.

THE IRISH GUARDS IN THE GREAT WAR - VOLUME 1 *by Rudyard Kipling*—Edited and Compiled from Their Diaries and Papers—The First Battalion.

THE IRISH GUARDS IN THE GREAT WAR - VOLUME 1 *by Rudyard Kipling*—Edited and Compiled from Their Diaries and Papers—The Second Battalion.

ARMOURED CARS IN EDEN *by K. Roosevelt*—An American President's son serving in Rolls Royce armoured cars with the British in Mesopatamia & with the American Artillery in France during the First World War.

CHASSEUR OF 1914 *by Marcel Dupont*—Experiences of the twilight of the French Light Cavalry by a young officer during the early battles of the great war in Europe.

TROOP HORSE & TRENCH *by R.A. Lloyd*—The experiences of a British Lifeguardsman of the household cavalry fighting on the western front during the First World War 1914-18.

THE EAST AFRICAN MOUNTED RIFLES *by C.J. Wilson*—Experiences of the campaign in the East African bush during the First World War.

THE LONG PATROL *by George Berrie*—A Novel of Light Horsemen from Gallipoli to the Palestine campaign of the First World War.

THE FIGHTING CAMELIERS *by Frank Reid*—The exploits of the Imperial Camel Corps in the desert and Palestine campaigns of the First World War.

STEEL CHARIOTS IN THE DESERT *by S. C. Rolls*—The first world war experiences of a Rolls Royce armoured car driver with the Duke of Westminster in Libya and in Arabia with T.E. Lawrence.

WITH THE IMPERIAL CAMEL CORPS IN THE GREAT WAR *by Geoffrey Inchbald*—The story of a serving officer with the British 2nd battalion against the Senussi and during the Palestine campaign.

AVAILABLE ONLINE AT **www.leonaur.com**
AND FROM ALL GOOD BOOK STORES

ALSO FROM LEONAUR
AVAILABLE IN SOFTCOVER OR HARDCOVER WITH DUST JACKET

ESCAPE FROM THE FRENCH *by Edward Boys*—A Young Royal Navy Midshipman's Adventures During the Napoleonic War.

THE VOYAGE OF H.M.S. PANDORA *by Edward Edwards R. N. & George Hamilton, edited by Basil Thomson*—In Pursuit of the Mutineers of the Bounty in the South Seas—1790-1791.

MEDUSA *by J. B. Henry Savigny and Alexander Correard and Charlotte-Adélaïde Dard*—Narrative of a Voyage to Senegal in 1816 & The Sufferings of the Picard Family After the Shipwreck of the Medusa.

THE SEA WAR OF 1812 VOLUME 1 *by A. T. Mahan*—A History of the Maritime Conflict.

THE SEA WAR OF 1812 VOLUME 2 *by A. T. Mahan*—A History of the Maritime Conflict.

WETHERELL OF H. M. S. HUSSAR *by John Wetherell*—The Recollections of an Ordinary Seaman of the Royal Navy During the Napoleonic Wars.

THE NAVAL BRIGADE IN NATAL *by C. R. N. Burne*—With the Guns of H. M. S. Terrible & H. M. S. Tartar during the Boer War 1899-1900.

THE VOYAGE OF H. M. S. BOUNTY *by William Bligh*—The True Story of an 18th Century Voyage of Exploration and Mutiny.

SHIPWRECK! *by William Gilly*—The Royal Navy's Disasters at Sea 1793-1849.

KING'S CUTTERS AND SMUGGLERS: 1700-1855 *by E. Keble Chatterton*—A unique period of maritime history-from the beginning of the eighteenth to the middle of the nineteenth century when British seamen risked all to smuggle valuable goods from wool to tea and spirits from and to the Continent.

CONFEDERATE BLOCKADE RUNNER *by John Wilkinson*—The Personal Recollections of an Officer of the Confederate Navy.

NAVAL BATTLES OF THE NAPOLEONIC WARS *by W. H. Fitchett*—Cape St. Vincent, the Nile, Cadiz, Copenhagen, Trafalgar & Others.

PRISONERS OF THE RED DESERT *by R. S. Gwatkin-Williams*—The Adventures of the Crew of the Tara During the First World War.

U-BOAT WAR 1914-1918 *by James B. Connolly/Karl von Schenk*—Two Contrasting Accounts from Both Sides of the Conflict at Sea During the Great War.

AVAILABLE ONLINE AT **www.leonaur.com**
AND FROM ALL GOOD BOOK STORES

www.ingramcontent.com/pod-product-compliance
Lightning Source LLC
Chambersburg PA
CBHW030215170426
43201CB00006B/91